IN THE KINGDOM OF SHOES

Bata, Zlín, Globalization, 1894–1945

One of the world's largest sellers of footwear, the Bata Company of Zlín, Moravia, has a remarkable history that touches on crucial aspects of what made the world modern. In the twilight of the Habsburg Empire, the company Americanized its production model while also trying to Americanize its workforce. It promised a technocratic form of governance in the chaos of postwar Czechoslovakia, and during the Roaring Twenties, it became synonymous with rationalization across Europe and thus a flashpoint for a continent-wide debate. While other companies contracted in response to the Great Depression, Bata did the opposite, becoming the first shoe company to unlock the potential of globalization.

As Bata expanded worldwide, it became an example of corporate national indifference, where company personnel were trained to be able to slip into and out of national identifications with ease. Such indifference, however, was seriously challenged by the geopolitical crisis of the 1930s, and by the cusp of the Second World War, Bata management had turned nationalist, even fascist.

In the Kingdom of Shoes unravels the way the Bata project swept away tradition and enmeshed the lives of thousands of people around the world in the industrial production of shoes. Using a rich array of archival materials from two continents, the book answers how Bata's rise to the world's largest producer of shoes challenged the nation-state, democracy, and Americanization.

ZACHARY AUSTIN DOLESHAL is a clinical assistant professor in the Department of History at Sam Houston State University.

ZACHARY AUSTIN DOLESHAL

In the Kingdom of Shoes

Bata, Zlín, Globalization, 1894–1945

UNIVERSITY OF TORONTO PRESS

Toronto Buffalo London

© University of Toronto Press 2021
Toronto Buffalo London
utorontopress.com
Printed and bound by CPI Group (UK) Ltd, Croydon, CR0 4YY

ISBN 978-1-4875-0658-2 (cloth)   ISBN 978-1-4875-3447-9 (EPUB)
ISBN 978-1-4875-2444-9 (paper)   ISBN 978-1-4875-3446-2 (PDF)

Library and Archives Canada Cataloguing in Publication

Title: In the kingdom of shoes : Bata, Zlín, globalization, 1894–1945 / Zachary Austin
   Doleshal.
Names: Doleshal, Zachary Austin, author.
Description: Includes bibliographical references and index.
Identifiers: Canadiana (print) 20210260807 | Canadiana (ebook) 20210264470 | ISBN
   9781487506582 (hardcover) | ISBN 9781487524449 (softcover) | ISBN 9781487534479
   (EPUB) | ISBN 9781487534462 (PDF)
Subjects: LCSH: Bata Shoe Company – History. | LCSH: Footwear industry – Czech
   Republic – Zlín – History – 20th century. | LCSH: Company towns – Czech Republic –
   Zlín – History – 20th century. | LCSH: Labor and globalization – Czech Republic –
   History – 20th century. | LCSH: World War, 1939–1945 – Czechoslovakia. | LCSH:
   Corporate culture – Czech Republic – Zlín – History – 20th century. | LCSH: Zlín
   (Czech Republic) – History – 20th century. | LCSH: Zlín (Czech Republic) – Social
   conditions – 20th century.
Classification: LCC HD9787.C944 B383 2021 | DDC 338.4/768530943725 – dc23

Chapter opening ornament from https://all-free-download.com/free-vector/different-shoes
.html.

Publication of this book was made possible, in part, by a grant from the First Book
Subvention Program of the Association for Slavic, East European, and Eurasian Studies.

University of Toronto Press acknowledges the financial assistance to its publishing program of
the Canada Council for the Arts and the Ontario Arts Council, an agency of the Government
of Ontario.

Canada Council   Conseil des Arts
for the Arts   du Canada

ONTARIO ARTS COUNCIL
CONSEIL DES ARTS DE L'ONTARIO
an Ontario government agency
un organisme du gouvernement de l'Ontario

Funded by the   Financé par le
Government   gouvernement
of Canada   du Canada

Canadä

For Leslie Lee

Contents

Illustrations

Figures

Table

Figures

Table

Acknowledgments

Like all scholarly work, this book was made possible through personal support and institutional nourishment. I am deeply thankful for both.

A fellowship from the American Council of Learned Societies made possible an essential year of research in the archives of the Czech Republic. Another from the University of Texas at Austin allowed for a year of writing. Grants from the Ministry of Culture of the Czech Republic and from the Foundation for Civic Space and Public Policy of Poland allowed drafts of this work a wider academic audience. The Department of History at Sam Houston State University provided financial support for several additional research trips as well as for other associated costs.

In the Czech Republic itself, individuals have been both academically generous and personally kind without exemption. Archivists at the no-longer-in-existence Moravian Regional Archive of Brno–Workplace Zlín were exceptionally helpful and friendly, as they allowed me to work outside of normal hours and directed me to fascinating documents. I am also deeply grateful to David Valůšek and Kamila Nečasová, respectively the director and archivist at the State Regional Archives of Zlín; they not only helped me find excellent sources but welcomed me into their lives with a rare generosity. Likewise, Martin Marek provided me with a steadfast companion in the archives and has since been always willing to expand my knowledge of Bat'a. The same is true for Vít Strobach and Ondřej Ševeček, whose scholarship and suggestions have been important for the development of this work. In addition, the staff at the National Archives and the National Library in Prague helped me locate a broad range of materials. Outside of archives and academia, a very warm thanks goes to the late Drahomíra Jílková, who allowed me to stay at her lovely house and patiently helped me with the beautifully complicated Czech language. May her memory be a blessing.

Among the scholars in the United States I wish to thank Mary Neuburger has to be among the first. She helped me to find my topic by opening up questions into industrial production and political economy in East-Central Europe. I was lucky to have her as my graduate mentor. Professor Neuburger's colleagues David Crew, Charters Wynn, Veronika Tuckerova, and Tatjana Lichtenstein all helped shape this project as well by offering insights and thoughtful critiques of the work in its early stages. The work also benefited from the Czech and Slovak Studies Workshop, a terrific resource for North American based scholars of the region.

Further on in this project, Jon Fox, Tara Zahra, and Maarten van Ginderachter greatly influenced the ways in which I consider national identification through their suggestions and edits. From Martin Jemelka, Tomasz Ochinowski, Michał Przeperski, and Lukasz Kaminski I received thoughtful recommendations on the manuscript. Martin Jemelka also shared important sources regarding Bata in Switzerland and the early days of German occupation. Over the last several years, he has communicated his deep knowledge of the labour history of the Czechlands, and I have tried my best to keep up.

The three anonymous reviewers of this work were also most helpful to me in cultivating the central arguments and letting go of loose ends.

I am deeply grateful to my editor Stephen Shapiro for believing in this project as soon as I brought it to his attention. Many thanks to him and his colleagues at University of Toronto Press, all of whom have been a joy to work with.

Colleagues here at SHSU have also supported this book in a variety of ways, most importantly by simply encouraging my research and creating a community. Brian Jordan, Mevhibe Emiralioglu, Brian Domitrovic, and Jim Olsen all helped to further the research for this project. Many others have provided friendship and encouragement.

My greatest debt is to my family. Along the entire journey, my parents, my sister and nephew, my daughter, and my wife, Brandy, have provided unwavering support and inspiration while I tried to make sense of a complicated story. Brandy especially deserves acknowledgment, for she unfailingly believes that what I write people will want to read. I am so very thankful that such a wonderful human is in my life.

Abbreviations and Terms

Bat'a Zlín A.S.   The central company organization
Batism   The Bat'a ideology
Batovci   Bat'a people (an identification used by many Bat'a employees)
Batovec   Bat'a person (a loyal employee)
BSP   Bat'a School of Work (Bat'ova škola práce)
Cisleithania   The Austrian half of Austria-Hungary
EJ   Endicott-Johnson (Company)
Vychovatel   A guardian and life coach for the students at the BSP
Young Woman/Young Man   The label for students at the BSP

IN THE KINGDOM OF SHOES

Introduction

At 8:35 on the morning of 1 May 1937 factory sirens in Zlín, Czechoslovakia, rang out, signalling to the entire Bat'a workforce that the most important day of the year had officially begun. Some forty thousand employees made their way to twelve meeting points to gather posters, double-check immaculate outfits, and climb aboard allegorical floats. The sirens sounded again eighteen minutes later to launch eleven organized sections of workers in a march through the factory complex and towards Labour Square. Giant standards flew at the head of each of the columns declaring, among other things, "Long Live J.A. Bat'a," "We Want to Go into the World," and "We Believe in Aviation." Marching bands playing pieces composed for and by these *Batovci*, or Bata people, followed the banners, and behind them, workers sang ditties in matching outfits.[1] At 9 a.m., the groups converged on the centre of the Bat'a empire, while some fifty thousand "guests," consisting of friends and family as well as visitors from all over the world, gathered around the square's boundary. Once in place, the workers and guests waited for the arrival of a twelfth group, with the "šef," chief executive Jan Bat'a, at its head.[2]

While the other groups were en route to the square, Jan's plane landed outside the factory perimeter. Though he had arrived in Central Europe several days earlier from a much-publicized trip around the world, he coordinated his arrival in Zlín with May Day in order to make a dramatic return. Stationed along the route, film crews, directed by a young Alexander Hackenschmied, captured his grand return. As he stepped off the plane, Dominik Čipera, the mayor of Zlín and long-time company executive, embraced Jan with intense affection, as did Thomas Bat'a Jr., Jan's nephew and son of company founder, Tomáš.[3] Behind the embracing dignitaries stood a line of saluting uniformed pilots-in-training from the ranks of the "Young Men" of the elite Bat'a management school, men who lived, worked, and studied under the close supervision of the company. After the salutations, Jan got into the first of two open-backed limousines. They drove the executive group to Zlín's Great Cinema, one of the largest movie houses in Europe at the time and the centrepiece of Labour Square.[4] For the May Day festivities, its entrance had been converted into an elaborate celebration of Jan's globe-trotting. Above the stage, an airplane jutted out over the dais. Jan climbed the steps to the speaker's platform. Below him, hundreds of banners and thousands of workers spread out into the factory complex, where the newly built Bat'a skyscraper, the "21," towered above the skyline. As Jan approached the microphone, the crowd erupted and Bat'a-built Zlín XII planes flew overhead; he then paused, acknowledging the crowd with a wave.[5]

After giving the perfunctory speech, "The Air Is Our Ocean!" Jan, his family, and a handful of other executives, set off on foot from the square to lead a parade through town. Behind the group, a banner fluttered, "Liberate Entrepreneurs!" Along the route, people cheered wildly. Some threw flowers as Jan walked by; the king of a "kingdom of shoes," whose sovereignty was based not on divine right but on industrial production.[6]

Jan and his companies, known legally as Bat'a Zlín A.S., along with dozens of subsidiaries, had harnessed the power of globalization. Bat'a connected leather buyers in French West Africa to tanners in Bengal to machinists in Zlín. By so doing, the company transcended the nation state and prefaced the rise of the transnational corporation in the latter half of the twentieth century.[7] As it developed, it created a culture, Batism, shorthand for Bat'a's ideology and the operating system its ideology produced. Undeniably, it was a culture that had much in common with the contemporary corporate world – here was a corporate project where people relinquished democracy for paternalism and privacy for profit.[8] Only 1937 was not 2021, and Bat'a then was not Nike now. The crucial difference of context, as always, decided the extraordinary nature of the Bat'a kingdom. Batism developed out of the cartel system of the Habsburg Empire, embraced Fordism with prophetic zeal, was hardened in the chaos of imperial collapse, sharpened through a protracted battle with Moravian Communists, globalized after the tariff wars of the early 1930s, and finally, in 1937, as Czechoslovakia came under siege from Hitler's Germany, was inspired by Italian fascism. Accordingly, it was never stable for long.

The 1937 Bat'a May Day's demands for mass conformity fit the times. In Germany of that year, at the Ninth Nazi Party Congress, better known as the Nuremberg Rally to the anglophone world, thousands of Hitler Youth with matching spades and camping backpacks assembled on the Zeppelin Field to chant in unison, "Firm in our belief and true to the command of the Führer, we march proudly into the future."[9] Italy's 1937 public spectacle "The Birth of Rome" celebrated the reign of Augustus. To enter the massive exhibit "Mostra Augustea della Romanità," visitors walked under a banner with Mussolini's words, "Italians, you must ensure that the glories of the past are surpassed

Figure I.1. Labour Square on 1 May 1937. Moravský zemský archiv v Brně, Státní okresní archiv Zlín, Sbírka fotografií Zlín, sign. 83, obálka č. 14295.

by the glories of the future."[10] In the Soviet Union, mass festivals prolifer-ated. Malte Rolf's descriptions of events held in the "new" towns of Voronezh and Novosibirsk eerily match those of Bat'a's May Day. "Rows of parading citizens, arranged according to city districts, marched toward the central place from different directions … They reached the central square in precise inter-vals, moving past the grandstand and regional leaders."[11] Amid the public spec-tacles of the Communists, Fascists, and Nazis, one would also find those of the Sokol organization within Czechoslovakia, whose members in 1937 were busily planning for the tenth "All-Sokol Gathering." Their event in 1938 would bring hundreds of thousands of spectators to watch tens of thousands of people perform synchronized gymnastics routines under the banner "Build and Pro-tect" ("Budovat a bránit").[12] Unmistakably, expressions of collective potential-ity had become normalized by the mid to late 1930s.[13]

A company-orchestrated mass event, especially on the level of Zlín's in 1937, however, was unique. None of the large welfare capitalist companies of the time, like the Ford Motor Company, Endicott-Johnson, or Siemens, could compare. In fact, while Bat'a workers marched in unison, the workers at Ford were engaged in a dramatic struggle against a management that routinely used violence against them. By 1937, Ford had long abandoned its "Americanization" program. In fact, it had shuttered its Sociological Department in 1923, which had been perhaps the most robust company-sponsored attempt at social engineering in North America.[14] Even Ford's ambitious project to build an idealized America, Fordlandia, and create ideal Americans for it in the jungles of Brazil, had proved to be a quixotic attempt based on bad science and misunderstood local customs. By 1937, it was "patchy and ragged."[15] Bat'a's fellow welfare capitalist shoe manufacturer Endicott-Johnson of New York (EJ) still held off the mounting demands of the National Labor Review Board and unionization, and continued to organize large public events such as their Fourth of July parade. But EJ's events were decidedly familial, casual, and often comedic. One such company event witnessed workers in drag or dressed in clown suits and festooned with silly beards.[16] Alcohol consumption at company events was common regardless of prohibition.[17] Closer to Zlín, the Nazi movement had quickly appropriated the huge electro-chemical Siemens Corporation and its company town, Siemensstadt, when they made it one of the first sites for a mass rally after taking power, turning it from a symbol of company to a symbol of state.[18] All of this is to suggest that Bat'a's power to organize employees was something that few companies could match, then or since. Indeed, when watching Hackenschmied's movie today, one is struck by the dramatic staging of the event, militarized precision of the actors, and pomposity of the chief executive. All of this, for a shoe company?

Creating such a scene was in reach of company executives because the company saturated everyday life. Three-quarters of Zlín's 37,342 citizens lived in company housing, over half worked for Bat'a, and nearly all shopped at the company stores and went to the company-run hospital. The one consistent source of information was the company's daily newspaper, *Zlín*, which was a mouthpiece for Batism. At least six neighbourhoods, out of nine, had been either entirely or partially built by the company along a master plan – red bricks, flat roofs, and green spaces laid out in a radial grid.[19] Like other welfare capitalist enterprises in the world, Bat'a strove for complete vertical integration. Bat'a-owned farms produced the eggs and milk that Bat'a employees ate at Bat'a-run canteens. Additionally, the company's footprint extended well outside of the town, as the factory complex stretched for seven miles down the Dřevnice River to its confluence with the Morava. There the company had built a satellite town named Bat'ov. (Bat'ov would be one of ten towns across the world named after the company by 1939.) *Batovci*, the true believers, dominated local government and controlled the police. They had been doing so since 1923, when citizens voted them into every major municipal office. Given the inescapable presence of the company, to survive in the "kingdom of shoes," workers had little choice but to line up and march.

Perhaps, as Eric Hoffer theorized nearly seventy years ago, mass movements are interchangeable. According to this theory, giving oneself over to a shoe company's demands for loyalty by marching around in the uniform of a leather tanner is not much different from marching in a Nuremberg rally. The decisive shared trait among those animating such events, according to Hoffer, is a boundless optimism in the future. "The hopeful can draw strength from the most ridiculous sources of power – a slogan, a word, a button."[20] So, why not from shoes?

Certainly, the Bat'a Company propagated such hope. "We are not afraid of the future" was one of company founder Tomáš Bat'a's most repeated expressions.[21] The company demonstrated its confidence through hiring preferences, democratizing shopping, and embracing modernity. Hiring policy inclined toward young, unskilled workers that the company would train. In 1937, a stunning 40 per cent of its workforce was between fourteen and twenty-one years of age, clear proof of the company's desire to create a new industrial worker.[22] Its retail stores projected such confidence by illuminating European cityscapes with glowing, electrified displays in modernist stores. Inside these stores, "customer first" policies encouraged browsing and offered a democratic shopping experience, with a strict policy of first come, first served. Czechoslovaks' consumption patterns were hitherto largely based on status and nationality, , but mass production and its attendant conveniences would make it possible for everyone to become a pampered customer. After all, Bat'a's industrial production process required a massive number of customers. Therefore, shopping for Bat'a shoes meant leaving class and nationality at the door. Not surprisingly, customers lined up for the experience. To many of them, Bat'a was the "acme of modernity."[23]

There was hope as well in the tremendous growth of the company in the face of the Great Depression. By 1939, the Bat'a Company employed over 84,000, ran 5,000 retail stores, and operated twenty-five factories in eleven countries across the globe.[24] It had become the largest shoe manufacturer in the world, with the ability to produce over half a million pairs of shoes a day.[25] In addition, the company produced tires, toys, electric motors, even airplanes, and operated Kotva, the largest import-export business in Czechoslovakia. Before the outbreak of the Second World War, Bat'a accounted for a staggering 43.2 per cent of all consumer goods exports from Czechoslovakia.[26] The unrivalled success had much to do with Tomáš's willingness to adopt Fordist and Taylorist principles of manufacturing and Endicott-Johnson's welfare capitalist company town model, which greatly reduced dissent and stabilized an industrial workforce. Yet Bat'a's approach was based on much more than mimicry. For the company developed its own management system, its own pricing plan – the now-ubiquitous "99" pricing model – and its own architectural style – the famed Bat'a functionalism of brick, iron, and glass. It also developed its distinctive company culture, Batism.

Batism held that an industrial utopia could be achieved through harmonizing man and machine, and through rationalizing society.[27] It maintained that the company could make a new industrial person, the *Batovec* (Bat'a person). In essence, particularly in Zlín, Bat'a created a company-run society, one which promoted new determinants for inclusion and exclusion. Instead of religion, class, and nationality, Batism prized sobriety, appearance, work ethic, and, above all, loyalty to the corporation; these were the key traits of the *Batovec*. And the company went to great lengths to inculcate these traits into its workforce. From an informal organization centred around personal relationships and profitability at the beginning of the 1920s, the company steadily moved toward a highly regulated system and a fully legible workforce, where employees' lives were to be opened, read, and further investigated if the bosses so chose. Following the rationalizing dreams of company founder, Tomáš, Bat'a in the early 1930s began issuing every employee a "personnel card," sent personal inspectors on regular investigations of employees' houses, and had over two hundred company informants reporting on the political habits of their neighbours in Zlín.[28] The project was an attempt to remake society into an efficient, machine-like organism with no interpersonal conflicts and harmonized to the rhythms of production. Of course, this project was beholden to the highly subjective values of its engineers (aka. top management), who were eager to change the moral attitudes and physical appearances of employees into what they saw as quintessentially modern. From out of the backwards Moravian past, which is how Tomáš and other executives perceived it, the Bat'a company would make athletic, sober, and obsessively clean standardized workers capable of going anywhere in the world to turn a profit.

As a result, Bat'a became Czechoslovakia's outstanding representative of James C. Scott's "high modernism," radiating "a strong, one might even say muscle-bound, version of the self-confidence about scientific and technical progress, the expansion of production, the growing satisfaction of human needs, the mastery of nature (including human nature), and above all, the rational design of social order commensurate with the scientific understanding of natural laws."[29] Scott traced the long-term Enlightenment project of making citizens legible through the standardization and rationalization of weights, measures, maps, and laws from the early modern to the modern period. The rise of modernity underlay a drive for greater legibility. He pointed to the utopian projects of Brasilia, Soviet collectivization, villagization in Tanzania and the Great Leap Forward as high-water marks for a high modernist mentality that sought to order humanity according to the Boolean logic of scientific planning. Scott viewed these utopian schemes with horror, as they led to unusable city spaces, famine, and wide-scale environmental devastation.

However, Scott's work curiously located similar corporate projects outside of the modern era. "While factories and forests might be planned by private entrepreneurs, the ambition of engineering whole societies was almost exclusively a project of the nation-state."[30] Scott suggested that in the twenty-first century corporate schemes for social engineering have become, and are becoming, the new threat to the metis, or local culture, while government has increasingly become a defender of the local. Thus, Bat'a suggests a false dichotomy in Scott's seminal book. States' social engineering projects and those of big business are presented as asynchronous, though with roughly the same deleterious effects. Yet, many of the massive social engineering projects that Scott explored came after the rise of the most well-defined company towns in world history. Consider Bat'a's Zlín, Ford's Dearborn, Olivetti's Ivrea, Endicott-Johnson's cities in Broome County, all corporate high modernist projects in the interwar era, where companies spent massive amounts of money and time trying to implement a scientific organization of factory and society.[31]

Placing Bat'a in the discussion of high modernism suggests that it too operated under an ethos that produced gross overreach, social engineering, and an aesthetic of rationalization. It connects the people of Bat'a's Zlín and the people of Highland Park, Johnson City, and Fordlandia, to name but a few, with those of Magnitogorsk and Roosevelt, New Jersey. Such a connection puts forward that in the interwar period, a significant number of people shared a global experience by living in environments built with a similar logic. And there was a good deal of cross-pollination. As it happened, Zlín was much recognized in its time by leading figures of rational planning. It attracted the likes of Le Corbusier, Jawarhalal Nehru, Indira Gandhi, Getulio Vargas, Hermann Goering, George F. Johnson, and a host of others who could be deemed "high modernists" under James Scott's now-famous definition.

Yet, attaching the interwar company town to the concept of high modernity also allows for crucial differentiation within the category. While these towns had remarkable similarities, such as authorities who strove to manage everyday life according to the principles of rationalization, their citizens had very different contexts. Bat'a's high modernism was far less brutal, haphazard, and destitute than that of Magnitogorsk.[32] That Zlín came from a high modernism not initiated by a state actor but by a corporation mattered a great deal.

After all, while the *Batovci*'s spectacles of conformity hinted at the potential power of companies operating on a global scale, the Nuremberg rallies and military parades on Red Square displayed the existent power of a despotic modernity that was far more sinister than uniformed employees marching to liberate entrepreneurs. Unlike Bat'a, some of the state actors interested in building a high modernist utopia had mass murder in their purview. Therefore, the goings on of the company town of Zlín in 1937 must be kept within the larger framework of the acceleration of the concentration camp system in Germany and the Great Terror in the Soviet Union. As Jan globetrotted, paraded, and harmonized industrial shoe production, social engineers in Germany were busy building a "road to a 'folk community' – a society homogenized, purified, and standardized by social technologies – [that] necessarily led through eradication, extermination, and violence."[33] The Nuremberg rally was meant to prove to the world that millions would be ready to kill for the nation and its "Führer." The Bat'a May Day was meant to prove to the world that management could count on their workers to resist unionizing, to enthusiastically travel abroad or relocate for the sake of the company, and to seamlessly fit into the overarching plans of a global enterprise.

The Bat'a Company harboured grand visions and brought about revolutionary changes, but these were generally of a far less destructive nature than the high modernism that surrounded them. Bat'a's city provided comparatively high wages for its workers, and an impressive array of social services found in company-built hospitals, schools, stadiums, theatres, and shopping malls. Employment allowed a largely provincial and impoverished group of people opportunities for world travel, greater material wealth, and education. These facts call for a nuanced approach when discussing the social environment of Zlín. Indeed, Jay Winter's work on "minor utopias" could just as easily apply to Zlín in the Bat'a era as to Scott's high modernism. Winter looked to people such as Albert Kahn, the global financier and passionate advocate of world peace, to balance postmodern condemnations of the utopian dreamers of the twentieth century. Focusing on people who fought for a range of utopian goals, such as universal human rights and world peace, Winter argues, provides another way of looking at the century; it can be seen not only as a series of disasters but also as an era full of hope and aspiration, with people who "tried in their separate ways to imagine a radically better world … who configured limited and much less sanguinary plans for partial transformations of the world."[34] However, Batism was hardly partial. It was, then, something between a "minor utopia" and "high modernism." It was Batism.

Batism, from its inception to the present, has sparked both fierce criticism and unwavering support in the historical literature. The study of Batism began in 1928 with Rudolph Phillip's widely distributed book *Der unbekannte Diktator Thomas Bata*, which internationalized local criticism from a communist point of view. Phillip's work focused on the inhuman pace of "rationalized work," the company's union busting, and the omnipotence of the company in everyday life. His critique framed an argument that could be found across decades.[35] Undoubtedly, the most comprehensive academic account of the company from a harshly critical perspective came from the historian Bohumil Lehár in 1960. A tour de force of economic and business history, the book made further research possible because of its statistical information drawn from company archives. Nevertheless, Lehár regularly criticized Bať'a for its omnipotence and repression. Lehár inserted and made central a "heroic" communist resistance in his narrative of an economic juggernaut. In its final assessment, Lehár's monumental history found the Bať'a system as "the pinnacle of exploitation."[36]

Such an approach toward the company in the Bať'a Era (1923–39) has been sustained by a dwindling but still vocal group of left-leaning academics like Stanislav Holubec. His short article, "Silní milují život: Utopie, ideologie a biopolitika baťovského Zlína" (The Strong Love Life: Utopia, Ideology, and the Biopolitics of Bať'a's Zlín), makes the claim that the company represented one particularly strong version of corporate fascism. Holubec was one of the first scholars to use Foucault's concept of biopolitics to discuss Bať'a, but nevertheless he falls in the category of commentators who view Batism as an accomplished totalitarianism that was set in place in the early 1920s and did not change over time. For him and other critics, Bať'a was entirely successful in its sinister high modernist project.[37] For the vast majority of leftist critiques, the Bať'a system's complete corporate hegemony represented a frightening stage of industrial capitalism: corporate fascism.

Meanwhile, the champions of the system, from company men in the Bať'a era and exiles to now-mainstream commentators, have maintained that life in Zlín under company rule was a glorious realization of utopian dreams. During the Cold War, such a viewpoint was championed in print almost exclusively by one man, Antonín Cekota. Cekota was the chief propagandist for the firm in the interwar period and never left his position while in exile in Canada. Cekota's biography of Tomáš Bať'a, while providing excellent anecdotes, is a hagiography, claiming that the man was a national hero and his system created democratization and opportunity for all.[38] High praise of the system has not been confined to self-proclaimed *Batovci*, however. Following the Velvet Revolution, Czech scholars re-envisioned the company in a more positive light. For example, Radomíra Sedláková, architectural collection curator at the National Gallery in Prague wrote, "what we could say, of course, is that in Zlín, they succeeded in realizing one of the great social utopias that European society had been contemplating since the beginning of the Modern Age."[39] Indeed, positivity has become the dominant trend among commentators of Bať'a. Milan Zelený, a professor of management at Fordham University and the Tomáš Bať'a University in Zlín, has routinely used Bať'a's success as a model for management in the present day.[40] Likewise, politicians and economists in the Czech Republic have used Bať'a as proof that capitalism works, and that, more importantly, the Czech nation has a long-standing tradition of successful entrepreneurship.[41] Therefore, much of Bať'a's historiography remains locked in the rhetorical constraints of the Cold War.

It has only been in the last decade that a significant, if small, group of scholars has moved away from the normative debates and the hegemonic descriptions surrounding Bat'a. Because of this, their work has dramatically expanded our knowledge of the company. Of these, six historians stand out as central to the project of writing a new history of Bat'a and Zlín – one which approaches the past with a much less abrasive ideological supposition: Lucie Galčanová, Martin Jemelka, Martin Marek, Ondřej Ševeček, Vít Strobach, and Barbora Vacková. Their professional ethos, along with their evidence-based approach, has guided a revision that allows for gender, race, class, identification, and contestation. In short, their work is now essential for any understanding of depth on the subject.[42]

Additionally, architectural historians, film scholars, and business historians outside of the Czech Republic have begun to extensively research the people involved with designing Bat'a's Zlín. The architectural historian Kimberly Zarecor has traced the development of apartment housing, the infamous *paneláky*, during socialism, back to the architects who worked for Bat'a in the interwar period. By doing so, she has made the rare connection between the socialist period and the Bat'a era, which has opened fascinating questions of continuity between the two systems.[43] Petr Szczepanik has followed the development of Bat'a's media network to argue that "Bata's organization of work and the respective media infrastructure were not typical examples of a disciplinary *dispositif* of surveillance in the Foucauldian sense, just as they were not a pure application of mechanistic models of management (Taylor, Ford). Bat'a was already partly exceeding the disciplinary mode and moving toward what Gilles Deleuze called 'societies of control.'"[44] The business historian Susanne Hilger has illustrated how Bat'a's "highly cost-oriented corporate policy" set it apart from other family-owned companies.[45] Taken together, such work has provided a more comprehensive outline for the company's development.

Still, there remain significant gaps in the historical literature which this work aims to fill. The most obvious is that there has not been a history of the company since Lehár's in 1960, and this was never translated into English. The others concern nationalism, globalization, gender, *Eigensinn*, and rationalization. The elaboration of these themes in the following chapters is the major contribution of this book.

One of the major arguments here is that while the trend throughout Central and Eastern Europe in the interwar era was a tightening of national loyalty, Zlín became a centre of a remarkable national indifference. National indifference, as Tara Zahra theoretically explored, was generally seen a problem by nationalists. Indeed, it is only through their negative construction of the indifferent that the category exists.[46] Bat'a much preferred "cosmopolitan" to describe its philosophy. However, national indifference is the better fit because of several commingling processes. In management, Bat'a needed employees who could move into and out of national identities while all the while maintaining a distance from them. Many managers, as will be seen, strove to "act nationally" wherever they went. For example, a manager in Switzerland would do their best to appear Swiss, with language and holidays conforming to the local custom. At the same time, the large retail operation within Czechoslovakia needed to essentially not care about nationality in order to sell the maximum number of shoes. Finally, the workers of Zlín themselves, while pulled almost entirely from the surrounding Moravian countryside, came into an educational system that sought to remake them into *Batovci*.

Dominik Čipera, the second most powerful executive in the company, summarized well Batism's approach to nationalism when he wrote in 1933 that "in the past people fought over religion – now they fight over nationalism – but in the future the fight will be over the economy. Victory will belong to those whose work best serves the people."[47] Nationalism was something in the present that had to be dealt with, but the company's goals were not in the nationalist present. Employees therefore needed to be trained so that they could move between and above the nationalists. They needed to be indifferent. At least in the eyes of top executives, the project of creating nationally indifferent *Batovci* seemed to be working. From as early as 1928, chief publicist Antonín Cekota declared the success of building a nationally indifferent company town.

> Here in this rather provincial town are people who are worldlier than citizens of the largest cities. English is heard on the streets as well as German. There isn't a European language that isn't heard here. The words, business contracts, tariffs, balance sheets, courses, import, export, etc. are not only theoretical but a part of daily life. The cosmopolitanism of the people of Zlín is the direct result of not having political corruption and bad blood.[48]

National belonging was not an ideal but an obstacle. This challenges the assumption of national indifference as a passive category of analysis by suggesting it was cultivated on purpose. Bat'a's "rationalization" did not countenance nationalist conflict. Here is a history where the "grip of the nation state" was "less than absolute."[49]

This particular brand of national indifference was possible because of industrial capitalism, "the most revolutionary invention of all."[50] This was a revolution that fundamentally changed shoe production in Central Europe by creating an extreme competitive edge for those who could concentrate capital into machinery. In this, Bat'a was peerless in the Austro-Hungarian Empire. Its success disrupted the region's entire shoemaking industry, and by 1937 was disrupting large swaths of the world's. Moreover, Zlín, which buzzed with the sound of motors, seemed like an entirely different country – visitors often remarked that it was as if they were travelling in America. This impression was by no means accidental. The migrants who moved to Zlín by the thousands in search of work, most of whom were rural, Catholic, and poor, witnessed their daily routines nearly completely upended. Baťa's futurism relentlessly attacked Moravian traditions and sought to bring in adolescents to reshape them for the task of industrial production. The nation, whichever one dominated at any given era, appears in the history of Baťa as more of a hindrance than a help. Such a statement seemingly goes against a growing literature about industrial capitalism in the modern era (1865–1950), much of which has shown that industrial capitalism had taken off *because* of state intervention.[51] In particular, Sven Beckert's work on cotton convincingly illustrated how industrial capitalism was "equally a project of governments."[52] Baťa's industrial capitalism undoubtedly benefited from certain moments of state intervention, such as huge orders for army boots during the First World War, but more often governments were ambiguous, conflicted, and at times hostile to the company. In fact, it would not be until after the shock of the Munich Agreement in September 1938, when the political order of Czechoslovakia collapsed, that the power of the company would enter the halls of national government.

For the thousands of May Day participants not on the dais in 1937 the spectacle remained something apart from the nation. It was a way to feel reassured that the revolutionary changes brought on by industrial capitalism were firmly under control. The contract was simple. Consent in exchange for economic security.

Such a trade-off infuriated those involved with the communist movement. According to their understanding of industrial capitalism, workers marching at a Baťa May Day could only be explained through a kind of brainwashing. As an unknown author wrote in the communist-leaning magazine *Tvorba* (Construction), "Baťa's system of rationalization demands that not only do people serve the interests of industrial production but that they also fully adapt to its ideology."[53] For communists, Batism was the "highest form of capitalist exploitation" through its seemingly total control of the proletariat.[54] In their eyes, the latest industrial technology and time management, when used in the interests of the bourgeoisie, created a "scientific exploitation of the working class." Of course, their critique could only go so far. For here was a company built upon the foundations of Ford, a system of production that captured the imagination of communists across the spectrum.[55] As they sniped away at Batism, they dreamed about having the power of its industrial production.

Batovci also defined their ideology through the rhetoric of class, only inverting Marx's historical process. "Our battle from the start was a battle against proletarianism," Jan Baťa informed readers a few months after his triumphant 1937 parade.[56] Just as Marxists strove to replace hierarchical titles of deference with "comrade," the *Batovci* sought to turn "workers" (*dělnici*) into "colleagues" (*spolupracovníky*). In Batism, the main enemy was communism. And the communists of Czechoslovakia returned the animosity. (It was no accident that the only major city in Czechoslovakia to have its name changed upon the Communist Party's seizure of power in 1948 was Zlín.) Their battles played out in the court system, in the press, and on May Day itself. After all, Bat'a had essentially co-opted the world's major socialist holiday. Moreover, especially to the people of Czechoslovakia in 1937, Batism seemed to be doing a better job of winning workers' loyalties.

Of course, underneath the May Day spectacle of uniformity, there were murmurs of disquiet among the disparate voices within and without Czechoslovakia's industrial utopia. The people, so uniform in appearance, held widely varied paths in getting to Labour Square, and widely varied interpretations as to what it meant to be standing there, cheering the *šef*. For on that day, workers such as Anna Čevelová and Vaclav Kamas, who would be soon pushed out of the firm for their communist sympathies, marched together with Jan Daněk and Vincenc Jaroněk. Jaroněk was the city police's most accomplished undercover agent and Daněk was the head of the company's intelligence service, whose lives were spent rooting out disloyal elements. Also there was Alexander Reinharcz, a struggling Jewish student from Podcarpathian Ruthenia, and Paul Zuppal, a German student who excelled at stitching and would go on to be a department manager. In the crowd, one would likely find Hans Tauber, a small business owner whose life would be twice rocked before the close of the decade by an affair with a younger woman and by the Aryanization of his store, as well as Ladislava Fornoušková, who as a teenager had been expelled from the city for ten years for living too promiscuous a life. And finally, there was Geza Stujlater, a local ne'er-do-well, who would be arrested some twenty-seven times for various minor offences over his lifetime. Even among those on the dais, and at the lead of the parade sections, the utopian project held varied promises.[57] For Jan's increasingly Il Duce style had begun to alienate the long-time general manager and mayor of Zlín, Dominík Čipera, and the executive Hugo Vavrečka. The Bat'a world, then, was not nearly as neat as the spectacle on the square would have us think. As the historian Alf Lüdtke has pointed out, everywhere one looks in the historical record one will find *Eigensinn*.[58] *Eigensinn* has been best defined in English by John Eidson as "putting up with political power to the degree that one must, while pursuing one's own ends to the degree that one can."[59] Across this narrative, one will find residents with an agency that the company could not control.[60]

Still, all of those thousands of people assembled on 1 May 1937 were historical actors in a play of considerable magnitude – the rise of the transnational corporation. And they were some of the first to rise to the stage. By 1937 the Bat'a Company was a central player in the development of a global political economy, as it helped to usher in a new era of globalization. When tariff walls went up across the world from 1929 to 1932, Bat'a jumped them by building satellite factories in its desired markets. The company did so by riding imperial pathways while simultaneously catering to local anti-colonial elites.

As Bat'a entered into markets around the globe and opened factories across the Global South, it was a bridge between "modern globalization" and "post-colonial globalization."[61] First defined by A.G. Hopkins, these two eras of globalization were distinguished by the imperialism of the former, and the rise of transnational corporations in the latter. In between, during the interwar era, one finds evidence for a "deglobalization," where markets collapsed and economic and political integration slowed. In this, 1914–50 is seen not as a growth period but a caution about the ways in which global integration is nonlinear. Adding Bat'a to the literature adjusts the picture of the transnational corporation in the interwar era, and provides clarity to the ways in which corporations used imperial pathways to globalize their operations. This adjustment matters because it confirms that the interwar era was not simply one of stagnation but one of significant transformation.[62]

As a progenitor of the transition to the era of the transnational corporation, Bat'a created a centralized organizational model, a decentralized system of production, and a mass-produced stylishness that it exported across the world. By so doing, the company participated in a process historian C.A. Bayly claimed as the fundamental feature of modernity – a growing global uniformity.[63] In this view, food, political ideas, dress, sport, leisure, and commodities all began to rapidly grow more uniform as people around the world shared in the complicated project of globalization. The history of Bat'a is essentially the story of a major actor in the process of this growing global uniformity. Bat'a zealously adopted certain American ideas – the company town model of EJ, the industrial technology of Lynn, Massachusetts, the time management and social outlook of Ford – tinkered with these, and then went on to create a standardized company town model that it exported around the world.

And yet in their remarkable similarity, these mini-Zlíns stood out in their local contexts. And so too did the people that came to manage them, Czech-speakers who were educated as *Batovci* and prized for their national indifference. Here, attention to gender and class differences is helpful in trying to explain Bat'a's successful globalization. Everywhere Bat'a went, it was met with protests. Through this conflict, management learned to essentially blend into the local culture so to be seen as resident and modern. Moreover, the company contracted with local, oftentimes remote, retailers that sold to the lower rungs of the socio-economic ladder. In many cases, Bat'a stores doubled as community centres. At the same time, the company built its global road on top of the maps of European empires. It expanded across well-worn imperial pathways, especially those made by the British. And it did so by making customers of white colonial elites. Racial and class differences mattered, and Bat'a remarkably managed to cater to the wealthy and to the poor, to anticolonial nationalists and to imperialists. Such a history suggests that globalization is just as much about recognizing differences in order to sell products as it is about acknowledging commonalities within a global modernity.

Indeed, the Bat'a model was uniform when it arrived in places like Calcutta and Jakarta. However, the company quickly realized it needed to become recognized as a local company, and not part of a global, uniform business to succeed. Just as the standardized flat-roofed red-bricked buildings were going up, the *Batovci* began the task of blending in. Such a history challenges much of globalization theory, which tends to present globalization as "the transcendence of nationalism" and as "having moved past colonialism and imperialism."[64] Bat'a did not transcend nationalism or imperialism, but used both to expand. All of this is to say that Bat'a, while being a key agent of global uniformity, was also forced to become highly sensitive to the local. Such a sensitivity is one of the major reasons one can buy their shoes today. It is also why Bat'a was and is *sui generis* among industrial shoemakers.

Bat'a's globalization also demonstrated the limits of transnational actors. Across the time period covered here, we see the hand of government. From the kid glove of Austria-Hungary to Nazi Germany's club, state actors were crucial to the success or failure of Bat'a's operations. As the last chapter will demonstrate, when so desired, state actors could bend Bat'a to their will. There was little space for indifference in the context of the Second World War. While Bat'a was large, complex, and remarkably adept at moving in and out of countries, it was no match for the US government. Similarly, once domestic critics of the company regained power in Czechoslovakia, they almost immediately nationalized the factory complex in Zlín. Indeed, Bat'a's history confirms the economist Robert Gilpin's argument that the "nation-state remains the dominant actor in both domestic and international affairs."[65]

While a secondary power, the company was nevertheless transformational. From 1923, when *Batovci* swept the municipal elections of Zlín and essentially eliminated all political parties from local contests, to the appointment of Dominik Čipera as minister of public works in 1938, a position of considerable power in post-Munich Czecho-Slovakia, Bat'a pushed for a radically modernist agenda. Throughout the interwar period *Batovci* vociferously called for public works projects inside Czechoslovakia using conscript labour. They argued for the elimination of all "politics," and for its replacement by scientific management. They sought to radically remake the country into a densely populated, thoroughly integrated modern state through parental incentives, countrywide infrastructure programs, and the elimination of local differences.[66] By so doing, Bat'a fit into a wider Czech and European context that has increasingly drawn the attention of historians.

During the first half of the century, academics across Europe developed a mania for public planning. Jan Janko and Emilie Těšínská have traced the spread of technical thinking throughout the crown lands of Bohemia and Moravia to reveal a circle of academics, authors, politicians, and industrialists pushing for a scientifically managed society.[67] The scientific management of everyday life came closest to reality during the First World War, as Rudolf Kučera has shown with his work on the Austro-Hungarian state's efforts to manage workers during wartime with nutritional "science."[68] Furthermore, recent work has shown how this network of technocrats created the foundation for a postwar Europe that relied on state planning on an unprecedented scale.[69] Bat'a's zeal for rationalization did not exist in a vacuum.

Yet, Bat'a exceeded the mandates of the technocrats in interwar Czechoslovakia. While these individuals pushed ambitious agendas through lectures and articles, mostly from the Masaryk Academy of Labour, Bat'a's capital allowed it to graft its industrial philosophies, many inspired by American examples, onto Moravian soil. The consequence was a unique brand of welfare capitalism.[70] While building a commercial concern, based on a society of small farmers, artisans, and aristocrats, into a global concern, the company developed a way of life, an operating system that was a radical departure from the past. It was an operating system that required demands of its population that other citizens of Czechoslovakia did not have and presented a unique challenge to the ideals of Thomas Masaryk's First Republic of Czechoslovakia. Life in Zlín offered an alternative to the nationalism and political perplexity of Central Europe, as it offered a vision of a rationalized industrial society where man and machine, family and factory, were supposed to work together seamlessly. From 1894 to 1945, Bat'a embarked on one of the most ambitious social engineering projects a private company has ever attempted. Southern Moravia did not cultivate its rationalization, but it was too weak to temper it. The result was a dramatic and rapid change in the everyday lives of the people of the Dřevnice Valley.

Stricter gender roles were foremost among the most significant changes brought by the rationalization of the valley. Company leadership tried to cultivate gender norms almost as fiercely as new markets. Their vision was a conservative industrial modernity, where women attended industrial schools, worked in the factory, though on specifically gendered tasks, and left to become housewives once married. Men were to be competitive sportsmen whose primary ambition was to work to make money. Administration was to be a male privilege. Such a perspective was not radical in the context of Czechoslovakia in the interwar period. As Melissa Feinburg has pointed out, women's political power waned in a context of conservative gender expectations.[71] What seems unique in the Bat'a context, though, was that the administrators encouraged both genders to embrace the speed of modernization through flying, driving, and incorporating other technologies into their lives. Young people were to be carefully separated to discourage premarital sex. All of this was implemented in company policies. However, as several examples contained herein will attest, the new world of industrial production created possibilities that undermined the conservative modernity – new spaces opened up for sexual exploration and some women used the acceleration of everyday life to defy expectations.

The pages that follow track these changes chronologically, from Bat'a's founding in 1894 to its dramatic split into three components in 1945. The work considers government officials' writings about Bat'a on both sides of the Atlantic, workers' reminiscences, newspapers, legal documents, and communist tracts. These records were mostly found in the Bat'a repository in the Moravian Regional Archive of Zlín, the Zlín City Archive, the National Archive of the Czech Republic, and the National Archives of the United States. It also rests on the shoulders of the aforementioned historians.

From the company's executives to those on its furthest periphery, from the sycophants to the critics, the voices of the "kingdom of shoes" are brought to light here in order to excavate a society largely covered in the political fallout after the Second World War. It was a society that did not move in lockstep, no matter how organized work and social life came to be. But it was a society identified by the centralized power of a company able to coordinate the industrial production of the most complex of textiles: the shoe. Bat'a was able to manufacture consent by providing its workforce with material goods and security, but in turn expected them to forgo democracy both at work and in society to maintain the technocratic order. This compromise was at all times challenged and imperfect. Indeed, the very threats the company were so concerned about were often the by-products of industrialization, such as high numbers of women in the workforce, drifters coming into town to beg and look for work, and increased opportunities for perceived moral transgressions.

After all, the radical futurism of the corporate regime corresponded with an intense fear and uncertainty. The disruptions brought by industrial capitalism, the First World War, the Great Depression, and the Second World War made the company's boundless optimism quixotic, yet understandable. In Europe's most brutal and uncertain years, Bat'a offered a promise of stability. Concurrently, it went about disrupting the global shoe trade and transfiguring a valley in Moravia. Its history, therefore, illustrates the multidirectional paths of modernity.[72]

"A New Fixed Existence": The Modernization of Zlín

That Zlín would be the setting for a spectacle like that of May Day 1937 was far from inevitable. After all, there are neither valuable mineral deposits nor particularly rich farmland in the valley of the river Dřevnice in southeastern Moravia. The river, prone to flooding in the spring, is little more than a creek by late summer and perennially unnavigable. Surrounded by the forested hills of the Western Carpathians, the valley has never been in the crossroads of major trade routes and remains an out-of-the-way location for even today's traveller. But for small farm plots, the occasional winery, and timber harvesting, the area's inhabitants have had few natural sources of revenue with which to entice development. And while the broken terrain, dense forests, and unpredictable rivers led to a rich cultural and linguistic diversity, with the Haná dialect in Wallachia, the Slovácko in Moravian Slovakia, and Romani travellers and German-speaking nobles and burghers carving out respective cultural zones in and around the area, the geography of the region ensured a political and economic marginality until the late Habsburg period (1900–18), when Bat'a transformed the valley into the centre of industrial shoe production in Central Europe.

Taking a long view, what follows outlines how industrial capital came to dominate the politics and landscape of the Zlín region by the eve of the First World War. As will be shown, it took a familiar path. Like factory production in other industrializing regions, such as Alsace, Catalonia, Saxony, Switzerland, and Lombardy, Bat'a's in Zlín used existing skill sets that had been developed in the putting-out system, which had workers performing labour in homes and small workshops, and took these regionally dispersed workers and concentrated them into larger sites. Industrialization occurred in a relatively small number of places in the nineteenth century, and in all of them, Zlín included, a family of craftsmen invested their capital derived from the putting-out system into mechanized production.[1] Therefore, the industrialization of shoemaking in Zlín resembled the history of manufacturing throughout Europe, which was defined by capital investment, usually by skilled craftsmen of a trade, going into regions with established networks of handicraft production and reorganizing people around mechanized production.

However, local particularities guarantee that no two industrial concerns are the same. And these differences can determine the longevity of an enterprise, the quality of life of workers, and the political power of a company. Bat'a's industrialization of the Zlín region fit no template, though it borrowed from many, because Zlín's particularities – its marginality, its local elites, its culture, and its shoemaking – blended with those of Moravia in the Austro-Hungarian Empire – with its cliquish world of finance, high tariffs, intense nationalist organizations, and explosions of social democracy – to deeply imprint the way in which this industrialization unfolded. From its brief embrace of Czech social democracy and attendant political alliance between managers and workers, its implementation of an idealized American system, and its subsequent drift away from Czech nationalism, Bat'a adopted an extraordinary path to industrialization. Indeed, while it is not until the middle of the 1920s that one can clearly see the outlines of Batism, the years preceding its manifestation are crucial to making sense of the ideology. It is in them that we find Bat'a's divergence.

Longue Durée

The people who participated in and witnessed Zlín's transformation were largely rural peoples who had for centuries attuned their routines to the seasonal patterns of Eastern Moravia. Daylight, temperature, and rainfall dictated the workday. Celebration was Catholic in name but often tied to much older traditions. At Easter, for example, girls of the village would be asked by the village's boys to give them brightly painted eggs. The boys were equipped with *pomlázky*, a whip made from willow branches. If the girl refused a boy's request, they were threatened with a beating. Thus, the pagan traditions of the early Slavic peoples continued under Catholicism, blending into a mix of practices and beliefs that can best be termed Moravian folk culture. Associated with brightly coloured costumes, Czech-Slovak dialects/ethnicities, charming folk architecture, music, wine-making, and strong brandy made from plums (*slivovice*) and pears (*hruškovice*), Moravian folk culture was the outcome of centuries of small communities interacting through religious festivals and pastoral trading in a marginal hill country.[2]

The valley, the town, and the serfs that lived there comprised the domain of Zlín, an estate of some 1,400 people in 1600. The local lords, who conducted all of the domain's official business at their castle, used the *robot* system of management, which was a forced labour obligation for the serfs. During the course of the sixteenth century, the labour obligation for the townspeople had changed into a regular tax of sixty gold pieces. The shift in obligations allowed the town to develop small-scale production and sell meat, soap, and wine. Yet this modest economic development was never able to compete with that of the royal town of Hradiště or the archbishop's town of Kroměříž.[3] While the region supported only a tiny market and meagre source of finished goods, its broken terrain and abundant rainfall, which brought lush grasslands and forests, were ideal for cattle. Medieval and early modern Zlín was a cow town.

Political events exacerbated the marginality of the region. During the Hussite Wars, 1419–34, Hungarian raiders repeatedly looted the area. Later, in 1605 during the Bocskai Rebellion, Hungarian rebels rode through and burned most of Zlín to the ground. During the Thirty Years War, the town experienced even more deprivations as the notorious Lisowczycy, an irregular light cavalry unit of the Polish-Lithuanian Commonwealth, and Hungarian armies marched across the area and confiscated whatever they could. The population of Zlín declined by half between 1600 and 1640.[4] Toward the end of the war, Protestant Wallachians staged a dramatic uprising against the Catholic armies of the Habsburg Empire and took control of the region for a time, even going so far as to ally with the invading Swedish and then Turkish armies, but their defeats in 1644 and again in 1663 sent the Wallachians back into the hills further east – their example serving as a harsh deterrent for future uprisings by the region's ethnic groups. When peace finally returned to the region at the end of the seventeenth century, Zlín had to overcome a "dislocation of the labour force, a decline in production, trade, and civil autonomy."[5] What little development that existed in 1600 had been thoroughly undone by almost a century of war.

Count Gabriel Serényi took over the estate and town after the Thirty Years War. Serényi, a veteran of the Battle of Vienna, never lived in Zlín. But his delegated authority stabilized the region by reaffirming the rights and responsibilities of the nobility.[6] Around this time, a shoemakers' guild emerged in the town; along with the butchers' guild, it would grow to be influential in town affairs. The cattle ranching of the region provided the raw materials and impetus for both guilds. Neither butchers nor shoemakers made much impact overall on the growth of the town in the 1700s, however. After Gabriel Serényi's death the estate passed to his descendants, who, judging from the stagnant population and very few construction projects that can be dated to their period of ownership, seem to have shown little interest in developing the area.[7] After the Serényis, a variety of middle- to lower-ranking noble families presided over the estate of Zlín. They profited from the property's cattle and timber, but, like the Serényis, invested little in the infrastructure of the area.[8]

This pattern of stagnation would change at the dawn of the nineteenth century, when Baron Claudius Bretton bought the estate and invested considerable resources into the town. Bretton spent substantial sums turning the castle into a chateau, rebuilding the Church of Saint Philip, developing a large park, overseeing the building of a gymnasium, and purchasing and renovating the chateau of Klečůvka. The infusion of resources led to a small increase in the town's population, and certainly helped the town's aesthetic. More important than Bretton's desire to update the landscape, however, was his commitment to the scientific method to create manufacturing and agricultural opportunities. In the *Moravian Wanderer* of 1854, Bretton appears as a leader of the silk industry, "overcoming prejudices against silk crops" to create "great mulberry plantations" and a model silk construction institute in Zlín.[9]

Bretton's development of the silk industry nudged the valley toward its industrial future. It also created the conditions for the privileges of people like Bretton to be publicly challenged. For Bretton's development scheme did not stop the liberal ideas of 1848 from briefly blowing through the valley. The first challenge to the social order since the 1660s occurred when students of the local gymnasium Bretton had funded led a takeover of the town's administration building, declaring solidarity with their counterparts in Vienna. While nothing came of the event, as the town soon returned to Claudius Bretton, the widespread uprisings ended serfdom for all of the agricultural workers of the empire. Bretton marked the momentous events of 1848–51 by affixing a note above the entrance to his Zlín chateau that read

> Rich, conservative embellisher,
> Or poor, wanton destroyer!
> Hear my words:
> The old stone which you have taken from its place
> Hides no other treasure than that of historical memory.
> It was put here three years after the revolution of 1848,
> Which tried in vain to destroy the nobility
> Along with the stony remains of a strong and aristocratic age,
> But which succeeded only in annihilating the last
> Remnants of feudal privilege: *robota*, tithe, and patrimonial court.
> Let this reminder and this historical example
> Be a lesson and a treasure
> To you, rich, conservative embellisher.[10]

The stone reminder of the fragility of the noble position and the need to look at the cause of the revolution through a clearer lens indicated Bretton's keen insight into the situation. The aristocracy's "stony" customs were threatening its survival. Bretton died two years after affixing the stone, but he seemed to have passed on to his son William the lessons of his generation. William continued to invest in the town by funding a brewery, granary, and a match factory. These were Zlín's fragile first shoots of industrial capitalism. It was then that a small but emergent manufacturing economy began a sustained challenge to the legitimacy of the economic and social system of the aristocracy and the clergy.[11] Yet, unlike Lancashire County, England, or Massachusetts – the cradles of industrial capitalism – capital in 1850s Zlín remained in the hands of an aristocrat who had no Peter Ewart – the engineer behind the genius of the Quarry Bank Mill – on hand. The match factory closed only a few years after opening. The small silk industry collapsed. By 1856, the estate's financial affairs were not good, and the Brettons had run out of capital to improve it. They put the entire property up for sale, some 2,400 hectares of land along with the Zlín castle.[12]

The property moved through others' hands before Leopold Alexander Haupt purchased it for 470,000 gulden in 1860.[13] Haupt's parents, one a wealthy linen manufacturer and the other a wealthy leather manufacturer, both died young. The young Leopold sold his mother's leather business, and moved that capital into banking, while keeping his father's linen manufacturing going. By all accounts he was remarkably wealthy. Though he made his wealth through manufacturing and banking, and lived in the centre of Brno, where he was on the municipal board, Leopold looked to Zlín as a way to move into the Austrian aristocracy. He used the estate as a summer residence for his extended family, and he invested very little in modernizing equipment, infrastructure, or housing.[14] Again, a crucial difference between nineteenth-century Zlín and the centres of industrialization like Lancashire County and Lynn, Massachusetts, was the outsized role of aristocratic privilege in Zlín. Life in the 1860s remained largely dictated by the powerful landowner, now Leopold Haupt, whose authority included the right to appoint the vicar of the church.

The spatial layout of the town provides a good example of the political economy of the town in this period. By the mid-nineteenth century, the town consisted of 260 buildings, with the church and the castle being the largest buildings among them. These two structures served to spatially reinforce the position of the Catholic Church and the aristocracy in local affairs. Interestingly, maps of the town from the period exaggerate these two edifices' size by depicting the chateau and the Church of Saints Phillip and Jacob larger than scale, thereby depicting the political and cultural power of the church and aristocracy in provincial areas of the Austrian Empire. At least that is how the unknown mapmakers viewed the town.[15] While Bretton proved himself something of a progressive aristocrat, the church in Zlín encouraged deference, clung to codes of honour, and put few resources into developing the public infrastructure. Ecclesiastical education taught a hierarchical worldview that disdained the liberal politics spreading throughout the education system in the larger cities of the empire.[16]

However, many residents surely visualized their surroundings differently. Another map, the cadastral survey created in 1910, depicts lives centred on small plots of land. The map illustrates a dense patchwork of slivers of farm plots, contrasted with the expansive church and estate grounds.[17] Until the end of the nineteenth century the majority of the people in the region were engaged in animal husbandry, forestry, and farming – none of which created vast amounts of wealth. Due to the practice of subdividing farmland among male heirs, the surrounding area around the town was a dense patchwork of small lots, often no larger than three acres and frequently exhausted. By all indicators a growing populace was beginning to encroach on more and more of the land surrounding the town.[18]

This poverty did not deter an enigmatic Frenchman named Robert Florimont to start up the region's first business with over one hundred employees. Florimont was from a family of shoe manufacturers with workshops in Paris and Egypt. He apparently set off to expand the business by opening the family's first shoe factory in Vienna in 1868. He sold this factory, though, and two years later moved to Zlín for either health reasons, or for the region's skilled shoemakers (sources disagree).[19] In 1870, at the height of unprecedented economic expansion throughout the Habsburg Empire (referred to as the *Grunderzeit*), Florimont established Zlín's first major business established by someone outside the ranks of the aristocracy. It grew in the following years to employ some two hundred people, which made it the largest enterprise in the town. The factory produced roughly two hundred pairs of stitched shoes per day, a ratio of one employee to one pair of shoes. The shoes were for the most part not made in the workshop of Florimont, but were the product of a cottage industry. Florimont's employees worked out of their homes and were paid by the shoe.[20] This type of production was common throughout the European shoemaking industry in the 1870s, but had vanished among other professions, such as weaving.[21]

The difference can be explained in the complexity of shoemaking and the particularities of Austria-Hungary. Before the mechanization of production, shoemaking typically required a seven-year apprenticeship, where the aspiring shoemakers would learn "the preparation of the insole and outsole ... to prepare pegs and drive them ... [to] familiarize themselves with making of turned and welt shoes ... rounding the sole, sewing the welt, and stitching the outsole."[22] However, the complexity of making a shoe had not prevented the industrialization of shoemaking in the United States, which began in the 1850s.[23] It was the strength of shoemakers' guilds in Austria-Hungary and elsewhere in Europe, as well as the relatively slow rate of the diffusion of new technology, that made shoemaking ostensibly resistant to the pressures of mechanized production. Thus, the tradition of handicraft production in shoemaking, as exemplified by Florimont's operation, continued as the dominant system of shoemaking in Europe through the nineteenth century.[24]

Florimont stayed for eight years in Zlín, enduring the depression of 1873. Little is known about his time there, but he and his family must have been outsiders, as they allegedly never learned Czech. Most likely the Florimonts used German as their language of interaction, which was the language of the aristocracy and bureaucracy. The one group the Florimonts did befriend was the Haupt family, who rented them a house on their land.[25] Thus, the local noble, Leopold, who was awarded the title of von Buchenrode in 1874, and the largest employer, Florimont, were on friendly terms and seemed to be much more compatible with each other than with their employees.[26] Their relationship ended in 1878 when, upon hearing the news that his brother and cousins were killed in an uprising in Egypt, the Florimonts abruptly left town. Robert eventually moved to the Suez region to work as an official with the post office; he died there of unknown causes. His factory kept on in his absence for two more years before closing.[27]

While far from revolutionary at the time, Florimont's factory marked the emergence of a small but powerful middle class that would come to replace the institutional and cultural power of the aristocracy and church. The middle-class revolution, well documented in the history of modern Europe, was relatively slow to take root in Zlín, as in the rest of Austria.[28] Yet once it began, the revolution happened in a compressed time of some twenty to thirty years (1890s–1910s). During that period groups of manufacturers, educators, and skilled workers formed organizations and started businesses that dramatically undermined the region's social hierarchy; these placed higher value on loyalty to nation and/or company than on social rank. These local organizations were nodes in a wide network that created the political and cultural values of the Austrian middle class.

The Making of Middle-Class Zlín

Toward the end of the nineteenth century, as the historian Geoff Eley has pointed out, these values came to create coherence across Central Europe "in which definite themes of national efficiency, social hygiene, and racialized nationalism coalesced."[29] The nodes of businessmen's clubs, parents' organizations, athletic associations, political organizations, and so on transmitted the criteria for this new culture, which included new conceptions of masculinity and femininity alongside information about the latest techniques in manufacturing, exercise, and education. The first transmissions into Zlín are difficult to precisely track, but what is clear is that in the last decade of the nineteenth century members of a new middle class changed the culture of the valley dramatically by bringing it in line with modern ideals that had been normalized in parts of Western and Central Europe since the end of the eighteenth century.[30]

The modern ideal, generally defined by a mentality that champions rationalism, industriousness, nationalism, science, and moderation, arrived in the valley a few years after the Austrian state enacted the Law on Assembly of 1867. The new law finally allowed for associations and interest groups to freely organize. Throughout the empire, the result of the law was a proliferation of associations and the beginning of mass politics.[31] In provincial Zlín, the law had less dramatic immediate effects, but all the same led to a profound shift in where people socialized, why they socialized, and what kinds of people organized their socialization. One of the first of these organizations was the Reader's Association, founded in 1886.

The Reader's Association, in the words of its chairman, the district pharmacist František Vrla, sought to "prevent cultural bankruptcy" by providing a reading room and library for the public and by organizing various events, such as poetry readings and musical performances. Its members were decidedly middle class: two teachers, three factory owners, a pharmacist, an accountant, and a doctor were among the thirty (all male) members in attendance at a meeting in 1903.[32] To these men of the association, preventing cultural bankruptcy meant embracing a Czech nationalist orientation – and steeping oneself in the writings of Czech nationalists. The library's inventory from 1893 showed a strong commitment to obtaining the works of the Czech "awakeners" (buditelé), from Karolína Světla to Alois Jirásek to František Palacký. Alongside the Czech nationalist pantheon, readers could find technical and travel books, while books concerning religion, and those written in German, were not priorities. Books were not the only focus of the organization – one of its biggest events in 1903 was to host an evening with František Bartoš, the Moravian ethnomusicologist and nationalist activist.[33]

To complement the Reader's Association, members of the growing middle class organized a Sokol chapter in 1898. The group, dedicated to the improvement of the physical fitness of the Czech nation through gymnastic exercise, began in Prague in 1862. Since that time, Sokol had slowly spread to the provinces, eventually coming to Zlín, when a group of locals decided to start a chapter.[34] Meeting in the newly built Emperor Franz Joseph I Public School, twenty-eight men and twelve adolescent boys exercised twice a week. They did so to promote the Sokol creed of "in a healthy body is a healthy soul." Largely, their meetings consisted of members taking part in synchronized gymnastics routines and Greco-Roman wrestling.[35] According to the organization's founder, Miroslav Tyrš, this exercise was "meaningless unless Sokol minted members with an attitude to help the present and future of our [Czech] nation."[36] That the Zlín group was interested in more than exercise is evidenced in Sokol's organization of social and educational events for the public.

A few years after its founding in Zlín, Sokol began working with the Reader's Association to host a series of cultural events in the recently built Citizen's Credit Union Building (itself a milestone in the middle-class revolution).[37] The two organizations brought in actors, intellectuals, and musicians to perform for the general public. While it remains unclear as to how many people attended such events, we do have records of the key personnel of the organizations. That

Figure 1.1. Sokol exercises in Zlín in 1903. Moravský zemský archiv v Brně, Státní okresní archiv Zlín, Sbírka fotografií Zlín, sign. 197, obálka č. 14407.

their memberships overlapped shows how the progressive citizens of the region actively brought about new patterns of everyday life. On both rosters one finds teachers, pharmacists, skilled tradesmen, and factory owners. Among the latter, we find the recently arrived Bat'a brothers, Tomáš and Antonín, who were among the founding members of Sokol and regular attendees of the Reading Association.[38] Energetic and young, the two shoe factory owners had quickly become central participants in the project to make Zlín modern.

The Bat'a siblings, Tomáš, Anna, and Antonín Jr., became central figures in Zlín's middle-class revolution when their unpredictable yet generous father, Antonín, himself a shoe manufacturer, gave them an early inheritance of 800 guldens, with which they started their own shoe factory in 1894. The siblings had moved from the nearby city of Uherské Hradiště, where they worked in a smattering of shoe workshops, sometimes their father's, while attending school. Antonín Sr. left a deep imprint on the siblings, as he had built up a successful shoe business only to watch it fail, becoming known for his gambling and drinking in his later years. A close acquaintance, Josef Macka, reported that Antonín Sr. had a "powerful beard from which protruded a long pipe," that he "liked to drink two or three mugs while he made shoes," and "he liked to play cards to midnight."[39] Perhaps because of this, when the Bat'a siblings moved to Zlín, their father did not join them. Investing their inheritance into their own workshop, the siblings began recruiting area shoemakers in much the same way Florimont employed them decades before – by hiring a few workers for work in a central shop and more to work out of their homes.

Their first employees were men and women like Rudolf Vachyněk and Aloisie Mlýnková, both of whom started working at Bat'a in the 1890s. Their letters to the amateur historian František Hodáč, which they wrote some years later about their experiences in the early days of the company, reveal the reliance Bat'a initially had on skilled workers and established networks of shoemakers. Vachyněk worked with Antonín Bat'a Sr. before moving from Uherské Hradiště to Zlín in order to work for Antonín's sons. In his recollection some forty years later, Vachyněk recalled how he "walked to Otrokovice [21 km] because transportation was too expensive at that time." He made such a journey because Tomáš Bat'a "was relentless."[40] Once settled, Vachyněk worked making shoes and slippers at the small factory the siblings had set up in the middle of town as well as at his own home. Except for stitching done on one sewing machine, all of the work was done by hand.[41]

Mlýnková was working stitching uppers out of a friend's house in Zlín when Antonín Bat'a Jr. asked her and several others to come and do the same work for his company. She recalled their workshop as being divided according to gender, with women doing all of the stitching of uppers and the men working on the lathes to assemble the rest of the shoes. She remembered starting out in a tough period when the company did not have enough money on hand to buy materials and Tomáš "alone did all the accounting, all the travelling, and made all the payments."[42] The early desperation gave way to expansion and profit when Tomáš won several sizable contracts. Mlýnková witnessed Bat'a hire accountants and managers for the first time. Among the new administrators was a former schoolteacher, František Štěpánek, whom Bat'a knew through Sokol and the Reader's Association. Štěpánek impressed Mlýnková with his intellect and easygoing manner. Since she was paid by the shoe, large orders meant long hours, often until 10 p.m. Singing with the other stitchers "from the moment we started to the moment we finished was incredibly helpful."[43]

Mlýnková's long hours were the result of Tomáš's push to make and sell the revolutionary *séglaky* (from the German *Segeltuch*), which he renamed the *batovky*. The *batovky* was a summer shoe with cotton-linen uppers and a thin leather sole, but styled as a high-fashion loafer. It was fashioned, in fact, on the oxford shoe, the low-cut closed lace shoe that was fashionable around the world at the time and synonymous with the "modern man."[44] Cheap to make and meant to be discarded after a few months, the *batovky* caused considerable uproar among local shoemakers at the time, but proved widely popular with customers who appreciated their light weight, availability, and price.[45] In Moravia, the shoe style became so popular and ubiquitous that Tomáš's *batovky* entered into the lexicon – indeed replacing *seglaky*. As it grew in popularity, the shoe, and by extension the company, became a lightning rod for controversy – and controversy was something that would routinely accompany Bat'a initiatives. Pressured by shoemakers' guilds, shoe vendors throughout the region banned the shoe from their shops. This in turn encouraged Bat'a to develop new business relationships with a variety of non-traditional retailers, such as grocery stores. Tomáš gave anyone who agreed to sell the shoe a large oval sign with a painting of the shoe in the centre and "Batovka" written underneath.[46]

These tactics led to a surge in new hires, some 104 people joined the company in 1896.[47] The expansion in employees put Bat'a in an exceptional position among shoe manufacturers, for, as table 1.1 illustrates, independent craftsmen working in shops with no more than five people continued to dominate shoe production throughout the empire. Still, even at Bat'a, production continued to be done by hand because the Austrian state showed little interest in supporting the mechanization of shoe manufacturing. Given the protectionist policies of the empire, no company had easy access to the machines being used in the United States or Germany, nor did anyone in the industry seem particularly interested in acquiring them.[48] This is evident in the way in which Tomáš Bat'a found his way to his first machines.

Upon the spread of the *batovky* into the Viennese market in 1896, Bat'a was given a large contract by a mercantile business there, which he soon realized he was not going to be able to fill.

Table 1.1. Shoe production in 1902 in Cisleithania*

Size of workshop	Number of shoe businesses	Total number of workers
1–5	49,471	76,140
6–10	799	5,627
11–20	116	1,592
21–50	60	1,877
51–100	25	1,684
101–1000	8	1,389
1001–	0	0

*Hodáč Collection, SOkA Zlín, Baťa fond I/3. č. 29 k. 19.

My name was again in jeopardy. This time it was a question as to whether I could fulfil my contract. I needed something out of the ordinary to help me. Could it be machines? ... I went to Prague to consult with a shoemaker in Vinohrady and the editor of a shoemaking magazine... he told me exactly what I had been hearing everywhere else in our country. That there were people in Germany who were making and using machines, but in fact demand everywhere was rising for hand-made shoes and not machine-made shoes.[49]

Tomáš remembered that a machinery company in Frankfurt had sent him a business card some months before his trip to Prague, and so he set off for Frankfurt. In Frankfurt, he went into the large showroom of A.G. Moenus, a machine works that specialized in shoemaking equipment largely based on the designs of American inventors. There he saw the German variants of the Blake Sole Stitching Machine (1858), the Goodyear Welt and Sole Stitchers (1880), and Matzeliger's Lasting Machine (1883). These were the most important inventions in the mechanization of shoe production, and had radically trans-formed the industry in the United States.[50] Yet their impact in the European continent had been highly variable, and within the confines of the Habsburg Empire, one encountered their effects not at all.

Thus, Tomáš encountered these machines as bolts from the blue. He would later write that he was immediately "awestruck" by them.[51] Yet he could not afford to purchase them, and the centralized banks of the empire were not in the habit of lending large sums to industrialists without the right connections. In the cartel system of the Habsburg Empire, connections had much to do with pedigree and established business relationships.[52] So Tomáš bought a magnetic hammer and scissors and went home to Zlín. While he was not going to kick off the industrial revolution of shoemaking with such meagre tools, the trip had shown him the possibility of mechanized production. When he returned, he began to discuss with his workers the reorganization of shoemaking around these machines. Meanwhile, business continued to grow – from 1897 to 1899 the company's balance sheet revealed a sixfold increase in profits (5,387 gulden to 30,711).[53]

Expansion dovetailed with several milestones in the development of Zlín. Foremost, the town became connected to the Austrian rail network, with a spur from Otrokovice to Zlín completed in 1899. A couple of years earlier, the estate of Zlín had passed from Leopold Haupt-Buchenrode to his son, Stefan. Stefan was much like his father in his conservative political and social views, yet quite progressive in his approach to remodelling the estate. Within six years, the Zlín castle was entirely updated with electricity and indoor plumbing.[54] Bat'a too upgraded its facilities. In 1900, Bat'a moved from its rented space on the town square to a new factory building of red brick and tall glass windows adjacent to the railway station. The company became a partnership, with Tomáš taking two-thirds and Antonín a third, while Anna was bought out of the business. The success of the *batovky* had allowed Bat'a to grow into a central player in the economic life of Zlín during the fin-de-siècle period, with the company employing 170 workers by 1900. This made the company not only the largest employer in town, but also one of the eight largest shoe producers in all of the Austrian Empire.[55] These employees, still largely pulled from the ranks of skilled cobbler families, were increasingly political – with the majority aligning themselves with the social democrats. The middle-class mentality swept into the valley in the 1880s and socialism was introduced at the turn of the century. Interestingly, Tomáš was among its early supporters.

Outside of the aristocratic network, as well as the German-speaking bourgeoisie (Tomáš was never fluent in German), which were the two groups with the most control over the Austrian economy, Tomáš had been interested in alternatives to the social and economic system of the empire since his schooldays.[56] By the turn of the century, he seems to have been swept into a wave of support for socialism. In 1903 he became a member and key supporter of the Social Democratic Party, which had grown into the largest political party in the Czech lands.[57] In the same year, he and Antonín co-founded a union with their employees, the Union of Shoemakers (Spolek obuvníků Zlín). What is especially of interest is that Bat'a offered a rare instance of a Czech-speaking employer interacting with Czech-speaking employees in an era historians have identified as crucial to the state's normalization of national identity.[58] Their interaction was an example of working-class identification merging with that of the owners of capital – the result of the heightened nationalism of the period.[59] In other words, the Bat'a brothers came to feel that they had more in common with their Czech-speaking workforce than with the largely German-speaking culture of the bourgeoisie. Essentially, socialism and nationalism were coming together, especially in the industrialized Czech lands. As the historian Jakub

Figure 1.2. Bat'a factory in Zlín, 1905. Moravský zemský archiv v Brně, Státní okresní archiv v Zlín, Sbírka fotografií Zlín, sign. 816, obálka č. 15022.

Beneš has illustrated, the Czech social democrats crafted a message that socialism was going to strengthen the nation and vice versa by including the working class in the national community. Such inclusion, in their thinking, would allow for a conscious, autonomous nation.[60] In provincial Zlín, this Austro-Marxist message fit well with the goals of the Sokol and the Reader's Association. For the Bat'a brothers and their allies, social democracy promised to bring the working class in step to the march of the middle-class revolution.

The Lessons of Lynn

This alliance between capital and labour at the Bat'a Company, however, proved short-lived. One year after the establishment of the Union of Shoemakers, Tomáš decided to use some of his increasing profits to travel to the United States with a handful of employees to work in and to study American shoe manufacturing. The trip would prove to be a turning point in the development of the company and valley. Bat'a chose Lynn, Massachusetts – the epicentre of industrial shoe production – to become his temporary home in America.

When Bat'a arrived in Lynn, he encountered a society that had long since abandoned the putting-out system still used by Cisleithanian shoemakers, as factory owners in Lynn had entirely transformed shoe production around a mechanized factory system by 1883. As historian William Mulligan writes, "with the introduction of machinery, making a shoe was divided into many distinct tasks, each performed by a different worker, and work was moved into a factory where it came under closer supervision."[61] These distinct tasks resulted in specialization. With over twenty-six different types of jobs at a given shoe factory in Lynn, it was no longer possible to apply the term shoemaker to any single worker.[62] The factory system had completely transformed the appearance of the town as well, which left one observer to remark that the town was "great masses of ugliness, red-brick, many windowed buildings."[63]

Tomáš would have observed, alongside the factories and the machines, the society of the industrial town. On one hand, a strict code of local laws had been put in place by town leaders following an influx of mostly young single men and women who came from the countryside looking for factory work.[64] In addition to its strict laws, Lynn had a strong temperance movement, which was supported by industrialists spending considerable sums on a variety of groups that spent their time trying to convince the workforce to give up drink.[65] Additionally, there was a clear gender division among the shoe workers, with women largely confined to the role of stitcher.[66] On the other hand, Lynn had an equally strong union tradition, and offered workers cheap lunches in city canteens, numerous union halls for leisure, and significant assistance in the case of strikes. The Knights of Labour had been remarkably active in the town in the 1890s, and unions continued to advocate for the end to open shops in the area.[67] In sum, Lynn was a town dominated by industrial shoemaking on a scale unique in the world, and it had yet to fully resolve the tensions that a transition into such a town had produced.

Tomáš did not seem to be impressed with these tensions. For he would later describe the experience as entirely positive: "I observed the shirt sleeves rolled up and the work being done with a smile. A father would look upon his six-year-old son as big enough to go into business for himself, and to handle the money he earned. That is how he learned to be independent."[68] On top of learning about the latest in American shoe manufacturing, it seems that Bat'a wholeheartedly took on the masculine identity of the American "self-made man." Bat'a reported that his first trip taught him that a place could exist where no difference existed between worker and manager, where instead everyone worked to the best of their ability and believed that by so doing, they would be able to improve their lot in life.

Bat'a's glorification of the American system was remarkably out of balance with the history of labour in the United States, especially that of the town of Lynn. For Bat'a conveniently left out of his reminisces and subsequent idealization of the American system the societal tensions shaking the city. Only a few months after his departure, Lynn experienced one of the more turbulent moments of labour unrest in its history when machinists organized a general strike for better hours and a closed shop system and the Molder's Union also organized a citywide strike for better pay.[69] In the context of American labour history, in fact, Lynn was a hotbed of union activity. This was no small feat, for the United States averaged "three new strikes a day for twenty years" between 1880 and 1900, many of which turned violent.[70] Thus, the realities of American production had little in common with the ideal of the America Tomáš Bat'a and later company propagandists would construct. Furthermore, the behaviour of the other employees who had come with him provides a much more nuanced perspective on the American experience for provincial Moravians. After all, these men, of whom little is otherwise known, seemed to have embraced a different side of American life. For when Bat'a came to collect them for the return trip to Zlín, he found them drunk and gambling in a dingy apartment. According to Bat'a, he fired them on the spot and made the return trip by himself.[71]

It is likely that what allowed Tomáš to craft such a glowing idea of America was the incredible efficiency and productivity of machine-based shoe production. Lynn factories made more shoes per worker at lower cost than any shoe factory in Austria-Hungary.[72] He also surely noticed the use of a rural, young, and mostly single workforce that had very little resemblance to the artisan cobblers of Moravia. For Tomáš, this young American workforce moved at a quicker pace than his employees back home. These three observations – the centrality of the machine, the use of unskilled labour, and the speed of worker movement – provided the foundation for the Bat'a philosophy of production. Upon returning, Bat'a began tirelessly reminding his workforce of the importance of efficiency and tempo while encouraging every employee to learn how to work with the increasing number of new machines entering the factory. To further the Americanization of his company, Tomáš had a new three-storey factory building constructed next to the rail depot in the style of the red-bricked and many-windowed factories of Lynn.[73]

For one worker, Bohuš Fimbingr, the expansion of machinery into the production process symbolized Americanization. Upon Bat'a's return, Fimbingr became a machinist in the newly operational machine works. Later, Fimbingr recalled the transformation as beginning with the purchase of a state-of-the-art milling machine from Schuchardt and Schütte. With it, Bat'a's machine works began building a variety of shoemaking machines modelled on American designs.[74] Antonín Ochsner, another worker from the time of transition, recalled a shift in the "soul" of the factory. "Up until that time [Tomáš's return from America] the soul of the factory was Antonín's and Štěpánek's. But after, Tomáš took it in his hands for the first time … it was a different pace."[75] Just what this "soul" transitioned from is elusive, as there are few records on Antonín Bat'a Jr. Given this, it is easy to imagine the two brothers as something of an odd couple, with Tomáš playing the part of the work-obsessed, disciplined visionary and Antonín as the gregarious, relaxed shoemaker. Yet, one should not go too far – the brothers kept to a strict gender division that determined who worked in what section of production, and Antonín left no record of protest against Americanization.

Key members of the business did protest Americanization, though. An immediate point of contention occurred when Tomáš required that workers pay for damaged shoes, which, he claimed, was how they did it in America.[76] His demands quickly led to conflict. Disaffected workers, citing Bat'a's desire to make shoes in the "American way," organized a strike in August of 1906. Supported by a union of shoe manufacturers in Prostějov, a town forty miles away, and the local social democrats, the strikers crippled production. They demanded a 20 per cent pay increase and the election of managers. The company's own union sided with the strikers. Tomáš Bat'a responded with layoffs and dissolution of the union. After a few tense months, the strike fizzled in the winter and ended in January 1907.[77] Never again would Bat'a tolerate union membership among its workforce. Moreover, the shattering of the remarkable solidarity between capitalist and worker meant that the nationalist fibres that had allowed for this solidarity came apart as well. The result was that Bat'a drifted away from Czech nationalism and into an internationalism that mirrored the philosophy of the Austrian nobility. The striking workers, however, were quick to use the language of nationalism as they framed Bat'a's Americanization as anti-Czech.[78]

The locked-out employees, many of them skilled craftsmen, did not have trouble finding new employment. For the strike ended as the former school-teacher-turned-accountant at Bat'a – and previously a close friend of Tomáš's, František Štěpánka, galvanized opponents of the new "American" system to start their own shoe factory. Štěpánka proved a capable organizer as dozens of disaffected workers left Bat'a to work for him, and within a year Štěpánka's factory became profitable. According to one observer, his shoes were "much more comfortable and flexible" than those that Bat'a was making with his new system.[79]

Štěpánka's popular stance against Americanization led him into politics. One year after starting his own factory, he became mayor of Zlín in 1908 – a position he would hold until 1919. His election marked a significant shift in the political traditions of the region, which transitioned from aristocratic to liberal to now social democratic. Štěpánka helped to organize a host of political committees, the majority of which advocated pacifist, humanist values tinged with pan-Slavism. In 1912, for example, Štěpánka led the Committee against the War in the Balkans, which advocated for strict neutrality for Austria-Hungary and a peace initiative on behalf of all Slavic peoples.[80] The committee proved widely popular. At a town hall–style discussion about the First Balkan War there was near unanimity among the Czech-speaking audience for the need for pacifism and solidarity with the South Slavs. At this same meeting, Tomáš, however, argued in favour of militarism and mobilization against the Serbs. This was a remarkably unpopular stance among Czech nationalists.[81] Bat'a's Americanization had led him away from Czech nationalism.

While staunchly opposed to the "American" methods of Bat'a, Štěpánka nevertheless embraced middle-class ideals of modernity. He was, after all, another of the founding members of the local Sokol. During his time as mayor, he spent significant resources to modernize the area by providing electrification, sewer systems, and flood control. Thanks to these efforts, the population of Zlín rose from approximately 1,100 residents in 1880 to 3,400 in 1910. All the while, Štěpánka's factory continued to turn out handcrafted shoes and make a profit.[82]

Bat'a meanwhile began a policy of hiring unskilled farmworkers to replace the skilled labourers who were leaving him in droves.[83] Their exodus, however, did not create a labour crisis. For an entire way of life in the hinterlands of Moravia was falling apart. A great exodus of rural Moravians was taking place at this time. With their plots subdivided, prices depressed, and family members writing enticing letters from America, thousands of people moved out of Eastern Moravia between 1900 and 1910. The immediate area to Zlín's east, Vizovice, was hit especially hard by the economic depression of the 1880s and had yet to recover; large numbers of its inhabitants had left or were planning to leave for America.[84] Making little profit from their increasingly debt-ridden farms, the remaining residents of the area found that work in a shoe factory provided them with a lifeline, one that would enable them to stay in the region. The company offered a source of stable employment to the agricultural workers of the area, many of whom witnessed relatives and friends leave for the United States.[85]

Not all of the rural people who came seeking employment could make the transition to industrial employment. Josef František, a woodsman, arrived in the Bat'a offices looking for work after walking from Ruthenia, a journey of some 300 miles. Josef František was sitting in the waiting room waiting for an interview when Tomáš walked in and asked him a few questions about himself. It was clear that the man from the east had had a hard life; he had apparently fled his home when a drunken rival murdered his wife. Josef František offered to help with collecting wood to store in the warehouse, and Tomáš hired him, with one warning – his new life demanded that he "found a new, fixed existence."[86] Things went well for a short while, gamekeepers from the area even came to have lunch with Josef František just to hear him sing Rusyn songs and tell stories about the wilderness of his homeland. But he soon began showing signs of restlessness by talking about his next trip and showing up at work drunk. After several complaints from his coworkers, and several days of being sent home to sleep it off, he was fired. The story became something of a legend among gamekeepers in Zlín, who sang a song about him for years afterwards.[87] Josef František's story illustrates the pull of Bat'a on rural people and the difficulty that many had in transitioning to industrial work. In fact, many never really embraced the "fixed existence." Many came and left after a few years. The challenge of rural workers' adjustment to factory life, however, did little to slow Bat'a down.

Working with a newly proletarianized group of workers, abandoned by his former friends and employees, and back from the multicultural world of industrial Massachusetts, Bat'a's owner drifted into a major economic crisis. People were not buying shoes, which left over 18,000 shoe makers unemployed in Austria-Hungary.[88] At the same time, Antonín – Tomáš's chief supporter, brother, and co-owner – died after a lengthy battle with tuberculosis in 1908. Remarkably, social isolation, unskilled labour, family loss, and economic crisis did not lead to contraction of the company. Instead, with the inventive retail solution developed in the 1890s and a commitment to machine production, Bat'a expanded from 1907 to 1912 in profit and number of employees.[89]

In 1911 Tomáš again travelled to the United States, only this time to Cincinnati. There he purchased "two modern lathes, one horizontal and one vertical boring mill and a great supply of tools capable of turning out with precision complicated gears, cams, shafts and moulds."[90] The machine shop would now be able to build the needed machines on site, thereby allowing the company to avoid one of the major problems Bat'a faced in the Cisleithanian economy – high tariffs on machinery imports. The focus on machinery further distanced Bat'a from its competitors. By 1914, the company, still the eighth largest in terms of employees, had the highest daily output of all shoe companies in Cisleithania.[91]

Soon after returning from Cincinnati, Tomáš met and married Marie Menčíková, a well-educated woman from a family with connections to powerful Czech politicians. Marie would become a central player in the Bat'a Company without ever having employment there; in the summer of 1912, she was new to Zlín and the shoe business. After the wedding, Marie experienced a foreshadowing of what her life was to be like when, on their honeymoon in Egypt, Tomáš became intensely focused on Egyptian women's footwear. What he noticed was the prevalence of slip-on shoes such as the open-backed black leather *bulgha* and the red-and-yellow *sarma*.[92] As the major manufacturer of slippers in Bohemia and Moravia, Tomáš was drawn to the slipper style of Egyptian footwear. He had found a new style for the Austrian market, a slip-on leather shoe, which he would make with a rubber soul. Fuelled by a vision of a new style for Cisleithania and armed with new machinery, the pace of revolution accelerated upon his arrival home.

Integration into Austrian Finance

In the Dřevnice Valley, the years 1912–14 proved to be a crucial period. In this time frame, the Bat'a Company came to establish a strong connection with financiers and other shoe manufacturers in Bohemia, Moravia, and Silesia, while solidifying a plan to create a vertically integrated company. Borrowing substantial capital from the Czech Union Bank, Bat'a invested in an expansion into the Austro-Hungarian market in 1912, signing contracts with retailers in Hungary, Croatia, Vienna, and Sarajevo. The company furthermore began exporting shoes to Germany and Egypt, which became long-term foci of Bat'a's expansion.[93] Market development coincided with a decision to join a cartel with seventy other shoe manufacturers in Bohemia and Moravia. The choice came in the face of rising material costs, and the cartel's goal was to raise shoe prices.[94] These factors resulted in a further change in the direction of the company.

In the cliquish world of Austrian capitalism, with its cartels, closely tied system of industry and finance, and protectionist policies, Bat'a had been an outlier. From 1902 to 1912, for example, the company did not borrow capital, which set it outside the influence of the small circle of large banks that dominated much of Austrian economic life. Bat'a was also a political exception in Austrian industry as it had been a company committed to the ideals of social democracy. After returning from Lynn, Massachusetts, the company shed its connection with socialism after a bitter struggle over the system of production. However, it distinguished itself from other shoe producers by hiring unskilled agricultural workers, building new factories in the style of American industrial architecture, and replicating American machinery.[95] After the economic crisis of 1907 and the loss of co-founder Antonín, the company moved into the mainstream of Austrian business culture by joining a cartel and borrowing capital. The move seemed to coincide with a shift in Tomáš Bat'a's worldview from that of a nationalist Czech social democrat to a more nationally indifferent Austrian capitalist.

The company also began to purchase the remnants of feudal Zlín – the estate lands of the now Baron Stefan Haupt-Buchenrode – some 100,000 square metres of land surrounding the factory and several hectares of land on the hillsides rising up from the Dřevnice Valley floor. On some of this land, Bat'a began building housing for workers, as well as his own modernist villa, which was built according to plans developed by the Prague-based architect Jan Kotěra, already a famed modernist. The villa and the American factory were now every bit as important in the mental map of the residents of the valley as the church and the castle. The Bat'a Company was becoming the primary source of stability for rural people in the area by providing employment and housing; meanwhile it continued steadily buying the land of the local nobility.[96] Florimont, the French shoe manufacturer in Zlín in the 1870s, had befriended the local nobility; Tomáš Baťa was overpowering them.

On top of all of this, sometime in 1912 the company did away with piece wages in favour of hourly wages. The task to track employee hours fell at first to the accounting department, which quickly needed more people to do the job. One of the new hires was Hyněk Matuška, who recalled his hiring interview as follows: "Tomáš Baťa said that 'our national duty was to raise the worker to the highest degree of responsibility. We will pick him and his welfare up by allowing him to earn more. And as for me, you will watch my hours as closely as the most recently hired employee, and the accountant that is mindful of his duties need not worry about retribution."[97] The transition to hourly wages was a significant step in the development of the Baťa operating system because it required careful surveillance of each employee's time. It was foundational in the process of creating legible employees.

The Austrian state, meanwhile, showed little interest in the local affairs of Zlín. In the archival material that can be found in the Zlín Regional Archives and the National Archive of the Czech Republic, in addition to the second- ary literature about the area, there is a remarkable absence of records of the Austrian state's role in the region's development. One key exception is the state-regulated expansion of the railway line linking Zlín to Otrokovice, which represented a significant state-sponsored investment. However, there are no records indicating state intervention in the Baťa strike or the Baťa purchases of area property, and certainly no help was given to Baťa to "Americanize" shoe production on the part of the Austrian state. While Tomáš came to inte- grate Baťa into the cartel networks of the Austrian economy, no evidence can be found of government support to assist him in the process. Baťa operated in the semi-autonomous sphere of provincial Czech-speaking Moravia, under the radar of the otherwise ubiquitous Austrian bureaucracy. Likewise, while the Union of Shoemakers called for a general boycott of Baťa, and labour inspec- tors from the regional capital of Uherské Hradiště admonished the company for unfair labour practices, meaningful intervention on the part of the state never came.[98]

Furthermore, the broader Cisleithanian public knew next to nothing about the goings-on in Zlín before 1914. Searching through the Austrian National Library's comprehensive newspaper database ANNO (which includes Czech and German newspapers), for example, reveals only two brief mentions of Baťa between 1902 and 1914.[99] The result was that the company's decisions, and its vision of how to make the Dřevnice Valley modern, were largely unfet- tered by governmental constraints and unknown to the Cisleithanian public. Thus, when Baťa came to reconfigure work around an American model, resis- tance arose locally and gained some outside support, but no legal restrictions were enforced to hinder Baťa. Thus, the new labour system to develop at the

Bat'a factory – a system that would soon come to dominate the entire town – developed outside of government oversight. In the early years of the company, the poverty and marginality of Zlín were crucial factors in allowing the area to become a company town. The state did not have a particular interest in the way in which shoes were made, or in how local affairs handled, in the out-of-the-way region. This would change once Bat'a captured the domestic market and began to dominate Czechoslovakian exports, but initially Bat'a developed largely outside of state intervention – the famous "visible hand" of the Habsburg state is barely evident in Bat'a's takeover of Zlín.

Upon closer inspection, the relatively remote, impoverished region was an ideal setting for a company town. For it commanded neither the attention of the major cities nor the investment of large landowners. It was out of the way and unimportant to the decision makers of the Habsburg Empire. Thus, the region could do little to resist the rationalization of everyday life brought on by the company, as local efforts to thwart the company's plans were, by and large, not supported by agents of the state. Bat'a revolutionized shoe production and, then, everyday life by existing outside of the spotlight while benefiting greatly from state infrastructure and the legal assurance of contracts. The benefits of this position became apparent when war broke out in August 1914.

Conclusion

The development of mechanized production ushered in turn new types of labour by creating a significant divide between manual and non-manual types of work concerning the mechanized factory. Those employed in these non-manual jobs, such as clerks, managers, retail operators, engineers, and so on, led a middle-class revolution, and often took over the local politics, education, and cultural life of their industrializing milieus. Such a process has been well-documented and need not be explained in detail here, but it is crucial to understand that the middle-class revolution that occurred in Zlín from 1894 to 1912 was but a small part of a global process – the growing uniformity of a middle-class perspective.[100] Such a perspective held that this was a new age, where traditional religion and its attendant authorities and customs no longer had authority. It embraced the symbols of modernity, like telephones and watches, and the speed that came with them. It was revolutionary in that it demanded a dramatic reorganization of social and political networks. Dynastic and ecclesiastical authority was weakened all around.[101]

The industrialization of shoemaking in Zlín followed the broad outline of other industrializing regions across the nineteenth century, yet diverged from the narrative in several important ways. The Habsburg shoe market was not under intense competition from foreign exports. Chiefly, when Bat'a began to mechanize there were no producers on the European market able to supply

Cisleithania with shoes produced on an industrial scale. Whereas textile manufacturers across Europe were confronted with cheap British exports, shoe
manufacturers had no such competition. Thus, Bat'a was relatively free to
introduce and experiment with mechanization. Also, in the second half of the
nineteenth century, when shoe manufacturing became industrialized, its centre
was in Lynn, Massachusetts. As in the case of textiles, the centre did produce
a coterie of agents to spread the industry's gains around the world – which was
done through the affiliates of the United Shoe Machinery Company of Boston.
However, the intense pressure to mechanize manufacturing that continental
producers felt due to the competition of cheap textiles produced in England did
not exist on the same scale for shoe production in Cisleithania. Therefore, few
shoe manufacturers in the Austro-Hungarian Empire were particularly interested in dramatically reorganizing production around the new machines being
used in Lynn. Of those that did have such an interest, their efforts were not
supported by the Habsburg state, which tended to side with the strong shoemakers' unions.

All of this led the chief architect of the Bat'a Company, Tomáš, who became
interested in the potential of mechanized shoe production largely out of desperation, to travel to the United States. Bat'a's affinity and reliance on the
United States developed into a highly idealized understanding of American
society and business practices and a strong commitment to a particular global
phenomenon of the early twentieth century – welfare capitalism, which he discovered in the United States – and an eventual realization that political capital
was crucial to reorganizing production.

This is not to say that Bat'a did not benefit from a strong state. Indeed, a key
in the industrialization of Zlín, as in the making of industrial capitalism seemingly everywhere, was a strong state that was "capable of legally, bureaucrati-
cally, infrastructurally, and militarily penetrating its own territory ... Forging
markets, protecting domestic industry, creating tools to raise revenues, policing borders, and fostering changes that allowed for the mobilization of wage
workers."[102] The Habsburg Empire was able to protect the shoe industry from
foreign competition by its use of tariffs and oversaw a dramatic expansion of
infrastructure in the late nineteenth century. Yet the state, according to the economic historian Eduard März and the economist Joseph Schumpeter, failed to
foster the level of entrepreneurial innovation that drove the American, British,
and German economies.[103]

This failure was linked to the culture of business in the Habsburg Empire,
which was defined by its German-speaking members' desire to mimic the aristocracy, a state sluggish to invest in innovation, and an alliance that largely did
not need external trading partners. The first problem, as historian David Good
and others have illustrated, was that bankers tended to lend to already established industrial firms – a conservative approach matched by their tendency

to identify with the aristocracy culturally. Second, the state seemed "immobilized"; it was reluctant to use novel techniques to encourage innovation in the face of nationalist struggles for resources. Third, the Austro-Hungarian Customs Union protected Habsburg industry from competition by providing a diverse resource pool within its territory.[104] All of this led to a concentration of economic power in the hands of a few large concerns, which were run and managed by individuals who had become "no longer concerned with the reconstruction but rather the preservation of existing conditions."[105]

The Bat'a story began in this pattern, but took an exceptional turn around 1904–6. From then on, Bat'a's trajectory challenges the narratives of industrial capitalism and Austrian ingenuity or lack thereof, for in the Bat'a case, wage workers were mobilized because of a general desperation among the inhabitants of Eastern Moravia, borders were hindrances, and protectionism was detrimental to the company. While legal contracts and infrastructure were crucial to company expansion, the keystone to Batism's development was a state that expressed little interest in the affairs of provincial Zlín. The company could and did expand to dominate the valley because the state did not take a strong interest in the region's inhabitants or economic life.

The most decisive influences in its turn away from Austro-Hungarian business culture came from the United States of America. The machinery of Lynn, Massachussetts, the writings of Henry Ford, and first-hand experiences working at an American shoe factory inspired the development of Batism. The company went far outside of the moral economy of the growing Czech-speaking middle class, which created a significant rift between Bat'a and its members' nationalist-tinged worldview. In sum, the Bat'a Company was central to the middle-class revolution in a provincial village, but when it turned in 1905 toward an idealized American model of production and daily life, the company alienated its skilled workers and former middle-class allies alike. These former allies organized into an opposition and took control of the town's administration. Bat'a retreated from public affairs, but grew into the seventh-largest employer of shoemakers and the largest producer of shoes in the empire by 1914. Using a largely unskilled workforce of young, single employees, Bat'a demanded a sped-up workday and the most up-to-date machinery. Tomáš began to dream of an Americanized future outside of the factory walls. All the while, both groups sought to transform the Dřevnice Valley around visions of modernity.

"Time Es Money": The Americanization of the Dřevnice Valley, 1914–1923

The relative obscurity of the Bat'a Company in Cisleithania ended during the First World War. For it was then that Bat'a came to be associated with a mission of patriotic significance, the shodding of the Austrian Army. This mission led to a rapid expansion of employees, profit, and space, which increased the profile of the company throughout the Habsburg Empire. The First World War allowed the Dřevnice Valley to become the epicentre of shoe production in the multinational empire, which in turn allowed Bat'a to expand and invest in its vision of progress. Correspondingly, the Bat'a name began appearing in the newspapers of major cities, like Vienna, Prague, and Budapest.[1]

Once Bat'a rose to the spotlight, one feature of the company reflected the strongest glare – its Americanization. When Cisleithanian observers reported on Bat'a's domain, they came to recognize it as "American." This Americanization sparked heated debates about the value of the Bat'a method, particularly in and around Zlín, where Tomáš moulded it into a mantra of individualistic efficiency; meanwhile workers chafed under the new methods. The methods that were under debate, though, were still gestating, and the exigencies of the war shaped them in unexpected ways. Americanization was never a stable phenomenon. Two of the largest changes the war brought on was an intense investment in the company on the part of the state, and the hastening of the consolidation of local responsibility, power, and control into company hands.

Americanization is a term that has been historicized, defined, and debated for over a century. In the United States from 1890 to 1923, the word meant to most people the process of turning immigrants into Americans by inculcating them with the "values" of the country.[2] The advocates of this process were typically members of the middle class who designed a curriculum for immigrants that focused on language, safety, civics, and nationalism. Advocates of Americanization often viewed their work as promoting democracy, literacy, and racial tolerance. Large industrial companies, such as International Harvester, the United States Steel Corporation, and the Ford Motor Company participated, designed, and promoted these programs.[3] Their effects were mixed, as turning immigrants into Americans was not a simple act of instilling patriotic feelings. For chambers of commerce across the United States, and for Henry Ford, anti-unionism was an integral component to Americanization. In the eyes of many managers, especially in the aftershocks of the Bolshevik Revolution of 1917, being American translated as being anti-union. Americanizing one's workforce became entangled with keeping an open shop.[4]

Such a connection fit well into Bat'a's plans for the Americanization of the Dřevnice, as Bat'a had held to an anti-union policy since 1905. However, in the framework of the Americanization of Europe, which historians have viewed as a kind of campaign where, instead of military personnel, American organizations such as the Rotary Club marched into the continent, Bat'a presented a challenge. Indeed, the narrative of the Americanization of Europe holds that American values and products swiftly and powerfully marched over the globe, which leaves little space for a company that adopted, interpreted, and implemented an Americanization program of their own only to later turn around and march into the United States.[5] Bat'a's Americanization, then, challenges a unidirectional view of American culture and interests. For it does not provide an example of how Americans thrust an idealized America upon a society, but rather one of how a local elite defined America for its own purposes. One could describe it as a quasi-religious conversion to an idealized society. Bat'a elites created the cult of America. It was theirs to define, to populate, and propagate. They did so by picking and choosing from the United States' playbook – borrowing from Ford's assembly line processes and attitudes on social engineering, looking to the Endicott-Johnson Company's version of welfare capitalism, and embracing an imagined work ethic based on their observations in Lynn, Massachusetts. They listened to the sober messages of Reverend Billy Sunday and tuned out the heady gaiety of Josephine Baker. They were hardly comfortable with ideas of democracy – the free press, party politics, and freedom of assembly were all subjects that caused the Bat'a managers considerable unease. Of course, by the end of the war, such democratic practices were causing American politicians, especially Woodrow Wilson, discomfort as well.

Thus, the Americanization of the Dřevnice Valley happened according to the specific imaginings of the Americanizers. It was not easy, not always successful, and always the product of interplay with the local environment, but it was, more or less, done. The valley became an outpost of American industrial technology, and certain American theories and practices, which had significant ramifications for the built environment, the mentalities, and experiences of the people of the region. The power to Americanize the culture of a Moravian valley, ironically, came from the expansion, disruption, and political collapse that grew from the First World War.

The First World War

The rise in Bat'a's prominence began when Tomáš made a trip to Vienna the day after the Austro-Hungarian Empire issued its call for mobilization on 25 July 1914. In the chaos of mustering in Vienna, he roamed from one ministerial office to another for three days until, according to him, a minister "no longer wanted any delays in the contracts" and gave him an order for 50,000 cavalry boots.[6] Tomáš returned home to a joyous welcome, but also to a serious problem. Despite having the only shoe factory in Cisleithania organized around machine production, Bat'a's initial contract exceeded its production capabilities. After all, Bat'a was only the seventh largest shoe factory in Austria in 1914, with 400 employees. And though its mechanization of shoe production allowed it to produce more shoes per day than any of the larger factories, Bat'a only had a total output of 50 pairs of military boots a day.[7] In light of this problem, Tomáš decided to subcontract parts of the work order to other local producers, including his old friend and later rival, František Štěpanek, whose factory had grown to employ nearly 200 people by the start of the war. The subcontracting of the military order quickly led to full employment in the city. However, even with every shoe manufacturer in town working at full employment, the company, which remained on the hook for fulfilling the order, struggled to meet the demands of the military. Bat'a and Zlín needed more workers.[8]

To find them, it turned to the rural networks previously developed when the company reduced its reliance on skilled labour in 1905. Having already established a policy of hiring young people from the countryside, Bat'a could expand its recruitment without having to compete against other shoe manufacturers that relied on skilled craftsmen. It could also use its existing employees to spread the word that Bat'a was hiring in their villages.

In addition, the company ran a series of help-wanted announcements in the small circulation newspapers of Eastern Moravia.[9] The recruitment drive brought in people like Anna Rektaríková, who was a seventeen-year-old with eight years of education when she started working for the company in July 1915. Rektaríková came from a working-class Zlín background, was single, and, like almost all other female employees at the time, was put to work stitching for the company during the war. There, in the high-ceilinged stitching room, Rektaríková sang with the other women to the hum of a thousand sewing machines. She would not leave the company until 1946.[10]

While Bat'a expanded its payroll, government officials continued to award the company contracts. What changed the attitude of government officials toward the industrialization of shoemaking were the priorities of a modern war. Bat'a's ability to outproduce all other shoe manufacturers per employee meant that the company was a preferred supplier for a state needing to shod some 3.2 million men in the shortest time possible.[11] Correspondingly, as Bat'a was able to meet the initial order for 50,000 cavalry boots, contracts continued to be signed with the company, which proved itself uniquely capable among the empire's shoe manufacturers. In a state with a remarkable centralization of industrial capital, Baťa's industrialization of a heretofore handicraft industry meant that Austrian officials, who operated under a mentality of centralization, came to view the company as the centre of shoe production during the war. This situation benefited the people of Zlín, as employment in the shoe factories exempted an employee from conscription into the Austrian military. In effect, shoe production saved the lives of the men in the valley.

The general manager of the military footwear division, Josef Blažek, recalled the meteoric rise in the company's output and command of the military's footwear production: "In the beginning we turned out 50 pairs [of boots] a day in the workshops, but when I assembled them all together in one building I immediately got 100 pairs a day, then 200 pairs a day, then 500 pairs a day, then 1,000 pairs, 2,000, 4,000, until by the end of the war we produced close to 6,000 pairs of military boots daily, which matched the entire output of every other factory in Austria-Hungary put together. I can say that we accounted for more than 50 per cent of Austria-Hungary's military shoes."[12]

The expansion of production corresponded with an increasing responsibility to organize shoe production for the entire empire. Having moved into the cliquish world of Austrian finance and industry before the war, Tomáš Baťa was in a good position from which to win these large contracts and be appointed to key positions. In October 1915, the government created the Kriegsschuhzentrale GmbH (Central Committee for Military Shoes) in order to increase shoe production throughout the empire and better distribute materials. Its chairperson was Tomáš Baťa. This organization, which was reorganized in 1916 under a new name, the Society for the Support of Leather and Shoes, was one of three organizations in Vienna in which Baťa served as chairperson during the war.[13]

Tomáš's connections and positions in these organizations led to large contracts and a steady supply of material with which to fill them. However, as the war dragged on into its second year, administrative chaos, military needs, and the loss of external markets created a serious shortage of foodstuffs and raw materials. The company responded by opening a cafeteria, then a grocery store, and then by buying farmland. To deal with the increasing scarcity of materials, Baťa built a tannery. Then it built a sawmill to obtain the lumber with which to build tannin-extracting stations. Next came a stone quarry for building material.[14] In essence, vertical integration, the foundation of the company's ability to create a company-run society, began out of the exigencies of wartime scarcity.

The war also led to an influx of workers to the city, in numbers it could barely handle. In a letter to the regional authorities in Uherské Hradiště, Mayor Štěpánka described the growing housing crisis as follows, "the growth of the population of the city during the war has been unimaginable ... Right now in the overcrowded dormitories three lodgers sleep in one bed. The frantic pace of building has not been able to prevent a situation in which many workers have been basically wandering the streets ... life in Zlín during the war has deteriorated significantly."[15]

In addition to the severe housing shortage, the demands of the war left people hungry and overworked. The company newsletter, which turned into a weekly and then a daily in 1917 and 1918, exhibited an overwhelming focus on food and the prices of basic household items. The paper served to inform its readers – who were largely Bat'a employees – as to what would be served in the cafeterias and on how to run a "war kitchen."[16] The company had begun operating on a twenty-four-hour schedule since September 1915, and workers were routinely working twelve-hour days.[17] To further deal with the labour shortage, Bat'a asked for and received Russian prisoners of war, who began arriving in 1916 and would total 144 by war's end. These workers caused considerable alarm among the rest of the workforce, especially the skilled machinists, who complained the use of prisoners as a form slave labour was undercutting wages. The POWs complained the loudest, however. Their lives consisted of walking from their barracks under guard to the factory where they worked twelve-hour shifts before walking back to the barracks. Several small groups of them escaped into the woods in 1916.[18]

The food crises, use of POW labour, and regular overtime created considerable dissatisfaction. In March 1918, the situation erupted into strikes and other forms of labour unrest. On 7 March, nineteen young workers walked off the job to protest the long hours of unpaid overtime. Gendarmes sent in from the county seat of Uherské Hradiště arrested fourteen of them the same day. Two weeks later, on 22 March, Russian prisoners of war held their own strike to demand better rations. Twenty-two were taken away from the factory.[19] The Union of Czech Shoemakers, Union of Czech Woodworkers, and Union of Czech Tanners then tried to step in and mediate on behalf of the workers. Their efforts yielded little reward and their protest was dealt with harshly; several workers who were arrested were sent into the army. During the war, the Austrian state had placed its local disciplinary forces at the full disposal of the company to maintain production.

In response to these grievances from hungry and overworked employees, the company played up the comparative safety of life at the factory. In one article, titled "Undernourishment and Working Overtime," Bat'a called workers to compare their lot with that of others in Cisleithania. "No one can claim that we have here in Zlín suffered undernourishment like that experienced in the other cities of our country. We still thank God we have something to eat; we have our daily bread and we often have a little piece of meat ... Ask kindly of yourself if it isn't true that many workers from Prague, from Pilsen, from Vienna, or from

Brno if they would not like to trade places with you a hundred times over, or if in those places there is not often hunger ... Why must you work overtime? Because of your fellow workers who are getting sick, taking holiday, or staying at home to rest – shirkers."[20]

Bat'a's comment was made in the context of dwindling food resources that the Austro-Hungarian state had been trying to desperately ration. As Rudolf Kučera skilfully illustrates, the state's "all-encompassing rationing system," based on the caloric calculations of scientists, led to a growing politicization of food within the empire during the war. Moreover, "the majority of the increasingly impoverished inhabitants of the whole country observed with growing bitterness the enormous profits of a narrow number of businessmen." By the time Tomáš was telling workers to consider themselves lucky, that is, in August 1918, the failure of the state to address the problems associated with food and inequality had "brought the total collapse of the basic social solidarity of wartime Austrian society."[21] Such a collapse was evident in the tensions between managers and labour at Bat'a, and would be evident in the immediate postwar period, when citizens would elect a socialist city council.

While not offering the warmest response to workers' frustrations, the company did respond to the housing crisis, which led Bat'a to again enlist the skills of architect Jan Kotěra. Kotěra, who had designed Tomáš Bat'a's villa in 1911, had become the pre-eminent Czech architect of his era and his approach seemed to complement the company's fascination with American methods. Kotěra had travelled extensively in the United States in 1904, where he was deeply impressed by the designs of Frank Lloyd Wright and other American influences. As well he was inspired by the famous Viennese architect Otto Wagner. These influences led Kotěra to envision a workers' colony for Zlín that looked like something out of a Vienna suburb, yet with the intent to harmoniously fuse housing and factory, perhaps in a manner inspired by Wright. This first plan, commissioned in 1915, was scrapped for reasons unknown. The second plan, begun in 1918, would determine the look and feel of Zlín for the next twenty years, when the town rapidly developed into a company town as its population expanded.[22] This plan reflected the strong influence, on both Bat'a and Kotěra, of the Garden City movement. The movement traced its start to the writings of Ebenezer Howard, who envisioned an industrialized countryside of modestly sized cities – the ideal population size being 32,000 – that would be planned out jointly by workers and managers. Howard wanted single-family houses with garden plots and plenty of space for recreation. In order to assure these clean, green, and pretty towns, Howard felt that the city and all of its land should be owned by a board of trustees, and everything would be leased out. As historian Marynel Ryan Van Zee has pointed out, "the appeal ... lay in the possibility of capturing an older, "traditional" agricultural household model within a "modern" framework."[23]

While the person most associated with the Garden City movement was Ebene-zer Howard, by the time Kotěra and Bat'a began dreaming, planning, and build-ing a large industrial complex, several other notable examples offered variants on Howard's model. In Europe, the most well known were Cadbury's Bourn-ville, Lever's Port Sunlight, and Krupp's Margarethenhöhe. All three of these company towns included features of the Garden City movement, such as sin-gle-family houses, ample green space, and recreational facilities, but in these communities housing was tied primarily to employment. The companies con-trolled who would get what.[24] In the United States, one could find a hybrid model involving the paternalistic company model of Krupp and the Garden City model of Howard. It also was found in connection with the shoe business. Since 1904, the Endicott-Johnson Company (EJ) had been building housing, mostly single-family bungalow and four-square houses, to sell at or below cost exclusively to workers.[25] In 1916, the company offered medical coverage to all workers and their immediate families. As EJ too experienced fast growth owing to its military contracts, its housing and social service program came to support the develop-ment of a sprawling three-city area in the valley of the Susquehanna River – a region similar to the environs of Zlín. It is unclear when exactly Bat'a took notice of EJ, but given his interest in American business models during the war, it is safe to assume that Bat'a knew about EJ by 1918. While formal study of EJ would have to wait until the close of the war, the EJ model that sought to integrate the city and the factory while putting considerable resources into social welfare intrigued Bat'a. Indeed, in the last year of the war, everywhere one looked in Zlín, one could find signs of a growing company's aspiration to Americanize.

The last months of the war seem to have further emboldened the company in its quest to convince its workforce that American practices were superior to their own. Throughout the summer of 1918, the company newspaper ran a series of articles relaying Andrew Carnegie's ideas on industrialism and indus-trial relations between workers and capitalists. On 3 August, the newspaper ran a stridently pro-American article, "The Intellectual Synergy of the Worker," which issued a challenge to its readers:

> Are our workers intellectually prepared? No ... Our worker still cannot be com-pared to the American worker, who can understand the reasons behind advance-ments offered by a machine and then help in its further development. It is barely two years since the second generation of our workers started working and we hope and look forward to them catching up with the fifth generation of American wor-kers. It is totally necessary to have their strength measure up to that of the Ameri-can industrial shoemaker or the very existence of our factory will be in danger.[26]

These articles culminated with a piece on 17 August called "The Honour of Work" ("Práci čest"). Written anonymously, the article gave the Bat'a interpretation of history. The history was Whiggish in its approach, offering a stage theory of development from the ancient past to the modern age. In this new age, the article claimed, America was providing the guiding motto, which the author wrote in broken English as "Time es money."[27]

Such praises of Americanization, one would think, would have provoked a strong response from the Austrian state, which was at war with the United States after all. No such response can be found in the historical record, however. As Mark Cornwall has shown, military authorities intensely feared this kind of laxity in the interior of the empire in 1918. And while they desperately tried to stamp out enemy propaganda among the troops, going so far as to detain and inspect every soldier returning from the Eastern Front in 1918, civil authorities seemed much more lenient.[28] Zlín is further proof that by the last years of the war, civil authorities had little enthusiasm for censorship and cared little about the praising of an enemy state. Unlike the Nazi regime, which brutally punished those deemed insufficiently patriotic, the Austro-Hungarian Empire allowed the only newspaper in what was becoming a vital industrial region to publish article after article glorifying an enemy nation.[29]

By the end of the war, more than just the company press admired the Americanization of Zlín. Influential writers began to take notice of the transformation as well. One such writer, František Obrtel, devoted a chapter in his 1918 book, *Come with Us (Pojd'te s námi)*, on the American influence in Zlín. Obrtel made the first mention of what would become an often-repeated anecdote about Zlín's exceptional status in Czechoslovakia: the story of a young worker on the train from Otrokovice to Zlín yelling out of the window, "Goodbye Europe, we are going to America!"[30] Obrtel himself was impressed by the spectacle. "Stepping off the train in Zlín ... you cannot believe your eyes – it seems like an American fairytale."[31] Bat'a's dramatic expansion and investment during the First World War had turned Zlín into an increasingly famous industrial site – the Detroit of Europe.

Or that was at least the image many Czech nationalists and optimistic literary characters wanted to portray. Indeed, one of the singular qualities about Czech national identification during this period was its fascination and admiration for the United States. From the writings of Tomáš and Karel Čapek to Tomáš and Lidia Garrigue Masaryk, the United States held a privileged place in the imaginations of cultural and political elites fighting for an independent Czechoslovakia. In May 1918 Masaryk gave one his clearest endorsements of "Americanization," which was, as he defined it, a political process:

> I am happy to note the recognition of the Government of the United States given by today's declaration of the Secretary of State; in it he states that the Government of the United States has earnest sympathy with the national aspirations of the

Czecho-Slovaks and the Jugo-Slavs. Yes, we accept with joy this declaration, all the more so because, though being Czecho-Slovaks or Jugo-Slavs by birth, we all, even I for my part, can say we are Americans already. And if you speak of Americanization today, there is an Americanization going on all over the world, because all nations must accept the principle of liberty proclaimed by the Declaration of Independence, proclaimed by Washington, by Lincoln, by Wilson, and by all Americans. Yes, if we are here in the United States and rejoice in the principles of the government of this country, we hope that soon there will be not only the United States of America, but a united mankind of all nations, great and small.[32]

The central place of America in the minds of elite Czechs could be found in artwork as well. One of the paintings of Alfons Mucha's massive *Slav Epic*, the final and triumphant *Apotheosis of the Slavs*, displays the US flag flying at the head of an array of Allied flags, as the allegorical Slavic nations celebrate underneath them. The painting is the symbolic representation of a conviction that, for many, a pro-American orientation was central to the process of *odrakousenit se* (de-Austrianization).[33]

Such an orientation was far from universally popular. In the German-language press, Americanization, a topic of discussion for several decades, often appeared as a humiliating process that worked to emasculate and flatten Austrian genius. "This Americanization can be seen in our youth, who run around with faces shaven like operetta tenors ... Our old idols, Wiener, Schubert, Strauss, and Lueger, would roll in their graves if they saw it."[34] By 1918, commentators were connecting the military campaign against America with the cultural struggle against Americanism. "If America brings war now, it brought pestilence before – that soulless, culturally abandoned, only-concerned-with-masses-and-numbers thing that is entangled with materialism – Americanization."[35] Clearly, Americanization was not going to unite the diverse peoples of Central Europe.

Thus, Obrtel's anecdote must be read in the context of the formation of the new state of Czechoslovakia and its supporters casting about for direction. The reality was that the Dřevnice Valley was still smaller and less technologically advanced than the River Rouge factory or the factory towns of Endicott-Johnson during the First World War. Still, one could not fault Obrtel and others for being optimistic, as Bat'a and the area experienced a revolutionary change during the war. From 500 workers in 1914, Bat'a now had 6,000 in August 1918 and a corresponding jump in the number of machines.[36] Rhetoric mattered in that it shaped the ways in which people approached the valley. Nevertheless, the ideal remained far away, and the economic and political situation at the end of the war was bleak.

Leftist, Poor, and Prone to Flood: The Dřevnice Valley in the Immediate Postwar Years

The company's commitment to, and propagation of, an idealized America only increased during the difficult postwar period, 1918–23. The transition back to a peacetime economy, accompanied by the political uncertainty of the breakup of the Austro-Hungarian Empire, led to a serious economic crisis. For Bat'a, previous markets, especially those in the new Hungarian and Polish states, became inaccessible owing to tariffs and political unrest. In addition, the large wartime orders ceased and production shifted to civilian footwear. To further exacerbate the economic problems of the immediate postwar period, Bat'a had to deal with much sharper and better-organized opposition than before or during the war. In the four-year window between 1919 and 1923, the company dealt with a hostile town council, pushback from the local elite, a sustained attack from shoemakers' unions, striking employees, communist agitation, and pressure to hire from the growing ranks of the unemployed.

At the beginning of 1919, Bat'a's large internal market shrank and Czechoslovakia's industries faced a serious crisis – the new state held just one-fifth of the Austro-Hungarian Empire's territory but three-quarters of its industrial capacity. Bat'a was left with the capacity to produce 45,000 shoes a day but because of the the shrinking market was able to sell only 50,000 shoes a week at best.[37] In January, the company fired the first round of employees. Wages remained stagnant. This, in turn, led to a radicalization of the workers. In April, skilled machinists walked off the job. They demanded an end to unpaid overtime and a minimum weekly wage of 120 crowns. Many in town, even schoolchildren, had been prepared for the strike by social democratic activists, who told them that a fire siren would announce the beginning of a strike. Several men from the tanning department offered their support. A major showdown neared.[38]

Management's strategy was to draw the workers into a series of negotiations, which ended up lasting three weeks. Tomáš, returning from a trip to Prague, announced with characteristic bluntness, "Those who want to work should come back to work, those who want to strike can stay on strike."[39] The workers' demands would not be met. Tomáš knew that workers would have to be let go anyway.

The strike created something of a political crisis in the valley as the citizens of the town supported the workers and their allies at the ballot box. The first municipal election after independence led to one of the company's major conflicts – the struggle between the town's administration – under the newly formed First Republic of Czechoslovakia – and Bat'a managers. The 1919 municipal elections, energized by the promise of the events in Russia as well the strike at home, ushered in a decidedly leftist town council. The majority of council seats and the newly elected mayor, František Novák, belonged to the Social Democratic Party. Novák was similar to Štěpanek, the mayor whom he replaced, in that he too owned a shoe factory in town that hired skilled craftsmen, though it was smaller than Štěpanek's.[40] Yet Novák was more critical of Bat'a than his predecessor, and, fuelled with the rhetoric of the Bolshevik Revolution, was more interested in taking over the company than in offering an alternative space for skilled workers to resist the pace of Americanization.[41] Shortly after becoming mayor, the Social Democratic Party in Zlín changed its name to the Communist Party, with Mayor Novák as chairman.[42] Though an owner of a shoe factory himself, Novák looked east for a way out of the financial crisis. For him, the Americanization of the Bat'a factory was a serious danger to the future worker's state.

Novák had limited leverage, however, vis-à-vis Bat'a, as the town's coffers emerged from the war significantly smaller than the company's. Especially after the large floods of August 1919, which completely destroyed some twenty-seven buildings in the town, Novák and the city had a considerable revenue crisis, which made Bat'a crucial for the day-to-day operation of city services.[43] The town tried to squeeze the company coffers. At one point in 1921, Mayor Novák sent the company notice that offering free movies to employees was a taxable expense. He demanded forty crowns for each movie the company had shown in the past year, six in all, and forty crowns for every movie from then on.[44] A small affair for sure, but the tax on movies was indicative of the kinds of pressure the town council sought to bring on the company and the desperate financial situation of municipal authorities.

A more serious challenge was the creation of the socialist alternative to Sokol – the Workers' Gymnastics Club (Dělnická tělocvičná jednota). The Workers' Gymnastics Club, created by Novák and others in the Social Democratic Party, focused on rhythmic gymnastics and group exercise, just as Sokol did. However, unlike Sokol, it was not founded and organized by the middle class of the town to cultivate the collective body of the Czech nation, but by communists interested in cultivating the collective body of revolutionary workers.[45] The conflict between town council and company management in the immediate postwar period marked the beginning of what was to become a prolonged conflict between the company and communists. Both sides were training the bodies of their respective cadres. The Bolshevik Revolution had altered the tone and political horizons of the town. From then on, the struggle between the owners of capital, chiefly Bat'a, and the socialists dominated the postwar political life of the valley.

In the larger context of Czechoslovakia, clouds were darkening over export industries. In early 1919, Alois Rašín, the minister of finance, began implementing policies that eventually pulled Czechoslovakia out of the inflationary tailspin that many other countries in the region could not correct. But in the meantime, the policies all but destroyed access to the large market of the former Austro-Hungarian Empire. Borders closed for three months in 1919 in an attempt to ensure that all in the new state would uniformly adopt the Czechoslovak crown.[46] While of limited efficacy, the measure generated a storm of controversy. Coupled with the political fallout over the border closing, the Hungarian Red Army under Béla Kun invaded Slovakia in May. Rašín lost his job; a new finance minister relaxed trade and banking regulations, which then quickly resulted in a dramatic fall of the Czechoslovak crown. From July to November the crown lost 220 per cent of its value.

In June, the Hungarian Red Army was defeated by the new Army of Czechoslovakia, but the vision of a Bolshevik-style seizure of power continued to haunt company executives. America, or at least the Bat'a vision of America, seemed to offer a way out of the economic and political crises, and top-ranking Bat'a managers returned to see if they could draw further inspiration to improve the company's prospects. A year and four months after the creation of Czechoslovakia, Tomáš Bat'a returned to Lynn, Massachusetts. This time the company started a subsidiary company there, the Bata Shoe and Leather Company. According to the company newspaper, "many of our *krajanů* (expatriates) ... have agreed to work with us."[47] Their focus in Lynn was on "highgrade" women's shoes and they sought to sell these direct to retailers in the major markets in the northern United States.[48]

Lynn in 1920 remained a hotbed of union activism and was home to a strong anarchist movement. In fact, as the historian Stephen Mostov has highlighted in his work on the Jewish shoemakers that immigrated to Lynn shortly before and after the First World War, Lynn experienced fifty-seven strikes between 1920 and 1923, nine of which were general strikes.[49] In keeping with the pattern of selective memory that Tomáš employed, by which he remembered only the idealized "American work ethic" gleaned from Lynn during his experience there in 1905 but not the significant labour unrest, the company never reported the news of Lynn radicalism. Knowledge of the strikes in Lynn would not find their way to the Bat'a workforce in Zlín.

Tomáš put two half-brothers of his, Jan and Bohumil, in charge of running the small factory in Lynn. Bohumil at that point was an American citizen who had emigrated before the war. Jan was a doughy twenty-one-year-old with an outgoing disposition and little experience in either shoemaking or with America. The factory, despite attempts to integrate into the manufacturing elite of Lynn, failed to turn a profit and closed in 1921. Jan was let go shortly before the factory closed, but remained in the United States, where he worked briefly for a variety of shoe companies. The closure of the factory did not mean that the entire enterprise was a failure, though, for Bat'a used its American outpost as a financial route between Zlín and other European states.[50] More importantly, the closure of the factory in the cradle of the shoemaking revolution did not slow down the Americanization of Zlín. It did, however, lead the company to look for other sources of inspiration and guidance in its quest to Americanize.

The Influence of Ford and Endicott-Johnson

In the fall of 1919 Tomáš made a whirlwind trip to the United States. In five weeks, he experienced first-hand two of the great company towns of the early twentieth century, the Ford Motor Company's River Rouge complex and Endicott-Johnson's sprawling factory-town system in the Susquehanna Valley of Broome County, New York. If 1905 marked the beginning of the Americanization of Bat'a, 1919 marked a watershed in the development of Batism. For it was during his trip that year that Tomáš came into contact with the manufacturing system of the Ford Motor Company and the welfare capitalism of Endicott-Johnson. Both companies were to make lasting impressions. His first stop was Michigan.

Unfortunately, no record exists of Bat'a's visit in 1919 to River Rouge. We know of it only through his remarks to a variety of individuals later. Most notably, we have the written record of Bat'a's biographer and company propagandist Antonín Cekota. Cekota writes of the visit, "It was love at first sight when he saw the conveyor ... the factory was a great organism linked by the maze of arteries and veins – the conveyors."[51] Henry Ford's personality also supposedly made an impact. "In Ford's simple, puritanical manners, and especially in his attitude toward money as the vehicle of business and its main operating tool ... he found a living example of his own basic principle."[52] Soon after this visit, Tomáš wrote a letter to Ford asking him to visit Zlín during an upcoming trip to Europe, and if such a visit proved impossible, offered, "I would gladly see you anyplace in Europe."[53]

While taken with Henry Ford's personality, Tomáš was deeply impressed with the Ford Motor Company's attempt to shape the "morals" and living habits of its workforce and the anti-union, vertically integrated structure of its operations. Tomáš became a devoted acolyte. Through expatriate networks, he had already heard something of Ford's social engineering project, begun in 1914, but he became well versed in it upon his trip to the United States in 1919. It was then that Tomáš could see for himself the famous profit-sharing plan that came to be known as the "five-dollar day." This plan, which raised the average Ford workers' wages far above the national average, came with substantial strings in the form of routine home inspections from members of the company's Social Department and a mandated savings plan. To be given the high wage, Ford workers needed to meet a set of criteria that ranged from how much the worker had in savings, to the conditions of their furniture. Inspectors commented on personal relationships, hygiene, political affiliations, drinking habits, and more. Their reports determined who could obtain the profit-sharing status, which ended up encompassing approximately 73 per cent of all its workers.[54] The lesson to Tomáš was clear; wages could be tools of behavioural change.

After River Rouge, Tomáš made his way to Broome County, New York, the home of the Endicott-Johnson Company (EJ). Stretched out between the three towns of Endicott, Johnson City, and Binghamton, EJ was growing into the largest shoe company in the United States, with nearly 14,000 employees in 1920. At the time, it was also growing into the most well-known example of welfare capitalism in the United States, with parks, a nascent company housing program, medical care for workers and their families, a profit-sharing plan, and numerous spaces for workers' entertainment. In turn, the workers did not unionize and EJ had a remarkably low worker turnover rate (quit rates were 40 to 60 per cent of the industry's average) and an almost non-existent record of strikes, especially remarkable for the volatile shoe business.[55] The exchange of welfare and leisure services for loyalty was the basic component of EJ's famous "Square Deal."

The visionary behind EJ was George F. Johnson, who had quickly worked his way up the ranks before becoming general manager, then co-owner, and finally chief executive. Johnson was a man of his time and was deeply influenced by the examples and theories of welfare capitalism (some 2,000 companies had some form of welfare in 1915). What set Johnson apart was his desire to rhetorically and physically make the workers feel as if all employees were a part of the same family. What this meant was that managers, including himself, lived in the same neighbourhoods, sent their children to the same schools, and routinely participated in some form of leisure with the workers. Johnson focused on "personal contact" between managers and workers, "close observation, living together, playing together."[56]

The small Bat'a entourage toured the EJ factories and the company towns sometime in the late summer of 1919. According to Cekota, there was little of interest for Tomáš in the machinery or production side of EJ operations, but the welfare practices left a lasting impression.[57]

After Tomáš's trip it did not take long for company men to return to Endicott-Johnson. In April 1921, Jan Bat'a and Joseph Krcmar travelled to Endicott in order to study the manufacturing process of EJ as well as its public services. They toured the "Ideal Home" and the "Library."[58] The library and home, built in 1916 to provide EJ workers with access to a sizable collection of reading material and a comfortable place in which to read them, were meant to double as meeting places and educational centres. Primarily, what the *Batovci* in 1919 and then in 1921 witnessed was a paternalistic company that championed loyalty, family, and workers' culture. Johnson was anti-Prohibition, encouraged worker intimacy, supported the maintenance of immigrant religious and social practices, and would build a racetrack that held its largest events on Sunday.[59]

What the Bat'a men selected from this package of practices was the close observation of workers, the rhetoric of paternalism, and the trade-off between welfare offerings and worker loyalty. Johnson's pro-working-class attitude, which was at odds with much of the Americanizing rhetoric of his day, did not make it back to Zlín.[60]

Tomáš returned home inspired to confront what he viewed as a host of enemies to be conquered, from worker morality and behaviour to political opponents, with his idealized American system. His targets for improvement were wide-ranging, and he seems to have become convinced of the concept of engineering a new industrial society alongside a new mode of manufacturing. After all, Tomáš became preoccupied with external opposition and an internal conflict – the struggle to manage the behaviour and attitudes of workers. Along with battling unions, communists, and collapsing markets, Bat'a launched a campaign to tend to worker morality by starting an abstinence movement, conducting anti-smoking campaigns, and encouraging workers to "change their work spirit so that they know perfectly every movement of their machine."[61] Already immersed in a spirit of struggle from his time in Sokol, in the factories of Massachusetts, and as an outsider to the cartel system of Austria, Tomáš came to synthesize his battles as a fight for a way of life. Fordism, with its emphasis on social engineering, was coming to the Dřevnice.

Bat'a was far from alone in looking to the American example as offering a way forward from the myriad problems facing the people of the new state of Czechoslovakia. In the eyes of the Americanizers, the powerful labour movement in Czechoslovakia had much to do with a problem of worker morale and the premodern conditions of their factories. Throughout 1920 one could find such arguments flowing within public discourse. Speakers engaged large audiences in Prague on topics such as "Experiences from America" that offered direct comparisons between Czech and American workers. A common point was that Czech workers had little work ethic, were chauvinistic, and entirely too collective in their thinking. American workers, so argued the speakers, were by comparison individualistic, hard-working, optimistic, and open to working with people from all over the world.[62] Newspapers echoed the positive lessons of America. An article titled "Amerikanismus," written under the pseudonym of "Nový Lid" (New People), offered Bat'a workers a clear message of the superiority of the American lifestyle and the correctness of Bat'a's interpretation of it:

> The American has the most opportunities for fun and diversion ... The American has the most reliable and most comfortable transportation: In Connecticut every tenth person, in Illinois, every eighth, and in Nebraska every sixth person has an automobile. The American has the greatest opportunity for education: schools and courses for free; institutes, museums, libraries are all available and offer a chance

for him to reach his highest potential. Materially or spiritually, the American has the greatest opportunities for a better life than citizens of all the other nations on earth.

And where can one find the source for this?

It is in work, in which everyone has the ability to create and build. America works like no other land. The American borrowed socialistic ideas for practical purposes, that work is the basis for all welfare, that without it there is no receiving, only poverty; and because of this principle all of America is one buzzing hive, or single ant mound, where everyone works with feverish intensity, where the dollar is the wheel and every citizen with it in their pockets can enjoy the benefits of its circulation. Europeans seem lazy in America; a true American could not stand not working; if he was down to his last dollar he would go to the nearest corner and start working shining shoes or working as a porter so that he would not waste time. Even the rich in America are not lazy, even the multi-millionaires. On the contrary, they are the hardest working people on the planet.[63]

Such a halcyon interpretation did not meet with universal acclaim in the diverse state of Czechoslovakia, or even in the town of Zlín. For the Americanizers, especially Bat'a, had become a symbol of a new exploitation – one of machines, time cards, and empty promises. As such, writers and politicians on different sides of the political and national spectrum came to formulate, or continue to propagate already formulated, negative definitions of Americanization. The Tradesmen's Party, the Social Democratic Party, the Communist Party, and even former champions of the American example in the bourgeois press attacked the idea of "amerikanismus" and its acolytes. The strong allure of America had lost much of its appeal in the tumultuous two-year period between 1918 and 1920.[64]

Aside from a growing scepticism on the benefits of Americanizing, one of the first difficulties to confront Tomáš upon his return to Zlín was a nasty rumour being spread by Novák that the company had illegally imported and exported goods in 1919. Given the myriad other continent-wide events, the affair caused only a small stir in public opinion, but Bat'a was quick to sue Novák for slander and libel. Bat'a won the lawsuit, and Novák had to issue a formal apology.[65] While the libel case proceeded through the courts, the Tradesmen's Party launched another attack on the company's name by making a formal accusation that Bat'a had robbed the state through inflated contracts with the army during the war. The company then asked, received, and reprinted an official statement from the Ministry of National Defence that stated the army contracts then and now were fair.[66]

In addition, Stefan Haupt-Buchenrode, who remained in possession of the Zlín estate, but whose title of baron no longer carried any advantages in Czechoslovakia, took Bat'a to court over a land usage issue. Apparently,

Haupt-Buchenrode had put in a clause in his land deal with Bat'a that asserted that no industrial buildings would be erected on a section of land close to Zlín Castle. According to Haupt-Buchenrode, "After the downfall of 1918, he (Tomáš) thought his position so strengthened that he could ignore the reserved rights in the purchase contract which were restricting his freedom of movement, that he started to build, without my consent, on the forbidden lots. The first step was to build a big annular brick kiln ... when he started with a sixty-metre-high chimney, I sent him a registered letter alerting him that I would have to stop this construction ... he didn't do this."[67] The case went before the local district court, where the judges sided with Bat'a. Haupt-Buchenrode, undeterred, would carry on about the issue for the next seven years.

Getting to Know the Workers

Alongside court cases and challenges from communists and former aristocrats, the year 1921 witnessed a concentrated effort on the part of the company to make the workforce visible and chaste. While company records are not nearly as voluminous as they are for later years, a steady stream of decrees in the company newspaper, accompanied by managers' accounts of the period, demonstrate that 1921 marked a significant moment in the history of the company when it applied management techniques learned largely from American practitioners. Some of these applications were not yet as comprehensive as they were elsewhere, like at the Ford Motor Company, but they were nevertheless the beginning of a systematic attempt to make legible the everyday lives of workers and their families and to discipline their habits.

The beginning of this campaign was seemingly benign. When Jan Bat'a returned to the company in August 1921, his first task was to compile a list of all the employees who were with the company longer than ten years and then systematically collect information on all employees' vacation plans.[68] On 1 October 1921, the company published an article based on the results of lengthy correspondence and research into employees' vacation habits – which provided evidence of both a slight uptick in the living conditions of Zlín and a growing desire to track employees' whereabouts outside of the factory. In some cases, the paper published what the employees did on their vacations, right down to the weather conditions in the Tatras.[69] Though the reports were lighthearted, the practice of tracking workers' holidays evidenced a growing desire for surveillance. The aftershocks of the First World War had left the company feeling boxed in by an oppositional city council, a nationwide smear campaign, and calls for a world revolution. Managers increasingly worried about workers' loyalty.

The next month, on 17 December 1921, the company announced the beginning of a systematic identification system that required all employees to have a photo on file that matched an identification card. Employees were instructed that they must have these cards with them at all times on the factory grounds, and that there were going to be periodic factory inspections to ensure their compliance.[70] Early files included short entries on the workers' length of employment and residences. They would prove to be the stepping stones to a society of surveillance, one that was not necessarily planned but led to a logical destination.

After all, the relatively limited goal of identifying workers dovetailed with an increasing interest in managing workers' lifestyles. While few internal records exist from this period, what the company newspaper published in 1922–3 offers convincing evidence of the beginning of a moral policy for employees and suggests a strong reliance on American examples. Beginning in early 1922, the company began publishing a translated series of articles from the Reverend Billy Sunday; these would run until 1926. The first article, "Stand with Abstinence," had a fiery tone and included the sentence "alcoholism is worse than war."[71] By 1922, Sunday was one of the most famous men in the United States, an evangelical preacher who was instrumental in the passing of the Eighteenth Amendment – which prohibited the manufacture and sale of alcohol.[72] In Czechoslovakia, where the Catholic press dubbed him "the charlatan preacher" and alcoholic consumption was deeply embedded in the social fabric, Sunday became one more radical voice in Bat'a's assault on the culture of the valley.[73]

Of course, the use of religion and religious figures to encourage workers to live chaste lives was a page directly out of Henry Ford's playbook. The Bat'a paper first began printing detailed information about Henry Ford and the Ford Motor Company in the spring of 1923. From then until 1932, with Tomáš's death, scarcely a week would go by without something from Ford printed in the paper. When Tomáš returned from his second trip to the United States, Ford became the company's principal teacher. Tomáš Bat'a later wrote a letter to Ford after reading his recently published book, *Moving Forward.* The letter revealed just how central Ford was to the company:

> We have already been working for several decades in a similar way to yourself and have had the same experiences. Each of your books is our teacher, an encouragement and a proof that our service is on the right line.
>
> We fight in our country against the same enemy, against the ignorance, indifference, and superstition of people, particularly regarding the purpose of machinery. With these thoughts in our mind we are approaching you in the hope that you would kindly give us your permission to translate and publish in the Czech language your book, *Moving Forward.* In this we do not seek any financial gain, we merely wish to serve the people of our Republic, because we are convinced that only economically right-minded people – and therefore people of substance – can work with success.[74]

Less constant than the example of Ford were the examples of Endicott-Johnson and George F. Johnson, whose work and speeches frequented the pages of the paper as well. Sunday, Johnson, and especially Ford were the backbone of Bat'a's program of Americanization.

In addition to highlighting the contributions of these "teachers," Bat'a was keen on providing basic instruction on how workers were to live their lives in a new age. There were frequent articles on personal hygiene, including on how to wash clothes and how to groom oneself. Instructions on how to raise children were also provided; children were encouraged to be independent and self-sufficient: "We should not worry that we do not hold their hand in leading them to the right path, but that it is our responsibility to fortify their strength so that they can find the right path on their own."[75] There were even articles about what was the ideal time to sleep, what was the ideal drink (water or warm milk), and what to do in one's free time (exercise and read). Nearly all such advice harkened back to an idealized American example: "Go find the practical Michigan man, and see there not only someone with self-control and parsimony, but someone who has an interest in everything that man has created and can create."[76]

The crusade to Americanize workers' behaviour was partly the result of the continued housing crisis, which did not subside after the war. Even with layoffs, the company had to take the step of reaching out to employees with housing to rent out rooms or beds to other employees. In every issue from 8 April to the end of May 1922, the company newspaper ran the following: "We kindly ask all residence owners that might have a free bed or couch to rent out that bed or couch to a worker of our factories. We recommend a contract to rent out a couch or bed and we can send you that contract if you contact us." The instability of housing left young workers floating in and out of Zlín, a situation the company wanted to end as quickly as possible. In the uncertainty of who was living with whom, and therefore what morals were rubbing off on young impressionable workers, the company launched its Americanization campaign. Of course, before such a campaign could be enforced, the company had to return to a sound financial footing.

While Bat'a crafted a moral compass for the factory, the Czechoslovak economy underwent the shock of deflation when Rašín, restored to finance minister, ushered in a series of policies designed to tighten money circulation and increase the value of the crown. This had the effect of both increasing the real burden on debtors and lowering consumer prices. Many people began to worry about covering the cost of groceries, as well as shoes, as their wages began to drop some 20 to 30 per cent across the country.[77] Bat'a had a significant stockpile of shoes due to the loss of the Austro-Hungarian market, which had cost the company considerably more to produce than prices would now allow. In other words, shoes had piled up in warehouses, credit had all but dried up, and wages were falling.

In this tense, and at times desperate, business climate of 1922, the company had the good fortune of having Dominik Čipera on its management team. Now largely forgotten, Čipera was a man of intense concentration, with perhaps one of the sharpest business minds of the twentieth century. Čipera had married Tomáš's niece Božena Klaus, who worked for Bat'a as a leather purchaser in 1918. A banker by trade, Čipera joined his wife at Bat'a in 1919 as a manager of the accounting department.[78] Faced with the crises of deflation, and runaway inflation in Germany, Tomáš and Dominik Čipera made the bold decision to cut the price on all of their shoes by half. The cut in shoe prices would be partially offset by a 40 per cent cut in all wages. In turn, all prices at Bat'a-run canteens and grocery stores would also be reduced 50 per cent. In what would become an iconic piece of advertising, the company announced their plans with a striking poster. In the image, a mighty fist smashes *"DRAHOTA"* (high prices). Customers poured into the Bat'a stores, workers largely remained loyal, and Bat'a stabilized its production. The company paid off all of its debt within one year.[79]

Conclusion

During the First World War, Bat'a moved to a central position in the economy of the Habsburg Empire as the state used its considerable power to underwrite company production. As a result, the factory began to resemble a labour camp, with forced overtime, food shortages, POW labour, and Austrian gendarmes prowling the area to arrest "shirkers." This situation then fed into the uncertainty of the immediate postwar years, which were marked by conflict. It was then that the Dřevnice Valley became the site of a struggle between the utopian dreams of Tomáš Bat'a, who sought to use the massive expansion that came with the First World War to "Americanize" the Central European industrial worker and workplace, and an array of socialist and tradesmen associations that sought to organize the company's and town's workers around their own visions of modernity. Changing local and national contexts shaped the contours of the struggle. After the war, the uncertainty accelerated. Indeed, the crisis years of 1919–22 saw the company at its most vulnerable. Bat'a lost its central position in the large market of the Habsburg Empire, was left with an outsized workforce, and faced a hostile city council. However, it also found itself at war's end with several important assets.

Perhaps its greatest asset was clarity of character. In Bat'a's view, its goal was to Americanize Zlín. While the First World War uprooted most citizens and officials literally and figuratively, the company began to create a robust disciplinary system girded by beliefs about gender and personal behaviour largely borrowed from an idealized America. To do so, it developed a worker identification method and broad employment practices that sought to impose worker legibility and control worker habits. This evolving disciplinary system drew from the examples of the Ford and Endicott-Johnson companies, and sprang from a rising fear of communism. From 1914 to 1923, Bat'a institutionalized its idols and demagogues, while building a vertically integrated system and modernized production processes. After this period, a few new enemies would be named, and certain thinkers would gain favour with the company elite, but the general orientation of the company had already been set. The Bat'a world pointed west.

However, Americanization, as defined by Bat'a, did not equate to American culture. Coca-Cola, jazz, segregation, and labour unrest were not part of the company's American mythology. Instead, the company promoted America in the form of the welfare capitalism of Endicott-Johnson and the sobriety, efficiency, and machinery of Ford. To the people of Bat'a, America meant time management and increased productivity. It meant accelerating everyday life, embracing individual competition in the labour market, and using welfare to insure loyalty. Eventually during the interwar period, Americanism would evolve into Batism, but in the critical years of 1914–23 Bat'a was largely an importer of select American ideas.

What resulted from this selective borrowing, and the company's responses to local conflicts, was that by 1923 the contours of Batism could be roughly sketched. The belief that humans could be engineered to fit the new machine-centred work, a popular one in the context of the interwar era, was the centrepiece. What they would be engineered into had much to do with Henry Ford and Tomáš Bat'a's romanticized view of American labour relations. But the social engineering that would be practised in the 1930s by the company was still a long way off. In many ways, the war pushed the company toward greater control over resources, especially by creating the momentum to move the company toward vertical integration.

The difficult postwar economic climate pressed the company to look for models to emulate, and the specific worldview of the head of the company pushed the company to find those models in America. Still, so much at the beginning of 1923 remained uncertain, especially on the political front. For having grand ideas of social engineering is one thing, but carrying those ideas out requires a level of governmental control. As Bat'a gained during the war, having the local authorities, especially those involved with law and order, working with and for a company gives a business tremendous power over the lives of its workforce.

By 1923, Bat'a was in position to strike a decisive blow against its local opponents and take such power. The upcoming municipal elections would provide the opportunity to do just that.

"An End to Politics," 1923–1926

If one had to give a definitive date for the start of the Bat'a kingdom, 16 September 1923 would be a good choice. For it was then that a Bat'a company ticket, with founder Tomáš Bat'a at the top of a list of forty-four other employees, won the municipal elections, sweeping out of office Mayor František Novák and the Communist Party. From then until the German occupation of the town in March/April 1939, Bat'a controlled the municipal affairs of Zlín. Holding the reins of employment and local authority allowed for a remarkable acceleration of processes begun earlier – the industrialization of shoe production and the social engineering of those that lived within its wake.

A cornerstone of Batism was that good management existed "above" politics. The Bat'a candidates were not interested, then, in allying with any existing political party. Instead, they created their own, the *Batovci* (Bat'a people), who were both candidates for city government and allegedly apolitical. The apolitical rhetoric came from the top. A couple of weeks before the election, Tomáš asked a crowd at his factory, "What do I need from you? Only for you to help me depoliticize the municipality as you helped me depoliticize the worker's council by voting for our candidates."[1] Ending politics meant eliminating the party system and managing the town according to a scientific rationality. Such rationality wanted little to do with the messiness of democracy, which had previously put the city council in an adversarial position with the major employer of the region. As seen in one of the *Batovci*'s campaign illustrations, Tomáš was going to lift Zlín out of the muck of politics and protect it from the political parties, depicted as predatory birds circling above the town.

The components for the Bat'a takeover had been assembled between 1918 and 1922. For it was then that the hostile relationship between city hall and the company grew into an intractable problem, which had to do with Bat'a's anti-union policy, unskilled labour, and growing reluctance to provide the city with additional funds, which the city sorely needed given the fluctuation in availability of labourers and the disastrous floods of 1919. It seems the sparks

Figure 3.1. Political illustration from 1923, Bat'a lifting Zlín out of the swamp of politics, In *Naše volby* (Zlín, 1925): 5, Moravský zemský archiv v Brně, Státní okresní archiv Zlín, Bat'a Fond, I.

that ignited this tinder of animosity were affairs over the new town council building, the price of electricity, and internal company politics.

In 1922, the old municipal building caught fire and was badly damaged. The city council approved a budget of six million crowns to build a replacement, which Tomáš argued was ten times what the city could afford to pay. Being a man who carefully tracked operational expenses, Tomáš was incensed by the city council's lack of fiscal responsibility. Ironically, the new building, which remains the town's administrative building today, was designed by František Lydia Gahura, the same architect Bat'a employed to design a large expansion for worker housing.[2]

In addition to the quarrel over the price of the new town hall, the price of electricity factored into Bat'a's decision to run for office. The electrification of Zlín had begun as early as 1896, but the construction of an Ericsson power station in 1913 greatly increased the supply of electricity to the town. In 1917, Bat'a bought this main power station, which gave the company a monopoly on electricity. Four years later, the company constructed another state-of-the-art power station. In 1922, with the new station online, the company sought to greatly expand its service network. To offset the costs of doing so, Bat'a planned to implement a 70 per cent increase in the price of electricity. The town council rejected the plan. Bat'a was incensed yet again.[3]

Perhaps the decisive reason for the creation of the Batovci Party, though, was a development within the ranks of the Bat'a workers. In May 1923, the workers of the company elected a socialist as chairman of the Worker's Council. This body served as a watered-down union, with a grievance process for its members, but no collective bargaining – a compromise resulting from the strike of 1918. The Worker's Council membership had been reduced to only 45 per cent of the total workforce since 1918, and it seems the workers had finally had enough of the anti-union policy, which left them completely at the whim of the managers. The company responded to their attempt to elect a pro-union chairman by using a provision in a statute which allowed them to veto the election results. Tomáš then personally selected the candidates for the Workers Council. This was "depoliticization."[4]

The Worker's Council election foreshadowed the municipal election. Just as they did with the Worker's Council, the company's executives decided to assert themselves in the municipal voting process. And while they could not very well personally elect the town council, Bat'a managers could overwhelm their socialist adversaries by wielding money and influence. Bat'a was, after all, responsible either directly or indirectly for well over half of the town's jobs as well as hundreds of housing units.

The campaign laid bare a deep anxiety the company elite felt about party politics. This anxiety partly originated from the strengthened position of political opponents after the First World War, partly from the experience of wartime, which showed how beneficial a military dictatorship could be for company expansion, and a still coalescing Batism, which held that the scientific planning of the public sphere could bring social harmony. Within this context, the party system of early postwar Czechoslovakia in general came to be seen by Bat'a as inefficient and counterproductive, especially as the town's debt grew and attacks on the company intensified: "The political parties have been treating us like we are the unbearable people."[5] The solution was to end partisanship with company rule.

It seems that such rhetoric played well to many potential voters. Dozens of citizens wrote in to the Bat'a newspaper, *Sdělení*, to offer their support – many specifically mentioning Bat'a's plan to depoliticize the town. "I completely agree that we need to depoliticize City Council, since its purpose is to manage municipal property in a reasonable and economical matter, not according to the policy of any party."[6] "Politicians should not enter into municipal affairs, only hardworking people who will act as one to improve the city and wealth of its citizens."[7] František Gahura, the architect, weighed in with a simple equation: "Bat'a is Zlín – and Zlín is Bat'a."[8]

Tomáš was already a father figure for company loyalists, and now he was to extend his role, protecting all of Zlín from the mire of partisan bickering. In turn, he would lead its citizens into a new and better age. Just what this new age was to bring was clear. Since 1906, and especially from 1919 on, the company offered a future inspired by the American way of life: "If we could change our citizens' thoughts so that they will think like Americans, we would have much greater prosperity in this country than we currently have."[9] It was a way of thinking found in Broome County, New York, and Dearborn, Michigan, where large industries provided a host of services for workers who in return gave unquestioned loyalty to their employers – this was what constituted American thoughts for the *Batovci*. The citizens of these towns engaged in a host of company-sponsored activities. Speed, machinery, and competition were the core masculine values. Motherhood, education, and material ambition defined the feminine. Bat'a, like many progressive politicians and academics of the time, promised a version of the future based on the scientific management of society. Only in the welfare capitalist variant the company, not the state, would manage it.

To create such a society, Bat'a had to remove its political opponents in city government. Promising that none of the Bat'a candidates would earn a single crown for their service in public office, Bat'a placed a vision of a "greater Zlín" – with the unpredictable Dřevnice River tamed by engineering, the transportation network impressively updated with broad boulevards and new bus routes, and a significant expansion of the city's footprint – in front of voters.

The results were not even close. The *Batovci* won 1,322 votes out of a total of 2,337, giving them 17 of the 30 seats at stake and the ability to elect the mayor. The second-place party, the Communists, won 454 votes and 6 seats.[10] Zlín was officially a company town.

Could the opposition have possibly found a way to prevent the company from taking control of the city government? Given the company's ability to mobilize its workers into voters, workers who had been hired young and educated on the job, it seems unlikely. On the other hand, the town had consistently elected anti-Bat'a candidates. The party in power, the Communists, tried to hit Bat'a in a variety of ways. The two most pronounced attacks were claims that the *Batovci* were motivated by greed and that they were not sufficiently patriotic: "The Bat'a workers were never allowed to fight for the freedom of Czechoslovakia or for their freedom from slavery ... Bat'a, like a capitalist, has no interest in the overall welfare and blossoming of the citizens of Zlín. He is only interested in the fact that as the largest landlord (*polatnik*) he will not have to pay his local taxes."[11] Though certainly appealing to their base, such rhetoric did little damage to the Bat'a promise of a "greater Zlín."

The *Batovci* delivered on this promise. Zlín experienced an unprecedented building boom and the town coffers increased sevenfold after the municipal elections. Taking over the town was of no financial gain to the company. After all, the town's entire budget in 1923 was 61,023 crowns. Given that the company did about 15.6 million crowns worth of business in 1922, the city budget was insignificant. The *Batovci* more than doubled this budget the next year, and by 1926 the city had an operating budget of 461,053 crowns.[12] In addition, the company provided a variety of construction materials for city projects at no cost, as well as free lunches for city employees and free laundry services.[13] A vast amount of the money and material went to infrastructure and transportation. Bus service expanded in these years; streetlights were added and roads were built. Connecting the company's and the town's budgets greatly accelerated construction in the region and turned city space into company space and vice versa. Entangling budgets was one part of the process.

The town's infrastructure grew concurrently with a reorientation of production methods. Between 1923 and 1924, Bat'a revamped its manufacturing by using an innovative process; instead of workshops focusing on one step in the production process, each workshop would focus on one type of shoe. The process relied on a conveyer belt system that moved the shoe to different stations in the workshop.[14] The Ford factories, which Tomáš had visited in 1919, undoubtedly provided the inspiration. Bat'a was the first to adopt such a system in shoe manufacturing.[15]

A rapid expansion of the enterprise corresponded with the reorientation of the production process. In 1924, Bat'a constructed three modern factory buildings, along with new "tanneries for chrome (or mineral) tanning, a new extractor, a grocery store, a brickworks, a transformer station, and numerous residential buildings."[16] With all the building and the infrastructure projects, it must have looked as if all of Zlín were under construction.

Voters in 1923 were perhaps also willing to back the *Batovci* because of a positive shift in the economic climate of the country as a whole. Economic historians estimate that in that year Czechoslovakia reached its prewar GDP. [17] The return to economic stability reduced the support for communism that the Bolshevik Revolution had earlier created. Coupled with the less-than-promising news coming out of Russia, many in Zlín had cooled to the appeals for a Bolshevik-style government by 1923. A similar revolutionary event in Czechoslovakia was unlikely. As a result, those in the opposition in Zlín did not look outward to inspire protest. They concentrated on the Bat'a Company and on Tomáš in particular. The Organization of Czechoslovak Socialists in Zlín accused Bat'a of imprisoning patriotic Czechs and other anti-Austrian persons in a prison on the factory grounds during the First World War. They also mocked Bat'a paternalism. "This is your Daddy Bat'a, children!"[18] While such accusations and strategies did not prevent them from losing the vote and control of the town, they did much to entrench a key tenet of Batism – enemies are everywhere.

The Bat'a System of Management

Alongside the us-against-the-world mentality, Tomáš developed a unique system of management that prioritized loyalty and competition. Working with Dominik Čipera, Tomáš decentralized all business units and set them in competition against each other. Each unit was responsible for meeting a quota, which was determined by the top management. Management also set levels for the price of needed materials, which established how many products needed to be "sold" either to other units or to customers. If the unit exceeded these quotas, a percentage of the profit went into the unit's paycheques, with managers getting 5 to 10 per cent more than everyone else. Similarly, workers from 1924 on were brought into a profit-sharing plan that essentially took a fixed amount out of their paychecks and bought company stock with it. They then earned a guaranteed 10 per cent interest on this not-so-voluntary investment. In a stroke of genius, Bat'a created a network of interdependent sections of a vertically integrated company. In other words, while the company expanded to include every phase of shoe manufacturing, from buying hides to selling shoes, each department competed to outdo the other on cost and quality.[19]

The system bred individual competition and ingenuity. For example, Čipera claimed that he never received a direct order from Tomáš; rather it was up to him to find solutions to problems. Indeed, an overwhelming number of people in management positions would make it there because they came up with a particularly bright idea on the job. In addition, Bat'a carefully embedded competition into everyday life, from stitching contests to athletic events. Athletic competition took off in 1924 when the local soccer club changed its name from F.K. Zlín to S.K. Bat'a. The company began to organize an array of sports teams, and built an impressive new stadium by the train station – a stone's throw from the factories.[20] Investment in creating a culture of competition continued at work, where gaining the highest profits for one's department earned a spot in the local newspaper, and various workplace contests were held throughout the interwar period. On the factory walls, one could find one of Tomáš's slogans: "Struggle – the father of all things."[21] Employees, students at the Bat'a School of Work (Bat'ova škola práce, or BSP), and low- and mid-level managers were to embrace a daily struggle at work and at home, where they were to compete in athletic events and overcome the lure of immorality, so that they could become *Batovci*.

Overwhelmingly, however, the top management, those twelve or so individuals who made up the inner circle, were mostly connected to Tomáš Bat'a through family and regional ties.[22] And while some showed remarkable ability, most were valued for their unquestioned loyalty to the boss. Dominik Čipera, the man most responsible for putting Bat'a's idea of industrial autonomy into an administrative and accounting system, married Bat'a's niece in 1922. John Hoza, eventually the head of the rubber division, entered as a teenager into Tomáš's service as his driver and mechanic before the war. Jan Bat'a was Tomáš's younger half-brother, and Josef Hlavnička, another corporate executive, married Tomáš's sister Marie in 1923. Thus, we see a company centred on familial piety. Despite claims to the contrary, most managers had no chance of moving into the top circles of the company, as these positions were reserved for men whose loyalty was guaranteed through family or regional connections.[23]

These family connections served to strengthen the sense of solidarity among management and to present a uniform model of masculinity at the factories. With Tomáš's three-piece suit, clean shave, and polished shoes setting the standard, the upper management came to model a masculine aesthetic at work and in public. There was very little need for discipline for the top-level managers, as they strove to emulate the appearance of the paternal figure of Tomáš. The rest of the workforce, however, was seen to need more guidance.

Making "Greater Zlín"

Keeping Zlín safe for the *Batovci* meant taking aim at four targets: the communists, the school system, workers, and the "new" woman. For these groups threatened to hold back Bat'a's new Americanized person, one who was to be above politics, trained in the industrial arts, sober, and monogamous. With only six uniformed city police, no personal inspectors, no health inspector, and very little municipal regulation of business, alcohol, or prostitution, the *Batovci* began their campaign of regulation and control.[24] Their plans, however, did not match the modesty of their resources.

One of the first goals of the company upon taking over municipal affairs was to temper radicalism. The *Batovci* did so at first by challenging the socialists and communists over space and followers. One of the first actions of Mayor Baťa was to forbid the Workers Gymnastics Club of Zlín, a group allied to the local Communist Party, from using school grounds or equipment to train. They would then have to find a private space.[25] As its next manoeuvre, the company sponsored a May Day rally in 1924 in order to compete with the Communist Party's own event in terms of both workers and space. Instead of marching through the old section of Zlín under the red banner, workers were to gather on the grounds of Tomáš Baťa's modernist estate and hear from the boss and mingle with management. It was a calculated and bold move. By going after May Day, the socialist and communist high holy day, the *Batovci* made clear that leftists were the arch-villains of the Baťa ethos.

While Baťa's May Day eventually became the largest May Day rally in all of Czechoslovakia, the first affair had a distinctly Sunday picnic feel, with guests strolling the grounds of the estate, playing games, eating from a buffet, and drinking lemonade (no alcohol was served).[26] Though a damp, chilly day, the event was considered a success, as turnout proved much larger than expected, and attendees, at least according to Marie Baťa, had a good time.[27] While employees dressed up for the occasion, they were given no explicit instructions on what to wear. Photographs of the day show many women in head scarves and a large number of the men in their Sunday suits.[28] This was to be a day when management and workers were on equal footing, a day intended to strengthen the Baťa family by giving workers the chance to carry on like gentlemen, rubbing shoulders with their bosses and letting their kids play together. It was very much like the Fourth of July parades of Endicott-Johnson. While the casual nature of the event would eventually give way to a spectacle of uniformity, certain May Day practices did become established: the boss made a speech and the loyalties of employees were put to a test, as just a few hundred metres away the local socialist organizations held their traditional May Day rally. The main purpose of the Baťa celebration was to counteract the influence of the Social Democratic and Communist Parties. For, just as the *Batovci* promised to do away with politics altogether, the Baťa May Day promised to turn its political rivals' most sacred day into an expression of fidelity to the company.

The next year, the company moved the affair into the streets, organizing the first Baťa parade. Armed with advertising posters, workers marched in a rather ragtag assembly through the town, the women and girls again mostly in traditional Moravian head scarves, the men and boys in overcoats and ties. A horse-drawn float displaying one of the latest machines for stitching uppers was the largest expense. Certainly, the 1925 May Day remained a local and casual affair, more akin to a country fair than a mass rally.[29] But it would not take long for this loosely organized event to change.

In 1926 the company amplified their May Day, turning it from a provincial celebration mostly aimed at undermining the socialist agenda into a focal point for the larger Bat'a enterprise and a platform from which to promote the Bat'a name across the continent. The expansion of the celebration coincided with a dramatic increase in the production of shoes from 8,785,000 pairs in 1925 to 15,205,000 a year later.[30] Financial success translated into a significant investment in the May Day celebrations of 1926, and other departments of the company outside of Zlín were brought in to join the festivities. The sales department of Brno, for example, showed up with a large float featuring a model of the company's proposed skyscraper, a functionalist design that had stirred up considerable controversy in the city. The day remained, though, more of a celebration than a political rally. The early Bat'a May Day events needed only to siphon workers from the socialist held events. As the company emerged from the financial and political crisis of the early 1920s, it recognized the power of self-promotion – a skill with which the chief executive had already proven himself remarkably adept.

While the *Batovci* were trying to marginalize communists and socialist activists, they took on another perceived enemy of their new society: alcohol. They saw drunkenness as being unproductive and a sign of the backward past – for Tomáš it was the hallmark of Moravian lethargy and he was committed to eradicate it: "Smoking and drinking beer in the pubs is a waste of time, health, and money. What circulates there are only old, dead ideas. Nausea and unhappiness are born there and then permeate family life."[31] Of course, by this time, the temperance movement had successfully ushered in the Prohibition era in the United States. In the mid-1920s, Americans were in the middle of a grand experiment, with the state mobilized to eradicate the evils of alcohol. Bat'a's commitment to temperance was yet one more link in its Americanization project. Like their idol Henry Ford, *Batovci* saw drink as one of the biggest threats to industrial capitalism. In 1925, they funded and founded the Abstinence Society in Zlín, an organization connected to a movement taking hold around the world.[32]

However, in Moravia, where there was a long tradition of alcohol consumption, Bat'a's temperance movement was considered radical and unpopular. While laws governing certain aspects of alcoholic consumption had been on the books since at least as early as 1891, they were considerably milder in their intent and language – the 1891 laws forbade the sale of hard liquor in bars next to industrial factories during their hours of operation.[33] Ultimately, few people at Bat'a and even fewer in Zlín, even when encouraged by job prospects to do so, made the commitment to give up alcohol. Even members of the upper management were known to drink. Tomáš Bat'a himself drank beer occasionally.[34] The anti-alcohol campaign, while effective at limiting the number of places that served alcohol for a time, was never able to stop workers from drinking, or businessmen from making a profit from it. Therefore, the abstinence movement in Zlín was led by men who looked at it as a way to increase worker productivity, and workers largely ignored it.[35] But for a while, between 1924 and 1927, Bat'a spent considerable energy trying to curb drinking in the town.

On 1 March 1924, after only three months in power, Tomáš Bat'a ran a public denunciation of a drunk in the company – soon to be city – newspaper: "This is a warning to all citizens that Karel Wernberger, in a drunken stupor, behaved in an offensive manner, threatening women on a public road and deriding children. Because of this I ask all citizens, especially pub owners, not to provide any intoxicants to him either for sale or for free."[36] This public shaming of a drunk marked the beginning of the campaign to marginalize alcoholics within the city. The excerpt also hinted at the still embryonic state of the Bat'a disciplinary system. For, essentially, the drunk's punishment was to be a public affair, meted out under the community's gaze.

The city council, firmly in the *Batovci*'s hands, followed suit and raised taxes on alcoholic beverages (not including beer or wine) by 40 per cent and limited concessions on purveyors of alcohol, which caused a minor uproar in town. The loudest critic was the former mayor, Novák, who railed against Bat'a's attack on free commerce and workers' personal freedom. To which Tomáš replied, "The vast majority of our citizens made it clear during the recent vote, that they do not wish their councilmen to expand pub life (*hospodský život*) at the expense of clean family living."[37] Furthermore, plans to have a pub in the new town hall were definitively scrapped.

Likewise, Bat'a asked the public to participate in the razing of "old Zlín" throughout the 1920s. The *Batovci* connected the crumbling façades of older buildings with the numerous bars and pubs scattered through the town. They were relics of a different age. In 1930, when the owner of a bar situated in the centre of town, next to a newly built school, refused to sell for less than 4 million crowns, the company asked all citizens to boycott the establishment: "[The issue of the city buying the pub] is a decision whether or not the owner of a bar can worsen the lives of a whole generation of children … or whether we give them the right conditions to be upstanding citizens."[38] Within a few months, the owner had sold and the building was torn down.

However, the company was not always so successful, as seen in one of the most astounding local setbacks the company experienced in the interwar period. A committed hotelier/pub owner named Antonin Máca fought the town council over two and a half years, through the courts, press, and public opinion.

The dispute began in 1927, when Máca approached the city council to get a building permit for a hotel and pub. He was denied, the council citing that his pub would be too close to an already existing pub, and too close to the Sokol hall.[39] Máca then petitioned the regional authorities in Uherské Hradiště, who also denied his request. At that point, Máca got much more involved and began attending city council meetings. He applied for a permit yet again, and was again rejected. Only now the council explained in much greater detail the reasons of their decision: "Today's Zlín has many young men and women workers and the administration has to look after them so that they do not suffer any moral harm."[40]

The moral argument had little effect on Máca, who once again went to regional authorities, only this time to the Moravian regional authorities in Brno. There, the case was sent back to Uherské Hradiště. Only this time the regional council sent a representative to Zlín to investigate both sides of the case. When the investigator returned to Uherské Hradiště, he brought a map with all of the bars and pubs in Zlín, which showed that in a rapidly growing town of around 18,000, there were only sixteen purveyors of alcohol.[41] Convinced of the illegitimacy of the Bat'a argument, the regional council overturned the city's ruling; Máca would have his pub and hotel. Bat'a representatives were furious. No one more so than Tomáš.

The company officially protested the decision, and while the appeal ran its course, Tomáš had a battle of words with Máca's lawyer, Jan Winkler. In April after his defeat in the courtroom, Tomáš printed on the front page of *Zlín* a letter Winkler wrote to him in which the lawyer claimed a "moral victory." Tomáš's responded, "Mr. Winkler, you boast of a victory over me, but over me you are not victorious. You were victorious, with the help of your powerful friends, over the health of our citizens." [42] Later, when their appeal failed, the *Batovci* ran a front-page article about the immorality of Máca, and asked citizens to join in another boycott.[43] This time, though, the boycott failed; Máca's establishment opened with a solid clientele and remained open throughout the interwar era. Thus, by going outside of the municipal authorities, an opponent of Bat'a successfully limited the company's reach into everyday life.

The success of Máca, the small business owner, was exceptional. For while the company lost a fight to restrict one hotelier from operating, it went about dramatically reorganizing the lives of the people of Zlín. Perhaps its most strenuous effort was on an overhaul of the educational system.

The Creation of the Bat'a School of Work

In the paternalistic rhetoric of welfare capitalism, the education of both school-aged kids and the workforce needed to connect with life in a large, vertically integrated company with global aspirations. The school system in

Zlín, however, fell far short of the mark in the eyes of the *Batovci*. So they went about remaking it in their image, starting with a private trade school for young men, the Bat'a School of Work (BSP), in 1925. Designed to be a trade school for a new type of shoemaker, in the beginning the BSP was meant to circumvent the traditional methods of education to provide the enterprise with a well-trained cadre of young, loyal workers.

The context of the founding of the school reveals its ad hoc nature. Tomáš's lengthy expedition to the United States, where he had visited both the Ford and Endicott-Johnson factories, convinced him of the comparatively poor training his new employees had for industrial work. Turnover was a constant problem, as workers came into the city only to leave a few months later when they either needed to help with the harvest or had tired of the monotony of industrial labour. He was especially interested in EJ's generous version of welfare capitalism, which seemed to have been able to keep unions out while also preventing strikes and high turnover. His aspirations went beyond promoting advanced industrial training in Zlín; Tomáš began dreaming of expansion into the Global South, and planned a trip to India in the summer of 1925. He saw limitless possibility in in a place where "half the world goes barefoot." The company would need trained workers for such an expansion.

After having weathered the difficult economy of post–First World War Europe, the company began rapidly expanding in 1923–4. The newspaper in these years ran daily announcements for new positions to be filled. Bat'a needed more workers, and more stable workers. And, still operating under the hiring policies established in 1905, Bat'a sought young people from the countryside. Every advertisement in 1924 was geared at those between the ages of sixteen and twenty-four.[44] As the company sought to make villagers into industrial workers, education could train and pull in people of an even more impressionable age. In the eyes of Tomáš, the school system, especially the troublesome public schools, neglected to offer the training an adolescent would need to become a *Batovci*. His first notion as mayor was to overhaul the school system to fit the company's needs. Such a plan, like the abstinence movement, did not go as he would have liked.

In the summer of 1924, a polemical battle raged in the local press and at city hall as the *Batovci* challenged school officials over building standards, curriculum, and pedagogy.[45] In 1925 to the list of chief threats to Bat'a's moral hegemony in Zlín, which included communists and barkeepers, were added the schoolmaster of Zlín, Jan Jaša, and the Teacher's Union. The struggle over education would go on for three years, with the public schools initially holding firm on their practices.

The tension increased at a meeting in City Hall on 3 July 1925; when Tomáš announced his vision for reforming education, Tomáš and Jaša clashed in public for the first time. Tomáš stated, "The industry of our community requests new types of teaching practices in our entire region, so that our young people maintain links with all parts of the world, and so that they acquire the skills necessary for their new employment." Jaša replied with clear frustration at the mayor's suggestions: "Work at a school is different from work at a factory."[46] The teachers' opposition initially blocked the company's plans for wide-ranging school reform.

Though having won control over city government in 1923 with a large majority, Bat'a's attempt at educational reform was proving more of a struggle. Education, like many aspects of life for the *Batovci*, was a contest, and they were going to win by going outside of the public school system. The company wanted a core of young, loyal employees, trained in the methods of industrial work and faithful to the moral code held by the executives. Faced with the hostility of local teachers, the company founded a school of its own. By the end of 1925, out of the conflict over educational reform, the BSP had been born.

The charter statement made clear that the school would be highly selective: "We will take only the best boys and girls from peasant and craftsman families for our factories."[47] Tomáš, like his hero Henry Ford, felt that the sons and daughters of the rural and industrial working classes would be the best candidates for life in the factories.[48] Thus, the first classes of "Young Men" comprised students from the surrounding Moravian countryside.[49] Before the bottom fell out of the world economy, the BSP remained very much a local concern.[50]

The BSP's first few years were rather modest compared to what would come later. The Young Men, the official title given to the boys enrolled, lived in various boarding houses throughout the city, and were largely responsible for finding their way to and from work and school, which were both held in one of the factory buildings. In the words of a company pamphlet sent out to prospective students, "we are looking for boys between the ages of fourteen and sixteen who have a love for work, an inclination for factory work, and want to specialize in this type of work. They want to put into this work not only their minds but also their hearts, and they will sign up for not only lifetime employment but to build an outstanding character."[51] In addition to their desire to find enthusiastic workers, executives also furthered their pedagogical goal to create workers capable of adapting and inventing in the midst of rapid advances in industrial technology.

The primary goal was to have young workers gain expertise in various aspects of shoe production by working in the factory and attending classes on the technical aspects of shoemaking. A Young Man's daily schedule from 1925 to 1930 therefore consisted of two main parts: work and school. From 7 a.m. to noon and from 3 p.m. to 5 p.m., the Young Men worked in various sections of the factory. Most would move to a new section each school year, though some would stay in one department their entire time. After 5 p.m., they would take evening classes in accounting, bookkeeping, machinery, electronics, shoe manufacturing, and business, and a class in either German or English.[52] Company executives hoped that such a schedule would create a new type of worker – one who could keep up with constantly changing technology. They also came to see the need for a new type of character for both men and women, which they believed could be created from a collective lifestyle and close supervision. The young men of the BSP were to grow into ideal *Batovci*, a group whose culture was increasingly being defined through newspaper articles, speeches, and styles of dress.

A New Morality

In 1924, the company outlawed all smoking on the factory grounds and began to strongly discourage drinking, firing anyone who came to work under the influence. The punitive measures went along with the abstinence clubs and weekly excerpts in the newspaper from prominent leaders of the temperance movement to create an ethos of sobriety. The attempt to sober up workers also corresponded with the regular instructions on grooming for an industrial lifestyle. One article about a young worker with long hair who worked well but slowly illustrated the practical aesthetics of rationalization: "The capable worker never figured out why (the floor manager) was disappointed with his work; his beautiful long hair fell in front of his eyes and he had to brush it away in order to see. He had to do this every 20 to 30 seconds, which meant he stopped work."[53]

Interest in managing men's appearances was matched by an interest in managing women's social behaviour. While the Social Democrats and Communists controlled the Zlín city government from 1918 to 1923, gender equality was not high on their lists of concerns, as the area was overwhelmingly rural, Catholic, and poor. Many women continued to wear the head scarf, a sign of Catholic piety throughout rural Moravia. Morality and decency laws from the Habsburg era, which gave authorities the right to banish transients and ne'er-do-wells, such as prostitutes and drunks, were not significantly altered. Nor were most citizens' ideas about gender roles, as the city's business and political life remained dominated by men. Still, liquor licensing was fairly loose in this period and the leftist city government did little to police the sexual conduct of its citizens.[54]

This non-interventionist attitude changed quickly upon the election of the *Batovci* in 1923. For while the Bat'a era's morality and decency laws maintained a consistency with the Habsburg and early Czechoslovak Republic legal code, the enforcement of such laws changed markedly. The *Batovci* strove to police the sexual conduct of the women of Zlín and were willing to use city police to do so. Over time this moral policing of perceived sexual transgressions turned from a community affair to one handled by so-called experts, ones who would detain suspects in private. However, as the population increased, and thousands of young people flocked to the city, so too did the frequency of "immoral" sexual behaviour. The Baťa era, then, became a period of both sexual repression and sexual opportunity.

In his autobiography, Thomas J. Baťa recalls a story about his dad becoming "incensed" at a young employee who travelled to Prague one evening to see Josephine Baker: "Spending time and money in pursuit of such entertainment seemed to him unconscionable."[55] Though Baťa constantly looked to new technologies to improve his factories' production, he abhorred modern, cosmopolitan attitudes toward sex. Baker's scandalous revue, and sensuality in general, was considered a waste of time, as they drained workers of energy needed elsewhere. Much like other contemporaries in positions of authority, Baťa saw sex as functional, and sexuality as dangerous. His moral conservatism found its way into a wide array of Baťa practices, from firing married women so that they would stay at home, to vigilantly policing perceived sexual transgressions of both its employees and Zlín residents.

The first record we have of the enforcement of Baťa morality concerns a young woman who was accused by the city council of being indiscriminate in her sex life. Seventeen-year-old Ludmila F. moved away from her parents in Uherský Brod to live with her grandmother in Zlín in 1925. There, her aunt found out about a rendezvous with an accountant for the Baťa Company who was ten years her senior: "She stayed out almost every night until 10 in the evening!"[56] It seems that from this information the police then brought Ludmila into the station to interview her about her sex life. From this interview they discovered that she had been having sex with other men as well, and that she "did not even remember their names." The health inspector, Rudolf Gerbec, who had been appointed in 1924, was then called in to give her an exam. He thought her a "potential carrier of a sexual disease" and had her sent off to the regional hospital at Olomouc. In the meantime, the city council, under the personal guidance of Tomáš Baťa, decided that she would be banished from the city for ten years for "leading an offensive moral life."[57] She spent three weeks in the hospital, even though she was declared to be healthy.[58] Within four years, she would be back in Zlín, where she was found working as an assistant at a small retail store by a police officer in 1930. The council reviewed her case again, and finding that she was not old enough to have been tried as an adult in 1925, overturned their ruling, writing in the decision that, after all, she "now behaves properly."[59]

Ludmila's case was enough of an exception that it became a city council matter, eliciting several letters from different council members, as well as from

Ludmila herself, as to what the city should do. That Bat'a took a personal interest also reflects on the size of the city at the time, and the small number of cases concerning immorality. Furthermore, it offers a glimpse of the limits to the sexual policing of Zlín, in that Ludmila was able to slip back into the city and remain undetected for several years. That the conduct of one young woman provoked such an interest speaks volumes about the small-town community feel of Zlín in the mid-1920s.

Without a doubt, though, the industrialization of the Dřevnice Valley was changing women's lives, giving them the opportunity to be wage earners away from their villages, introducing them to western fashions, and at times giving them the chance to "lead an offensive moral life." For many, the transition into the Bat'a world meant new clothes, ballroom dances, and the opportunity to have a little fun. Batism also called for women to go to school, learn languages, learn how to drive a car, and play sports. For the desire to control woman's bodies, to make them "modern," also meant distancing them from the Moravian past, a past that at least to the *Batovci* was marked by rural poverty, ignorance, alcoholism, and a backwards approach to work. For while women were to be housewives, they were to be modern housewives, bringing their children up according to the "bustle and haste" of an industrial society. To this end the company created several educational outlets for young women, all with the intent to wean them from their mothers' and grandmothers' influence.

One of the first such initiatives was a "Women's Section" in the company newspaper. Begun in 1925, the section ran throughout the rest of the interwar period. Here, reporters addressed a variety issues in articles such as "How to Dress at Work," "What Type of Man Should You Marry," and "Grandmothers Are Bad Governesses."[60] Through such articles the company encouraged young women to separate themselves from the past and to see themselves as the vanguard of modernity. This distancing of the "new woman" from the "grandmothers" constituted a central part of the Bat'a discourse:

From your grandmothers you heard how young women used to work with feathers. At that time they would gather together with their neighbours and while working they would spin fairy tales. These tales were terrifying – filled with ghosts, the undead, graveyards, monsters, and full moons. Happy tales could not be told because laughter would blow away the feathers.

That's how it used to be ...

Look at the young girls of our era.

They have an entirely different function (*poslání*). When they sit in the halls with their sewing machines ... there you have an example that a new generation is growing. While their mothers go stitch by stitch to embroider something on a personal handkerchief, these girls will have done a thousand stitches, not for the benefit of one, but for thousands.

And these girls carry on with their own young romantic lives, but in an entirely different way. Their minds and hearts are different from those of their grandmothers or mothers. They have set their eyes on the factories, they are participants in a new life; responsibility is placed on them, but they also feel free and independent. Work is replacing personal hobbies. But every spin of the wheel fills the pay envelope and with it comes the feeling of freedom.

It is clear that this generation of women will look at the world with different eyes than the previous generation, because they know not only responsibility but also the benefits of the work they are performing. It is easy to assume that these girls will make better housewives because they will be able to understand what it means for a man to go out to work and to thrive there amid the hustle and bustle.

The modern working girl does not sew handkerchiefs, but when she sits down to the day's work, and dreams about the future alongside her chosen one, she has set the proper foundations for her relationship to a working man.

Nowhere is it written that in life young girls must and will remain in the workshops for many years. They sooner or later will leave, when it is their time, in order to begin a common household, and then they will surely say how good it was that they experienced what it means to earn a living with their own industry and labour.[61]

The excerpt above is clear evidence of the Bat'a feminine ideal. A woman was to go to high school, work for a bit in the factories (so that she could relate to her husband), get married, and leave to become a housewife in one of the semi-detached company houses on a leafy street. There she would raise children according to the latest trends in pediatrics and make sure that when her husband came home from work he would enjoy a restful, clean space. She and her family would be well turned out when they left the house, as she kept up with the latest styles.[62] The women's clothes were to be clean; their make-up restrained; their stockings in perfect order. They were not to wear complicated clothing or ostentatious jewellery. Their men should be ambitious, sober, sportsmanlike. And their models of child care and home economics would move from the past to a rationalized future. The new woman, therefore, was encouraged to turn away from her grandmother and mother and look to scientific management, namely in the guise of the company, for guidance. It was a message that executives maintained throughout the era.

Marriage policy was one of the company's foremost tools in upholding the gendered hierarchy. For men, upward mobility often depended on marriage. For example, the company's social workers, first organized under direction of the Social Department in 1924, had to be "married, over 35 – with a family" to be considered for the job.[63] These men of the Social Department, which was modelled after the Ford Company's Sociological Department, were responsible for checking workers' requests for assistance and inspecting their homes. Married employees were expected to be more dependent on the company and therefore more loyal and vigorous in their duties. Likewise, sales managers were expected to marry before taking over control of a store. In addition, all top management was married. Eventually, these executives succeeded in creating a system where marriage was a fundamental step to higher wages for men, and one of the only ways a woman could escape the crowded dormitories in Zlín.

Conclusion

In 1924, the policies of social control, while still in their infancy, promised an acceleration of the radical changes industrial production brought to the everyday lives of those living in Zlín. Electing the *Batovci* to run the city resolved a significant tension between the company and the socialist-run city. The previous year swept away local opposition; the quick implementation of a series of disciplinary and financial manoeuvres solidified the company's grip on the town. Promising technocratic rule and an American vision of welfare capitalism, the *Batovci* set about remaking society.

Their efforts, though, were often met with resistance. Their temperance campaign could not stop workers from drinking. Their educational overhaul did not go as planned. In both examples, limits on company ambition are apparent. These limits did little to temper the high modernist vision, however. For in the mid-1920s, Tomáš had hired Jan Kotěra to sketch out Greater Zlín, and then to go about building it. The BSP circumvented the teacher's union. The May Day celebrations undermined the socialists. Company and city were joining forces to impose a middle-class morality.

Outside of the confines of Zlín, though, Bat'a faced greater opposition. Its successful model bred divisiveness. This divisiveness had less to do with nationalist divisions than with attitudes toward industrial production. For as Bat'a took over the Czechoslovak market, thousands of shoemakers faced unemployment. They tried to stop Bat'a from taking over the industry, setting off a fierce debate across the country.

"Speak Briefly": Rationalization and Everyday Life, 1926–1932[1]

The Czech shoemakers of Prostějov, long a bastion of traditional shoemaking, offered the first countrywide resistance to Bat'a in 1923 when they appealed to Czech nationalism by suggesting that the company's "inhuman" factory system of Bat'a was undermining a long Czech tradition of handmade shoes. Following quickly on the heels of the Prostějov protests, a nationwide anti-Bat'a movement linked the Verband der Gewerbe-Genossenschaften and its fifty-four German-language chapters of commercial shoe cooperatives with some 215 Czech-language organizations to protest the expansion of the company into shoe repair and personal services.[2] The groups called for a total boycott of all Bat'a products and tried to pressure politicians into outlawing shoe repair in department stores. Their primary argument was that shoe repair services and handmade shoes were crucial industries not only for economic reasons but for national ones as well. Their protest made its way onto the platform of the Tradesmen's Party (Československá živnostensko-obchodnická strana středostavovská), a party led by a native son of Prostějov, Rudolf Mlčoch. Mlčoch went as far as to question the legitimacy of Tomáš Bat'a's shoemaking apprenticeship and claim to have descended from a family of shoemakers. The Tradesmen's Party, under its slogan, "honourable nationalism, assertive democracy, and the protection of small businesses" ("poctivého nacionalismu, důsledné demokracie a zachování soukromého podnikání"), wanted to force the government to ban Bat'a from offering shoe repair in its retail stores. In 1924, they were unable to enact legislation against Bat'a's shoe repair services, at least for the time being. However, their nationwide protest provided a preview of the intense animosity Bat'a's expansion would provoke.

Bat'a had won Zlín, but Czechoslovakia was proving more difficult. As the company prevailed in local political struggles, the national stage was galvanized over a new term that Bat'a seemed to exemplify: rationalization.

Rationalization

It is difficult, if not impossible, to know exactly when the first use of the word *racionalizace* (rationalization) appeared in the Czech language, but its adoption across the country can be traced in a wealth of archival data and secondary literature.[3] In the Kramerius system, which is the National Library of the Czech Republic's impressive digital wing, the word first appears in 1922 in the periodical *Čas* (Time) in a short article about the new methods of industrial organization. From there, the word came into use fairly slowly in the mainstream press, averaging twenty-four mentions a year over the next seven years. Then, in 1930, it appears all over the place.[4] As Jan Stocký wrote in the opening line of his 1930 book, *Economic Rationalization*, "Whether in conversation or in writing, in this age almost everyone is hearing the word."[5]

Why then? The answer lies in the uncertainty of the moment, when a broad segment of society looked to the planning dreams of high modernists in order to secure a volatile world of collapsing markets. In parliaments, in newspapers, in lecture halls, and on the street, rationalization framed a volatile debate over the future of industrial capitalism. For some, especially those employed in handicraft work or operating small businesses, the word came to mean unemployment at the hands of larger manufacturers. For others, it meant simply a cost-cutting strategy that sought to find the most efficient way to produce goods. For Bat'a, it meant efficiency not only in production but also in everyday life. It became a buzzword for a reorganization of households, infrastructure, and the economy, and when the economic crises spread across the world in 1930, it seemed to offer a solution.

Of course, intellectuals had come upon and discussed the term much earlier than the general public, and that discussion provided the foundation of the word's usage among mass society. The most important critical definition came from Max Weber; he theorized rationalization as the key component of modernity in several of his works between 1904 and 1920.[6] Weber's concept of rationalization, which has now been the subject of hundreds of books and thousands of theses, revolved around the idea of "disenchantment." Essentially, for Weber, there were positive and negative rationalizations, which together led toward a secularized, bureaucratic future of technical proficiency.

While Weber explicated and unlocked the significance of the expression, Frederick Winslow Taylor's work established its use in academic circles and provided the basis of its meaning for Bat'a. The term, which later social scientists, journalists, and others applied to Bat'a, was synonymous with Taylor's concept of scientific management. In short, rationalization for Taylor was "accurate time knowledge."[7] His 1911 book on the subject transformed the industrializing world. In the United States, Taylor's ideas, such as on managing industrial workers with stopwatches, quickly became central to a larger discourse on efficiency. From there "a massive industrial engineering crusade" took Taylor's ideas into Europe and Asia.[8] The historian Mary Nolan has traced this discourse through Germany, where a flood of commentators equated rationalization with Americanization and held up Ford as the foremost example of rationalization in action. Germans responded to the concept in a variety of ways, from wholehearted embrace to fiery opposition.[9] In the mid-1920s, Fordism, scientific management, and rationalization were the buzzwords of the day, though they held different connotations for their users. The discourse over rationalization worked in Czechoslovakia much the same way it worked through Germany, with philosophical battle lines being drawn between people from diverse occupations.

Taylor's philosophy of management moved into Czechoslovakia shortly at the close of the First World War. As Elizabeth van Meer has shown, a host of like-minded individuals created international engineering organizations in the early to mid 1920s to discuss and promote Taylorism. "Technocratic internationalism" guided one of them, the World Engineering Federation (WEF), which was founded in 1921 in order to argue for engineers to be "in charge of technological cooperation among nation-states."[10] The WEF was largely an American-Czech organization; its makeup confirmed the idea that engineers and scientists governing the public sphere were under American influence.

In 1924, Prague hosted the International Congress for Scientific Organization; there Taylor's associate, the well-known public speaker and author Fred J. Miller, gave a keynote address. Miller, acting as an acolyte of a new faith, told the audience, "Taylor was the first to understand that management is a true science, resting on rules, laws, and principles, and that they could be clearly defined and put to every human effort from the simplest individual task to the largest corporation requiring extensive teamwork."[11] Miller's words resonated with Václav Verunáč, a professor at the Czech Technical University (ČVUT) and at Masaryk's Academy of Work; he became a prolific supporter of Taylorism and helped popularize it among academics and the general public alike. By 1926, Taylor was famous within Czechoslovak academic and intellectual circles as a proponent of timing workers' movements and matching pay incentives with performance. Taylorism was a significant piece to a growing intellectual movement that emphasized "technical thinking."[12]

Following Miller's influential speech, the Social Institute of the Republic of Czechoslovakia entered into a multi-year study of rationalization and its effects by creating the Commission on the Social Results of Rationalization. The report of the commission, published in 1930, illuminated a European network of institutions discussing the term and its applications. The authors also explained why Czechoslovakia was better suited to *racionalizace* rather than to "scientific management." Translating "management" into Czech moved the word out of its correct context, said the authors. The work offered the following definition: "The technical and organizational methods that limit the loss of materials and work to the smallest possibilities; in it lies the scientific management of labour, the standardization of material, the simplification of the production process, and the improvement of methods of transport and distribution."[13] In sum, rationalization was Taylorism.

The report also acknowledged Bat'a as "our representative of a specific type [of rationalization], that involving the combination of factory equipment, factory production, and retail."[14] Ladislav Dvořák, a professor of economics, agreed. In a 1928 speech in Prague he told his audience that Bat'a was the Czech example of Taylorism: "Mr. Bat'a worked according to the American pattern to show how to expand in the domestic market."[15] Professor Dvořák made it clear to his audience that companies would do well if they followed Bat'a's example.

Rationalization, however, was extended beyond what Taylor had in mind. In Czechoslovakia, intellectuals who championed rationalization, like Verunač and Dvořák, pressed it into the ideology of "laboretism" (*laboretismus*). Laboretism held that scientific management/rationalization could provide social harmony. Never a large-scale movement, the ideology appealed to economists, intellectuals, and businessmen who saw it as a way to stifle rising class discord. The system championed "technical thinking, a moral conception of work, and on principles of scientific organization."[16] Batism was very much a sibling of laboretism. Understandably, for some laborites, the company was a primary example of what laboretism hoped to achieve for the nation.[17] Yet Batism encompassed key differences, from its specifically gendered understanding of modernity to its obsession with competition; most importantly, Batism gave its adherents a specific object to be loyal to: the company. Laboretism struggled with defining just who would be the scientific managers and who the managed. Batism did not.

While economists and academics were lauding Bat'a's rationalization of the shoe industry, Bat'a's opponents did the opposite. Rudolph Philipp, a journalist and Communist Party member of the Trotskyist persuasion from Austria, launched an impressive attack on Bat'a's operations with his book *Der unbekannte Diktator Thomas Bat'a*. Published in 1928 by Agis, a German-language press with ties to the Communist Party, the book, with its bleak depictions of life in Zlín, caused a minor sensation in Central Europe, selling some 12,000 copies the first year of its publication. In it, Philipp crystallized major charges against the Bat'a system. The charge of price fixing, or dumping, was a key component. Philipp described it accordingly, "The Taylor system is applied so rationally in Zlín that Bat'a determines the sales prices of shoes at his discretion, and his competitors have to meet it."[18] Philipp added to the accusation of unfairness with an attack on rationalization. "Bat'a: proof that capitalism, even in its highest forms, as soon as certain inhibitions disappear and the proletariat is weak, is not satisfied with technological rationalization but falls back into the methods of its predatory years to rationalize the brains of its slave labour."[19]

Filled with such dramatic expressions, Philipp's book was a sensationalized, partisan account. However, the writer offered one prescient insight, that the future of Europe hinged on two choices: "The two poles of 'anxiety over hunger' and 'fear of hunger' correspond in today's economy to Americanism and socialism."[20] In Philipp's eyes, Americanism meant the economic philosophy of Henry Ford, who had been regarded in Europe as a "new messiah." Bat'a' and the "young nation of Czechoslovakia" had been taken in by the new messiah, according to Philipp, and were now beholden to the economic philosophy of Fordism. Bat'a's method was all the more threatening because it produced shoes, items "which every single person needs."[21] The choice of the unknown, the Americanism of Ford-Taylor-Bata, would not change the inexorable march of socialism for Philipp, however: "We let Bat'a calmly develop his philosophy; we have time, for nothing exposes the Zlín conditions better than the juxtaposition of theory and practice, poetry and truth ... the future will show that Bat'a's system does not abolish the crises but offers only a distraction."[22]

The Zlín press responded to the popularity of Philipp's book with a remarkable tactic. Instead of condemning Philipp's basic description of the rationalization of the factory, the *Batovci* embraced its general claims and found fault with the culture of the audience that would condemn them: "If the author of *Unbekannter Bat'a* translated his book into English, the entire American and English public would applaud Bat'a. If he thinks people would have a problem with a factory protecting its workshops from political agitation, he does not know the Anglo-Saxon nations' mentality. He does not know the American mentality if he thinks that they will be howling over there if it is proven that communists are thrown out with the chickens in Bat'a's factories."[23] The company essentially agreed with Philipp's notion that Europeans faced a momentous choice between Americanism and socialism – and Bat'a clearly had chosen America.

Perhaps the most interesting moment in this back and forth over rationalization occurred in 1929, when Communist Party activists, inspired by Philipp's book, organized a public meeting over "rationalization, workers, and resistance" in Zlín. The speakers, Jan Nováček and Jiří Valchař, explained to a packed audience that Bat'a's rationalization led to overproduction, unemployment, and economic crises.[24] Nováček told the audience that "every new machine replaces one if not more workers." Valchař "hypnotized the audience" with his booming voice to tell them that the one goal of the union was to rationalize the workers to protect them against Bat'a's rationalization. After the formal speeches, chief company propagandist Antonín Cekota responded: "We believe that the helpfulness of machines and the wisdom of science are the

most reliable means to improving the lives of the greatest number of people."
Toward the end of the back and forth, a worker, identified only as Mr. Kovář,
addressed the speakers: "At this meeting you tell us that the rationalization of
Mr. Srba [Antonín Srba was a trade union leader and prominent social dem-
ocrat] will provide the greatest welfare. But such rationalization we do not
believe in. It may help Mr. Srba, but not the 12,000 workers. Our people can
benefit from the kind of rationalization provided by Tomáš Baťa."[25] When the
debate over rationalization came to Zlín, at least some of the workers understood it as a term claimed by both sides of an ideological debate.

Rationalization Baťa-Style

The issue of course, was how to rationalize humans. The company had guide-
lines for such a project through its mix of American sources of inspiration,
like Henry Ford, Frederick Taylor, George F. Johnson, and Andrew Carnegie.
These were matched by Tomáš Baťa's own sense of order. Putting such guide-
lines into action under the direction of Tomáš, the *Batovci* became representative of a particular kind of rationalization. Alongside the more ubiquitous
aspects of time management, surveillance, efficiency, continuity of operations,
and calculation of results, Baťa's rationalization included a particular type of
education, a gendered order, and a drive to regulate sexual conduct.

  In 1926, Baťa took a small but important step to rationalize its workforce.
Inspired by Endicott-Johnson, which was located in the same city as the Com-
puting Tabulating Recording Corporation (later IBM), which made timecard
machines, Baťa mandated that every employee have a time card. Employees
were held responsible for these cards. If lost, the worker faced a fine of ten
crowns. Walking to the factory gates, all employees punched their card before
moving into the facility. From then on, an employee's time could be accounted
down to the minute. Not surprisingly, shortly thereafter watches became much
more commonly advertised in the company press – in the newspaper and archival photographs it was rare to see a company man without a watch after 1926.[26]
With the timecard, Baťa management took a step forward in the practical
application of Taylorism, a step that would lead to the development of one of
the most comprehensive accounting and personnel management systems in the
world.

  In addition to utilizing timecards, the company developed a much more thorough file system for employees. Paper file folders, intended for each full-time
employee and meant to provide a running list of their time in the company,
became the central depositories of the evidence needed to prove an individual
was a true *Batovec*. Extremely valuable as historical objects, the "personnel
cards" reveal extraordinary detail about the *Batovci* in the interwar period.
They show the dates of when an employee began and stopped working for the

company, as well as details on their religion, languages spoken, family members, debt, what kind of jobs they worked over their careers. They included a yearly, though brief, evaluation, and, depending on how long they worked at the company and how exceptional they were, a list of all of their mistakes and successes. In addition, the cards commonly referenced employees' politics and personal financial statements, and usually included a photograph. Unfortunately, these cards have yet to be thoroughly catalogued; thus, outside of a handful of cards that have attracted archivists' interest over the years, it is almost impossible to get a wide-ranging statistical analysis of employees. Still, the cards point to the institutionalization of behavioural surveillance. By allowing managers to keep an ongoing file on the behaviour and appearance of each worker, they provided a way to read their employees.

The company also began issuing instructions to its workforce on diet (a big English-style breakfast and a smaller lunch was preferred to the Central European-style meals), how to use the telephone ("don't shout!"), what to do on holidays (hike and exercise), and how to raise children.[27] Bat'a also championed a simple, utilitarian approach to dress. In an article entitled "How to Dress at Work" the company told workers that a "practical and efficient" style of dress was preferred.[28] In the interwar context, this meant that managers should wear the short suit, rather than a frock coat, and women should wear long blouses.[29] The masculine ideal was fast becoming tied to the aestheticization of modern industry. In the 1920s a key part of this aestheticization was efficiency, which became a mantra that permeated the factories. "Be quick," one article reminded readers.[30] Another slogan painted on factory walls was "the day has 86,400 seconds."[31] Clearly, dress and style had to be in the service of efficiency. Of course, putting on a tie and suit and shaving daily is not at all the most efficient way to prepare for work.[32] This trend toward short suits and straight razors was embedded in a much larger movement in the fashion and business world that established the style of the modern man, a man whose life was to be rationalized and mechanized, and required that he spend more time on his appearance.

As evidenced by these and many other similar articles throughout the time period, the rationalization of workers' habits had much to do with the emulation of Anglo-American lifestyles. It also, of course, had much to do with time management, as Bat'a further mechanized production.

Along with dispensing behavioural advice, the company trained workers to handle new machines and the conveyor, which were bought in with speed and regularity between 1925 and 1927. Both demanded a further increase in the pace of work. One article captured Bat'a's ideal worker succinctly, "no wasted time, no theories, no illusions, only concentration, activity, and tempo, tempo, tempo."[33] In 1926, a variety of new shoemaking machines, each with its own electric motor, came in to replace older machines that operated on shared motors. This, in turn, led to an increase in the size and output of the Bat'a-owned power plant, and also guaranteed that if one machine went down, work on the line would continue uninterrupted. Around the same time the company introduced a conveyor system, one which could move products quickly between manufacturing units and floors. Together, these initiatives led to a dramatic increase in production, from 8,785,00 pairs of shoes in 1927 to 15,205,000 in 1928, and a noticeable acceleration in the pace of work, as the number of employees increased during the same period by only 35 per cent.[34] To match the worker with the new work environment, the company advertised the laws of rationalization. One article, "Our Ten Commandments," was only one among hundreds of articles with rationalizing instructions.

Our Ten Commandments

1. Arrange your work space according to our exact plan. Always leave it in such a state so that it is ready for new work.
2. Have a daily work plan and do not leave work before all of the plan is completed.
3. During work, do not have anything on the table that could hinder the perfection of the task. After every workday always have your table completely clear.
4. Keep your notepad in order.
5. Keep your timecard in order.
6. Do not go personally to answer a telephone call or page when a reply in your notebook will suffice.
7. Know the value of one minute of your work time.
8. Collect the evidence of every great book you read.
9. Speak briefly and directly.
10. Set your own life goal, and if you cannot achieve it at our factories, then resign from the company. [35]

Intentionally replacing Mosaic Law, even if lightheartedly, these commandments symbolized the spiritual demands of Bat'a's form of rationalization.

Crafting the *Batovci* ethic meant pushing male employees to be competitive. As well as meeting the demands of efficiency, men were to strive to outperform coworkers. Once comfortably in control of the town, Bat'a funded an impressive array of athletic events; these enmeshed athletic competition into everyday life. First the local soccer club changed its name from F.K. Zlín to S.K. Bat'a in 1924. Then the company built a brand-new multi-purpose stadium in 1926. By 1928, the company had organized six sports teams competing on the international level. At the end of the decade, Bat'a could boast of having trained Olympic champion Ladislav Vácha, a gold medallist on the uneven bars, a women's handball team that won the national title in 1927, and a car racing team that won major events in Europe.[36] From the humble beginnings of Sokol exercises in a school auditorium, Bat'a was turning Zlín into an athletic powerhouse.

The spirit of competition extended into the factory. Above all, the Bat'a masculine ethos centred on working hard and "getting ahead." One of the Bat'a creeds, "Life Is a Battle," reflected this ideal. Much as the Stakhanovite movement did in the Soviet Union, Bat'a celebrated men for their industrial stamina.[37] From 1925 onward, the company had male workers compete in a variety of contests, from athletic events to rubber boot production. Bat'a believed that competition led to happier, more independent men. Achieving the highest profits for one's department earned a spot in the local newspaper, and workplace contests were held throughout the interwar period. In the Bat'a conception of masculinity, a man should compete in order to prove his manliness, and therefore Tomáš pitted his workers against each other to see who could rise above the rest. The system pitted each department against the other, institutionalizing competition at work. All of the individual units were in a constant struggle to outproduce, outsell, and show up their counterparts.

This conception of the masculine ideal, famously dubbed "muscular masculinity" by George Mosse, was in step with a general trend found in industrializing nations; it emerged from the crises brought on by the replacement of physical labour due to mechanization. The managerial classes, however, tended to disguise their male bodies through the short suit.[38] The class division was stark in the paternalistic Bat'a world., For instance, the young people at the centre of the Bat'a labour force were expected to be physically fit while managers had no such expectations placed on them. Indeed, part of the rationalization of Zlín, according to Bat'a, was the implementation of paternalism. All workers were part of one family, and thus the *Batovci* existed in a familial hierarchy. Managers had a duty to guide workers, executives a duty to guide managers, all men a duty to guide their families, and the company a duty to guide the citizens of its factory town. Thus, competition was tempered by paternalism. One had to face constant competition to prove oneself, but the more important quality was loyalty to the fathers of the company.

The company had already set about organizing society along a cascading series of paternal relationships by controlling housing, education, and policing, but it would not be until 1926 to 1930, when the company would be in a strong enough position politically, financially, and structurally, that distinct outlines of a unique civilization emerged. Having control over these three aspects of everyday life – housing, education, and the police – gave tremendous power to the company's drive to rationalize. Building these structures for the reorganization of everyday life, Bat'a could attempt to create new industrial people, and, much like other social engineering projects, these people were to be made under a comprehensive surveillance network.

Figure 4.1. Young Men from the BSP race in the 1933 "Celebration of Sport."
Moravský zemský archiv v Brně, Státní okresní archiv Zlín, Sbírka fotografií Zlín,
sign. 152, obálka č. 14364.

Housing

As Bat'a rapidly expanded, thousands of newcomers arrived in Zlín each year. Most were single young people from lower-class backgrounds from rural Moravia. Others came from more distant places in search of work. Bat'a tried to solve the housing crises this expansion created by building workers' dormitories. In 1925 the first such dormitory was constructed. Two years later, the dormitories became "rationalized" by the architect František Lydie Gahura, who had already had taken on a major role in the design and look of Bat'a's Zlín. In 1924–5, Gahura designed what became the standardized construction pattern, a reinforced concrete and iron skeleton with square pillars, flat roof, brick parapets, large windows, and a floor space of 80 x 20 metres. The standard size for interior units became 6.15 x 6.15 metres, "a uniform measurement which literally served as a standardization of work and life."[39] This same pattern he then applied to the dormitories. Gahura's eight dormitories, began in 1927 and completed in 1930, were massive, having a total capacity of 9,600 occupants. The dormitories, which led up a hill to the south of the factory complex, were both the homes of the new workers and their places of education.[40]

Those moving into the newly built workers' dormitories were strictly divided by their gender and separated from previous structures of family and hierarchy. This was a new social arrangement, one in which the company controlled all of the workers' used space and dictated their daily life, down to how often they would shower. Despite the steady construction of single-family housing over these years, completed by Bat'a's newly formed subsidiary construction company, most workers of both sexes would live in the dormitories throughout the Bat'a era.[41] Those who wanted to continue working and living at Bat'a – and were not forcibly removed for transgressions against the company – had to conform to the ideals of the company if they were to move up from this barrack-like existence.

The company had clear criteria for who could move out of the dormitories and into the functionalist semi-detached two-storey duplexes and triplexes in leafy garden neighbourhoods being built on the hills above the factory complex. These criteria did much to enforce the company's gendered ideals. No worker moved up unless he or she was married, had proven his or her loyalty, or had arrived with a family and a needed skill. The keys to these coveted houses were almost exclusively given to men. For a single woman, the only way to move out of the dormitories was to marry, which meant termination of employment in most cases.[42] Pregnancy was grounds for dismissal in every case – a company policy since 1923. While these measures hurt women's careers, marriage and children were crucial for men to achieve promotions. They also led to raises in salaries and were often accompanied with monetary gifts from the company. The goal was to create a distinctly gendered town, where women stayed at home with children while their men continued to climb the company ladder.

Figure 4.2. An aerial photo of the factory complex looking south, 1937. The dormitories are the long rectangular buildings going up the slope in the middle of the photograph. Moravský zemský archiv v Brně, Státní okresní archiv Zlín, Sbírka fotografií Zlín, sign. 825, obálka č. 15031.

Only the logic of Batism went further than devaluing women's labour in the factories. For Baťa executives dreamed that in the rationalized future housework would become obsolete in the face of technological progress. Indeed, as seen in numerous articles written by executives predicting the future, housework was considered drudgery. According to the *Batovci*, machines would eliminate it. As Tomáš said in a speech in 1927, "Our ambition is to release all our womenfolk from the last remnants of household drudgery and to help them to establish homes of which they may justly be proud." "Women's work," then, fit into a remarkably limiting box – that of childcare and emotional support.

Through gifts for having children, increases in salary for married men, and most of all, better housing for husbands/fathers, mothers/ wives, the company pressured workers to pair up and procreate. The idea was that a family man would be less prone to radical thoughts and actions, more dependent on his paycheque, and more likely to embrace the paternalism of the company. After all, encouraging a highly patriarchal structure for worker's families would mean that they in turn would align with the highly patriarchal structure of the company town. Indeed, company statistics on firing illustrate that the housing policy created a core group of loyal employees over time. In the first half of 1938, for example, Bat'a dismissed 572 employees who lived in company housing; of these only 29 lived in "family housing," while the rest were staying in the dormitories.[43]

Rationalizing through Gendered Education

Though using housing to further a gendered worldview of labour and purpose, Bat'a employed a small army of women to work in its factories, and these women needed to be trained for their new industrial lifestyle. As a result, in 1929, the BSP opened its doors to women. Having already seen the results of its first male cohort, which graduated from the school the year the women's school opened, Bat'a executives now sought to educate women in the skills they thought would be necessary for the modern age. Similar time management principles applied to Bat'a's Young Women, but women were continually treated in a paternalistic manner; they were paid less, kept out of executive positions, and ultimately valued primarily as homemakers. Such patriarchal policies flew in the face of the fact that in 1929 the company employed over four thousand women, over two thousand as sewing machine operators alone, and increasingly looked to them to staff the sales departments.[44] The Young Women in the BSP, like their older counterparts throughout the factories, were in a paradoxical situation.

The Young Women were ultimately prepared for a life of middle-class domesticity. Chiefly, the school was designed to "instil in the female student a strong character from which she can independently make moral decisions that benefit the public and strengthen her family."[45] The emphasis on family and character led to a holistic teaching philosophy that demanded they be monitored at all times: "The method of training such young women involves carefully following their behaviour in the dormitories as well as their wages. Elevating their moral qualities takes place at school, in the factory, and at the dormitories and it requires [us] to devote our full attention."[46] Like the Young Men, the Young Women were to be carefully watched and guided to improve their character, but with different expectations. Whereas the Young Men were constantly encouraged to compete with one another, Young Women were put in classes such as "rhythmics," which was the practice of synchronized movement. Young Women had to take courses in sewing, family behaviour, health, "home culture" (*bytová kultura*), and home economics.[47] There would also be

Figure 4.3. A typical bedroom for the Young Women, 1933. The picture in the middle of the room is of Marie Bat'a. Moravský zemský archiv v Brně, Státní okresní archiv Zlín, Sbírka fotografií Zlín, sign. 153, obálka č. 14365.

significantly fewer spots for women in the BSP than for men: 1,318 Young Women as compared to 2,500 Young Men in 1931.[48]

From the vantage point of enrolment and applications, the school was a success, mostly because it offered young, poor, and rural teens gainful employment. By 1931 there were 3,820 Young Men and Women and a massive expansion of living quarters was complete. With the BSP, the company was encouraging a new generation of workers to conform to new gender and work roles. The school gave its pupils technical skills, while providing them with a moral education crafted around Batism. Meanwhile, the company took control over the public schools.

While creating the unique, and intense, way of life of the BSP, the company launched an ambitious program to modernize the public school system. One of the more ingenious ways the company gained control over the schools in Zlín was through the Parents' Association (Spolek Rodičů), an organization founded at the height of the battle with the schoolmasters of Zlín in 1925–6.

The Parents' Association, chaired by Tomáš Baťa, consisted of top executives of the company. Their main goal was to deliver the school system into the hands of the company so as to create a new type of relationship between parent and student, and a new way of discipline that did not involve the heavy-handed practices of the past, such as whippings and public humiliation in the classroom. Instead, the Parents' Association called for a type of education that encouraged individualism, freedom of thought, and, above all, skills of immediate value to the shoe industry.[49]

The group found that the most efficient way to reform the system was with monetary funding. And spend the group did. For the 1935–6 school year, for example, the Parents' Association gave 156,000 crowns to deserving city schools and individual teachers.[50] This was slightly over 11 per cent of the city's entire budget for education. Moreover, the bonuses given to teachers were instrumental in raising their income above the modest salary of a Moravian schoolteacher; this meant Zlín could recruit the finest teachers in the country. Furthermore, by tying teachers' salaries to the Parents' Association, the company was able to gain leverage over teachers, making them de facto Baťa employees.

Another key strategy of the *Batovci* was to reach out to school reformers in Prague, something they did with considerable success. They were most successful in convincing Václav Příhoda, a professor of education at Charles University and long a voice for educational reform, to use Zlín as a testing ground for new ideas about education. Příhoda travelled to the United States in 1928 and came back with a scathing report comparing the Czechoslovak and American school systems. Primarily, Příhoda argued that the American system encouraged a type of student who asked questions, was encouraged to experiment, and enjoyed physical fitness. It was also to "strengthen and rationalize" education by dividing students according to their ability.[51]

Very much in line with what Tomáš had argued for in 1925, Příhoda's report had a significant impact on the Ministry of Education and created a strong connection between educational reformers in Prague and Zlín. Like many other ideas implemented in Zlín, educational reform was initially modelled after the American educational system. Within one year of the publication of Příhoda's report, in 1929, support for Baťa's educational reform could be found in all of the necessary places in Brno and Prague. Once the regional and national authorities signed off on Baťa's so-called experimental school plan, the company had the leverage needed to overcome opposition from the teacher's union and in 1930 established the first experimental school in Czechoslovakia, the Masarýk Experimental Public School.[52]

The Masarýk Experimental School, which was entirely Baťa-funded, had the ambitious mission to change the entire country's educational system. The school's primary interest was to assign students hands-on experiments, almost exclusively in the sciences, that could prepare them for a life in modern industry. Students gained experience in chemistry, electronics, mechanics, and applied geometry. Mathematics was heavily emphasized. In addition, the Masarýk, compared to the municipal school, devoted more time to physical education. The school also included the state-mandated requirements in religion, Czech language, and history, though there is little evidence that instruction in these subjects was innovative.[53] Essentially, the company designed the curriculum to prepare the students of Zlín to excel in the hard sciences in order to make them ideal employees. All of which is to say that the Masarýk curriculum coincided with the curriculum at the BSP.

Enforcing Rationalization

As Bat'a went about rationalizing education – making it work in line with the goals of the company – it also set about using its municipal powers to police behaviour. In the evolving Bat'a ideology, one of the main threats was laziness. And the source of this laziness, to paraphrase Tomáš, could be found at home, as evidenced in the slogan "Enthusiastic Woman – Successful Man; Timid Woman – Lazy Man."[54] Therefore, workers' home lives, and workers' choice of a partner, became of interest to the company. Men's and women's bodies were placed in the service of the company, and sexuality became a company concern. To regulate relationships, the company called upon the town's police to restrain female "enthusiasm."

One case, of the more than 400 that went before the city courts that dealt with some type of moral transgression between 1925 and 1935, exemplified the company's need to "see" the private affairs of the people of Zlín. This was the case of Anna T., whose liaisons were discovered by authorities after launching an extensive investigation into her private life. Though it remains unclear as to exactly why the police took Anna into the station for questioning on 16 January 1930, it seems that someone in town had reported on her sexual history. Regardless of the reason, once there, she revealed a detailed saga of her sexual encounters and the steps she took to get an abortion.

Anna's story began at a dance party in the Založna Hotel, where she met and left with a local businessman, Jan Svoboda, one night in November 1929. They had sex in the back of one of his friend's cars in a parking garage. From there she revealed a series of affairs, one in the coatroom of the sports club S.K. Bat'a, another again after a night of dancing in the Založna, and finally an affair with Karel Kalinovský, an adulterer who left her pregnant. From there, she went to a doctor in Zlín, Hanna Gutmannová, who provided her with a recommendation to terminate the pregnancy due to medical issues, which was the only way for a woman to have a legal abortion at the time. With this recommendation, Anna travelled to Brno by train with another doctor, Jan Opletal, who took her to an unnamed specialist. After the operation, Anna went to her family home in Kroměřiž, where "she laid down for an entire four days." The operation cost 1,000 crowns, which Anna had to borrow. After being somehow found out once she returned to Zlín, she was placed on trial for having an illegal abortion. Her confession, though, resulted in a reduced sentence. Instead of being sent to prison she was banished from the town for life. The authorities then tried to find out who performed the abortion; eventually a Dr. Boček was identified. He was tried in Brno, but his fate remains unknown.[55]

One can only surmise that there were many other Annas, especially given the numbers of unmarried pregnant women working in the Bat'a Company. And while their stories will never be fully told, we can assume that abortion was fairly common and the choices surrounding the decision greatly impacted women's employment and housing. Furthermore, that a network of doctors existed to perform abortions suggests that this was not an isolated event. This network shows how people negotiated and subverted Bat'a's control over women's bodies even within the scientific establishment. At the least, these doctors rejected the notion that healthcare was subject to the company's and state's morality.

The way the authorities handled the case reflects the institutionalization of a sexually repressed mentality, but it also reveals a prurient interest on the part of the authorities in every detail of Anna T.'s sex life. In the margins of her confession, for example, someone with excellent handwriting, more than likely Mayor D. Čipera, wrote out and underlined the names of all of her partners. The police report gives an address for everyone she mentions in her account, something that seems to have become standard practice by 1928. That there are no records of such incidents before 1925 suggests that, as Foucault has proposed, with modernization sex becomes more talked about within the context of scientific enquiry despite evidence of its repression.[56] Sex education, after all, was not taught in Zlín until after the Second World War, and as the authorities tried to eradicate sex outside of marriage, a general silence is noticeable throughout the era on the topic. It seems that while Bat'a authorities did not promote sex education, they took a rather extreme interest in uncovering the sex lives of their people. And their techniques grew ever more "scientific" as the interwar period went on.

Indeed, by 1937 one could not find the city council banishing young women based on their allegedly loose morals, but instead sending a team of inspectors under the direction of the city doctor, Jan Gerbec, to look into the private lives of workers and ordinary citizens.[57] Gerbec had full authority to take in whomever he so chose to test for sexually transmitted diseases, and suspects were carefully tracked. These persons were overwhelmingly female. From 1931 to 1934, for example, women made up 91 per cent of all the reported cases of STDs in Zlín.[58] Only a few of these women were professionals, some 12 per cent. The rest were mostly young factory workers from Moravia. The men identified with STDs were a mix of travelling businessmen and factory workers, whose average age was 22. In the rest of Czechoslovakia, the state had established the "health police" in 1920, which had a wide-ranging mandate to supervise public places. However, the state did not pass any laws that granted these authorities the power to inspect suspected "loose women" and prostitutes.[59] It was not until 1943, during the years of the Protectorate of Bohemia and Moravia that the Ministry of the Interior established a law mandating suspected prostitutes be inspected for STDs. Zlín, then, was decidedly ahead of the curve.[60]

In many places the paternalistic company town was invested in regulating female sexuality.[61] However, Bat'a's town was unique in the level of interest the company showed in its sexual policing. Its conservatism was paired with an insistence on the "science" of sexual relations. This mentality led to an increasingly sophisticated surveillance of women, who were seen as in need of protection, yet also as a threat capable of upsetting the entire gendered order.

Still there was nuance and complexity in Bat'a's gendered order. Some women were not only able to cross the gender divide but were celebrated for doing so. Eliška Junková, for example, was one of the few women who moved into a position of authority within the company. Junková joined the Bat'a racing team in the 1920s as the one and only female driver. She went on to win an impressive victory in Sicily in 1928 before leaving racing after the death of her husband. She then went into tire sales, and was instrumental in dissuading Tomáš Bat'a from going into car production.[62]

Junková was an exception to the rationalization of gender roles that was perhaps best captured in a cartoon in the company newspaper. The cartoon comes across to today's viewer as a sarcastic take on the monotony of life in Zlín. After all, the artist presents the homes in the neighbourhood as being exactly the same – so much so that even the numbers on the houses are identical. The children are faceless and play with identical toys. The mothers standing in front of their "Bat'a cottages" appear as uniform characters cut from one maternal mould. Even the plants conform to one standard. Yet this illustration was not intended to poke fun at the standardized ideals of the Bat'a Company. Rather, it was meant to evoke a triumphant achievement: the establishment of a middle-class gender order in working-class neighbourhoods. To company executives, women and children waiting in perfectly ordered neighbourhoods for their labouring husbands and fathers was the outward sign of a long-term project to rationalize everyday life. All of the homes have electricity, as seen in the wires above them, signifying that life in the company town of Zlín was not a conservative retreat, but a significant achievement in "modern" living. In this one cartoon, then, we can see the company's imagined "rationalized" gender

Jak to vypadá v Baťově čtvrti, když odhouká 5 hodin

Figure 4.4. "How the Baťa neighbourhood looks when the five o'clock whistle blows," *Sděleni*, 2 July 1927. Moravský zemský archiv v Brně, Státní okresní archiv Zlín.

relationships, which tied women's success to motherhood, the home, and consumption, and men's success to labour and money.

However, as in the example of Junková, the standardized picture championed by the company press fails to capture the complex roles women ended up having in Zlín. For, as Susan Porter Benson found for American women working and consuming in mass retail and Donica Belisle found for Canadian women in retail, though routinely reminded in subtle and not-so-subtle ways that their place was at home taking care of children and as consumers, women simultaneously experienced new opportunities for work, travel, and socialization in the interwar period. Indeed, the company's twofold desire to shape women into ideal citizen-mothers and avid consumers opened new educational possibilities for women while giving them a certain amount of power in their economic choices. Women in Zlín in the interwar period, therefore, experienced Baťa's paternalistic company town in contradictory and complex ways.[63]

Figure 4.5. The all-male design team inspects a model's shoes (date unknown).
Moravský zemský archiv v Brně, Státní okresní archiv Zlín, Sbírka fotografií Zlín,
sign. 1006, obálka č. 15212.

One sees in the years of rationalization considerable changes in what women,
especially young women, were encouraged to try, as well as the expansion of
a paternalistic environment that severely limited women's opportunities for
professional advancement. The company routinely let women go when they
married or became pregnant; it closely monitored their sex lives, and kept up a
steady stream of rhetoric about their place in society, which was as caretakers to
children and husbands, and consumers of the latest fashions. However, women
were also expected to know how to drive, to have an interest in literature, to
speak another language, and to exercise outdoors. All of these requirements,
no matter how far from reality, meant that the Bat'a woman's life was significantly different from her mother's and grandmother's, though it would be hard
to argue that it was any more empowered. Women, who made up slightly over
one-third of the workforce from 1926 onward, were almost non-existent in the

managerial ranks and in city government.[64] And yet they were a constant focus for Bat'a, for they were the primary customers (the company produced many more women's shoes than men's)[65] and they were the supposed driving force behind male ambition. They were presumably the reason why men worked.

Conclusion

The rationalization of relationships had much to do with the holistic philosophy of the company and its commitment to its social engineering project. And along with propagating the practices of the *Batovci*, the company carefully regulated its workforce. Utilizing the labels "sick," "unsatisfactory," and "unreliable," the company removed 2,910 employees in 1927 alone. Along with the workers that voluntarily left, 70 per cent of the entire workforce in 1927, mostly young workers, left the firm.[66] Such heavy turnover did not slow down production, as it seems there were no shortages of workers ready to replace those who had been let go. As the Czechoslovak economy, especially the light industries such as textile and shoemaking, fell into a slump in 1928, workers flocked to Zlín, hoping to grab a spot recently vacated by those deemed unfit.

Bat'a's policies did grab the attention of the opposition, namely the Communist Party. At the fourth conference of the International Meeting of Revolutionary Leather Workers, convened in Moscow in April 1928, one of the delegates warned, "The system of rationalization, which Bat'a has implemented in all of its workshops and retail outlets, is one of the most refined exploitations of working people's strengths that the capitalist mind has ever imagined, and stands as one of the prime examples for other capitalists who wish to harm the international proletariat."[67] The conference delegates then issued forth a call to boycott Bat'a.

These protests, however, did little damage to many people's enthusiasm for rationalization. Rationalization as exemplified by Bat'a came to be seen by many within Czechoslovakia as positive for the nation. From 1929 on, writers across the state began praising the results of Bat'a's approach.[68] In a series of articles in 1931, the most intellectually influential magazine in Czechoslovakia, *Přítomnost*, came to the conclusion that Bat'a's form of rationalization and even its expansion abroad was good for the nation. "[Because Bat'a's shoes are so affordable] The wages of Bavarian farmers go toward buying boots made by Czech workers in Zlín rather than by German shoe manufacturers. Bat'a's expansion into the international market has opened a new source of wages for the ČSR, for national pride … those shoemakers put out of work by Bat'a pale in comparison to the 17,000 people employed by the firm."[69] Indeed, Bavarian farmers were buying Bat'a boots in 1931, which created its own controversy.

By 1930 the Bat'a Company surpassed the entire German shoe industry in yearly output, and opened a satellite town in Ottmuth, in what was then Upper Silesia.[70] Soon afterwards, Bat'a shoes flooded the German market. In turn, German shoe manufacturers and labour unions banded together to try to fight off what was increasingly referred to in the German press as a Slavic expansion. No matter how well organized, the protests could not keep German customers from wanting the experience of shopping at Bat'a or from buying its cheap, well-made shoes. The American public was no different. In 1927, Bat'a shoes made a significant inroad into the American market; it was then that Bat'a shoes were sold at Macy's in New York City. According to company reports, "they sold immediately on the first day more than 2000 pairs and they are saying that customers' interest is still rising."[71] Within three years, the United States was Bat'a's largest export market, with 300,000 pairs of shoes entering the country every year.[72]

The examples of the United States and Germany serve the purpose of illustrating just how successful Bat'a had become. This success convinced those within and without the company that Bat'a's version of rationalization was the optimal one. Indeed, it clearly benefited the development of shoe production. As Dr. Eugen Belavsky, the chief scientist of the tanning department during this period, later recalled, "the central laboratory was being developed to determine the optimum process for every component of every kind of shoe. When this was established, standards had to be set. Then procedures had to be laid down to maintain the standards and finally, inspection methods devised to check continuity of production."[73] In the eyes of the *Batovci*, rationalization paid off: "The results are clear. Statistics show it. Lower prices on shoes, increased salaries for workers in the factory, more shoes exported, and increased production capacities at the factories ... There is no better program for the next ten years within our state."[74]

The debate over rationalization swung further toward Bat'a's favour in 1936 when the Central Committee of Czechoslovak Business and Commerce released its report entitled "Influence of Rationalization on the Health of the Workers."[75] This lengthy report used Bat'a as an example to show how rationalization increased the health of the workers by providing healthcare and more opportunities to exercise. The investigators concluded, "if done correctly and justly, rationalization brings a great good to the nation."[76] Over time, Bat'a's rationalization became widely accepted in powerful circles, especially once the effects of the worldwide economic depression hit every sector of the economy.

Such reports show considerable variation in how rationalization affected different Central European societies. Mary Nolan has convincingly argued that in Germany "rationalization ... produced new economic problems and intensified the political and social crisis of late Weimar." However, in Czechoslovakia rationalization had fewer negative effects, largely owing to Bat'a's approach.[77]

Bat'a increased markets, decreased costs, and grew to dizzying heights while other companys' collapsed. Just how it did so had everything to do with its embrace of globalization. Of course, rationalizing society and rationalizing shoe production are two very different matters, but Batism did not see the distinction. Thus, for the *Batovci*, optimization could be applied to both shoe production and social relationships.

"Half the World Is Barefoot": The Globalization of the Bat'a System, 1931–1937

Historians of globalization regularly posit that the First World War marked the beginning of a deglobalization process that ended only after the Second World War.[1] This narrative, first put forth by John Maynard Keynes, suggests that around the turn of the century, growing interconnected markets allowed the middle-class Englishman to access a world of consumer goods without ever leaving home.[2] Then, the shock of the First World War cut these markets off from each other, a situation which could not be repaired afterward owing to wartime inflation and the loss of wealth. With imperialism on the ebb, and its total collapse in Central and Eastern Europe, nationalist economic policies prevailed. Such policies led to a proliferation of tariffs, which further impeded the restoration of global trade. The return to international cooperation only then came about by necessity in the face of the Second World War.

This Anglo-centred narrative has little relevance to the former Austro-Hungarian Empire, which, because of the protected nature of the Habsburg economy, meant that many of the items produced around the world were not as readily available for the well-heeled Austrian as for her English counterpart. And this was the case throughout the First World War.[3] The middle-class Austrian was connected to the wider world in a variety of ways, but remained essentially outside of the vast material and economic web associated with globalization.[4]

Certainly the First World War, the collapse of empires, and the Great Depression slowed down or reversed the processes of globalization. But while such a slowdown undoubtedly occurred on a macro level, it was not the only economic story of the 1930s. Instead of stagnation and contraction, the Bat'a Company experienced tremendous global expansion in the period between 1929 and 1937. In its case, the Great Depression provided the backdrop for a worldwide expansion, rather than collapse.

From the perspective of the historical stages of globalization theorized by A.G. Hopkins and others, Bat'a provides a startling case of post-colonial globalization, a process which supposedly did not happen until after 1945.[5] Tapping into the power of local labour markets by exporting the Zlín model, Bat'a set up a transnational behemoth that by the end of the decade would be the largest shoe company in the world. This was all the more impressive considering it did so during a transfer of power at the top, following Tomáš's death in an airplane crash in 1932. How and why the company expanded so quickly during the Depression, while withstanding a major shift in leadership, can be explained by the advantages it gained by globalizing its manufacturing. Furthermore, a marked shift in nationalist identification attended this globalizing project. Bat'a's globalization brought a perspective of national indifference into its corporate ideology, as it began integrating workers from an array of cultures into its fold. This integration would give it a platform on which to stand well into the twenty-first century.

High Tariffs, Aggressive Nationalists, and the Bat'a Response

The global depression that began in 1929 cannot be attributed to a single cause; however, the tariff situation greatly affected its longevity and severity. After the US stock market lost a quarter of its value in four days, 24–29 October 1929, countries on both sides of the Atlantic entered into a game of one-upmanship, raising tariffs and writing tough import laws in the belief that this would save jobs. Though far from the first to begin raising tariffs, the United States was the catalyst for the catastrophe. Senator Reed Smoot and Representative Willis Hawley put their names to a comprehensive tariff policy – the last that Congress would pass – the Smoot-Hawley Tariff Act. Duties shot up to their highest levels since the mid-nineteenth century. Then deflation set in after France and the United States refused to loosen monetary policy. The collapse of Creditanstalt, the primary lending bank in Austria, sent further shocks around the world. Together, high tariffs and declining prices made trading outside of borders considerably more difficult. The result was that, between 1929 and 1932, a quarter of global trade disappeared.[6]

The great powers tried to protect their industries from foreign competition by returning to mercantilism. After the stock market crash in late October, politicians scrambled to find solutions to save American businesses. While Bat'a's 300,000 pairs of shoes were a tiny fraction of the output of one of the largest American shoe companies, Endicott-Johnson, they were enough to alarm the shoe industry. George F. Johnson encouraged his local Broome County congressman, John Clarke, to argue in favour of shoe tariffs, which Clarke did with force.[7] EJ's previously futile calls for tariffs were now met with near total acclaim. The United States began issuing substantial tariffs on shoe imports in 1930, when the disastrous Smoot-Hawley Tariff went into effect. In this milieu, the American shoe industry lobbied furiously for protective tariffs, and

Congress conceded. Shoes were a key piece of the Smoot-Hawley legislation – Congress placed a duty of between 35 and 65 per cent ad valorem on all shoes except expensive leather shoes. This meant that most of Bat'a's exports to the United States faced on average a 30 per cent tariff.

The American tariffs on the Czechoslovak shoe industry were not the beginning of the global tariff war, but a significant escalation to the one already under way. The first country to legislate a high shoe tariff on Czechoslovakia was the Kingdom of Yugoslavia, which did so in April 1928. Citing the need to "make the path of rationalization more expensive," the Economic Council pushed a 20 to 30 per cent increase on all shoe imports.[8] Hungary was next, then Germany, where trade unions, politicians, and industrialists called for a 200 per cent increase in the import tariff on shoes, toys, and aluminum in December 1929.[9] The German tariffs went into effect at the beginning of 1931, all but banning Bat'a shoes from crossing into the German Republic. The year 1931 was a watershed for shoe quotas, which set a fixed total number of shoe imports. Germany led the way in imposing a shoe quota in addition to high tariffs, followed by Switzerland, France, the United Kingdom, Poland, Turkey, Sweden, Greece, and Austria, all of whom raised tariffs and implemented quota systems.[10] The channels of commerce for the Bat'a Company were soon clogged.

The company responded with a simple but bold strategy: export factories rather than shoes. By opening up a subsidiary company within the boundaries of a country, Bat'a could circumvent high tariffs and possibly circumvent nationalists' ire. After all, if countries would view Bat'a as "theirs," the boycotts and negative commentary about Bat'a "dumping" shoes and killing local shoemaking traditions would end. Moving factories abroad would also allow for greater specialization in product, closer access to key materials such as leather and rubber, and creation of an outlet for excess product made in Zlín – as long as satellite factories could place a heel to an upper, they would likely avoid the tariff.

Bat'a's export of its factories coincided with the timeline of the tariffs. The company opened its first satellite factories outside of Czechoslovakia in Borovo, Yugoslavia, in July 1931, and their second in Ottmuth, Germany, in November. Chełmek, Poland, came next (February 1932), then Möhlin, Switzerland (August 1932), Hellocorte, France (September 1932), East Tilbury, United Kingdom (July 1933), Batadorp, Netherlands (1934), Baghdad, Iraq (September 1934), Batanagar, British India (December 1934), Beirut, French-Occupied Lebanon (1935), Kalibata, Dutch-occupied Indonesia (August 1938), Alexandria, Egypt (October 1938), Batawa, Canada (August 1939), Belcamp, USA (October 1939), Martfu, Hungary (July 1942), and Batapur, Lahore (1942).[11] Along with building these new factories, Bat'a built seven company towns within Czechoslovakia in the same ten-year period.[12]

Not all of these factories were the same. Of the fifteen factories built abroad, eleven of them were true factory towns built along the same lines as Zlín, with worker colonies and new factories constructed in a rural area but close to a major population centre. These were the factories in Borovo, Ottmuth, Chełmek, Möhlin, Hellocourt, East Tilbury, Batadorp, Batanagar, Kalibata, Batawa, and Belcamp. The factories in Alexandria, Beirut, Batapur, and Baghdad were initially small and operated out of older buildings in the cities, with no worker colonies.[13]

The list provides clear evidence of company strategy: Jump tariff walls to access crucial export markets. On the list of countries, though, were locations that were not considered valuable markets by other industrial shoemakers like Bally and EJ. These were locations unlike the others. Indeed, two factories stand out – Batanagar and Kalibata. Both held a playbook for the transition from "modern" to "post-colonial" globalization[14] in terms of transitioning from empires to nation-states, from plantations to factories. In India, Egypt, and the Dutch East Indies, Bat'a found cheap labour, large population centres, close proximity to the natural resources needed to mass-produce shoes, and anti-colonial elites who craved industrial production. In other words, these outposts exemplified the possibilities of the Global South.

A Trip to Batavia

On 10 December 1931, Tomáš, along with two pilots, a telegraph operator, and four managers from the export department, set off on an ambitious business trip. They travelled from Zlín to Batavia (Jakarta), Indonesia, then under Dutch control, and back again entirely by plane. Along the way they made stops in Tunis, Cairo, Damascus, Jerusalem, Tel Aviv, Baghdad, Tehran, Jask, Delhi, Calcutta, Bangkok, and Singapore – mostly places Bat'a had established prior connections and, in many cases, had opened retail stores.[15] Many of these retail outlets, though, were still in their infancy.

In terms of the history of air travel, the trip was ambitious. The route stretched some 16,571 miles, a distance just slightly shorter than that of the longest commercial route in the world at the time, the Amsterdam to Batavia route operated by the Royal Dutch Airline (KLM).[16] In 1924, KLM pieced together a twenty-three-stop trip that linked Northern Europe with the Middle East, India, and Southeast Asia. These trips were arduous, with frequent delays, freezing cabins, and bouncy landings. Long-haul air routes were mostly for the maintenance of empires – the Netherlands and the United Kingdom heavily subsidized their imperial airlines. Beyond Europe, the route extended only past current or former territories of the British or Dutch Empires in Iran. Still, when Bat'a embarked on his journey, the route was exploratory. Imperial Airways' London to Singapore route opened two years after Bat'a's trip took place. Even in the commercial world of air travel, then, the trip anticipated a new pace of globalization.[17]

In Egypt, the *Batovci* met with King Fuad, who seemed eager to embrace the company. Already, the country imported some 215,000 pairs of Bat'a shoes. These were sold in five Bat'a stores located in the major population centres of Cairo and Alexandria.[18] For Egypt, Bat'a represented yet another foreign investor in its economy, which was crowded with major European businesses by the 1930s.[19] For Egyptian shoemakers, Bat'a offered a considerable challenge, as most were making shoes by hand in 1932. For consumers, Bat'a was becoming a wildly popular shoe brand. As Nancy Reynolds has pointed out in her study on the commerce and politics of twentieth-century Cairo, "Bata became known for its cheaply priced but stylish shoes, competitive in the local market since they were affordable." Furthermore, Reynolds attributes Bat'a's success to its ability to connect to Egyptian elites' ideas about the "superiority of mechanization."[20] Indeed, one of the keys to Bat'a's global expansion was its ability to present itself as the acme of modernity. Bat'a's cheap yet sturdy mass-produced shoes had the look and feel of modernity, something Egyptians readily embraced. In the seven years after Tomáš's visit, Bat'a expanded its Egyptian retail network to thirty stores and began operating a factory in Alexandria.

The group travelled on to several stops in the Middle East. In British Mandate Palestine, the entourage visited Tel Aviv and Jerusalem, where Bat'a stores largely catered to Jewish clientele. This was likely owing to the fact that Arab Palestinians attempted a boycott of Bat'a in the late 1920s to stop it from destroying the traditional shoe industry.[21] Though police were summoned to protect Bat'a stores, the boycott in Palestine, like elsewhere, did little to slow down operations in the area. Bat'a opened twelve stores in Mandate Palestine in 1932 and exported some 120,000 pairs of shoes in the same year, a 400 per cent increase over exports in 1930.[22] In Beirut and Damascus, Bat'a found similar opportunities, and created a plan to increase shoe imports as well as scout for possible factory locations. In Iraq, Bat'a had no previous stores and so the entourage travelled to Baghdad to open the Iraqi market. Shortly after Tomáš's visit in January 1932, Bat'a stores opened for business in Baghdad, Basra, and Mosul. Two years later, Bat'a opened a factory in Baghdad out of a small warehouse in the heart of the city.[23]

The trip revealed that political elites throughout the Middle East were clearly interested in bringing the company into their countries and that the company recognized the region's people as promising potential customers and workers. The company carefully followed the pathways of British and French imperialism, which were populated with a ready-made clientele of European colonizers already familiar with the brand. The corresponding anti-colonial local elites, meanwhile, tended to view the company as a potential force of modernization that did not have the stain of imperialism.[24] For example, Benoy Kumar Sarkar, one of India's key social scientists in the first half of the twentieth century and a fervent nationalist, saw Bat'a as a "model of the Indian future."[25]

Why Iran proved more of a stopover than a place for future expansion remains to be explored by the future historian, but it seems that there was no effort to move into the Iranian market. The next stops would turn out to be the most important in Tomáš's itinerary – those in India. India represented a huge market, as well as a potential source of seemingly inexhaustible supplies of leather and labour.

The 1932 expedition was not the first time Tomáš had travelled to the Indian subcontinent. He had already journeyed by boat to India in 1925 in order to find contracts for leather and cow hides. During this first trip, Tomáš adopted a worldview of the Global North and South based on the racist theories of human evolution so popular among Europeans at the time. Though the nations of Europe and North America were equal in his eyes, Tomáš initially held that the world was divided by race, and that the races were distinguished by a marked difference in abilities. For all of the man's cosmopolitanism, he was not able to move outside of the racist mentalities of his day. Some of Tomáš's clearest statements on the question of race can be found in the company newspaper around the time of his trip to India in 1925. Bat'a wrote:

> the world is divided into two parts. The lands that have regular cold rains and the lands that are in the eternal sunshine, where life does not require a lot of material ... Through his battle with nature the man of the north had to learn complex tasks and become more of a man than his brother in the south ... The northern man produces for the sun-drenched man what he cannot himself, chiefly science, organized government, and industrial goods ... When you are in these lands you find that the northern man is pumping the life blood into a new era. It feels like the differences among the various nationalities become meaningless and those of the north, those white ones, all look like the same race ... Luckily there is no danger that this man (the southern man) can win over the European as long as he cannot win over himself and his ignorance. A nation has a right to sovereignty only as long as it can manage its land in such a way to best benefit humanity in general.[26]

Such a bifurcated approach toward humanity in 1925 conformed to what the Ford Motor Company had implemented in its Michigan factories. There, immigrant European workers were given the same job and housing opportunities as native whites, while black workers were given "the worst possible working conditions."[27] Henry Ford, after all, was Tomáš's most important teacher.

In addition to holding this racist worldview, Bat'a may have taken Ford's guidance in the globalization of his company. He was developing his company into a transnational behemoth, just as Ford was doing, and at the same time. In

1931, in fact, the first European-built Model A rolled out of Ford's new factory in Cologne, Germany. The same year, Ford opened a sales subsidiary in Romania and a factory in Istanbul, and witnessed the first vehicle to drive out of its impressive factory in Dagenham, England. In 1932, Ford opened a subsidiary company in Egypt. Ford also ventured into India in the 1920s, opening a small assembly plant there through its subsidiary company, Ford Canada.[28] Bat'a and Ford, then, were globalizing in tandem.

However, on Tomáš's second visit to India, he may have experienced an ideological shift. His notes of the trip contain the following: "Aviation brings home to man the necessity to serve others. It teaches him that his life is continuously in the hands of other people. It cures man of hate toward other nations."[29] Bat'a very may well have been breaking free of Henry Ford's ideological grip.

Tomáš's second visit to India in 1932 differed from his earlier trip in 1925 in its purpose as well. His first visit was for the purpose of gaining contracts for raw materials. This time, he arrived to investigate the possibility of expanding into the subcontinent. Significant groundwork had been laid before he had even embarked. In the spring of 1931, the company carefully selected and sent fourteen men between the ages of twenty and thirty-two to India. They arrived in Calcutta in June of 1931, along with several thousand pairs of shoes, and quickly formed and registered the Bata Shoe Company Limited. These young men opened four retail shops across the city, but apparently their sales figures were underwhelming. Part of Tomáš's visit was to investigate as to what was going wrong.[30]

When the group arrived, they went to work investigating the economic context of Bengal. Local elites, who in turn had the confidence of colonial officials, determined economic success in India at the time. It was a system of connections and cartels – a system similar to the one Bat'a navigated during the days of the late Austro-Hungarian Empire. Accordingly, the *Batovci* sought and found a key ally in Bahadur B.M. Das, the manager of the National Tannery and superintendent of the Bengal Tanning Institute. A year before Tomáš's arrival, the British had conferred upon Das the title of Rai Bahadur, an honorific reflecting his significance in the leather trade. He proved to be an excellent contact. In a series of meetings between the two men, Das helped to convince Tomáš that India would make a fine location for a modern shoe factory. Three days after arriving in Calcutta, Tomáš made his decision. In the fields surrounding the sprawling city, he would build a new Zlín on a rural spot close to a major population centre and a navigable river. They bought 155 acres of this land from the Port Authority and named it Batanagar. Three years later, on 28 October 1934, a group of *Batovci*, who had made a harrowing journey from Gdansk to Calcutta in a leaky boat, laid the foundation stone of the first factory building. From then on, Batanagar would be the Bat'a Company's flagship factory complex in India, and one of its largest worldwide.[31]

Figure 5.1. The Bat'a complex in Batanagar, India, sometime in the late 1930s.
Moravský zemský archiv v Brně, Státní okresní archiv Zlín, Sbírka fotografií Zlín,
sign. 930, obálka č. 15136.

After deciding on the location of Batanagar, and the direction the company
was to take in India overall, the group continued on to Bangkok and Singapore.
In Bangkok, the executives acquired the company's first retail store. Singapore,
with its proximity to abundant supplies of rubber, had been on the map as a key
location in which to expand since at least as early as 1926, when the company
first exported shoes to the city. When Tomáš arrived in July, the first Bat'a-
owned store had been open for five months, and business was good. Perhaps
because of this success, while touring the city and meeting with local elites
Tomáš dropped a few hints that Singapore could become another major manufacturing centre. He even went as far as to tell a local *Straits Times* reporter
that the company was going to create an air route from Czechoslovakia to
Southeast Asia.[32] Such an air route never came to be, and it would take eight
years until the factory in Singapore came into existence, but when it did so, it
provided yet another strong base for the company.

The last stop of the trip was to what was then called Batavia, Dutch
East Indies, now Jakarta, Indonesia. By the time of the *Batovci*'s arrival,

Indonesia, along with Malaysia and Singapore, had dramatically surpassed Brazil as the world's most productive rubber region. One of the reasons for their success lay in the ability of the colonial states to structure natural rubber production around intensive cultivation. In rubber plantations in Southeast Asia, workers lived in communities with better healthcare and working conditions. They could also work year-round. This increased production and drove down labour costs.[33] Connecting the shoe industry to Southeast Asia's rubber boom would allow Bat'a to dominate the rubber shoe market. It was therefore a pivotal location.

In addition, as in India, many people in Indonesia had never worn a western shoe, and many went barefoot. One recollection found in the work of historian Adrian Vickers, relates a fairly typical Indonesian experience in the 1930s. Pramoedya Ananta Toer recalled, "when I moved to Surabaya I picked up two new habits ... smoking kretek and wearing shoes." As Vickers states, Bat'a made those shoes.[34] Toer's recollection was one that hundreds of thousands of Indonesians shared, as Bat'a became the first shoe company to cater to Indonesians. The company did so by creating a large network of retail shops across the country, as well as contracting with local merchants to sell their shoes in remote villages. The latter method of distribution accelerated dramatically after 1939, when the Bat'a factory of Kalibata opened. Afterwards, Bat'a shoes were everywhere. The anthropologist Clifford Geertz found Bat'a in small locally owned shops across Indonesia and argued that the rights to sell the shoes led to significant economic opportunity for the local merchants. "Bata has thus contributed more to stimulating small-scale local entrepreneurship than any other foreign-owned company in Indonesia."[35] As the furthest stop on Tomáš's trip, the islands of Indonesia were to be some of the most fertile ground for the global shoe industry.

When the group finally returned to Zlín in April 1932, a crowd gathered at the airfield to welcome them home. A camera crew was among this welcome party and recorded Tomáš addressing the crowd. His speech revealed the trip's impact. "We are not afraid of the future. Half of the people on earth go barefoot and about 5 per cent of the citizens of the world have quality shoes. We see in fact just how little we have done so far, and just how much work waits for the world's shoemakers."[36] It would become his most quoted and iconic speech. For it conveyed the global orientation of the company and the confidence that came with it. This global vision – to realize the potential of the peoples labouring under the yoke of European imperialism – was Tomáš's greatest achievement.

Training for Globalization

Looking at the trip from the perspective of the twenty-first century, after the huge shift in industrial production to the Global South, it was a prescient

Figure 5.2. Benin rubber planters with two Bat'a buyers, F. Peřimon and Česmír Němec. Moravský zemský archiv v Brně, Státní okresní archiv Zlín, Sbírka fotografií Zlín, sign. 139, obálka č. 14351.

itinerary. Indonesia, with its abundant supply of rubber would go on to become the fifth-largest producer of footwear in the world; India is currently the second-largest producer of footwear in the world, and its people comprise the second-largest market.[37] Planting the company flag in India, Singapore, and Indonesia allowed Bat'a to thrive and survive during the globalization of the shoe industry. Of course, the company men on the trip did not predict the collapse of manufacturing in Europe and the United States at the time; in fact their trip was something of a gamble. After all, travel times between Zlín and Batanagar were formidable, and expertise on how to build, operate, and maintain the latest machinery was not something the host countries could provide.

It was no coincidence, then, that during this same period, Bat'a opened the doors of its management-training program to foreign students while it aggressively expanded around the globe. As early as 1927, the BSP accepted its first foreign students. They came mostly from Poland, Germany, and Yugoslavia.

A few years later nearly every country Bat'a was moving into had students living in Zlín, some twenty countries in all.[38] In 1931, the BSP began accepting its first groups of non-white students, a group of Egyptians and Indians who caused considerable curiosity in Zlín. They were reported to have begun "learning Czech on the boat ride over."[39] Many of these teenagers had little or no idea about where they were going or what to expect.

One of the Young Men from abroad was Reg Field, a teenager from East Tilbury, England. Reg remembered the experience of going to Zlín decades later for a Bata East Tilbury reminiscence project.

> We eventually arrived at this little tiny station, no platform, just wooden kind of sleepers laid down and it turned out to be Zlín, where the original place was. That was the nearest railway station and we got on a small bus and it took us right down to the factory and we were quite surprised because although it looked barren there from the train, when we got down we found it was quite big, quite a big industry, a massive factory for the place where it was. They welcomed us in and then showed us where we would be staying, it was called INTERNAT, that's a kind of dormitory effort, but there were quite a few of us. We settled down and after a couple of hours or so I then went to get something to eat and we found we were sitting with quite a variety of people. There were Germans, Arabs, Czechoslovakians, Americans, Canadians, quite a lot of different nationalities, which rather surprised us. Anyhow they all got round us, kind of patted us on the back, shaking hands, "Good boys, good boys, etc" all in Czechoslovakian. So we said have we got any French people here "French caw no, frogs pooh pooh" they said "the French are down the other end somewhere" that's what they thought about the French blokes. We didn't want to start no war so we just took it with a pinch of salt and carried on.[40]

A few of these students stayed in Zlín through the Second World War, marrying Czechs and assimilating into the town. Most though, like Reg, returned to their countries of origin, where they became managers and engineers in Bat'a's burgeoning company towns.[41]

Accordingly, there was no industrial Czechoslovakization in Zlín. Instead, students from abroad marched under the national flags of their home countries during the May Day celebrations, and lived, studied, and worked in groups arranged according to their countries of origin. Such internationalism was a point of divergence from the Ford model. Bat'a would never replicate the elaborate graduation ceremony of Ford Motor Company's English School, where foreign worker graduates walked from a symbolic boat into a giant pot stirred by their teachers, to emerge "dressed in their best American clothes and waving American flags."[42] However, not trying to nationalize foreign employees did not mean that the company did not want to assimilate its workers.

Bat'a employees were not to be assimilated to a national identity but to a corporate one, which promoted a universalism rooted in its own high modernist ethos. They were not to become Czech or German or any other nationality, but *Batovci*, which meant being able to adapt to new cultures around the world on one hand and uphold a company aesthetic on the other.

The National Indifference of the Bat'a Company

How does one label Bat'a's approach? Was this a case of transnationalism, cosmopolitanism, internationalism, supranationalism, or national indifference? Does one label give us a clearer insight into the historical development of the Bat'a Company?

The historian Tara Zahra has argued for "national indifference," a new label for an old phenomenon that went by several names, one of the more common labels being "cosmopolitanism."[43] So why not use cosmopolitanism in the Bat'a case? Paul Lerner, in his work on Jewish-owned department stores in Germany, argues that cosmopolitanism is a useful category of analysis as it helps us to understand the mentality behind both the shopping experience and the ways in which Jewish retailers were able to look above narrow ways of defining consumption.[44] The Bat'a story is certainly in line with the stories of these department stores, such as Schocken and Tiertz, in that its retail stores also offered customers a standardized, pampered way of shopping that encouraged browsing, had a first come, first served rule, the company embraced modern architecture, and its executive elites freely referred to themselves as cosmopolitan. Yet the problem with cosmopolitanism as a category of analysis is twofold: it assumes an opposition to national identification and its ideal of a self-proclaimed citizen of the world often limits its catch to an educated elite. Looking at the transnational company under the broader category of national indifference seems to offer a way out of both problems.

First, the *Batovci* were opportunists in their use of nationality. When "hej Slované" (Yeah Slavs!) sold shoes, they could wave a flag as well as anyone.[45] Indeed, in the words and actions of company personnel we see flexibility in nationalists' demands that people promote the national interest.[46] When nationalism hurt sales, which was often the case in the multinational context of Central and Eastern Europe between the wars, the *Batovci* responded with indifference and even protest. But when it helped, many acted nationally.

Moreover, Bat'a recruited mostly young people from agricultural backgrounds to run its expanding empire. These employees rarely considered themselves citizens of the world. Instead, in Zlín at least, they identified as *Batovci* and Moravian. Undoubtedly the cosmopolitanism of company managers held sway over these thousands of workers and may have influenced how they

Figure 5.3. National indifference on display. The Young Men march under their various flags in Zlín. Moravský zemský archiv v Brně, Státní okresní archiv Zlín. Sbírka fotografií Zlín, sign. 83, obálka č. 14296.

self-identified. Yet we do not have a single reminiscence or quote from a rank-and-file employee that uses the word "cosmopolitan" as a marker of identity. Instead, in the numerous memoirs and short biographies of employees found in company publications and on the still active batastory.net website, we see the word *Batovci* or the gendered equivalent.[47] First used in the 1923 municipal elections as the name for the company's candidates, *Batovci* came to largely replace Czechoslovak or Czech in the company-controlled press to refer to its workforce. It became a term of identification that served to further the globalization of the company. National indifference therefore seems to give us a way to connect self-identifying cosmopolitan executives with workers who identified as company people.

The most obvious examples of the benefits of such national indifference are found among the Czech-speaking employees who moved into management. Augustin Doležal, for instance, entered employment as a poor seventeen-year-old from the small town of Fryšták in the winter of 1929. He proved skilful at rubber processing, which led management to select him for work abroad. Between 1931 and 1934, Doležal travelled to the Bat'a factories in Hello-court, France; East Tilbury, Great Britain; and the plant in Borovo, Yugoslavia, in order to train workers in the vulcanization process. Then, while back in Zlín, the director of Batanagar, Jan Baroš, requested Doležal for the new factory in India. He moved to India, where he lived for eight years before taking over operations at the new Bat'a plant in Batapur, which was right outside of Lahore. In 1960, the company asked him to move yet again, this time to Bel-camp, Maryland.[48] In one man's lifetime, we see the new realities of managerial life within a transnational company. Nationalism, with its implicit privilege of one group over the other, was a fundamental obstacle to someone who must work and succeed abroad.

Top-ranking *Batovci* understood the necessity of national indifference. Dominik Čipera and Antonín Cekota, a corporate executive and the leader of the advertising department respectively, consistently advocated international-ism within the company's workforce as well as in Czechoslovak society. From as early as 1928, Cekota touted the internationalism of the company town: "Here in this rather provincial town are people who are worldlier than citizens of the largest cities. English is heard on the streets as well as German. There isn't a European language that isn't heard here. The terms 'business contracts,' 'tariffs, 'balance sheets,' 'courses,' 'import,' 'export,' etc. are not only theoreti-cal but a part of daily life. The cosmopolitanism of the people of Zlín is the direct result of not having political corruption and bad blood."[49]

Like Cekota, Čipera felt that the underlying purpose for the company was to serve mankind. Nationality should not get in the way of service, he argued. Writing about the uncharted waters the company found itself in during the chaos of the Depression, Čipera described the globalizing process: "We had to find our own unique path. We had to build our own new nation – the nation of shoe workers (*ševců*). In this nation there were many different languages, but only one way of speaking – the speech of the shoe worker."[50] In order to function as a global enterprise, then, the workers would have to let go of any national chauvinism. In order to inculcate this nationally indifferent philoso-phy in their workforce, executives selected training materials that reflected a profoundly international outlook. Richard Coudenhove-Calergi, certainly the most well-known pan-European of the time, was routinely on the list, as was Alexis Carrel, an advocate of eugenics.[51]

As Čipera realized, national indifference gave the globalizing company an essential purpose. Tomáš had known this for a long time, at least as early as 1905. But it would not be until 1929–32, when tariff walls forced the com-pany to reorient toward building factories abroad, that a significant number of employees would have had the motivation to reorient their own nationalistic ways of thinking. This reorientation took years and was never really complete.

But, in a host of examples, there is evidence that in the mid-1930s Zlín and the Bat'a workforce displayed a remarkable degree of national indifference. Unfortunately, Tomáš would not be there to see most of the transition.

Transition of Leadership

As the dormitories of Bat'a's School of Work began to reflect the company's global aspirations, and Czechoslovak employees travelled across the world to build on these aspirations, tragedy struck. On 12 July 1932, Tomáš arose early to fly to Switzerland, where his eighteen-year-old son, Tomáš Jr., known at that time as Tomík, would be waiting. Tomík was working in the newly built Bat'a factory in Möhlin, and his dad was coming to check on its progress. A thick fog covered the valley, but it did not deter Tomáš and his pilot Jindřich Brouček. They stepped into the company's Junker Ju 52 plane and took off. Within minutes, the plane tumbled to the earth, the victim of an apparent electrical malfunction. Both men on board were killed.

Writing about the event twenty-six years later in 1958, Dominik Čipera emphasized just how central Tomáš had become for the national economy:

> It [the death of Tomas] was not simply one of our problems; it was a problem for many leaders in the country, especially those who felt responsible for the balance of the national economy. The premier of the Czechoslovak government, František Udržal, flew to Zlín the day of Tomáš's accident ... [the leaders] were afraid of the many repercussions of Tomáš Bat'a's death. That was the reason the government understood our delicate situation and did not interfere with us more than was necessary; instead they helped us as much as their power allowed.[52]

Udržal's concerns were understandable. By the time of Bat'a's death, the company accounted for four-fifths of the shoe industry of Czechoslovakia.[53]

While causing concern among political elites in Czechoslovakia and speculation abroad that the company would not survive the death of its founder, Tomáš's death did not pose much of an actual threat to the future of the company. For Bat'a had become a transnational company with unparalleled access to markets, materials, and labour.

To attain such a position, the company had made a crucial decision in February 1931 to create Leader A.G., a holding company in St. Moritz, Switzerland. This decision allowed Bat'a a haven for its capital in neutral Switzerland. It could then use this capital to further its expansion through investments in foreign operations, investments which would not carry the Bat'a name – a significant point when considering the anti-Bat'a campaigns that followed the company seemingly everywhere it went.[54] With its capital unfettered in its Swiss holding company, the company could act on its ambition to become

Figure 5.4. T. Bat'a at the Autoklub in Zlín, 1931. Moravský zemský archiv v Brně, Státní okresní archiv Zlín, Sbírka fotografií Zlín, obálka č. 110.

the only shoe company in the world to globalize in the aftermath of the tariff war.[55] As a result, when Tomáš's half-brother Jan took over as chief executive, following the execution of a will that would later come under scrutiny, he was stepping into a position with a company that had tremendous potential for growth. He only needed to follow the path already traced – which is what he and the other chief executives did. Though Jan was somewhat eclectic in his management style, he remained fully committed to the globalization scheme outlined by his half-brother.

Tomáš's life quickly became the yardstick with which to measure all other managers, and his maxims came to be taken as gospel truth. After his death in 1932, the *Batovci* made him the object of a long-lasting cult of personality. Thereafter they memorized his dictums, which were frequently painted on walls around town and on the factory walls, and were constantly published in the press. František Gahura's impressive public memorial to him, which overlooked the factory, was a focal point of the town. In short, by the mid-1930s the company press was comparing Tomáš Bat'a with Tomáš Masaryk, the founder and first president of the Republic of Czechoslovakia. And such comparisons favoured Bat'a. For if Masarýk founded a country, Tomáš led a region to greatness and created the mould for the "new industrial man."[56] He had created the way of life of the *Batovci*.

This way of life was mobile and, at least initially, centred on uniformity. As the satellite towns began going up, their architecture conformed to the basic Bat'a specifications for proportion and style. Workers' housing and recreational buildings were modelled after the flat-roofed red-brick houses and structures of Zlín. In Borovo, Yugoslavia, which would become the largest Bat'a factory outside of Zlín in the interwar period, Bat'a architects V. Karfík and F.L. Gahura designed a factory town with thirteen standardized factory buildings based on the plans for a factory building in Zlín. They added a "Social House" like the one in Zlín, which served as a social gathering place with shops and a cafeteria, a stadium, and a school. Housing took the familiar form of the two-storey duplexes, a few single-family houses, and two dormitories – one for single male workers and the other for single female workers. Bat'a also exported its family policy. As the chief manager of the complex, Tomo Maksimovic, explained to workers, "Only a married man committed to family life can be a good co-worker, not to mention a manager of a unit."[57] Emanating from its standardized philosophy, the new factory towns were to be imports not of Czechoslovakia, but of Batism.

While the built environment conformed to the Bat'a aesthetic, the societies where they were to operate had specific nationalist criteria. Bat'a therefore had to weave its new company towns into local and national identities. Two cases, Möhlin, Switzerland, and Chełmek, Poland, reveal how Bat'a tried to integrate its new factory towns, and its brand name, into these environments. Their examples reveal a high-wire act of a transnational company trying to make its way in the fiercely nationalistic context of 1930s Europe.

Chełmek

On 17 February 1935, the Bat'a Company's Polish language-magazine, *Echa Chełmku* (*The Chelmek Echo*) ran an article that suggested that the Czech managers and their children in the Bat'a satellite town of Chełmek were fast becoming Poles. "If we take into consideration that one of the Czechoslovaks got married in February to a Polish girl from Vadovice, the second of their number to recently do so, we will understand that the children of these married Czechoslovaks will forget their mother tongue in three years. It is unbelievable that at first we actually thought we were going to have a 'terribly dangerous Czechification' in Chełmek."[58] Surprisingly, in the nationalist hothouse of mid-1930s Central Europe, the managers' deference toward Polishness deserved praise in the opinion of the company press. Upbeat in tone, the article intended to pacify a Polish audience shaken by their country's economic collapse and wary of foreigners running industries.

The factory complex at Chełmek, founded in 1931, was part of Bat'a's initiative to expand manufacturing abroad in the face of sharp tariff increases and import quotas that nearly every industrial country in the world began implementing after 1929. Bat'a's response to these tariffs was to build factory towns across the globe modelled on Zlín. By 1935, eight such company towns operated abroad.[59] Since these new factory towns often met serious local opposition, Bat'a management was keenly aware of the importance of putting a local face on what was widely viewed as a Czechoslovak brand.[60] The *Echa Chełmku*'s prognosis of the seamless Polinization of company management was a part of the project to quell fears that Czechoslovaks were taking over what should be *their* jobs. For the *Batovci*, such local concerns had no place in the rationalized future. Yet the locals needed to be placated so that business could move along as smoothly as possible. Hence the magazine article on managers' Polish assimilation.

However, the company's attempt at smoothing the transition of its managers from one national milieu to another had the unintended consequence of inciting the Czechoslovak consul in Krakow, and subsequently the entire Czechoslovak foreign service. Almost as soon as the article was published, Arthur Maixner, a consular officer in Krakow, wrote to his superiors at the embassy in Warsaw that "if the children of Czechoslovak couples in Chełmek are forgetting their mother tongue in three years then this is a poor testament not only to the parents' national pride but to the pride of the company, which helps in founding the Towartzystwa Skoly Ludovej (Society of People's Schools), but doesn't lift a finger to protest the denationalizing of Czechoslovak children."[61] Playing on the fears of Czech nationalists, many of whom were already deeply suspicious of Bat'a, the consul used the article as evidence of what to nationalists amounted to treason: the erosion of Czech national identity. The attack found favour with the Czechoslovak ambassador to Poland in Warsaw, Václav Girsa, who alerted the long-time minister of foreign affairs, Edvard Beneš.[62] In a letter sent out on 28 June 1935, Girsa bemoaned the fact that only nine Czechoslovaks worked at a factory that employed 1,500: "that is not even 1 per cent. This is proof of the Polish character of the Bat'a Corporation."[63] Girsa went on to describe the "dangerous Polonization" of the Bat'a employees, who even joined the Sport Club of Chełmek, "whose goals to lift up Polish society with sporting victories are well known."[64] Beneš, who would become president of Czechoslovakia by the end of the year, agreed that the Bat'a project in Poland, and perhaps in general, posed a threat to national pride.

Five months after the publication of article, the Czechoslovak government refused Bat'a's request to bring in an unspecified number of young employees from outside of Czechoslovakia to be trained at the Bat'a School of Work in Zlín.[65] Though the practice had become commonplace by 1935, Prague now viewed foreign worker-students in Zlín as agents of denationalization. After all, in the eyes of Beneš and others, these students were being trained for management jobs that should have gone to Czechs. Furthermore, when these students finished their coursework they would return home as representatives of a name brand these Czech nationalists increasingly saw as "theirs."[66] Bat'a's rare success in the difficult economic climate of the 1930s, expanding rapidly from 1930 to 1935, had much to do with such an attitude. Thus the rather innocuous goings-on in the small industrializing town of Chełmek mattered a great deal to powerful government officials. The rejection letter for the requested visas specifically mentioned the "troubling events in Poland."[67]

Bat'a tried to influence the ministers in the midst of their deliberations. One of the company's letters, written by executive Hugo Vavrečka and read by at least six officials in four different ministries, laid out the Bat'a position in full. Vavrečka, a former ambassador to Austria, played up the necessity of training foreigners so that Bat'a can "propagate Czechoslovak goods and Czechoslovak enterprise." Yet underneath his appeals to the nationalism of his audience, one can find the national indifference of a global corporation. "We have young men in our factory from Yugoslavia, Bulgaria, Poland, France. England, Egypt, India, etc., to train them ... because everywhere there is a strong reaction against foreigners. It pays to know the details of your customers, to be able to know their local dialects, their various religious habits, especially in Egypt and India."[68] For the transnational company, slipping in and out of identifications was good for business.

Through a series of legal and diplomatic manoeuvres the company was able to lift the ban on work and study visas for its promising foreign employees in January 1936. Yet the attacks on Bat'a's operations in Poland carried on well after the end of the visa issue – another letter in which Consul Maixner sustained his attack on Bat'a went straight to Beneš' office, and then made the rounds to four ministries in May 1936. Maixner again used an article in the *Echa Chełmku*, "From the Lives of Young Poles in Zlín" ("Ze života mladých Poláků ve Zlíně"), to prove that the company fully intended to put Polish workers in charge of the growing factory in Chełmek. In Maixner's eyes its products would then compete with Czechoslovak products, especially tanned leather.[69] For the nationalists Maixner, Beneš, and Girsa, the transnational company was another manifestation of a historical problem, the incursion of "amphibians" – those who could move between national identifications.[70] The nationalists' hostile reaction conformed to a well-established pattern about how to deal with the nationally indifferent. Their goal was to make Bat'a Czech. After all, by their definition, the company, whose workforce in Zlín was 92 per cent Moravian and whose top management all spoke Czech as their mother tongue, belonged to the nation.

Elsewhere, other nationalists felt that Bat'a's system could not be reconciled to the nation at all. In the same year in which the trouble in Poland occurred, the fiercely nationalistic Czechoslovak Tradesmen's Party (Československá živnostensko-obchodnická strana středostavovská) called for a nationwide boycott of all company products.[71] It was the latest in a string of conflicts between Bat'a and nationalist activists loosely organized by the Tradesmen's Party.

Just the year before, in 1934, the leader of the Tradesmen's Party and soon-to-be deputy chairman of parliament, Rudolf Mlčoch, proposed legislation banning Bat'a from shoe repair, from having cafeterias inside their shoe stores, and, in what would be the most damaging aspect of the legislation, from selling shoes directly from the factory. The Bat'a stores, especially in the larger cities of the country, had become one-stop shops for all footwear, as well as for pedicures, and began offering hot lunches for remarkably cheap prices in 1933. Self-identifying German and Czech unions of cobblers united with the food service lobby to support Mlčoch's legislation. They argued Bat'a's industrialization of shoemaking and rationalization of shopping left tens of thousands of cobblers, tanners, lathe makers, shoe peddlers, and so on unemployed. Without state intervention, they felt, nothing could stop the company from destroying small businesses.[72]

Bat'a responded to the proposed legislation by taking out advertisements in nearly every daily newspaper in Czechoslovakia.[73] The advertisements warned that the proposal would increase the cost of shoes by 50 per cent, a "ruthless attack on your pocket." Following up on the advertising campaign, the company organized a nationwide protest and petition against the legislation in September 1934. According to *Národní Politika*, within a week, 3.1 million people had joined the protest across "every city of the republic." The corresponding petition amassed over one million signatures. Though the forces behind the legislation remained undeterred, it would not be signed into law. Such a showing stymied Mlčoch's plan. While nationalists railed against the transnational corporation, the people of Czechoslovakia and Poland seemed to care more about cheap, sleek, and well-made footwear.

Möhlin and Beyond

A remarkably similar story unfolded in the small town of Möhlin, Switzerland, a story which has been told from the Swiss point of view by historian Tobias Ehrenbold and from the Bat'a point of view by historian Martin Jemelka. Taken together, their work provides compelling evidence that the company's push for a global uniformity encountered resistance strong enough to change key components of the template.

Bat'a moved into Switzerland in force in 1929, when it organized Bata-Schuh AG. This company, based in Zurich, opened a clear channel for Bat'a shoes to flood into the Swiss market, where they were sold at twenty-three company stores at highly competitive prices. The entry of low-cost quality shoes paired with the pampering offered by the Bat'a sales employees represented a threat to the rest of the Swiss shoe business. Swiss politicians joined with the rest of the world and implemented higher shoe tariffs in 1931. Bat'a responded, as it did elsewhere, by looking to build a manufacturing centre in the country. Tomáš identified a spot that conformed to the template – Möhlin.[74]

Möhlin was rural, poor, and desperate. It was also right next to the Rhine River. Bat'a bought a large parcel of farmland next to the town and began building a mini-Zlín. The citizens of Möhlin considered the laying of the foundation stone as a "highly important and pivotal event for our village."[75] Bat'a designed Möhlin along the same architectural principles as applied in Chełmek and Borovo. The design, of course, originated in Zlín and was unambiguously modern. First to be erected were two three-storey, red-bricked factory buildings with large windows, two dormitories of the same style, three "standardized" duplexes to the west of the dormitories, and three "standardized" detached buildings to the east of them.[76]

The company also planned to export Batism. In 1934, the company created a publishing house and began printing a newspaper, the *Möhlinger Anzeiger.* Its first series of articles included translations from Antony Cekota's *Tomáš Bat'a: Thoughts and Work.* We can surmise that reprinting excerpts from the book was done in the hope that the new satellite town would be infused with reverence for the founder. The newspaper also printed a series of articles from Paul Metzger, a former farmworker from Möhlin who had gone to study and work in Zlín.[77] Metzger was introduced as a pioneer among the Swiss *Batovci.* Young people of the community were to go to Zlín to study at the School of Work, and then return to Switzerland to lead Swiss operations. In addition, the company emphasized physical activity by organizing collective exercises on a field next to the factory buildings, as well as other sporting events. It also imported the company version of May Day.[78] However, even before the buildings went up, the project became enmeshed in the nationalistic attitudes of its locale.

The rest of Switzerland was more divided in its reception of the company's presence. As Ehrenbold puts it, a "colourful bouquet of enemies" met Bat'a's expansion into Switzerland. Fascists, communists, and above all shoe manufacturers went to great lengths to weaken or even remove the company from the country. Bally, one the largest shoe companies in Europe and based in

Switzerland, supported a boycott that lasted until 1948. It had lost to Bat'a in a variety of European markets in the 1920s and was alarmed by the arrival of its larger competitor on its home turf. The fascists saw Bat'a as a foreign influence; the communists saw it as the height of exploitation.[79]

In order to succeed in such a hostile environment, Bat'a did what it did in Poland – it switched its image to capture the nationalism of its context. In fact, just when Switzerland turned to a managed economy in 1933, Bat'a found a way around what were strict quotas over its rubber production and sales. As it turned out, Bat'a was the only European shoe company at the time that could make all-rubber galoshes. Influential people in Switzerland liked the idea of having this technology in the country, and the government reversed course and allowed Bat'a to expand its production, though modestly.[80]

As Bat'a became the only producer of galoshes in Switzerland, it carefully tied its image to the nation. The transition of the *Batovci*'s most important holiday illustrates the shift. In 1934, the May Day celebration looked very much like the one in Zlín, but in miniature. There was a "parade through the factory grounds ... an afternoon concert, speeches, a tour of the factory, a communal lunch ... soccer and boxing contests."[81] But the ongoing boycott and sustained criticism of the company operating on Swiss soil led to a noticeable shift in the event the next year. The company decided to turn the large May Day celebrations at Möhlin into a display of Swiss nationalism. On May Day in 1935, the company bedecked the entire colony in Swiss flags, and banners read "The Swiss Galosh – our product!"[82] It seems even this was not enough. Swiss groups continued to complain about the company's May Day, saying that it channelled workers from other organized events. So, Bat'a cancelled its May Day in Möhlin. Instead, it moved its major holiday to Swiss National Day, on 1 August. Its advertising, all the while, moved to focus on the idea of its galoshes as being "made in Switzerland."[83]

According to Tobias Ehrenbold, "Bat'a had set the nationalistic signs in its bricolage so unerringly, that by the end of the decade its shoes were hardly identified anymore in broad circles of the population with the idea of foreignness. The medium of Bat'a shoes now ran in a Swiss product. Made in Möhlin."[84] In other words, Bat'a proved to be a quick student of local preference. Standardization, uniformity, and rationalization at its satellite factories around the world met with serious opposition. Bat'a responded by blending in.

This ability to capture nationalistic sentiment by having locals identify the company with their nation was not confined to Europe. It also applied in India. Jan Bat'a moved away from the white man's burden rhetoric of his deceased half-brother, finding Indians to be "beautiful people, clean, tall, intelligent, and with high goals ... The shoemaker entrepreneur is free here like nowhere else in Europe."[85] He went about carefully cultivating ties to Indian elites, and, as the company increased their presence on the subcontinent, *Batovci* increasingly softened on the idea of Indian sovereignty. In 1938, Indira Gandhi and Jawaha-rlal Nehru visited Zlín on their travels across Europe. Their visit was sparked by Bat'a's operations on the subcontinent, which Nehru looked to as a model for the industrialization of an independent India. In Zlín they were treated as honoured guests; they were invited to meetings with top executives and given a private tour of the factory complex.[86]

Bat'a's relationships with India, Poland, and Switzerland were symptomatic of its ability to adapt its global strategy to the conditions on the ground. The politics of the country were of concern only as far as they affected production. Seeing the imminence of Indian independence, the company courted India's future leaders. Politics, race, and nation mattered little as long as profits kept coming in. One could argue that even the racial and national stereotypes of the executives were erased by the apolitical, rational Bat'a system. As a result, Bata's company town Batanagar became the largest industrial concern in India during the Second World War and remained so into the 1960s. To this day it is rare to meet an Indian unfamiliar with the brand name, and, for that matter, one that associates the Bata brand with anything other than India.[87]

Conclusion

Bat'a's expansion during the Great Depression provides an important moment in the history of globalization. It confirms what Robert Holton argued in his groundbreaking *Globalization and the Nation-State*. Globalization does not destroy nationalism, which in many cases becomes enflamed by the arrival of a global brand, but it offers a significant alternative to the absolute grip of the nation-state.[88] Bat'a's expansion in the nationalistic hothouses of the 1930s left the company with little choice but to blend in with the colours of whatever flag flew over the local market. Yet its global expansion also facilitated a remarkable multiculturalism in Zlín, influenced a managerial philosophy of national indifference, and created standardized company towns across the world.

Bat'a elites viewed nationalism with open suspicion. In 1933, top executive and mayor of Zlín, Dominik Čipera, contended in the town newspaper that "in the past people fought over religion. In the present people fight over nationalism. The future belongs to those who fight for the economy. Victory will belong to those whose work best serves the people. We must learn to work well – to serve well – and we will be victorious."[89] Armed with such reasoning, Bat'a executives strove to create relatively nation-free spaces in their stores, factories, and towns. While capturing nationalism to operate in certain markets and attract customers, Bat'a stores operated around a customer first policy – regardless of nationality. Democratization and standardization of shoe shopping meshed with the demands of the nation-state.

Bat'a's global expansion is an important outlier on the timeline of globalization. On this timeline, the powerful transnational corporation does not appear until the 1950s, when economic recovery efforts following the Second World War revived international trade. There is little doubt that when trying to address the interwar period as a retreat from globalization one must consider Bat'a an exception.[90] In particular, when we consider historians' understanding of the rise of the Global South, we must put Bat'a as a forerunner in industrialists' emancipation "from their age-old dependence on particular states."[91] Narratives of globalization are typically associated with industrial expansion of the 1970s.[92] However, Bat'a expanded its kingdom of shoes into India, Malaysia, and Indonesia in the 1930s and 1940s. Its initiative was therefore without precedent. And its brand of globalization was guaranteed a long reign.

"The Path of Perfection": Engineering the *Batovci* for an Uncertain World, 1933–1938

Bat'a's rapid expansion abroad did not lead to immediate benefits for workers in Zlín. Faced with quotas and tariffs that clogged the flow of exports, Bat'a's business slowed down and its warehouses began filling with shoes. This time, though, the company did not cut wages while it reduced prices at its company stores and restaurants, as it did in 1923, but instead responded by downsizing the workforce at its flagship factory complex. In a series of firings, Bat'a let go 5,436 workers between January and December 1932.[1] It also introduced a five-day work week, which negatively affected the majority of its employees who worked on the piece-rate system. This in turn fuelled a radicalization of some of the workers, who went to great lengths to organize resistance to the company's austerity measures. As the company attracted protests on the national stage, a growing chorus of disaffected voices could be heard in Zlín. To quiet these voices of protest, and encouraged by new chief executive Jan's decidedly more wide-ranging approach to social control, from 1933 to 1939 company authorities accelerated their social engineering project – turning Zlín into a tightly controlled company town.

This chapter examines Bat'a's social engineering project by looking at the personnel department, the educators, and the upper management within the company, as well as the city police. Evidence of Bat'a's network of surveillance suggests that by 1937 managers had spread the task of enforcing Batism throughout the community, and the use of informants, everyday inspections, and frequent expulsions had become normalized. Furthermore, the ability of the company to "own" space, to encourage self-regulation through wage and housing incentives, and to regulate their workforce with technologies of control such as time and personnel cards, radios, health inspections, and informants led to a markedly non-violent society, at least in terms of physical violence. Indeed, the city had one of the lowest violent crime rates in Czechoslovakia, and, after sifting through some seventeen years of company and city police records, only three cases of police brutality were found.[2] As Zlín became

Europe's pre-eminent utopian industrial town, its social engineering became increasingly sophisticated, with surveillance being used in place of force. Such power turned Zlín into Czechoslovakia's outpost of "high modernism."

However, the resulting cityscape resembled what Jane Jacobs found in her analysis of modernist planning in New York City – a flattening of diversity and a "mask of pretended order."[3] Looking at the experiences of a variety of ordinary people living in Zlín during its "high modern" phase, as seen through the fragments of their lives left behind in the archives, pulls off this "mask" of order to reveal that though ubiquitous, the surveillance network was never complete. Within each piece of Bat'a's social engineering scheme, one can find the *Eigensinn* of people living in the kingdom of shoes. Their ability to evade the disciplinary mechanisms of the company town highlights the ambiguities intrinsic in forms of control.[4]

"A gram of allegiance is better than a pound of intelligence"

Manager's Guidebook (1938)[5]

The death of Tomáš and the rise of his successor, Jan, significantly changed the ways in which Bat'a promoted its image. Whereas in the past leaders were told to focus on encouraging their team to exceed production quotas, by the mid-1930s they were given these instructions:

> Follow how people act during the parade on May 1st. Watch how people conduct themselves during overtime (at work). Watch those who do not have enough respect and confidence in their personal affairs. In all of these contexts you can point your finger at the unfaithful.
>
> It is also worth taking note of those who ignore their appearance and those who care too much about it. The latter tend to be superficial. After all, a boy who takes care to groom his eyebrows must not be a man who is a serious thinker. Always exercise caution with people who have very pretty faces whether they are men or women. They always have a greater tendency toward superficiality than those to whom nature was not so kind.[6]

Delivered to upper management in 1937, Jan's speech is evidence that the Bat'a system required managers to become active participants in cultivating a corporate body. They were to manage loyalty by monitoring appearance.

The Bat'a obsession with appearance extended to all levels of employees and the students of the BSP, but it seemed especially intense with regard to women. With typically scientific language, Bat'a told women that "the ideal woman's height is 168 cm and weight is 56 kg ... If you are under this height you can at least try to make yourself look taller by wearing clothes that present a the illusion [namely, never where shoes without heels]."[7] Bat'a's standard-ized, paternalistic, and, to them at least, modern, list of life instructions helped company executives conceive ideal types and go about cultivating these ideals in the residents of the Dřevnice.

Jan's promotion of pseudo-behavioural psychology to identify the unfaith-ful harkened back to the days when fidelity to the Bat'a project was the most important attribute an employee could have. In fact, the company demand for absolute loyalty was one of the links that connected Tomáš's approach to that of Jan's. Yet how workers' loyalty should be measured, and what lengths the company would go to in order to take that measurement, underwent a notice-able shift between the two bosses, from an emphasis on familial piety to a more "scientific" approach. During the 1920s, workers' political affiliations and their work habits were the main focus of management outside of profitability. Tomáš asked managers to monitor the workforce for the presence of commu-nist sympathies and signs of alcoholism. Jan, however, requested that his man-agers approach with suspicion employees who were beautiful or showed a lack of self-confidence – a significant extension of the company's biopolitics. This mentality, which required managers' active participation, led to the greatest excesses of the Bat'a system, for it became a system committed to disciplining nearly every aspect of the lives of those within Bat'a's sphere.

The reasons for the ratcheting up of social control has much to do with the character of Jan Bat'a and also with the phenomenal expansion of the com-pany. After a brief period of domestic contraction from 1932 to 1933, Bat'a found new success. Over the next six years, Bat'a grew its global retail chain from 1,045 sales stores to 5,810. Employment went from 16,560 to 65,064.[8] Such a considerable rise in company personnel meant that more traditional techniques of control – the kind that relied on Tomáš's paternalism of company picnics, shared meals, and word of mouth – were ineffective. New methods of tracking loyalty and skill were needed. The complications to management that accompanied the scaling up of the workforce, however, were not enough to create a society like that of Zlín in 1937. Personality was also a crucial factor. Jan's obsession over appearance and order had a definite imprint on the ways in which the company's social engineering project developed.

Jan began intensifying the means of social control early in his tenure. In a memo to managers just weeks after taking power, Jan declared, "we will fire any-one in the courtyard who does not have a pass."[9] Such instruction corresponded to a new policy that all workers had to get written permission in the form of a pass to go between the factory buildings. This was at a time of uncertainty – large layoffs led to disgruntled employees. Everywhere Jan looked he saw communists and saboteurs.

Jan's suspicion led him to create the personnel department in 1934; it was designed to scrutinize the private lives of employees, offer help to those who could benefit from it, and remove disloyal elements. Drawing heavily on the management theories coming out of the United States and England, the personnel department's reading list included works by industrial psychologist R.B. Hersey, psychologist Harry D. Kitson, Dr. L.G. Giberson of Metropolitan Life Insurance, and director of the Ford Schools Frederick E. Searle.[10] Collectively the authors argued for the need to invest significant resources into uncovering the psychology of employees. Building on their work, Bat'a wrote up a "Catechism for the Leaders of Departments," which instructed managers across the company on who to hire and how to build new industrial people. "Our actions are always decided by authority. It is in us or outside of us. But it always requires obedience. People who cannot be obedient to their internal authority must get used to being obedient to an external one ... We will divide their time according to advances in their health, intelligence, character, and will. We can mark their progress on their personnel cards ... This will be how we will raise and prepare a cadre of strong-willed people."[11]

Overseeing the department was Vincenc Jaroněk. As per Jan's expectations, Jaroněk was married with children, in his mid-forties, and well-groomed. He sported a carefully trimmed mustache and closely cropped haircut.[12] He wore a suit and tie, like all other executives, and, as chief of the burgeoning surveillance network, was to make sure that employees dress and grooming conformed to Bat'a standards. In one of his first acts on the new job, Jaroněk issued a list of orders to remind company managers that "it pays to watch the employees in the factories and between the factories so that we can find out the behaviour and thoughts of those who would live and eat with us ... misunderstandings and unaware employees should be brought to an understanding by the personnel officer."[13] Jaroněk worked as an accountant for the organization before becoming the first and only head of the personnel department. Employed since 1914, his loyalty was without question when he took the job in 1934. His background lent itself to overseeing all personnel officers; after all, with employees numbering around fifty thousand, one had to be good with numbers.[14] The trail of evidence he left in the personnel department files from 1935 to 1940 offers a compelling glimpse into the lives of the *Batovci*.

Although head of the most invasive surveillance apparatus of the company, Jaroněk was held responsible for situations well beyond his control. In one of the male dormitories in Zlín, for example, Jan Bat'a found several employees sleeping at noon. When asked as to why, they responded that they simply had not been given anything to do. Outraged, Jan insisted that the incident be written on Jaroněk's personnel card, "for not knowing what is going on in our dormitories."[15] Likewise, he was similarly punished for not knowing that for thirteen weeks employees in Třebic had not worked the appropriate number of hours.[16]

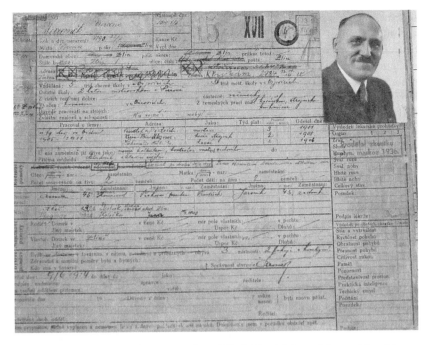

Figure 6.1. Vincenc Jaroněk, personnel card, Bat'a Fond, Moravský zemský archiv v Brně, Státní okresní archiv Zlín. K. 1023 č.14.

Jaroněk, in turn, oversaw a number of "personal inspectors" whom he assigned to each company unit. After 1934, on any given day, these company inspectors visited workers and their families in their homes and at the factories to report on their overall health. Just what the inspectors were looking for was revealed at a conference for all personnel officials on 29 November 1937. At the conference the personnel department's major tasks were specified as follows: finding out what organizations employees belong to, uncovering any political ties they may have, keeping track of their financial status, and ascertaining employees' character traits. "The personnel inspector must perfect his ability to read a person's character. In meeting with people, he must be able to sort out and summarize their innate emotional dispositions."[17]

The personnel inspector exemplified the increased scope of the company in everyday life. Manifesting the "light" and "dark" sides of the Bat'a world, the personnel inspectors were in effect both social workers and company spies. They personify the intrusive nature of Batism. One collection of reports from the personnel inspectors of the sales department reveals just how wide-ranging was their field of concern. One report on machinist Jaroslav Sáha discusses his relationship to his daughter, another, on Irena Karlová, guesses that her meagre sales results have to do with her emotional state.[18] Another batch of reports, concerning the facilities department, reveals descriptions of the cleanliness of employees' windows and card-playing habits, and discusses dissatisfied janitors.[19]

Hundreds of other such examples of "improper" behaviour exist within the records of the personnel department; these illustrate the oftentimes wide gap between the ideal and the reality, even for those who were supposed to be the embodiment of Bat'a ideals. When managers went afoul of the moral standards of the company they were rarely punished or reported to the police.[20] Instead they were subject to a much greater level of scrutiny by the company's personnel inspectors and executives, who sought to ensure that managers conformed to the company's code of morality. Bat'a managers under the tight surveillance of the company frequently acted outside of Bat'a morality. Bat'a managers often quit because they "needed to explore other possibilities." They fooled around with subordinates, got involved in elaborate skimming schemes, and even dared to keep an untidy shop. Through myriad examples of management acting out of line, the grey areas between the ideals and the rules reveal themselves.

The personnel department also helped to oversee the company's social welfare spending. Alois Šafařík provides a good example of how the company maintained worker loyalty through its personnel inspectors and expansive social welfare program. Šafařík, who started working at Bat'a in 1927, transferred from a machine shop in Brno to Zlín in 1934 largely because his wife suffered from bad asthma. When one of the company's personnel inspectors found out about her condition, they gave him 1,000 crowns for medicine and doctor visits.[21] After a year of work in Zlín he was also given keys to one of the Bat'a cottages – the two-storey brick duplexes that still characterize the town. In return, Šafařík worked for the company beyond the Second World War, and remains active in promoting the idea of the Bat'a era as the golden age of industry.[22] Šafařík's seemingly mundane story reveals the company's interest in the intimate details of its employees, and how its ability to help workers in need promoted intense worker loyalty.

To assist with the personnel department's oversight, all managers from 1934 onward had to fill out a quarterly evaluation of their employees. The sales managers, for example, completed a detailed one-page form, culminating in a recommendation for the employee. The evaluation form covered fifteen topics: relationship status, place of residence, living arrangements, children, education and training courses taken, languages spoken, salary and expenses (including car ownership), yearly bonus amounts, and finally, an eight-part section on behaviour. In this section managers had to rate the employees' quality of work, performance, behaviour, temperament, leadership abilities, creative abilities, and relationship to the factory. Then the manager decided whether the person was "on the rise," "good," "falling," or "fired."[23] The use of intelligence tests became widespread around 1934; nearly every new hire was expected to take one. These tests ascertained the candidates' abilities in arithmetic, grammar, and writing. The evaluations, unfortunately, were not as faithfully archived as the personnel cards, and thus we have precious few forms of this type that were actually filled out.

These evaluations and requirements reveal a great deal about the increasing influence of industrial psychology on the company. As with the personnel cards, the quarterly evaluation furthered the goal of creating a legible employee, giving managers one more tool with which to examine their employees' lives and determine whether or not they had the right character for the Bat'a project. These methods of oversight were being adopted throughout the world, though more by states than by companies, and have come to be such a routinized way of managing populations that today we hardly pay them notice.[24]

While the personnel department established itself in the lives of those in Bat'a's sphere, the company turned its attention toward Zlín itself. Particularly troubling for Jan and the other executives was the rise of communist rhetoric in the Dřevnice Valley. Accordingly, they turned to the Zlín city police to quell the threat. In turn, the police became central players in the company's social engineering project.

Policing Communists

On 20 June 1934, the Zlín police, acting on a tip from a Bat'a Company informant, entered the apartment of Antonie Hřívová. There they found her sister, the "known communist activist" Růžena Urbancová, with a bundle of illegal pamphlets. They arrested both sisters and took them to the city jail.[25] The police collected the pamphlets, placed them on file, and notified both the company and the authorities of Urbancová's legal residence in Uherské Hradiště.[26] The pamphlets were none other than the *Bat'ovák*, a newspaper published intermittently throughout the 1930s, providing locals with a communist critique of the Bat'a system. Written for the average worker, the paper strove to amplify potential sources of discord in the Bat'a workers' daily lives.[27] The two most common attacks found in the *Bat'ovák* concerned the pace of work at the factories, which was argued to be inhumanly fast, and the tight regulation of employees' personal lives, particularly those of young workers. The *Bat'ovák* was perhaps the most circulated of all "illegal" pamphlets.

As Hřívová's case illustrates, one of the most common ways the police and the company tried to root out communists was through keeping track of individuals' personal relationships. The police built a large database of suspected communists by frequenting rallies held in the region, making reports for all persons caught with leftist material, and using Bat'a Company information regarding locals' political affiliations (and vice versa). They then checked new arrivals and new potential Bat'a employees against their database. If a person's parents or siblings were suspect, then they would not be hired by the company or given a residence permit by the city.[28] If the new arrival was suspected of being friends with a communist, the police usually began an investigation into the person's past, contacting authorities at their places of residence and sending plainclothes officers to follow them. Likewise, if a person had visited the Soviet Union, they went on the watch list, and were not likely to find employment in town.[29] Finally, reports by local informants could also open a case against a suspected political undesirable. Some cases proved nothing more than idle gossip, as when the police investigated Václav Berka after the company received a letter from an ex-lover that falsely stated he was a communist activist.[30] Still, the threat of denunciation, and the real danger of losing one's job through association kept socialists isolated, as few Zlínians wanted to be friends with people who could get them expelled from the town.

As the power of the company rose, communist influence, and its ability to marshal any forces of opposition, conversely fell. In fact, in 1936, after the Communist Party requested space to hold its May Day rally, the city told its representative that they could have "the bus stop on Zarámí Street."[31] After sending several letters protesting the restrictions, the party held its rally, drawing a handful of supporters and a nearly equal number of police, who, after one hour, requested the small crowd to disperse, which it did.[32] In essence, communism had been effectively forced into the shadows of the kingdom of shoes. Activists were closely followed by the agents of the Bat'a surveillance network; the communist opposition could be found only on the very fringes of society, but it was not yet extinguished.

This resiliency is seen that same year when Communist Party members began holding meetings in secret camps in the woods around the town. There, they set up a printing press for their Bat'ovák and a socialist library of sorts. Indeed, it would have been the only place in Zlín that a curious worker could borrow a copy of the Communist Manifesto. Their shacks, three in all, escaped demolition for several months and attracted, at least by police estimates, some fifty people from the town.[33] What seems to have broken their secrecy was when villagers turned in a railway worker, Jan Martinec, for distributing illegal communist flyers at a train station. Martinec then revealed that meetings were taking place in the woods.[34] At this point, the head of Bat'a's personnel department, Vincenc Jaroněk, read a confiscated copy of Bat'ovák and got involved.

Jaroněk ordered the police to search the woods around Zlín, going all the way into the ethnic region of Slovácko if necessary.[35] (That he was able to take such an action is of course testament to the company's control of the police force.) The police found the "tramps' huts" in the forests between the villages of Provodov and Ludkovice, just a few kilometres south of Zlín, and raided them in the early hours of 20 September. They arrested eight people, two women and six men. Among them were two current Baťa employees, one former employee, and Jaroslav Hošek, the secretary of the Union of Industrial Leather Workers and a member of the Communist Party. Hošek had photographs of the Spanish Civil War along with numerous brochures and magazines associated with the communist movement. During the search, one of the men allegedly said, "so, this is our free republic." All of them ended up in the Zlín jail, where they faced charges of "vagrancy" (*tuláci*).[36]

The camps represented both the shadowy fate of socialist activists and their continued ability to present a radical alternative to the Baťa system. The activists' influence should not be overestimated, though, as has been done in the past by Marxist-Leninist historians in the Czechoslovak Socialist Republic. Communists were a small fraction of the population of Zlín, and the company town's surveillance network effectively kept them out. The Simajchl family provides an example of how company personnel, city police, and local officials worked to frustrate and alienate those on the far left of the political spectrum.

One year before the discovery of the forest huts, Josef Simajchl, a known Communist Party activist from Zlín, requested to put up posters before the upcoming national elections. The town council denied his request on the basis that the posters would disturb the "public peace and calm."[37] It seems that not long after denying him the right to display propaganda posters, the police launched an investigation into Simajchl and his family. They used a family photograph to identify four people closest to him and then compiled a report for each person in the photo. Their final report, which is in the records of Baťa's personnel department, offered statements about each of the individuals' places of residence, employment, and political opinions. All of them were labelled as "communist" and were blacklisted by the company. According to the police statistics, these tactics were effective: in 1934 communists caused five "disturbances," in 1935 six, in 1937 four, in 1938 only one.[38]

It is tempting to celebrate the underground movement of socialists fighting a giant corporation, but ultimately these activists, whether conscious of it or not, were championing a system that was eerily similar to that of the Soviet Union. For communists in Zlín were fighting against a system built on the principles of Taylor and Ford, while the Soviet Union was simultaneously trying to implement Fordist and Taylorist practices in its factories.[39] Furthermore, Soviet policing techniques were similar to those used in Zlín; personnel cards, home inspections, and expulsions were used as means to uphold a utopian social

Figure 6.2. Josef Simajchl's poster: "Make the Rich Pay! Vote Communist for the
Worker's Party to Represent the People." "Pan Josef Simajchl" 29 November 1935.
Moravský zemský archiv v Brně, Státní okresní archiv Zlín. č. 263.

order that celebrated hard work, sobriety, technology, and loyalty.[40] Indeed, as Jan Bat'a once commented, "we are as decisive and strict about firing untrustworthy employees as they are in Soviet Russia."[41] The Soviets too were interested in the rationalization of production and in intervening in people's lives to build a new industrial society. In essence, communists in Zlín were trying to throw off one version of high modernism for another. Fortunately, for the people of the Dřevnice Valley, the Bat'a version of high modernism had to make significant compromises, even within its pre-eminent company town, as regional authorities, townspeople, and even radicals prevented the company from realizing its most extreme ambitions.

Jan's Social Protection

Along with driving away communists, the company was committed to expelling prostitutes and promiscuous women who "disturbed the peace." The campaign against sexual promiscuity, like that against alcohol, was a community project that gave way to a "scientific" approach. And as with their efforts to contain communism and alcoholism, the authorities' attempts to enforce a rigidly conservative sex life was an ongoing project. What follows is an examination of Bat'a's policing of sex under Jan's time as chief executive.[42]

The story of Marie U. reveals the efforts by police to control women's bodies and people's sex lives, and the ability of individuals to thwart these efforts. Marie's case began when Jan Daněk, the most highly regarded of all undercover police agents, was in Café Beseda on 28 December 1936. There he recognized a woman whom he thought was named Žofia Hradilová, known to him for "sitting with random men and then taking them later in the night to pubs to fuck for money."[43] He also suspected that she carried a venereal disease, which allowed him by law to arrest her for inspection. He placed her under arrest as she got up to leave the cafe, searching her wallet.[44] Once under investigation, Hradilová, aka Marie U., cooperated with authorities by giving them the names of everyone she had slept with recently; the police proceeded to track down her partners so that they could be examined for sexually transmitted diseases. In her statement to the police she related how she became a prostitute in Zlín, claiming that while looking for legitimate work, she was brought into the business by two local women and three men who set her up in a hotel in a nearby town. While working there she contracted gonorrhea. After taking her statement, the police sent her to the hospital in Olomouc and tried to contact her city of residence. It was then that they discovered she was someone else, twenty-year-old Marie U., who was wanted all over the country for swindling and theft.[45]

With Marie, we see Bat'a's interventionist approach, as she became known to police in a very short time, though under a false identity. Anecdotally, her presence on the authorities' watch list suggests that the surveillance network in Zlín was much stronger than that of all of the other places where she had committed crimes. Her story also suggests that the police in Zlín could be led astray on false tips, leading to detention of people based on evidence of unreliable witnesses. The incident was not an isolated one, as women across the Bat'a sphere were subject to police surveillance for perceived sexual transgressions.[46]

By 1937, however, such sexual incidents had become commonplace even among factory employees who lived in the closely supervised dormitories. As the number of Bat'a employees multiplied, outside of higher-ranking employees, company and city managers had little time to deal with individual cases of sexual promiscuity. Instead, they tried to create a network of surveillance and policies of exclusion to combat what many feared was an epidemic of sexual transgressions.

In this context, Jan issued a directive on "the social protection of women at work." The document finely illustrated both the inability of the company to control employees' sex lives as well as its commitment to substantially increase its presence in the private lives of female workers. Therefore, it is worth quoting at length:

Women in the factory are often alienated by their intimacy with men at work. Frequently, the establishing of familiarity – and we have had several cases – has had a decisive influence on the lives of all our women.

It is necessary to find out about these actions and attitudes, which have to be watched and brought to the attention of the personnel department, so that they can look into certain cases.

1. Single women employed in our factory have to be enlightened as to what our way of life requires of them. It has to be made clear to them that we have an interest in [their private lives] so that we can help them solve every important problem in their lives, even the question of choosing the right life partner ...

3. There should be created in the factory a department of wedding affairs, which will be responsible for looking after wedding issues of our co-workers.

4. To avoid unwanted numbers of single women, we have arranged the following: we will announce that we are letting go single pregnant women.

5. But this will happen only when the personnel department cannot find a normal, humane way to solve to the problem. In the case where the future father is reluctant to fulfil his duties, we must use moral, psychological reasoning, or legal arguments, and then it will be possible to persuade the man to become a good husband.

It has to be known throughout the neighbourhood, that in every case of an afflicted (postižené) girl, we will protect her with our considerable legal and material resources.

If we cannot solve the girl's problem in a simple, humane way, we will remove her from our partnership.

The philosophical reasons for this are that a woman has stopped being a desirable member of our work family if it is no longer possible for her to attain a life full of happiness and satisfaction.[47]

Thus Jan's justification for firing single pregnant woman was that they tempted other women into an unfulfilled life. The codification of this policy was a part of an increased presence of the company in the daily lives of the workers, and its motivation had much to do with a rapidly expanding workforce. For it seems that the young Bat'a workforce frequently slipped away from the company's surveillance system to have sex in all kinds of places and with all kinds of people. And as the company banned premarital sex in all of its housing, couples were forced to go to unlikely places. Those who were caught or found out often had their transgressions written up in personnel officers' records. We therefore have hundreds if not thousands of reports of illicit affairs and sexual acts in parking lots, forests and parks, retail stores, hotels, and so on.[48]

One of the personnel inspectors' major tasks was to uncover illicit affairs among its employees, something for which Bat'a had little tolerance. In fact, the company often fired their managers in such cases. Out of twenty-one cases found from 1936 to 1938 of improper relationships between managers and employees, twelve managers were fired immediately for their actions.[49] The others were either demoted, transferred, or let go. In each case a male manager had become involved with a female employee. One case, that of Josef Tillburger and Eta Ollarková, illustrates both the role of the inspector and the intense interest of Bat'a in the personal lives of its employees.

Tillburger was the manager of the Bat'a retail store in Zvolen, a medium-sized town in central Slovakia. Ollarková worked in the sales department in Zvolen, while her brother Robert was the manager of the sales department in Čadca, a Slovakian town on the border of Moravia and Poland. When the company inspector travelled to Čadca for his normal quality control checks, he was told by Robert that his sister was not at work in Zvolen but rather back in her hometown because she "had been accused of causing strife in a marriage and of being a whore." Upon further investigation, the inspector discovered that Ollarková had recently attempted suicide by way of a scalpel after being confronted by Tillburger's suspicious wife. The inspector asked Ollarková to return to Zlín and make a detailed report of the incident, which she did. He then travelled to Zvolen to confirm her report. Eventually, the inspector produced an account of the affair, including details of the circumstances of the first sexual encounter (Tillburger's wife was at a spa), and handed it over to the personnel department. The personnel department decided to transfer Ollarková to the shop in Bratislava and demoted Tillburger to a "manager without personnel" in Spišské Podhradie.[50]

In addition to facing personal investigations by the city and company into their love lives, female workers faced the threat of losing their jobs should they become pregnant. For the company never abandoned the policy set forth by Tomáš, which at first was more of an understanding, that women left the factory if they became pregnant. In 1937, though, the company codified the policy: "single pregnant women will be fired."[51] This policy affected thousands of women. In the last half of 1938 alone the company fired 191 women for pregnancy.[52] This was not forced maternity leave, though the company gave marriage and maternity gifts to loyal employees; it was a policy of forced expulsion from the factory. In the case of unmarried pregnant workers, their release meant having to move away from Zlín altogether. As the vast majority of single women were housed in the large dormitories, and these dormitories had strict moral codes of conduct, anyone let go from the factory would lose her bed. This ensured that single pregnant women would not "pollute" the other young workers. And as abortion remained illegal in all of Czechoslovakia throughout the interwar period, unmarried women had few options but to have the child and leave the company town.[53]

For those women who went about the "proper" way of having a relationship, through marriage, pregnancy also resulted in termination of employment. In the mid-1930s, executives succeeded in creating a system where marriage was a fundamental step to higher wages for men, and one of the only ways a couple could escape the crowded dormitories in Zlín. However, for women, this pro-marriage policy often translated into the loss of their jobs. Like the pregnancy policy, the marriage policy was at first an unwritten understanding, and then sometime in the early 1930s/late 1920s the policy came to be codified; managers had to dismiss women who married and became pregnant.[54] This policy, like the pregnancy policy, had a significant impact. In the last half of 1938, 161 women were let go from the factory for getting married and having children.[55] What they received in return, assuming that they married a Bat'a employee, was a better house, a marriage gift, usually around 500 crowns, and often the opportunity to travel with their husbands abroad. And while these incentives may seem trivial in light of losing their professional careers, moving into a semi-detached house from an overcrowded women's dormitory, where their actions were closely monitored, must have had tremendous appeal.[56]

Dominik Čipera summarized the vision of these policies on domesticity in 1934: "housewives of greater Zlin are not forced to do the heavy household work and can devote themselves fully to family life instead, bringing up the next generation and attending to their husbands, to whom they provide support and advice."[57] Likewise, the company's architect and urban planner Vladimir

Karfík wrote the following in 1934 when asked to predict what the future would look like in 1974.

> What will the life of the future family that has paid for our services look like? The family of the teacher Klement, consisting of five members, has a beautiful house surrounded by greenery at the Štákovy Paseky location, near one of our department stores.
>
> Every morning, life in this residential area is symbolized by Bat'a helicopters which hover in the air and then descend to the flat roofs of the small villas, delivering ready-to-eat English breakfasts to their occupants ... the children leave for school and the parents for work. Mrs. Klement does not have to do any cooking or cleaning – or washing, for that matter, since breakfast was served by the department store on aesthetic and hygienic paper plates, which are simply discarded after use; the same routine takes place at midday and in the evening.
>
> Keeping the houses tidy is taken care of by our employees who come every morning and, in a few minutes, clean the living space with the help of efficient machinery.[58]

The company was determined to get women to buy into its vision of a modern lifestyle, in its own Bat'a-wrapped package. The Bat'a newspapers continuously ran articles with titles such as "The Woman and the Airplane," "Why a Woman Loves America," and "Modern Young Women and Sport."[59] This modern lifestyle required training women (as well as men) to become comfortable with air travel, automobiles, and sports that had been recently introduced into the country such as handball, ice hockey, and basketball. Zlín's automotive and aviation programs were not only designed for men. As the company developed its own airplanes, pilot school, and airports, it sent thousands of managers on flights abroad (one of the first companies in the world to do so).[60] Of course, the vast majority of these managers were men. Still, the company encouraged wives to fly with them, even on short business trips.[61] The modern woman, according to Bat'a, should know how to drive, and, in Zlín, the city with the highest percentage of automobiles in the country, it was common to see women behind the wheel.[62] In Zlín, as in the United States, the act of driving was seen as a form of emancipation for women.[63] Nevertheless political constraints persisted. The lack of political power for the women of Zlín reflected the broader Czechoslovak context.

In her study on gender and democracy in Czechoslovakia from 1918 to 1950, Melissa Feinberg finds a steady decline in the women's rights movement during the interwar period. She sees the heady days of early democracy, and the promise of full gender equality, giving way to fears about the loss of traditional family structures. For Feinberg, the Women's National Council, and indeed a democratic Czechoslovakia committed to individual rights, lost its struggle to overturn a patriarchal mentality that placed men and women in a gendered hierarchy. When faced with the uncertainty of interwar Europe, Czechs turned away from full civil equality. Instead, Feinberg finds myriad groups squashing efforts to enact reform in civil law and the government placing limits on women's rights, as in the reinstitution of the *celibát* laws for female civil servants.[64] All of this, argues Feinberg, underscores a general uneasiness with democracy – an uneasiness that eventually led to widespread acceptance of authoritarian government.

This political context is where the Bat'a world began and never really left. Unsurprisingly, in a patriarchal company town, women's movements never had the chance to form independent, meaningful organizations, even at the start of the First Republic. For the traditional gendered model of the family that most Czechs accepted was the foundation of the Bat'a Company's organization. The patriarch, Tomáš, created a familial structure of management that had an interrelated group of men overseeing thousands of employees. Their wives stayed out of the factory but were visible in the community, participating in organizations such as the Red Cross and local relief efforts. This middle-class model was then applied through the ranks of workers so that every woman who worked for Bat'a was in an unequal relationship with her male coworkers from the day she began her job. Indeed, Bat'a maintained that women should quit the factory after a time to become wives and mothers. Then, mostly by becoming a ravenous consumer, she should aggressively push her man to rise in the company.[65] Her labour, particularly at home, was seen as drudgery by the Bat'a ideologues, who dreamed of a future free of housework for the wife, with machines, cleaning services, and food deliveries (all company-run) taking care of everything. Thus, women were explicitly positioned outside the world of work, outside of the narrative of labour. Their sexuality was seen as a threat to the rational order of the "Garden City" and their voices were marginalized.

Bat'a developed a patriarchal business structure with little to no interference from women's groups, a structure that upheld traditional ideals, similar to those of the authoritarian Second Republic of Czechoslovakia. Throughout the Bat'a era Zlín's form of governance anticipated that of Czechoslovak society as a whole in 1938 – a sanctioned system of inequality.

Such visions of modernity did not emancipate women from their second-class status in the workforce. If anything, Bat'a's social engineering project called for a division of labour between the sexes to a minute degree. When one looks at each department, for example, a clear picture emerges as to what types of jobs men and women could or could not do. Men represented more than 85 per cent of all tanners, machine workers, advertising personnel, engineers, dyers, shoe repair employees, and managers. Women made up over 75 per cent of all secretaries, stitchers, sales clerks, and pedicurists.[66] This strict division extended into the town's public schools, where all elementary teachers were women and all principals were male. This strict division of the sexes could even be seen in the hallways of the factories, where "women's coats hung on the right; and men's on the left."[67]

Policing Vagrants and "Gypsies"

While cases of moral and gender policing and political repression were routine in interwar Zlín, they did not occupy nearly as much time as did "beggars," "vagrants," and "gypsies." There were two reasons for this. First, far more economically marginal people were interested in employment than in politics. By the 1930s the mundane act of begging had come to be seen by Bat'a executives as a grave social illness which weakened the body politic. This mentality coincided with the Great Depression, as hundreds of unemployed men and dozens of women arrived in Zlín each week in search of work. Their presence led to almost a siege mentality among the upper management of the company and town; the elite saw their utopia threatened by a large influx of desperate people. Second, the previously fluid borders dividing local Moravians and local Roma were made sharp by the company's social engineering project.

Authorities' preferred way to deal with perceived social threats was expulsion. For, as Zlín's population was largely from elsewhere, and the residency statutes of Czechoslovakia allowed local authorities to expel anyone who did not have a local residency permit, it was easy for authorities to arrest and send off anyone caught begging. In 1937, for example, the police expelled 208 people, all of them labelled "beggars," "vagrants," or "gypsies."[68] In the Bat'a mentality, these people represented the irrational, lazy, and backward of Czechoslovak society and, like housework and communists, they had no place in its future.

In the context of this rationalized discourse, authorities perceived Roma (whom they referred to as *cikáni*, or gypsy) as being especially threatening. To them, the Roma represented transience, spontaneity, superstition, and sexual depravity. In addition, and perhaps most frustrating to the leaders of the company and town, they were unknowable. Roma groups were almost impossible for the authorities to track, register, and control. Indeed, the state-issued identification cards, which all Czechoslovak citizens were required to carry, would often be swapped between Roma, leading to much confusion.[69] Even when they did have the correct identification, their histories were only made legible to the authorities through criminal records. The company had no informants or personal inspectors among the Roma, who typically lived in camps outside of town. Thus, the authorities had no awareness of the skills, experiences, or politics of people of Roma descent. As a result of this profound culture clash, the company hired almost no Roma and the city often refused to allow them residence permits; they were de facto second-class citizens, and substantial effort was made to drive them out of the utopian space of Zlín.[70] They were a striking exception to the purported cosmopolitanism of the company and their social alienation suggests that, despite the company's claims of rationality, authorities perpetuated local prejudice. In sum, the Roma way of life became criminalized in the kingdom of shoes.

While the authorities consistently viewed the "gypsy" camps with consternation and went to some lengths to harass and drive them out, Roma people played a vital, if at times blurry, role in the life of the city. Their camps served as counterbalances to the highly ordered, regimented life the people of Zlín were expected to lead. They provided frequent visual reminders that an entire way of life outside the Bat'a operating system was only a stone's throw away. We know of several instances, for example, where Czech men (I found nothing concerning Czech women) visited the camps for entertainment.[71] In addition, Roma were key sources of labour as the valley expanded. They frequently worked on the numerous infrastructure projects in and around the city.[72]

Police reports filled with stories of Roma gambling, begging, drinking, and violence outweigh the documentary evidence we have on their gainful employment. This discrepancy perhaps reveals the largest disconnect that existed between Bat'a social engineers and another group. The Batovci were simply not able to control the Roma. Anna Šubertová's interaction with Zlín authorities typifies the collection of evidence concerning Roma interactions with the city. Police arrested Šubertová on the afternoon of 14 December 1934. She was apparently begging in front of a local shop when a police officer saw her. She ducked into the store to hide, but to no avail. She was caught and taken to jail. There, she reported that she came to Zlín only occasionally to sell herbs. The police officer taking the report, though, wrote that her real reason for being in Zlín was in order to beg. The police report also informs us that she was an illiterate mother of two. She had 4.40 crowns on her, which the police assumed came from begging. She was processed, fined, and told that she had to stay away.[73]

Another, much less mundane, story emerges from the police files – the saga of a large Roma family with the surname Daniel. From 1931 to 1940, city police made fifty-two arrests of people with the Daniel surname. Most of these arrests concerned begging, drunk and disorderly conduct, or failing to have their "cikánska legitmace" – their citizenship papers. But a few of these records are larger and more detailed than the others – the ones that cover violent crimes. In 1933, Ludvík Daniel went on a crime spree in the Dřevnice Valley, robbing homes and holding up a bar at gunpoint. In 1937, Gabriel Daniel allegedly stabbed a young man in the chest with a pike. Also in 1937, Vladislav Daniel stabbed a young Bat'a accountant in the head with a knife; the accountant survived.

Ludvík Daniel's confession tracks his whereabouts and his associates over a two-month period, from July to September, 1933. During these two months Ludvík Daniel and his accomplices went on a spree stealing, bartering, and drinking. They lived nomadic lives as they did so. They spent much time in the forests surrounding the valley, where Ludvík reports on having many days simply lounging around under the trees with his friends. They came in and out of town as they saw fit and moved to different forests every few days. Then one day Ludvík found himself in a bar in Zlín, the U Kaláčů, and noticed that there was a window above the storage cellar. He hatched a plan with his friends, and on the night of 8 September they robbed the place. While Ludvík was stealing as many bottles of beer as he could, a man showed up unexpectedly. Ludvík, who had brought a rifle, fired at the man. Ludvík carried on after the man retreated and then took all of his booty to a Roma camp named Lidora, which was in easy walking distance in the forest. There he distributed the beer to whomever wanted it. The next morning he took five bottles of beer and headed off to throw his rifle in the Morava River. Police caught Ludvík sometime after that and brought him to the station in Miškovice, where they took his confession; they later shot him to death during an escape attempt.[74]

Vladislav Daniel's and Gabriel Daniel's reports reveal a similar way of life. Gabriel and his friend were at a popular sledding hill, eating bacon on a wooden spike, which the police report claims had been stolen. A fifteen-year-old boy sledded into them and Gabriel stabbed him with the object ("sharpened for the purposes of warfare").[75] Vladislav Daniel was a local twenty-four-year-old who worked for the city as a labourer and lived in the Roma camp in northeastern Zlín. He came back to his home drunk on 29 August 1937. There he found Jaroslav Boubrava, a twenty-one-year-old accountant at Bat'a, also drunk, and trying to take the necklace off of his girlfriend, Anna, whom the police report refered to as Vladislav's "concubine." Convinced that Boubrava was trying to rape his partner, Vladislav confronted him. The two got in an argument that led to a fight. During which, Vladislav pulled a pocket knife out and stabbed Boubrava in the head. Both men were injured; Vladislav's hand was badly cut. They ended up in hospital, where the police investigated and made one arrest, that of Vladislav Daniel.[76]

These Roma camps, whether just a handful of men living in the forest or the more established camps like the one Vladislav lived in, were the antithesis of what the *Batovci* were trying to engineer. They were difficult for authorities to keep track of, sometimes being entirely out of sight, and all times being porous. Their casual mobility and violence seemed to embrace a very different set of rules, ones that were unwritten. Perhaps that is why the police reports consistently assume criminality. What is certain is that the reports are biased and distorted. Certainly, begging and violence were a part of Roma life, but we cannot assume that they played a larger role than sober business transactions, hard work, and powerful artistic expressions. While prejudice toward the Roma has a long history in Central and Eastern Europe and continues to be a major obstacle for their equal rights in the region, the relationship between Roma and the *Batovci* has yet to be discussed in the historiography of the region. Indeed, in regional histories of Zlín, both from then and now, the Roma are entirely left out.[77]

Likewise, the stories of the thousands of unemployed vagrants and beggars that moved into and through the city have yet to be told. In fact, cases of begging and vagrancy made up 60 per cent of the total number of arrests made by city police from 1923 to 1938.[78] Many of them were men like Jaroslav Bubík, who came from poor areas around Zlín in hope of some type of employment. Bubík, a former factory worker, had tattered shoes and bad teeth, but was literate. He was caught begging from house to house by a patrolman, who took him to jail and ran a background check on him. Like so many others who were picked up for begging, he had been found guilty of the offence before. He was sentenced to two nights in jail and ordered to return to his place of residence, a few miles away in Paskov.[79]

Because vagrants were not from the city authorities considered them foreigners, and thus outside the city's responsibility. On 8 May 1934, police found seven men sleeping in a forest behind the brickworks. They were all in their twenties and were all looking for work at Bat'a. When they failed to find a room, they decided to camp in the woods, where they were discovered by a patrol. All of them were fined for vagrancy and ordered to leave the area. They complied.[80] The seven men were but one among many groups to be bounced out of the kingdom of shoes: "In 1936 … all of those arrested for begging (205 in all) were foreign persons."[81]

By 1937, the company's domination over the spaces of Zlín was decisive. Police worked closely with company personnel and were largely successful at keeping out those on the margins of society. While the company charged the police to keep away out-of-work individuals, communists, and prostitutes, they were bringing in thousands of young people yearly from all over the country. As Bat'a went through another rapid expansion in production and workforce, it felt compelled to invest significant resources in educating its workforce. As police patrolled the perimeters of the company town, educators tried to shape the right kind of people to live within them.

Perfecting Education

During Jan's tenure, educational reform rapidly accelerated in Zlín. However, throughout most of Czechoslovakia's educational system, discipline was uneven and private trade schools were rare.[82] Indeed, the vast majority of Czechoslovak youth in the interwar period went to schools where lessons were conducted in Czech, German, Slovak, or Hungarian; classes were based on official curricula and most after-school activities were offered by various nationalist associations. By contrast, Zlín youth had five "experimental" public schools, two industrial schools (including the 8,500-pupil Bat'a School of Work), a business academy, a private language school, a women's trade school, and a music academy to choose from by 1938. In addition, the company built workshops and laboratories, two gymnasiums, and nine libraries, and brought in over two hundred teachers, engineers, and even former military leaders to teach the town's youth.[83] Bat'a had the youngest average hiring age in Czechoslovakia, and Zlín supported a web of schools infused with the mission to train students for Bat'a's modern industrial society.

At the centre of this educational web rested the Bat'a School of Work. The BSP grew rapidly after 1933, when the company overhauled it to reflect both its globalization as well as the ideas of the new chief executive. Indeed, the change in leadership from Tomáš to Jan Bat'a had a direct effect on the lives of the Young Men and Women. While Tomáš seemed to have cared largely about creating loyal skilled workers, Jan tried to design a curriculum that would mould them into young renaissance men, capable of speaking four languages, dancing, painting, and even flying aircraft.[84] As early as 1936, the BSP required Young Men and Women to put on a play "no less than twice a year."[85] There was more emphasis on training Young Men as general managers rather than as skilled workers. All Young Men were expected to know "the entire layout of the factory by their third year," when they could then test into a special program for managers.[86] Jan saw the BSP as the centre for future upper management, whereas Tomáš had looked at the school as a way to ensure a loyal workforce, both foreign and domestic. Clearly both leaders aimed to propagate the ethics of Batism, as the school was focused on moulding students' character from its beginnings. Thus, while Tomáš created the company's educational system, Jan expanded and refined it.

Reflecting Jan's growing expectations, the BSP expanded into a five-year program in 1934, with a revised curriculum and schedule. Classes were no longer held in the evening but in the afternoon. The Young Men and Women had their evenings entirely filled with study and collective activities, such as singing, sports, and cleaning. Character became more important than in the past. The pamphlet for interested applicants in 1936 is indicative of this change, as physical health, cleanliness, and discipline were stressed under the rules of the school. "Successful work depends upon a healthy body and a quick spirit."[87] Ironically, the new rules were similar to those of the Soviet state in its attempt to transform society; the Bolsheviks also sought to inculcate in their youth "punctuality, cleanliness, businesslike directness, polite modesty, and good, but never showy manners."[88] Regardless of the demands, the school was flooded with applications. By 1937, the BSP had an 11 per cent acceptance rate, which gave the company confidence in its code of strict discipline.[89]

As the BSP grew, the Young Women and Men became subject to a much more organized experiment in social engineering when, in 1929, the company created the *vychovatels*. A *vychovatel* was something between a security guard, a tutor, and a section manager. Two *vychovatels* lived on each floor of the dormitories with their charges, which meant they had about 100 to 120 students each to manage. The *vychovatel* was the key to the social engineering project of the BSP. "The *vychovatel* must be a strict father and a loving mother."[90] After 1934, the typical day of a *vychovatel* in the Young Men's dormitory began at 6 a.m., when they were required to make sure the Young Men washed the "top half of their body" and brushed their teeth. After breakfast, the *vychovatel* would arrive at the factory by 7:20, where they inspected the Young Men for appearance. Every day these inspections were recorded for future reference. As the Young Men began working at the factory, the *vychovatels* would meet between 7:20 and 8:00 to discuss any problems with their students. They would then walk back to the factories and check in on each of their charges to make sure they were behaving and keeping a tidy appearance and workspace. At lunchtime they had to investigate "how much and how the young men eat." They also needed to make sure the Young Men left their tables clean after lunch. The *vychovatels* had their only free period while the Young Men were in school, from 1:30 to 5:00. Afterwards, the *vychovatels* arrived at the dormitories to make sure everyone ate dinner and studied. Then they went over attendance records and personal finances. After study time, they checked that everyone washed themselves and their shoes, and inquired about the health of everyone in their group. They were responsible for anyone arriving to work the next morning tired or dishevelled. Thus, they carefully patrolled the hallways after lights out at 9:15 p.m. They could go home only when "their group is completely calm." Helping the *vychovatels* were "captains," Young Men selected to be the leaders within their sleeping quarters. They had the task of "keeping order and cleanliness" and maintaining their room's "honour." Maintaining honour largely meant ensuring that no alcohol, girls, or gambling went on in the room.[91]

Housing was central to the project of shaping a loyal cadre of young employees with the necessary skill sets. Accordingly, the company built carefully designed dormitories between 1929 and 1937. The construction project followed a common pattern seen in Zlín: local resistance, Bat'a persistence, and eventual triumph by the company. In 1929, the local aristocratic family, the Haupts, refused to allow the company to buy the land to build the dormitories on their large, and increasingly surrounded, estate. The struggle between aristocracy and industry in Zlín ended in a total Bat'a victory when the company, through the auspices of the city, bought all of the land as well as the noble estate house within the year.[92] Having gained ownership of the land, Bat'a began building the campus for its new workers. The eight dormitories exemplified the Bat'a architectural style: large rectangular structures made of iron, red brick, and glass whose proportions were all based on the Bat'a standard size of 6.15 by 6.15 metres. The dormitories made up a profoundly functionalist campus, with six thousand inhabitants living in a tightly packed area within an easy walk to the factory. Life in this mini-city was characterized by strict rules, tight surveillance, and an almost non-stop schedule of events.

Students wore specific outfits on special days in the Bat'a calendar and followed a strict dress code while in the factories. Likewise, the company regulated what students listened to. Radios, installed throughout the factory in the early 1930s, made their way into the dormitories in 1937 at Jan's order: "Put a special radio in all of the bedrooms so that we can speak to the Young Men after the curfew whistle." As the radios could not be turned off by the students, Young Men had no choice but to listen to the company announcements.[93]

The adolescents who entered the BSP program also had to agree to limited company control over their own finances. Regulating students' bank accounts was perhaps the most effective method of control of them all. In addition, guardians carefully monitored spending so as to eliminate frivolity. In fact, the company required the *vychovatel*s to keep track of five separate forms regarding their charges' finances. These consisted of a general account of all expenses and income, and specific forms related to borrowing, lodging, school accounts, and wages.[94] A student could be written up and possibly expelled for improper spending, such as the purchase of expensive jewellery.

According to the company's accounts, the guardians and their captain helpers were remarkably successful at their jobs. On a schoolwide inspection for cleanliness and order in 1939, for example, each of the twenty-one groups of Young Men in one of the dormitories achieved a mark of 95 per cent or higher. The success was the result of a policy of collective responsibility, and the company's ability to find highly disciplined men to become *vychovatel*s. In fact, the Czechoslovak military contributed several to their ranks. A former general, lieutenant, and captain could be found among the *vychovatel*s.[95] Strict discipline was a clear priority.

Despite such discipline, dormitory life elicited considerable loyalty and nostalgia on the part of many who experienced it. Stanislav Štětkář, a Young Man from 1937 to 1941, has written perhaps the fullest account of life in the dormitories.[96] In his memoir, he details a life almost constantly in movement, and with very little privacy. He is overwhelmingly positive about his time as a Young Man, as are most others who have written memoirs about the experience. The strict discipline led to a lifelong shrewdness with money, Štětkář writes, and a solid work ethic.

František Šumpela's story is similar to that of Štětkář. Šumpela entered the BSP in 1934 and specialized in tanning. He quickly rose to the position of manager, and then general director, which allowed him the opportunity for travel abroad. Later in life Šumpela became an outspoken advocate for the Bat'a philosophy, participating and organizing numerous events for the Club of Bat'a School Alumni.[97] For him, the BSP provided an iron discipline that served him well during the vicissitudes of the twentieth century. Being a student in the BSP for many years created an affection and a nostalgia for the Bat'a system that survives today.[98]

Life in the dormitories did not create total conformity of course. Antonín Vavra, a young man from Strážnice who graduated from the BSP in 1930, was fired from the company in 1934 for insubordination. According to his *vychovatel*, when asked to write an essay about the principles of a *Batovec* for incoming students, Vavra replied, "I am a *Batovec*, but I am not going to write this because it is stupid (*blbost*)."[99] There was also a steady stream of petty thefts. As the young students' schedules were highly predictable, thieves regularly pilfered their valuables while they were at work. Many of these crimes proved impossible to solve. The thieves that were caught usually turned out to be students.[100] One of the worst of them, Rudolf Paták, a former Young Man from the neighbouring village of Klečůvka, was caught by police after witnesses saw him trying to open a dresser in one of the rooms of a dormitory. Police later found over 6,000 crowns' worth of stolen goods in his room at his parent's house.[101] For others, life as a Young Man or Woman did not produce outright defiance, but a deep ambivalence about the entire experience. Madla Vaculíková, in an interview with Pavel Kosatík in 2002, commented that living as a Young Woman in Zlín "was terribly unfree, like the worst kind of military experience."[102]

Life in the BSP, then, produced a complex array of memories among its alumni. On one hand, it allowed a generation of youth the chance to live, work, and study under the protection of a uniquely successful company – it was a way out of the poverty of rural life. On the other, students had to sacrifice privacy and freedom of choice – sublimating their individuality for employment. While everyone came under the company's gaze in the city of Zlín, the young adults at the Bat'a School of Work experienced a level of control far more intensive than the rest of the populace. From mandatory radio hours to the company's tight grip on their personal finances, the experience allowed few moments of individual freedom. This level of control, however, did not translate to widespread unhappiness and revolt. In fact, the young people in the dormitories were often energetic partners in Bat'a's educational project. They volunteered for tasks and kept watch on potential troublemakers, and many would later join the alumni club of the BSP, the Klub absolventů Baťovy Školy Práce (ABS), cultivating the Bat'a myth.

Figure 6.3. Young Women perform a rhythmic gymnastic routine in 1933. Moravský zemský archiv v Brně, Státní okresní archiv Zlín, Sbírka fotografií Zlín, sign. 152, obálka č. 14364.

Interestingly, the rigour of the BSP was not enough for Jan. In 1937 he further stratified the educational system by founding the Tomášov School. It was based on the English public school model as well as on the increasingly sophisticated organizational models of upper and middle management. Tomášov was supposed to be more elite than the BSP, a kind of executive training program for the best and brightest Young Men. There would never be more than sixty students in the program, all men and all recruited from the first-year students of the BSP. Predictably, women were not permitted as students in Tomášov.

The adolescents picked for the inaugural class were a carefully selected group of outstanding students, and the company's expectations for them were tremendous:

They will have to work hard in order to reach their desired station. Just being in this institution does not assure them of a leadership role.

In the Tomášov there will be fun. Fun and joyful youth. So, for example, every student of this school must learn how to play tennis or cricket, golf and polo. They have to know how to fly a plane and drive a car – as well as to drive a motorcycle and a carriage with a pair of horses.

They have to master two languages outside of their mother tongue and become moderately proficient in another.

They have to be a person who is not aligned with the proletariat in their feelings or in their thoughts, but one who believes in their own strength, in the strength of their character.

And they have to do all of these things on their own initiative.[103]

The most ambitious of all of the company's education projects, the new leadership academy sought to engineer future leaders as modern-day renaissance men. Tomáš Bat'a's only child, Tomas Jr., fit the bill and became the public face of Batism. As he began his life as a Young Man in the early 1930s, he came to be the embodiment of the Bat'a ideal: a sportsman, worker, and leader who spoke foreign languages and maintained a well-groomed appearance at all times. The records from Tomášov's *vychovatel*, Rudolf Hub, provide an intimate look at the lives of the best of the best. Hub's reports are, not surprisingly, filled with glowing reviews, and show a tight-knit group that had a remarkable work ethic and athleticism. The group regularly trounced other sports teams from the surrounding area, including teams of adult factory workers.[104] Their prowess was due to physical attributes used as criteria for acceptance, the closeness of the group, and impressive opportunities for physical activity. In one week in February of 1940 the group had a boxing tournament, a table tennis tournament, and a ski outing.[105] Not all the workers could be so lucky, of course, to have even been the right age to be considered for such a school.

To guide the workers who were too old to benefit from the BSP or the Tomášov, the company established the Pedagogic Department in 1935. This department was headed by a former schoolmaster, Antonín Grác, who was an unabashed *Batovci* in his ideas of the future. "We in Zlín feel very strongly and clearly that the purpose of life is to progress in many different ways toward the path of perfection. Illuminating human understanding and strengthening the collective will create infinite progress in all fields of human endeavour and enterprise."[106] With their lofty goal of human perfection, the department went about offering a staggering number of "educational opportunities" for adults from 1935 to 1939. In six months in 1938, for example, the department oversaw 183 events for 5,924 people.[107] The courses were offered at a nominal cost, typically ten crowns per course. These courses were mostly technical; there were very few offerings in the liberal arts. It was as if the *Batovci* were not at all interested in teaching the past to their adult employees. Instead, the stress was on modernity, scientific principles, and the rationalization of industry and society. Still, the courses offered a way for workers to obtain a very affordable education on everything from "hygiene" to human behaviour and hydroelectricity.[108]

Another key addition to the educational landscape was the Private Foreign Language School in Zlín. While technically private, and therefore largely filled with the children of the managerial class, it operated under the direct supervision of the company, which made it really another extension of the municipal educational system. Its purpose was to give certain elite members of the community the chance to immerse their children in foreign language instruction. At its founding in 1934, the four-year school's languages of instruction were English, French, and German.[109] Upon entering the school in the fifth grade, the student had to pick one of the languages and would thereafter receive almost all instruction in that language. The only courses that would be taught in Czech were Czechoslovak language, religion, civil affairs, and homemaking. In 1936, a total of 212 students were in the school, 86 in English, 32 in French, and 89 in German. These students would, of course, become excellent candidates for the Bat'a School of Work, which highly prized foreign language skills.[110]

One year after the establishment of the Private Foreign Language School, the city created the Professional School for the Female Sex. The school recruited poor young women who "haven not had luck with their education."[111] These were women, age sixteen and older, who had very little chance of making it into the School of Work or a local high school. The school functioned as a kind of auxiliary for the company's welfare program, as it strove to train women in childcare, home economics, cooking, and healthcare. The goal was to turn the future wives of workers into capable housewives. To this end the school offered schooling for work in the home: three-month, five-month, and two-year programs. For Ladislav Vlček, the director of the school, the purpose of the short three- and five-month programs was to provide "all of the girls and women who have not had luck in the women's schools with a chance to learn the basic knowledge and expertise needed to become managers of the modern household in the shortest amount of time possible."[112] The three-month program was almost entirely designed around taking care of children, while the five-month program had a few extra courses in sewing, language, and physical fitness.

The BSP, the Masarýk School, the Professional School for the Female Sex, the Foreign Language School, and the adult education classes all served to create an educational atmosphere unique to Czechoslovakia, one in which self-improvement through company-approved curricula was available to almost all strata of society. By extending Batism into local schools, the company tried to ensure that the populace would embrace its values and be able to join its workforce, or become wives and mothers, with the necessary skills already in hand.

In Bat'a's Zlín, nationalism was muted by the desire to create a workforce capable of doing business around the world. Students, like managers, needed to be world citizens. This led to an unusually international education in Zlín: trilingualism was expected, international students were recruited, and Young Men and Women were trained to go abroad. Of course, those students who were not among the elite BSP students had fewer global options but were nevertheless subject to a wide-ranging experiment in education as the company took control of all public and private schools in the area. The quest to capture students' souls was no less important to the *Batovci* than it was to the nationalists. [113] In the linear, future-oriented ideology of Bataism, youth were to move far beyond their parents' horizons as they harnessed technology, embraced a rational way of life, and put aside national differences to compete economically in the world. While other pedagogues in other parts of Czechoslovakia struggled to organize children into nationalist cadres, Batism strove to remake them into new industrial humans, whose rhythms would be synchronized with the fast pace of the factory and the movements of their fellow workers.

Conclusion

On 25 November 1937, thirteen uniformed officers, two plainclothes officers, and one "assistant officer" patrolled the public spaces of Czechoslovakia's pre-eminent company town. All of them were white Czech-speaking men. All but one was between the ages of twenty-five and forty. They had an average of four and a half years' experience on the force. Their day was typical: the men tracked down beggars, arrested a "professional hobo," wrote up reports of items stolen from the workers' dormitory, and "shoved out" a twenty-year-old male from the city for crimes unknown.[114] At the end of the day, when filing the daily report, police commissioner Jaroslav Durdík added a slight reprimand to those who brought in an incarcerated individual the day before and did not immediately file a report with the chief social inspector. [115]

Meanwhile, five men in the employ of the Bat'a Company walked through the residential and commercial spaces of the town, "visiting" workers' families in their two-storey semi-detached homes, listening to conversations in the street, and carefully marking down their observations. These men, the personal inspectors (*osobní inspektory*), took notes on everything from carpets to literature that day, remarking on family relationships and neighbourhood gossip.[116] On the front line of the company's drive to engineer *Batovci*, their job was to carefully watch for signs of any transgression of the Bat'a ideals of sobriety, loyalty, cleanliness, frugality, and industriousness. Furthermore, they were expected to report on transgressions against a gender order constructed from traditional Moravian paternalism as well as Midwestern values (Bat'a's inspiration was, after all, Henry Ford), letting company executives know of illicit affairs, family discord, and marital problems among their workers. Their reports could lead to the loss of someone's home, job, and residence card; however, these inspectors mostly served as roaming counsellors, giving out advice, trying to save marriages, and doling out money to workers' families in need.[117] Their work was largely concerned with long-time skilled workers who were privileged by the company; most workers did not live in the well-appointed semi-detached company houses that the personal inspectors visited. The majority of the workforce lived in large dormitories, under the even more watchful gaze of building and floor managers, the *vychovatel*s, who had twenty-four-hour access to every room, and a mandate to remove all workers who drank, engaged in sex, or broke curfew.[118]

Clearly by 1937, the Bat'a Company had turned Zlín into one of the most tightly regulated towns in interwar Europe, where the task of policing the social order was spread throughout the community, and informants, everyday inspections, and frequent expulsions had become normalized. Furthermore, the ability of the company to "own" space, to encourage self-regulation through wage and housing incentives, and to regulate their workforce with technologies of control such as timecards, personnel cards, and radios, coupled with the fact that the company remained under the administration of state authorities in Brno and Prague, led to a markedly non-violent (at least in the physical sense) society. Indeed, the city had one of the lowest violent crime rates in Czechoslovakia, and, after sifting through some seventeen years of company and city police records, my research discovered only three cases of police brutality.[119] Hence, as Zlín became Europe's pre-eminent utopian industrial town, its policing became increasingly sophisticated, using surveillance in place of force. And yet, was this surveillance network effective in eliminating dissent? Was Zlín so controlled?

For on that same day in November, one would likely find communists printing illegal fliers in cramped apartments, drunks gathered at bars, including Máca's notorious watering hole, workers showing up late to the factories, vagrants begging, people engaged in scandalous affairs, and Roma playing *pod skořapku* (shell game) on the street.[120] In addition, prostitutes plied their trade in unlicensed rooms and groups of the unemployed slept in makeshift camps in the forests.[121] Thus, no matter how omnipresent the company seemed, the multivalent desires of the human soul muddied the Bat'a executives' drive to create the "new industrial man."

At first glance, these stories from the social engineers of Zlín seem insignificant. But when unpacked, stories about the policing of communists, alcoholics, prostitutes, beggars, vagrants, and "gypsies," along with those about the education and the inspection of workers, reveal a wealth of information about who was a threat to the utopian city and what measures the authorities would take in order to remove them. While we see a company town very much involved in a high modernist project, trying to engineer a rationalized society, we also see the people and spaces that eluded the forces of law and order. For life in the company town was not always under the gaze of the company, nor was it free from everyday sin. Still, one wonders what life would have been like for the people of Zlín had there been no way around the Bat'a system, if all of Czechoslovakia had embraced the high modernist mentality of the company. If policing the kingdom of shoes was continually frustrated by the elements beyond company control and the influences from the rest of Czechoslovak society, then surely the removal of those elements would have resulted in an even more tightly monitored society. And that seems to be what followed when Bat'a principles metamorphosed into governmental principles after the Munich Agreement of 1938, when key personnel of the company became key personnel of the state.

"Everyone Gives Their Soul to Their Country," 1937–1939

On 11 February 1937, the National Committee of Fascists held a public meeting in Zlín. Some four hundred people gathered in the events hall of the Hotel Založna to hear three speeches about "the economy, a politically strong national state, and the defence of the nation."[1] A long-time *Batovec*, František Jaroš, chaired the event and gave the opening remarks. He attacked Hitler for his "dirty propaganda" while praising Jan Baťa for his "courageous" trip around the world (which was currently in progress). He singled out Baťa's recent favourable comments about Italy published in the company newspaper only two weeks prior to the meeting. To Jaroš, Jan's words were proof of the righteousness of the fascist cause. Jan's admiration for what was going on in Italy energized the local fascist, who clearly felt that the *Batovci* would be swayed by the movement. Regardless of Jaroš's appeal to Baťa loyalty, however, it seemed most in the room were less than overwhelmed by his speech. To one of the three undercover city police agents who were writing all of this down, Jaroš's brief speech "proved he was not much of a speaker."[2]

Jaroš yielded to the next presenter, an operative of the organization from Prague, Alois Šlechta. Šlechta peppered his speech with comments about eliminating the "foreign" capital of the Jews and Germans in the country. He was as combative as he was anti-Semitic: "Šlechta called the Jews slaves to foreign capital and was really upset that people in the crowd had said that fascism was funded by the Jews. He called all of those decrying his leadership capitalism's workhands."[3] Many in the crowd reacted and "shouted him down" at several points. He shouted back so loudly that he began coughing, and Jaroš had to return to the podium to continue the lectures.

The next speaker, a professor Kalus from Uherské Hradiště, fared a little better, but then "general" Radola Gajda walked onto the stage in the middle of Kalus's speech, sat down right in front of the podium "and smiled." The shouting from the crowd began again. Eventually, the postmaster of Zlín, a Mr. Rozehnal, got on the stage to intervene. "Look, friends, am I a fascist?,"

Rozehnal reportedly asked the rowdy audience. "You know well enough that I am no fascist. Leave the speaker alone and let him finish his speech." Kalus continued, managing to quiet the crowd with what one undercover police officer referred to as "beautiful words."[4]

The keynote speaker, Radola Gajda, then took the podium. Gajda was a former legionnaire who had become the face of the Czech fascist movement. His was the speech that the crowd came to hear. And, at least according to the police officer reporting on the meeting, he delivered.

> Czechoslovak fascism calls for a reformation because today's leaders in government are completely incapable and unwilling to help all strata of workers. In producing results in getting all capital into Czechoslovak hands, we have Bat'a as a leading example. Bat'a is very wealthy but watches out so that all have work and are rightly honoured for it. If there was no Bat'a, today everyone would pay three times as much for a pair of shoes.
>
> It is truly regrettable that there are so few examples like Bat'a in the Czechoslovak Republic. Just think if all the capital and national wealth were in the hands of people like Bat'a instead of the Jews and Germans, who steal our national wealth.[5]

Gajda added how the country needed to flex its military muscles in the face of Nazi aggression. Then he referred directly to Jan Bat'a's recent letters from Italy, which had celebrated fascism's accomplishments there. "Jan Bat'a has seen what fascism can do."[6]

The meeting concluded with further animosity. During the question-and-answer session, two known communists stood up to speak. Before they could get a word out, Jaroš exclaimed, "livestock will not be allowed to dirty this place. Communists are swine and not people."[7] A deafening roar went up from the crowd. Whistles and shouting blasted Jaroš, who then left the stage with the rest of the speakers. The hall emptied and the event ended with no further incidents. It was a full house, and police estimated perhaps 120 of the 400 attendees were pro-fascist.[8]

Even though many were there to protest, the large turnout revealed the effect of Jan Bat'a's letters from Italy. Published two weeks before the event at the Založna, they signified Jan's turn toward politics – and toward nationalism. They also marked the beginning of a phase in Jan's life that would profoundly differentiate him from his half-brother Tomáš – a turn toward fascism.

The Path of Fascism

At the beginning of 1937, Jan decided to set off on his own globe-trotting mission, mirroring that of Tomáš's in 1932. Travelling by air, Jan mostly followed the route of Tomáš, from North Africa to India and Southeast Asia, but went further by adding China, Japan, and the United States to the itinerary. It promised a true circumnavigation of the world, perhaps the first such trip by air by a chief executive. Jan would be gone for slightly over four months. He planned his arrival to coincide with the annual May Day celebration. During the journey, he reported back to Zlín with weekly updates. His first updates came from Italy.

Two of his letters from Italy were meant for publication, and one was meant only for specific directors. All of them contained unabashed admiration for the projects he witnessed and the government that was funding them.

His first article, "In Turin," marvelled at the "path" of fascism: "It is a path to greatness and patriotism. Chiefly [the fascists] are building a new man. They instil pride not in ideas but in his own work and that of his nation. Not for freedom, but for decency ... The people walk on clean streets. They are building train stations, hospitals, schools, streets."[9] The *autostrada* from Turin to Milan, a recently completed stretch of the national Italian motorway system, especially impressed him: "It is important, this *autostrada*. It is a service to the public."[10]

The next week Jan dispatched a longer piece for the company newspaper that provided another enthusiastic endorsement of fascism. The first section compared Italy's massive project to dry out the Pontine Marshes with the Czechoslovak government's stalled plan to dry out the black marshland of Otrokovice: "In the words of President Beneš democracy is a dynamic force. But [left to him clearing the Otrokovice marshland] would have never happened."[11] Jan wrote that the Bat'a Company itself cleared the land and it was the only organization in the country that could do so efficiently. He ended the section with a quote from Tomáš: "We will not run away from water like some rabbits."

The article then went on to discuss the Italian government.

> The government in Italy pretends like it's a tailor constructing something for the land ... everything revolves around factories, industries, and construction ... There is no, or hardly any, unemployment as the whole endeavour takes the entire work force. They know neither strikes nor social strife – and everyone gives their soul to their country, to Italy.

Jan ended his praise of the fascist order, however, with something unique to the *Batovci* – a statement of national indifference. "We do not want to conquer the world and rule it, and we are not the sons and daughters of lords ... our goal and our position in the world is not to rule over people, but to serve people. All people, regardless of their nationality, religion, language, race, or origin."[12] The conclusion is strange, as if Jan had forgotten his audience for most of his letter, including a nod to the *Batovci*'s commitment to national indifference only at the very end.

Outside of the two articles, Jan sent a private note to four Bat'a directors. It stated quite simply, "Mussolini is a teacher."[13] The letter praised the fascist leader's vision for national education, and, moreover, his ability to inculcate individualism. Jan even drew inspiration from Mussolini's imperialism. "Our children can be a bit more imperialistic. But they and their collective – the nation – will succeed in this world only if they understand that each one of them depends on each other realizing that they are responsible for carrying out the tasks we ask of them for the nation."[14] In other words, young people should act nationally as empire builders for a global company.

Jan's flirtation with fascism took place amid widespread anxiety over the political situation in Europe. Hitler's rise to power had changed the mood across the country, which was still struggling to recover from the economic depression. A clear external threat and ongoing unemployment pushed many away from the political establishment in Prague, and Czechs and Germans in Bohemia began to turn on each other with remarkable speed.[15]

Within the Czech-speaking political realm there was a unity not seen since independence in 1918. Czech fascists were fiercely opposed to Germany, as were the Social Democrats, National Socialists, Communists, and so on. Political debates in the Czech language in 1937–8 centred on strengthening the nation, not on rationalization or cosmopolitanism. The changing political context lent itself to a reformation of Bat'a in the nationalists' imagination and moved the *Batovci* closer to national identification. The move happened quickly. After all, as late as 1936 nationalist groups were lined up to protest Bat'a's rationalization and globalization. Now it was a talking point for the most rabidly nationalist group in the country, Gajda's National Committee of Fascists. In one year, Bat'a had come a long way.

Two and a half months after the fascists' event in Zlín, and on the biggest day in the Bat'a calendar, May Day, the company publishing house, Zlín, released Jan's book *We Will Build a State for 40,000,000*. The book signalled Jan's ambitions to enter into national politics. Released to coincide with Jan's return from his world tour and the now famous Bat'a May Day celebration, the book argued for massive public works projects, much like those in the United States, Italy, the Soviet Union, and Germany, to improve the country's transportation infrastructure and unite a regionally divided state. Jan intended his book for a wide audience, filling it with finely drawn maps and colourful graphs. Written in a simple, direct style, *We Will Build a State* marked a dramatic leap onto the national stage for Jan's evolving concept of Batism.[16]

While not a huge commercial success, the book reached fourth place on the Czechoslovak nonfiction bestseller list in 1937.[17] It caught the attention of certain newspapers and received some positive reviews.[18] Mostly, though, the major publications of the day, like *Lidové Noviny*, neglected to review the book. Jan Bat'a was making headway within Czechoslovak political discourse, but not as quickly as he would have liked.[19] Still, the book offered a clear plan for the future:

> Our plan to build a state has two categories of reforms. The first is related to technical aspects, while the second concerns administration ...
>
> The technical category deals with building superhighways (*magistrály*) and canals, harnessing hydroelectric power, organizing research into natural wealth, expanding trade and business schools, reforming train and automobile links, building airports, and expanding telephone services and radio.
>
> The administration category consists of reforms of the basic laws of business, consolidating the legal aspects of taxes on trade, and providing a fixed currency. Here we understandably request a modern and flexible business administration, one that is accountable to the leaders of the citizens and responsible for the outcomes of its decisions, as well as new business schools that are oriented to an export economy.
>
> The purpose of building this state is to end unemployment and unify the state so that we can perfect a strategy of economic union, and finally guide the economy to grow so that the next generation of citizens will find a wealthy, strong Czechoslovakia of forty million citizens.[20]

The accessible and visually appealing book, which went into a second printing, laid out Baťa's political platform: lower taxes for a more technologically advanced society, with better railways and more air links; technical and administrative reforms; business school reforms; and revival of the "Old Tradesman's Council."[21] Rumours began to circulate about a potential place for Jan in government, but these seemed to be contained within the right.[22]

While Jan aspired to increased national presence, the company in 1937 planned for two major exhibits to open the next year in Prague and Zlín. The exhibits, named "Baťa's Plan for an Ideal City," aimed to convince Czechoslovaks of the wisdom of the Baťa system – and for its expansion within Czechoslovakia. They featured a fifteen-square-metre model of the factory complex and immediate neighbourhoods of Zlín, along with large displays of infrastructure plans for all of Czechoslovakia along the lines of Jan's book. Slogans and brochures on the Baťa way of life accompanied the displays. These promised a "future of the industrial man" that would mean better working conditions and higher wages through mechanization: "We are seeing how this age of machines can make mankind king of the earth."[23]

While these exhibits were planned, the *Batovci* assembled a lengthy manual for internal company use that laid out the principles of Batism. The manual was entitled "The Ideal Industrial Town of the Future" (*Ideální průmyslové město budoucnosti*). Running to some four hundred pages, the manual was remarkably comprehensive. In its vision it collated the ideas of key thinkers such as Henry Ford, George F. Johnson, Richard Coudenhove-Kalergi, and provided precise directions on how to build the perfect factory town: "It would be in the shape of a fan or leaf, with the leaf stalk heading toward the entrance to the plant."[24]It also discussed the importance of media, such as telephone lines, radio stations, cinemas, and even television. As the scholar Petr Szczepanik has written, "media was the key to the internal and external function [of the ideal factory town]." For it allowed the company to remind workers of the factory rules, provide advice on social questions, connect with satellite towns, and "propagate Bat'a principles in the wider world."[25] What is perhaps most impressive about the manual is its unwavering confidence in a carefully planned industrial future.

It was this confidence that animated the company's advertising that was embedded in all of the large marketing projects of the mid to late 1930s. In the five years from 1934 to 1939, Bat'a funded nineteen major displays, ranging from airplane trade shows to a massive poster project in the Moravian countryside.[26] While these exhibits intended to increase brand recognition and impress customers, they also propagated the Bat'a philosophy. All of them evinced a future made better by machines. With the book, the exhibits, and the manual, the *Batovci* were increasingly looking to themselves as a solution to the world's economic and political problems.

In 1937 Batism was not the same ideology that it was in 1932, though it went by the same name. It was still a brand of industrial paternalism along the lines of Fordism, a system in which workers were given relatively good wages, healthcare, education, and housing in exchange for loyalty and obedience. It still held to a teleological view of technology and a belief that machines would overcome the limitations of both factory and domestic labour. Furthermore, the ideal city was still to be thoroughly rationalized and every section of the city to be designed by urban planners and city officials. Work was still central. All other aspects of city life were still to emanate outward from the factory complex along broad, well-paved streets. The "Garden City" philosophy was maintained. So too, was Frederick Winslow Taylor's philosophy of time management. Indeed, modern life was still to be organized down to the second.[27] By 1937, though, new sources of inspiration had been added and one was dangerously fading. Bat'a liberally added to Fordism and Taylorism Italian fascist ideas, notions of British gentlemanliness, and even concepts from the Soviet Stakhanovite movement into the porridge of Batism.[28] The most distinctive tenet of Batism, that nationalism would fade as men organized around economic competition, remained. However, this attitude of national indifference proved to be the most fragile piece of the ideology. From 1937 onward, nationalism increasingly crept into the frame. This development pulled at Batism's global future. The tension this caused began to twist the ideology into a complicated blend of nationalist and nationally indifferent rhetoric.

Ideological principles can of course be toned down by reality, and this happened in Zlín as it did elsewhere. But the ideology on display in the Baťa world headquarters of Zlín, its satellite towns, its leaders' books and articles, and its exhibitions remained robust in 1937. The collage clearly showed that, to Baťa, competition was essential, the leader's will was unquestioned, and modern man was rationalized through order, function, and technology. As chief company propagandist, Antonín Cekota, wrote during the height of the Great Depression:

> Today, when all the world is uncertain, unsatisfied and on edge, our Zlín stands like an island from another world. An island on which crowds of visitors wander so that they may witness with their own eyes the truth of our reputation and the bounty of our work, which brings wealth and satisfaction ... Assertiveness, determination, the taste for work, the battle for first place, the competition for the best result, this is not a slogan but a fact which directly charges the air of Zlín.[29]

Thus, for the *Batovci*, future success seemed to depend on the expansion of the Zlín model throughout the world. And while Batism changed over time, one of its constants was futurism, with Tomáš Baťa's maxim in 1932 guiding the way: "The future will be better than the present, but only for those who have confidence in the future."[30]

The Nationalist Present

The problem was that the future seemed to be turning ever further from the Baťa vision of a global market, one in which companies could operate wherever and for whomever. And Baťa could not avoid becoming embroiled in nationalism, particularly after 1935, when the tense political situation in Czechoslovakia brought national divisions to the forefront of company concerns. The national election year of 1935 saw the Sudeten German Party (SdP) of Konrad Henlein win the most votes, 14.7 per cent overall. The SdP, consisting largely of German speakers from the borderland areas of the country, demanded autonomy for those areas. Additionally, Hlinka's Slovakian People's Party, allied with other Slovak nationalist groups in a "Autonomy Bloc," captured the most votes in Slovakia by a wide margin. They too demanded autonomy from Prague.[31] Though neither party could form a majority to govern the country, their mandates – especially that of the SdP – emboldened their nationalist-minded constituents. By 1937, the peripheries of Czechoslovakia were aggressively pushing separationist agendas.

In response, for the first time in the history of the company, executives requested all managers to report on the nationality of their employees. The non-Czech employees' responses were at times accompanied by a short description of their loyalty from their managers: "Rayonista #20308, Becker, Helmüt, arrived from Germany in 1935, not a Henleinist."[32] The move to scrutinize nationality revealed the heightened pitch of nationalist discourse.

The tallies, of which only partial records remain, show that the workforce in Zlín was overwhelmingly Czech, some 92 per cent, but with a significant number of Germans, Slovaks, and Ruthenians (Rusyns) working in retail stores throughout Czechoslovakia.[33] Of course, each factory abroad was filled with workers of the predominant nationality, with a handful of Czechoslovaks (here the company did not differentiate between Slovaks and Czechs) in leadership positions. At home and abroad, Czechoslovaks dominated management. Only three of the eighty-nine top executives of 1937 were not Czechoslovak citizens, and only one was of a nationality other than "Czechoslovak." Two managers, Rudolf Chlud and John Hoza, had American citizenship but claimed Czech nationality.[34] Indeed, in spite of the internationalist rhetoric and outlook of the *Batovci*, throughout the Second World War the upper echelons of the company continued to be "an essentially Czechoslovakian team."[35]

Still, there were managers who continued to reject nationalist demands. Antonín Cekota, for one, remained an unwavering voice for Bat'a cosmopolitanism even in the middle of the nationalist fervour. In a speech given to top management in October 1937, Cekota ordered his press corps to continue to appeal to citizens of the world: "Do not support chauvinism and do not give it any space in the newspapers. Our work serves all of the people of the world and cooperates with all nations. Give space to that which brings people together and connects people as people."[36] Such cosmopolitanism proved a useful sentiment to the Bat'a elite in the coming chaos of Nazi occupation. However, the events of 1938 would make it difficult for the largely Czech company to remain a citizen of the world.

In the first month of the year Zlín plunged into darkness with scheduled blackouts and air defence drills.[37] The town's cinemas started a new tradition by preceding every movie with a short patriotic clip showing President Beneš in front of the Czechoslovak flag. A newspaper editorial reminded its readers that "honouring the flag is honouring everyone around us; honouring the flag makes a statement that we can trust each other."[38] Patriotic appeals to defend the nation could be found everywhere one looked.

Some of those appeals were more bizarre than others. Also in January, Jan suggested the capital be moved from Prague to the East Moravian, and German-speaking, border town of Javorník. It was the best way to defend the nation, he thought, because no foreign power would ask the country to give up its capital.[39] After presenting this idea that went nowhere, Jan turned to social engineering when he gave a widely publicized speech that called for the country to build new "Czechoslovak people." Jan gave the speech while receiving an honorary doctorate from the Edvard Beneš Technical College in Brno – he would go on to use his honorary title for the rest of his life. The speech, with its orientation toward the future, was a classic statement of Batism: "We have to make [the new citizens] from the collective, from the masses ... we have to teach them new things. What do you think makes us successful in Zlín? ... Our success lies in the Czechoslovak people. We have liberated them from the aristocrats' feudal obligations, from the proletariat and the past where they crouched behind their stoves. We have made from them world citizens that are not afraid of people and the world, people who know that they can do anything because they want to do it."[40] Despite such statements and proposals, there was plenty to be afraid of in the world during the spring of 1938.

The Anschluss, the aggressive absorption of the Austrian state into the Third Reich, led to another noticeable crack to the company's national indifference. As Martin Wein's *The History of the Jews in the Bohemian Lands* points out, one of the immediate effects of the Anschluss was Czechoslovakia's complete reversal of its asylum policy; thousands of desperate refugees were turned away at its border.[41] Romania had already begun persecuting its Jewish population after a right-wing takeover in January, sending thousands of people into Czechoslovakia's easternmost state of Subcarpathian Ruthenia. With the swastika flying over Vienna, tens of thousands of Christians and Jews now tried to move into Czechoslovakia from Austria. State authorities, along with many influential public intellectuals, felt that the entry of a flood of people, enemies of the Nazi state, would create a dangerous situation within the country.[42] Borders across Central Europe were changing and hardening.

Jan Bat'a made no public statement on the situation in the first few months of 1938, but privately began imagining a future outside of Czechoslovakia, somewhere on a seacoast. General manager Hugo Vavrečka reported on Jan's ruminations sometime in the spring of 1938:

> Jan wanted to build a new enterprise somewhere along a coastline, because it appeared to him that the development of Zlín was getting close to its end and further economic expansion and improvement of the business in Czechoslovakia was no longer possible to do from Zlín, but only from foreign lands, where there is plenty of raw material, skins, rubber, cotton ... He therefore wished to move the seat of the company to the coast, but in the meantime he had to think about how to keep Zlín in reliable hands.[43]

Impending conflict notwithstanding, the company had considerable assets to fund such a move. Bat'a continued to increase its production at home and abroad and its sales expanded worldwide. At the beginning of 1938, the Zlín parent company alone had 526.2 million crowns in equity capital and 412.8 million crowns in reserve funds.[44] Long the largest shoe company in Europe, two years earlier the company took over the top spot in the world from the St.

Louis–based International Shoe Company. Moreover, the company had gone through major diversification, and was now producing tires, toys, stockings, electric motors, and airplanes. In short, Baťa had enough liquidity and assets to undertake a major geographical shift.

While Jan plotted to build the "new Zlín," Baťa's famous May Day celebration went ahead as scheduled. The 1938 event set a record, in fact; some 65,000 people participated and tens of thousands more came as onlookers. It was again a spectacle of uniformity and optimism. The personnel department put on an exhibit entitled "Future of Industrial Man" in the newly opened "21," Zlín's, and one of Central Europe's, first skyscrapers. The exhibit, a chronological depiction of the working man from ancient times to the present, declared triumphantly that "this new era's revolutionary culture of the machine has liberated man from difficult physical labour."[45] Jan's speech crowning the day's events was full of praise for the culture of Zlín.

> We have taken the best ideas and orders from the world and brought them to Zlín and adapted them to its needs.
>
> In Zlín you will find today elements of capitalism, but without the defects of capitalism.
>
> You will find elements of humanism, but without sentimentality and weakness.
>
> Elements of collectivism, but without collectivism's irresponsibility.
>
> Elements of individualism, but without the criminal selfishness.[46]

Jan's speech coincided with the city's growth into "Greater Zlín." A few weeks after May Day, Zlín incorporated five smaller surrounding villages and "rationalized" administration for the Dřevnice Valley. The number of people serving on municipal councils dropped from 150 people to 42.[47]

The local vote to incorporate was indicative of what was happening to the Zlín culture Jan had, intentionally or not, eulogized in his speech. The culture was being overwhelmed by nationalist feelings, which were accelerated by external threats. Czechoslovakia instituted readiness drills, which would soon include gas masks, and issued a partial mobilization of its military in May. These developments further infused the citizens of the city with nationalist fervour and instilled in Czechoslovaks across political lines a sense of togetherness. During the partial mobilization, the efficiency and high morale of the troops impressed observers, who concluded that, with the exception of the Henleinists, the country was united in its fight against Germany.[48]

Such observations were not entirely correct. Around the same time as the partial mobilization, Jan was hosting Alberto Pirelli, a major Italian industrialist and recent addition to Mussolini's cabinet, in Zlín. The visit incensed President Beneš, who saw it as more than just business. His relationship with Jan cooled.[49]

A few months later, as the crisis with Germany reached its tipping point, the government issued a full mobilization. This time, the city prepared for war, and Jan did not entertain controversial fascist visitors or make suggestions to move the capital. No one seemed to panic. "Zlín is used to organization," the Zlín paper read.[50] War, while absolutely the worst possible outcome for a global shoe empire, was not something the city or company would ignore. In the build-up, Bat'a fired employees considered to be "German" with remarkable speed. Between 27 and 29 September, it let go 504 of these "Germans."[51] Most of these employees were German speakers in the Sudeten areas, Czechoslovakia's fortified borderlands. These areas held considerable industrial capital and a great number of German speakers – many of whom favoured Germany over Czechoslovakia in the coming conflict. War seemed inevitable.

On 29 September 1938, the editor of the company newspaper, Antonín Cekota, printed the next day's issue. It was entirely devoted to war preparations. One article urged residents "to not take a step without having a [gas] mask!" Others told citizens how to protect children during an air attack and where to give blood, and explained the basics of the city's air defence system.[52] In the brief time it took the paper to get into the hands of its readers, however, the political situation had changed. The elected leaders of the "great" democracies of Europe – Great Britain and France – had capitulated, resulting in the surrender of the Sudetenland to Germany.

Cekota was not the only *Batovec* caught off guard. Thanks to the remarkable memoir of Jan's personal attendant, the lawyer Vladimír Krejčí, Jan Bat'a's actions during the crisis years of 1938–9 are well documented. The remarks suggest a great deal of confusion and uncertainty. When German troops marched across the old Czechoslovak border into the Sudetenland during the first week of October 1938, Jan was in Yugoslavia, where the largest satellite factory at the time was located. Only Jan was not on a normal visit to the factory in Borovo. As the likelihood of war increased into September, he had gone to a resort on Lake Bled, Slovenia, with his family and other close associates for safety. As war grew closer, Jan and his group then moved to Borovo, where Jan planned to build a school for his kids and wait out the conflict.[53] When word reached them of the Czechoslovak government's decision to stand down and accept the Munich Agreement, Jan decided to return to Zlín.

The group flew to Romania, where they had to bribe the director of the airport in Oradea Mare to allow them to leave, and then to return home. Upon arrival, Jan stayed for less than twenty-four hours in Zlín before flying to Prague. There he had a meeting with soon-to-be-former President Beneš and Prime Minister Milan Hodža. According to Krejčí, the meeting "was tense, with some kind of mutual antipathy in the air."[54]

Once back in Zlín, Krejčí found letters all over his desk. They were from a variety of "citizens of the Republic, who were asking Bat'a to stand for election as head of state and president of the republic in the critical situation." Krejčí guessed the letters were planted by Cekota, whom he saw as someone with "Machiavellian" skills and "dictatorial" opinions.[55] Bat'a's name did briefly circulate as a possible pick for the vacated post of president. Yet it is hard to tell if the campaign was largely the work of chief Bat'a publicist Cekota, or a genuine wave of support for a Jan Bat'a presidency in the wake of the collapse of Beneš's network of alliances.

What is certain, though, is that Czechoslovakia after the Munich Agreement experienced a crisis of governance when, facing a near total loss of international support, the government of the First Republic of Czechoslovakia capitulated to the cessation of territory to Nazi Germany. President Beneš had had to make the agonizing decision, and he left office almost immediately thereafter. Citizen Beneš went into exile in England, where he would spend most of the war years fighting to overturn the Munich Agreement.[56] In tandem with Hitler's demands, the Polish government pressed for the disputed district of Český Těšín. Czechoslovakia conceded. Hungary began demanding its claim to a strip of southern Slovakia. Czechoslovakia, left out of the negotiations in Munich, had been abruptly abandoned. For many outside of the country, the rising tide of an inevitable war seemed to have vanished; for those living within, however, it felt like a war had been lost.

Life after Munich

A new government organized itself under the name of the Second Republic of Czecho-Slovakia. The republic had indefensible borders and far fewer minority groups. Slovak nationalists under the Slovak People's Party gained wide-ranging autonomy, as did the Ruthenians (many of whom had begun to see themselves as Ukrainian). The central government in Prague would be left with control over only defence, foreign affairs, and finances. This government appeared to be far more right-wing than the government of its predecessor. Before he left, Beneš appointed General Jan Syrový as prime minister. Syrový, General Inspector of the Czechoslovak Army since 1933, was no politician: "They needed men to take up positions in government in uniform to calm the public. I stayed a soldier."[57] Syrový left the politics to a close ally in the Agrarian Party, Rudolf Beran.

In the political fallout, Beran was instrumental in creating and promoting a new kind of politics – "authoritarian democracy."[58] This new system would do away with pluralism and be called the Party of National Unity, which in Beran's words, would be a "state party of clean, active nationalism. The delusion of internationalism will be replaced by the spirit of national community."[59] For many on the right the capitulation after Munich was reason for optimism and hope. To them, the fall of the First Republic of Czechoslovakia was their "Fall Revolution."[60]

Upon returning to Zlín, Jan took to the airwaves to give a speech about the event:

> We have to look for a new way. But we do not have to go far. Four years ago, I began writing a memorandum, "We Will Build a State for 40 Million People." Even today we cannot find anything from that program to discount ... We need to above all stop being led by a head filled with different ideologies, some which want to teach other nations how to do democracy and others that want to promote their religious or racial views. It is necessary to let go of politics and focus on building the state. It is necessary to build a new democracy. A democracy that will select people and not political parties.[61]

Jan's message was starting to resonate in Prague, and Baťa was becoming central to the political decisions of the new state. Jan's turn toward fascism and nationalism were well timed. Bat'a was becoming a pillar for the authoritarian democracy of the Second Republic of Czecho-Slovakia.

In the political shake up that followed the Munich Agreement, Beran's Party of National Unity filled the major political posts. One of the most important of these was that of the foreign minister, which Beran staffed with František Chvalkovský, a noted Germanophile. He was intensely interested in improving relations with fascist Italy, which became the major diplomatic manoeuvre of the Second Republic.[62] There was also the matter of deciding who was to be president after Beneš stepped down from the office. Jan Bat'a's name once again began to circulate as a possibility for the position. Antonín Cekota, chief publicist for the company, organized a campaign for Jan, mostly through indirect channels, and the rumours that Jan Bat'a would be offered the position intensified.[63] Jan seemed to like the idea. He travelled to Prague and Slovakia to meet with key individuals to ascertain their support for his candidacy. In the end, though, his campaign for the post came to nothing, as Bat'a executives, most likely Hugo Vavrečka, talked Jan out of the idea. Beran decided on Emil Hácha, an elderly lawyer.[64]

However, the Bat'a Company cemented its political clout in the republic when the new government appointed long-time general manager and mayor of Zlín Dominik Čipera as minister for public works, and general manager Hugo Vavrečka as minister without portfolio and chief commissioner for Czecho-Slovakia for the 1939 New York World's Fair.[65] Both men had good reputations among the ruling circles of the country, and were seemingly able to bridge the divide between the Beneš and Beran governments. At their core, they were *Batovci*. Their appointments led to the development of programs that resembled those laid out in Jan's book. In October, the government announced new public works legislation authorizing the formation of labour corps from the ranks of the unemployed. These labour corps were to work on large infrastructure projects and were organized along military lines. In November, the Ministry of Public Works released plans for the first superhighway, which was practically copied right out of the pages of *We Will Build a State*. [66]

Jan Bat'a now charged the *Batovci* with guarding the nation. As the state began to implement programs long championed by Bat'a, such as work camps for the unemployed, massive infrastructure improvement projects, and widespread school reform, Jan encouraged employees to act nationally: "The 10,000 *Batovci* throughout the world have to guard our nation so that it can be respected and taken into account by all."[67] For the first time in public, the chief executive began to support the "Czecho-Slovak" nation at the expense of other minority groups within the country.

Upon returning home to Zlín on the first of October, Jan gave an unprecedented company order: all remaining German personnel were to be carefully watched and all stores in the Sudetenland were to be closed. By the end of the month, the order had been carried out. Bat'a closed all of its retail stores in the annexed areas and began the complicated task of moving Czech-speaking personnel into the newly formed Second Republic of Czecho-Slovakia.[68] In post-Munich Agreement Czecho-Slovakia one needed to abandon internationalism.

Nowhere was this shift in attitude more apparent than in a series of editorials Jan wrote for Zlín's newspaper about what should be done with the thousands of people fleeing the expanding Nazi state into the rump state of Czecho-Slovakia. Bat'a's response to the wave of political emigrants was to argue that the state should help the "runaways" by finding them other countries to live in: "There are other states where there are barely 10 people per square kilometre; meanwhile the western part of our state is around 150 people per square kilometre ... We have to clearly say that it is truly too much for us and that we cannot bear it and thus we will not take it."[69] After arguing in 1937 in *We Will Build a State for 40,000,000* that Czechoslovakia needed to increase its population density to roughly that of Belgium's in order to compete among the advanced nations of the world, Jan's concern about overpopulation was particularly shallow.[70] Indeed, what he was really afraid of had little to do with population density. His fear was that the country would be inundated with Jews.

In the same article he overtly separated the refugees into co-nationals and foreigners, by which he meant Jews. It was the latter that should not receive a welcome in the Second Republic: "We do not have any race hate for the Jews. But we understand that they could share their own unwanted danger with us, which would easily endanger the entire Czechoslovak nation ... It is extremely rare that one of them feels nationally Czech."[71]

As with most things in the company town, the attitude of the boss was put into action by the city in short order: two weeks after the article's publication, the city council banned all "refugees from foreign areas" from living or working in Zlín.[72] The refugee ban, as well as its larger context, affected an unknown number of people in the area. Yet it certainly had an effect and could be seen in the lives of the some of the most vulnerable students at the BSP, as in the case of Alexander Reinhartz.

Reinhartz arrived in Zlín on 22 September 1937, to begin his training as one of the Young Men in the BSP.[73] He was a fifteen-year-old from Mukachevo, in what was then Subcarpathian Ruthenia, the easternmost and least industrialized province of Czechoslovakia.[74] Reinhartz was the son of Jewish agricultural workers; his acceptance into the prestigious school promised him an opportunity to become one of the company's elite Young Men, a group who could expect world travel, excellent salaries, and generous benefits – all unheard of for a poor peasant from the east. It was with considerable disappointment, therefore, when Alexander's father Miksha found out that his son was not doing well in Zlín.

In November 1938, around the same time that the city council imposed a ban on "refugees from foreign areas," news reached Mukachevo of Alexander's trouble with school authorities. When Miksha heard that Alexander was on the verge of being kicked out of the school, he wrote a desperate plea to the company. Miksha himself had "no prospects," so Alexander "cannot find work here." His letter blamed the family's poverty on recent political changes, which transferred Mukachevo from Czechoslovakian to Hungarian authority after the Vienna Award of 1938: "After this change I have been left with three sons who are all minors and who cannot be employed. I have no way to make money any more. Sending my son home would worsen this terrible situation … Please, if you send him away from this school it will destroy his young life … If you have to punish him please at least consider removing him to one of your sister factories in Hungary."[75]

Two weeks after Miksha's letter arrived at company headquarters, the *vychovatel*s met and decided to fire Alexander and suspend him from the BSP on 18 December 1938. His *vychovatel*, Jan Hoček, explained: "I requested 300 crowns for him so that he could go home. He never went. He lied: he kept they money, claiming that he sent 200 to his family. He does not have a receipt for this. This is a very bad boy, who on the whole doesn't care about being with us."[76] In a world where money management was seen as a window into character, every crown had to be accounted for and dishonest financial transactions were anathema. Alexander had little chance of remaining a Young Man if the accusations were true. He would have a final review in February before being removed from Zlín.

Ten days after the company's decision to suspend Alexander, he received a letter from his mother, Rosalia, which contradicted Hoček's accusations. In it, Rosalia thanked Alexander for sending money home – exactly 200 crowns.

While aware of some kind of trouble at Bat'a, Rosalia seemed to have no idea that her son was going to be kicked out over the money. "Please complete your studies and always remember that you are in a good position, you do not suffer from hunger, and because of this you have to be completely satisfied." She added, "Father doesn't work at all and has no chance to do so."[77] The two letters paint a grim portrait of Jewish life in Mukachevo, where Jews were increasingly isolated and marginalized. Staying in the BSP meant life or death for Alexander.

The *vychovatel*s certainly read this letter, as they included it in his file, but it did not change their decision. Alexander's disregard of the absolute transparency the company demanded of its students' affairs was unforgivable – at least for a Jewish boy from Ruthenia. The BSP guardians deemed Alexander unfit for continued employment and he had to leave Zlín. The final judgment came on 21 February 1939, just three weeks before the Nazis would invade Czecho-Slovakia. He was, in the words of the *vychovatel* Hrušecký, "unreliable, unconscionable, and dishonest in his work reports. He was weak in his performance."[78]

Yet Alexander's "weakness" was not as well defined as the company's final report made out. The young man aspired to become a retail manager, spoke five languages fluently, and later somehow survived the Second World War; all three of which hint at ambition, intellect, and luck.[79] However, he was not an ideal Young Man, as his record was marked by mixed reviews from his superiors. He seemed to have done well as a rubber worker but struggled a year later when he was moved to the machine works division; there he was caught smoking, which nearly led to his termination. Alexander's smoking notwithstanding, the *vychovatel*s had consistently rated him as being "good" at his job.[80] Evidently, the reasons given for his removal were spurious.

Reinhartz, the son of Jewish peasants from the far east of the country, was accepted into the highly competitive school because of his multilingualism and his poor, rural background. His story reveals the mechanisms of control the company used on the students inside its school. His guardians carefully tracked his spending and read his private letters, typical treatment for a Young Man. His removal, though, illustrated changing priorities. In the past, what mattered most was one's attitude toward the company, rather than one's place of origin. Given the timing of Alexander's removal from the BSP and the city's ban on foreign refugees, it seems that the company had adopted a new criterion for employment by the end of 1938.

Still, the efforts to prevent Jewish refugees and one BSP student from finding succor in Zlín should not be taken to mean that Bat'a had abandoned the position of national indifference entirely. After all, Jan's new-found nationalism did not interfere with the plan to move company headquarters, or with continuing to operate wherever it could. After Poland took over the Těšín district, for example, Bat'a executives were pleased that "all of the sales and shoe repair shops are operating normally, not a one of them has closed."[81] In Trutnov, the company decided that a known Sudeten Party sympathizer, Emil Seidel, should keep his job because "he only works in sales."[82] In fact, a case can be made to suggest that Bat'a was playing a double game during the tumultuous Second Republic. While embracing their new nationalist credentials, and wielding considerable influence on state policy, Bat'a executives wanted to continue selling shoes everywhere and to everyone. Furthermore, they were busy secretly preparing an exit strategy.

This strategy to move headquarters came into focus when Jan Bat'a was arrested by the Gestapo in the resort town of Marienbad (Mariánské Lázně) in the middle of October 1938. He was on a stopover on a trip through Germany and the Netherlands to England, but it remains a mystery why he made his entourage stop in Marienbad. It was also a mystery why he left this entourage, which included Krejčí and Thomas Bat'a Jr., at the train station while he went into town alone. After taking longer than planned, Krejčí and Thomas went looking for Jan. They eventually found him working at his typewriter in the former city police building, which had been turned over to the Gestapo. He "calmly" told the two that he was going to be taken to give a "longer disposition at the Gestapo regional headquarters in Karlovy Vary."[83] The Gestapo then took Jan, in isolation, to Karlovy Vary, where he wrote out the disposition. His aide Krejčí did manage to see him while in custody, and "brought him coffee and little sandwiches." Krejčí was then also detained. The men spent the night in jail. They were released the next morning, after answering a number of brief questions, such as, "Name? Are you a Jew? Are you a friend of the Jews?" Krejčí recalled, "Then, while answering the last question, some other officer entered the room, turned all red, and nervously whispered something into the ear of another officer. This one interrupted the proceedings and announced to Bat'a and me that we were free to go and asked if we could use their help."[84] Krejčí told them they needed a ride to the train station in Cheb to catch the express train to Brussels. The Gestapo obliged the request. "We made ourselves comfortable at the back of the train, and then went through towns and villages where freshly burnt synagogues smouldered."[85]

Jan's "arrest" signalled to the *Batovci* that the Nazi government was not going to destroy the company if it got the chance. Targetting of the company was a legitimate fear given the intense anti-Bat'a propaganda coming out of Germany in the mid to late 1930s. The incident suggested, though, that an arbitrary and violent future awaited; it was not going to be pleasant in Central Europe. Sensing this, shortly after his arrest in 1938, Jan decided to turn his sights on the small factory town to be built in Belcamp, Maryland, as the new world headquarters of Bat'a.

The Dream of Belcamp

Only twenty-seven miles from downtown Baltimore, but in a rural setting with excellent access to major transportation routes, Belcamp met all of the prerequisites for the company's model factory town. In 1933, a team of executives, including Jan and Thomas Jr., purchased 2,000 acres of what once was a large dairy farm.[86] The farm had riverfront acreage on the Bush River, which flows into the Chesapeake, and was right off of US 40, a major highway completed in 1927, which itself followed the historically significant Philadelphia Road, dating to colonial times. US 40 was a modern marvel, a paved highway that connected the Midwest and West with the mid-Atlantic. It was also close to the Baltimore and Ohio Railroad line. The surrounding population consisted mostly of farmers, whose sons and daughters could be recruited into the Bat'a system without bringing any of the baggage of seasoned industrial workers.[87] The property was one of Jan's earliest acquisitions of land as chief executive officer, and it was a sound one.

But Bat'a proved to be in no hurry to develop the area. As late as 1 December 1938, no work had begun on building the factories. Apart from an undated, pre-1938 master plan for the site, which was most likely designed in 1933 by architect Vladimir Karfík, nothing suggests that Belcamp was a priority for the company. By the end of the year, this was to change. Jan issued a directive to redesign the master plan; Karfík quickly revised the original. Karfík's new design was similar to other Bat'a factory towns, many of which he also had designed. The complex had three functional zones: manufacturing area, municipal buildings, and residential quarters. The residential section was based on a radial design and included ample greenspace. There were to be churches, schools, a retirement home, and athletic facilities.[88] One of those schools was to be another BSP, which would be the only other such school outside of Zlín. It was to be a city of 30,000, with 10,000 workers, which was considered the most desirable size for "the ideal industrial city."[89]

In January 1939, a team of executives began drawing up a list of the best and brightest Bat'a people to send to the United States. An undated letter written by an unnamed author, although most likely from Jan himself, gave managers clear directions on who they should select to be sent to Maryland. "They should be no older than thirty, have musical abilities, language skills, and construction skills."[90] Jan expected to have 300 names and the personnel files from which to select 100 to go to Maryland in a few months.

While the list was being drawn up, the drive toward authoritarian democracy seemed to be going well in Zlín. The Party of National Unity, the party of "clean, active nationalism," was finding Zlín to be fertile ground for recruitment. In January 1939 alone, 1,891 people joined its ranks.[91] Led by manager and long-time *Batovci* Josef Hlavníček, the group organized nationalist activities and fund drives across the Dřevnice Valley. One such activity, involving the youth wing of the party in Zlín that month, "ended with the singing of Hey, Slavs," the unofficial anthem for Slavic nationalists.[92] Patriotic speeches, fundraising balls for the party, and member movie nights filled Zlín's social calendar in early 1939. The party's barrage of activities tried to turn every citizen into patriotic Czechoslovaks.

Beneath the nationalism, though, hints of Batism remained. The newspaper continued to publish articles about labour and cooking contests, social advice for women, and calls for national indifference. Jan even offered a strident denunciation of nationalist hatred.

> I surely love my nation … But I have never offended any nation and I have never hated one either! I want to work together with everyone and learn from everyone so that I can help our work … Religion, race, and nationality are not for sale. And in Zlín we will pay nothing for them. This house is a house of equal opportunity for all who work honestly … This house was and will be a house of lords, not of derelicts. And it will not become a house of derelict nationalists. I am a lord – you are a lord.[93]

Written after an incident in which a German employee in Zlín faced ridicule, the article suggested that while the elimination of the messiness of a democracy was something Baťa encouraged, national chauvinism remained deeply troubling to him. Jan's flirtation with fascism had not in the end created a rabid nationalist.

Conclusion

In many ways, it was a time of contradictions. The company reached its political zenith with the formation of Czecho-Slovakia, after the otherwise disastrous Munich Agreement; but, at the very same point, it also began planning to move hundreds of key personnel and millions of crowns in capital outside of the country. The authoritarian democracy and its Party of National Unity promised to do away with political parties – a goal of the *Batovci* since 1923 – and invest in massive infrastructure projects using the unemployed, while at the same time simplifying the tax code. These were all undertakings Jan promoted in *We Will Build a State*. The elite young workers of the BSP were told to participate in nationalist activities: "The fate of our homeland rests in the hands of every one of us," implored Dominik Čipera.[94] At the same time, the *Batovci* were to remain nationally indifferent at work and to be prepared to move abroad on short notice.

Clearly, the period of the Second Republic, October 1938 to March 1939, was a strange time to live in the headquarters of a transnational company in

Czecho-Slovakia. After all, the centre of Europe fast became the centre of a new world war. Germany's aggressive foreign policy focused on destabilizing Czechoslovak society and colonizing its businesses, causing tremendous anxiety among Bat'a company executives. Indeed, the decisions and actions of its belligerent neighbouring country pushed the company to consider alternative locations for its headquarters and new depositories for its cash. But at the same time, the removal of Beneš from power and the turn toward the authoritarian democracy opened up avenues through which Bat'a executives could ascend to high positions in government. In the spring/summer of 1938, the constant rhetoric of war turned the company town of Zlín away from its national indifference and toward nationalism, gas masks, and readiness drills. The tension forced executives to further define Batism. Their efforts only muddied the waters. The Bat'a company town model as laid out in the company manual "The Ideal Industrial City" existed in a cosmopolitan bubble, resting on the exclusionary realities of Jewish refugees, Czech workers, and German salespeople. By the winter of 1938–9, a chaotic push and pull between defence of the nation and exit from the nation defined the Bat'a experience. Soon, such conflicting positions would become all the more acute.

"Not a Nazi, but More or Less a Fool," 1939–1945

On a snowy day in March, German soldiers moved across the borders of the Second Republic of Czecho-Slovakia, ending the brief life of the "authoritarian democracy." As the rump state withered away, the Bat'a Company faced its most serious challenge since the economic and political chaos of 1919: Nazi occupation. The invasion did not surprise many at Bat'a; contingency plans for a move to Maryland were forming as early as November 1938. But the timing of the occupation caught the company off guard. Little had been done about selection of the people who would go abroad. Much of the company's gold reserve remained in Zlín. In the midst of the crisis, Batism, with its apolitical technocratic vision of industrial society, became lost in the fog that lies between collaboration and resistance.

After the March invasion, Bat'a sped up its removal of the best and brightest young *Batovci*, while dealing with a different set of political leaders at home. With Nazi occupation came anti-Semitic laws, a reorientation of production for the Nazi military, and the establishment of a racial hierarchy, with Germans at the top. Company managers responded to the effects of occupation in myriad, sometimes contradictory, ways, as they played a double game with the Axis and the Allies. Often frantic and chaotic, their actions reflected the state of the world in 1939–40. The Bat'a managers prepared outstanding students at the BSP for lives abroad and tried to move headquarters to the United States. All the while, other *Batovci* successfully negotiated with German authorities to maintain control of Bat'a Zlín, and company personnel began bending policy to the new racist dictates of the Nazi state. Meanwhile the Nazis unravelled Bat'a's democratic shopping experience in Central Europe.

Within Zlín, nationalist thoughts and actions commingled with persistent national indifference. Largely in response to the occupation, displays of nationalism abounded in Zlín. From small acts, like shouting at German actors when they came on screen in cinemas, or hurling rocks at the Oberlandrat's house, to large ones, like police officers' deserting their posts, defiance to Nazi

Figure 8.1. Werhmacht band plays in Zlín's town square while workers look on, May 1939. Moravský zemský archiv v Brně, Státní okresní archiv Zlín, Sbírka fotografií Zlín, sign. 199, obálka č. 14409.

authority was not hard to find.[1] At the same time, company executives did their best to maintain control over Zlín by working with German authorities. Workers, for the most part, kept on working. Dominik Čipera, Bat'a's chief financial officer and Zlín mayor since 1932, stayed in office. The only change to the composition of the city council was the addition of two German speakers, who were added as late as March 1941.[2] Indeed, Bat'a's Zlín kept producing with remarkable efficiency until Allied bombs flattened the factories on 20 November 1944.

This push and pull between collaboration and resistance was evident at the top levels of the company, especially between Thomas Jr. and his uncle Jan. Secret deals may have been made with high-ranking Nazi officials to allow Jan Bat'a to move personnel into the Americas, and purchase property in Brazil. Certainly the move abroad happened with full German knowledge. During the first five months of the occupation, executives sent cadres of new international managers through Bremen with German approval. After Germany's invasion of Poland in September 1939, Jan refused to issue a statement of loyalty to the Allied cause. At the same time, an enormous pile of workboots stockpiled in Norway curiously fell into Nazi hands. Meanwhile, Thomas Bat'a Jr. migrated with a handful of *Batovci* to build a satellite factory near the Trent River in

Prince Edward County in Ontario, Canada. The site would become Batawa. While Jan hedged, Thomas Jr. pledged his allegiance to the Allied cause. He was unequivocal in his support for the Allies and transparent in his financial transactions with Canadian authorities.[3]

Unsurprisingly, the intelligence communities in the United Kingdom and then the United States did not understand the company's intentions. Nor were these intentions clear to many key figures in the Czechoslovak resistance movement. Such uncertainty led to a showdown between the power of the state and that of the transnational corporation, and Bat'a came close to being wiped out of existence. The near disaster had to do with the decisions and wavering of Jan. Ultimately, Bat'a was far too large to be destroyed by the mistakes of one man. In Zlín, the *Batovci* basically kept their heads down and served the Reich under the direction of Čipera. Abroad, the decisiveness of a host of Bat'a people to support the Allied cause, especially that of Thomas Bat'a Jr., saved the company from outright takeover by the Allies.

Preparing for North America

For Jan, when the Nazis invaded the Second Republic of Czecho-Slovakia in March, things got downright bizarre. Perhaps terrified after his interrogation by the Gestapo in Karlovy Vary only five months earlier, Jan appeared to have temporarily lost his nerve. The day after German troops marched into the Czech part of Czecho-Slovakia, Jan boarded a company plane and flew to Yugoslavia. As German soldiers paraded through Zlín, Jan was safe in a hotel in Belgrade.[4]

From Belgrade, he could have fled Europe, which would have left much unsettled but would have ensured his personal safety. However, his immediate family was still in Zlín. After staying just a few days in Yugoslavia, Jan decided to return to what had become the Protectorate of Bohemia and Moravia. It appears that guarantees from Nazi authorities convinced him to return. The US consul general in Prague, Irving N. Linnell, reported that Jan told him a few days after returning from Yugoslavia that Hermann Goering had reached out to him through channels in Belgrade and offered him safe passage and unmolested travel to "any factory in the world." Linnell also reported that the German Ministry of Economics agreed to let previous anti-Nazi statements made by Jan slide if he "would return to Zlín and continue operation of the plant."[5]

Jan did return to Zlín, but for only two months, April–May 1939. It was during that time that Jan's notorious "Patagonia Plan" created trouble for him. As early as April 1938, when Europe seemed poised for a second world war, Jan began circulating a curious idea in the company newspaper. There he argued that the entire Czech population, some ten million people, should relocate entirely to either Brazil or the Patagonia region of Argentina: "Brazil, a country as big as the whole of Europe, has 44 million citizens. Europe has 480 million. Why look for land for development in a tightened Europe? Why not there? Better to move out. The last war cost the world 8 billion crowns. Bringing 10 million people to South America would cost 14 million. And for 140 million, they can buy beautiful farms. Why get involved in something so stupid, so detrimental, like war? Patagonia, in southern Argentina is very suitable for us."[6] The idea belied Jan's thinking that the Germans would be in control of Bohemia and Moravia for perhaps hundreds of years, so it was time to move.

Jan's remarks only raised eyebrows. It was outlandish and perhaps treasonous to promote moving the entire Czech population. But for Jan, near total emigration was going to save lives. The idea manifested itself because Jan had personally decided he was going to emigrate – and move company headquarters – around the same time as he devised his Patagonia Plan. All the same, it was pure fantasy. Of course, for Czech leaders like Edvard Beneš, Vladimír Hurban, and Jan Masaryk, once the Nazis occupied the country a removal of all Czech speakers was looking more like a reality. In any event, the Patagonia Plan marked Jan Bat'a as persona non grata in influential émigré circles.[7] Regardless of what the political elite of the former Czechoslovakia thought, Jan seems to have remained convinced of its wisdom. Writing about a meeting with his uncle that occurred sometime in June 1939, Thomas Bat'a Jr. noted that Jan brought up and defended the plan: "He reasoned, with considerable conviction, that the Germans would be pleased to endorse a scheme that would rid them of their ancient enemies ... I couldn't believe that my uncle could have hatched anything so absurd."[8] However absurd to Thomas, moving populations en masse was entirely within the normative framework of the high modernist Jan.

Instead of moving all of the Czechs, Jan would have to settle for moving the *Batovci* and making a new Zlín in America. Even this, though, proved no easy task, as the tight discipline of the Bat'a system began showing signs of collapse. At two public speaking engagements Jan demonstrated the slippage of Bat'a's authority in the new world of Nazi occupation.

Before leaving Zlín, Jan began paying a lot of attention to the young cadres. On 14 April 1939, he spoke to an auditorium packed with the Young Women of the BSP. The night was devoted to two themes, the girls' appearances and life abroad. Unscripted, Jan began by complaining that young women were not making themselves look nice enough.

> I imagined that in Zlín we would have been an example. Truly, though, after half
> an hour [of being in Zlín] I met with girls who just about shook me out of my cloak
> the way they looked in the stores. Scuffed shoes, worn-out heels, torn pockets ...
> hair like a boy, torn stockings, smeared make-up ... I don't like telling you this!

He went on to say that the source of all dishevelment and personal uncleanliness lies at home, the domain of the woman, of the mother, " the one who raises you."

> You might be wondering why we are sitting here and why I am talking to you about this so seriously ... But I will tell you that it can happen that when I see a girl going from the factory or to the factory in scuffed shoes, when I see a girl with torn stockings, a dirty coat, it not only reflects on your patrons, your caretakers, and even yourselves, but it introduces this slovenliness into the factory. And I wish that such girls be brought to me, because as you know, I am your father, and I will not tolerate this type of slovenliness for a minute. I will call not only the girls but their caretakers and overseers, and I will write on their cards. Because we cannot tolerate such people ... who are supposed to help others but cannot even help themselves.[9]

This obsession with appearance was nothing new to the Young Women, for most of them had had to live up to the double standards of working fast in a modern factory while being dressed in pantyhose and make-up. At this talk, though, some of the Young Women had had enough of Jan's unrealistic demands: "How are we supposed to have clean, nice stockings when the machines in the factory constantly tear at them? How can we wear sweaters (in the factory) when it is so hot in there?"[10] The Young Women, it seemed, were growing weary of the patriarchal dictates of the company. Jan changed the subject to travel and emigration: "It is better to be unemployed in America," he said, "than to be the prime minister of Turkey."[11] His rambling speech concluded that being open to a life abroad was by far the most important attribute the Young Women should cultivate.

A month later, on 15 May 1939, executives held a panel conference for all of the adolescents of the city, which was entirely focused on preparing students for a life abroad. Several weeks earlier, managers had been given the task of compiling a list of young employees to go abroad; it was thought the students would have been clamouring to get on it. Apparently they were not. Their reluctance prompted the conference, which turned out to be a public admonishment. Jan began by bringing up František Klátil, a factory planner and manager who helped develop the new factories in East Tilbury, England, in Brest, Holland, and in Hellocourt, France: "Klátil is not afraid of working abroad. He does not care a bit about the difficulties that await him there."[12] The discussion that followed focused on the courage of Klátil and the disappointment that the managers were now feeling toward the young Bat'a people. "Our man does not have enough courage to go out into the world," remarked Hugo Vavrečka. "When I see our people's attitude toward travel I get the sense that they would rather be home with their mommies."[13] Jan continued, "Only one [of the Bat'a people sent abroad] did not return. It is true that Josef Sedlář died in the Sahara Desert. But whoever thinks that they should not go because of what happened to Sedlář is not the right person for our work."[14] Jan went on and stressed that the workers need not fear emigration, because life was "more desirable abroad."[15]

Already, 100 employees had made it onto a list to be transferred to Belcamp, Maryland, to oversee the development of the area. The majority of them were between the ages of twenty and twenty-seven and graduates of one of the Bat'a schools. Upper management had devised criteria for who would be sent as early as February 1939. Then they decided that the people they wanted would have language skills, musical abilities, construction skills, and could be no older than thirty. They did have exceptions to the age limit: "We cannot allow even one young or old leader who has served abroad successfully or in the construction services to stay in Zlín." Still, the focus was on bringing young people across the Atlantic: "These youths we have to very intensively prepare for their special task right now."[16] Finding the right people, though, proved difficult.

Under the pressure of Nazi rule, upper management decided to add 300 people to the list of who would be sent to Belcamp, all of them proven Young Men and Women. To locate employees within a giant multinational corporation, however, was not easy. In a letter to four executives, Jan made clear his frustrations with the process: "Finally received the 300 personnel cards of people on the rise. But only by accident do I know where some of these people are. It is written on many of the cards that they're in Zlín, but they are not in Zlín at all ... it makes little sense to have all of these cards if they cannot tell us where the employee is."[17] Still, the men and women were tracked down for the most part and arrived in the United States between April 1939 and October 1940.

Several were graduates of the "best of the best," the Tomášov School. These were true *Batovci*, praised by their mentors and managers across the board. They were people like Karel Aster, Josefa Hanáková, Marie Kouřilová, and Arnošt Meisler. The company sent nineteen-year-old Karel Aster to New York and then Belcamp because he "was above all a *Batovec* ... he not only has all the prerequisites of a Tomášov student but is always the first in behaviour and success at work."[18] One of the more interesting stories comes from Josefa "Pepča" Hanáková, who was sent with this first group of outstanding graduates to the United States in 1939 at the age of twenty. From Maryland, Hanáková was sent with a very small group, some four people, to Haiti, where she helped establish a small shoe factory in Port-au-Prince. There she oversaw some 300 Haitians. The Protektorat press picked up her story in 1941 and several newspapers ran it as a human interest story.[19] It is not clear what happened to the bold Hanáková after this, but her story suggests that by the time of the Nazi occupation, the company had all but abandoned its rigid gender divisions, preferring to send the best and brightest abroad. The best and brightest included

Marie Kouřilová, and Arnošt Meisler, both of whom were young, exceptional, and unquestionably loyal. All were sent to Belcamp in 1939. Seventeen-year-old Kouřilová graduated from the Baťa School of Work with excellent marks, and her "attitude toward the factory was always very good."[20] Meisler, Jewish and likely a genius, spoke five languages fluently. Older than most of those chosen, at age thirty-five he had a family and years of experience as a correspondent and rayon worker. In any case, these young, loyal workers found themselves at the New York World's Fair on tourist visas before being quickly sent south to Maryland.

In the case of Meisler, we have one of the great debates of Baťa's past – was the decision to move certain employees carefully considered in order to save Jewish lives? On one side of the debate, John Nash-Baťa, Jan's grandson and key researcher in support of Baťa's righteousness, has argued that Jan intentionally saved hundreds of Jewish lives. He points to the testimonies of Marie and Charles Morgenstern, who ended up moving, working, and living out the rest of their lives at the Belcamp complex, and of Otto Heilig, who ended up in Brazil. All three testimonies recount that Jan intentionally saved the lives of Jews.[21] Marie's testimony in particular is compelling evidence. For in it she recounts how Jan responded to her husband's request to rescue his brother Julius from Vienna after the Anschluss. She states that Jan found him employment with Baťa and sent him to Zlín. Jan then provided funds for the family for their passage across the Atlantic to New York and then Maryland.[22] The Morgensterns believed Jan saved their lives.

On the other hand, the historians Martin Marek and Vít Strobach have come to a convincing, if painful, conclusion that the decision to move personnel abroad had little to nothing to do with their religion or race and everything to do with the practical needs of the company. Scouring the personnel files of the Jewish employees of Baťa, Marek has illustrated that the 70 Jewish employees who were sent abroad in 1939–40, out of a total of 1,100, were highly skilled and multilingual. The Jewish employees who were not chosen did not possess these attributes. The same profile fit the non-Jewish employees who were sent abroad in the wake of the occupation. In other words, Baťa moved the best and the brightest abroad, but did not go out of its way to shelter the most vulnerable group.[23] Furthermore, through a careful study of the wartime history of Baťa satellite factories in Ottmuth, Sezimově Ústí, Chełmek, and Radom, Marek has found that the firm used at least 1,500 Jewish prisoners to perform the most arduous tasks. Managerial records suggest that this use of slave labour was intentional.[24]

As with most things, the truth is somewhere in the middle. Jan undoubtedly went out of his way to get key Jewish personnel, and their families, out of Europe and beyond the reach of the Nazis. But to label his actions an underground railroad is grossly misleading. As Marek and Strobach have clearly argued, the vast majority of Jewish employees did not receive special consideration.[25] As for rescuing Jews, Bat'a acted in a predictable way. What mattered was aptitude for the work and loyalty to the company. Bat'a saved hundreds of Jewish lives, but in the eyes of Bat'a the people who were sent abroad were not Jews, they were *Batovci*.[26]

Soon, all of these *Batovci* would be labelled dangerous elements by the FBI, as Bat'a's move to the United States turned into a near disaster.

The Nightmare of Maryland

As the Young Men and Women were leaving for North America in May, Jan assembled an entourage of assistants, artists, and a few extended family members to leave for New York. At the beginning of June, they left Zlín. It would be Jan's last departure from the town.

He and his group travelled under tourist visas ostensibly to see the New York World's Fair, where the company had by far the largest exhibit of the now orphaned Czechoslovak Pavilion.[27] It was a period of great uncertainty; by the time the Bat'a entourage arrived in New York, Czechoslovakia had been occupied for three months by the Nazis, and the company's future was in doubt. German authorities had detained Jan in November of 1938 in Karlsbad, and the German press had made allusions to Jan's possible Semitic heritage the same year.[28] After the invasion, Jan likely expected that the Nazis would take control over the factories in Zlín. Indeed, even with Nazi guarantees, it seems Jan did not have much faith in the Protectorate. At the end of March, Jan had moved his immediate family to London.

Despite the stress, Jan arrived in Manhattan with considerable confidence, and did not utter a word to the public condemning the Nazi occupation. Furthermore, Jan almost immediately complicated his standing with Czechoslovak political leaders in exile. Sometime in the two weeks he was in New York, Jan met with Edvard Beneš, former president of Czechoslovakia and soon-to-be president of the Czechoslovak government-in-exile. During their conversation, Jan reportedly said, "so now maybe, Mr. Beneš, you can try your hand at making shoes and come and work for me." To which Beneš replied icily, "Mr. Bat'a, I have other plans."[29]

New York was otherwise a place of amusement for Jan. His real business was in Belcamp, Maryland, where Bat'a personnel were busy trying to open what was hoped would be their new company headquarters. Executives earmarked US$2,200,000 for the Belcamp plant, which would come largely out their holdings in Switzerland. Created by Tomáš Bat'a in 1928 and overseen by his business associate Dr. George Wettstein, Bat'a's Swiss portfolio was substantial and out of the Germans' reach. As moving money out of Zlín was growing difficult, the "Swiss Trust" as it came to be called, allowed the

Figure 8.2. Jan Bat'a, at centre, and entourage in New York City, May 1939.
Moravský zemský archiv v Brně, Státní okresní archiv Zlín, Sbírka fotografií Zlín,
sign. 496, obálka č. 14702.

company to build two large-scale factory complexes in North America at the
same time.[30] One was in Canada in southeastern Ontario, under the direction of
Thomas Jr., and the other in Maryland under the direction of Jan.

Jan travelled to Belcamp in early June 1939. There, with Senator Millard Tydings, he laid the official cornerstone of the factory to considerable
fanfare. The event was filmed.[31] This video, it would appear, marked the
beginning of a beautiful relationship between the US government and the
Bat'a Company. Tydings "heartily welcomes Jan" and the factory that will
employ "10,000 American workmen." The narrator then explained that Bata
was "the first big industry to bolt from German-occupied Czechoslovakia."[32]
As the cliché has it, appearances can be deceiving. The relationship would

be anything but beautiful. Moreover, Bat'a had not bolted from German-occupied Czechoslovakia. It maintained control of its city under new and difficult circumstances.

Occupied Zlín

While Bat'a prepared its future managers for a life abroad and Jan left with his entourage for the United States, the people of Zlín faced the initial demands of a harsh regime. On the same day that Jan declared that being unemployed in America was better than ruling Turkey, the city arranged for, and paid out of its pension account, fifteen young male workers, all between the ages of eighteen and twenty-eight, to go to work in Germany.[33] A week later, the company announced that there would be no May Day celebration. Also in April, company executives made the astute decision to name a German, Albrecht Miesbach, as chief director of the Zlín factories. Miesbach ran a small shoe manufacturing operation in Augsburg, had an accomplished military career, and proved essential in mitigating the worst of the Nazi demands on the *Batovci*.[34] All the same, his arrival sent a clear message. The Nazi occupation was a serious threat to the company town's sovereignty.

The people of Zlín grew defiant and nationalistic in response. In June 1939, three city police officers, all of them recently hired, abandoned their posts to help distribute anti-German leaflets.[35] They were caught and all faced criminal charges for doing so. In July, the police that remained on duty had an added responsibility. After several instances of heckling in movie houses, they now had to attend every film. Apparently, crowds had whistled and shouted when any German actor came on the screen.[36] In addition, anti-German graffiti, vandalism of the Oberlandrat's house, and numerous reports of anti-German outbursts in social establishments were evidence of hostility to Germans.[37] While German could be heard more frequently on the streets, and education came to focus more and more on German language and culture, in the movie houses, bars, and private homes of Zlín, German came to be scorned as the language of the occupier. Zlín's exceptionalism, where German-Czech conflict seemed a world away, was no more.

This became especially apparent in the world of retail, where employees had constant interaction with the public. There, in short order, Bat'a's customer first policies were undone by Nazi dictates and the hypernationalism that accompanied them. Retail employees had to operate under a set of rules written with racial hierarchy in mind. The democratic shopping experience, where the "Our Customer, Our Lord" motto reigned, came to be dismantled by the occupation authorities. The case of cashier Helena Kutějová reveals just how quickly the nationally indifferent policies of the Bat'a retail stores were undone by a rising tide of intolerance.

Bat'a social inspectors heard of Helena Kutějová in the first weeks of April 1939. She was working as a cashier at the Bat'a store in Trenčín, a town which had become part of newly independent Slovakia on 14 March 1939. Previously, the personnel department had not given much attention to either the store or Kutějová. Both were minor characters in Bat'a's vast retail system; Trenčín was a relatively quiet town of 12,000, only seventy kilometres away from Zlín, and Kutějová a twenty-something cashier without a negative mark on her record. Authorities took notice, however, when the store suddenly reorganized its sales department.[38] This unusual act led to an inquiry from the sales department's social inspector, Karel Huták. Huták discovered that the store's roster of saleswomen had all been rearranged because the mild-mannered Kutějová had attempted suicide sometime at the end of March 1939.

After launching an investigation into her suicide attempt, which had become standard procedure by the late 1930s, social inspector Huták found national conflict to be the reason why Kutějová tried to take too many of the pills her doctor prescribed "for calm and sleep."[39] Huták wrote,

> Kutějová is Czech; the other personnel are of Slovak nationality, including the manager and his family. The store is often politicized, so much so that even customers have written warning letters to Zlín. This situation had a negative effect on sales. The manager became interested in enterprises other than our store. He began thinking about retirement, but he needed more cash to do so. Because of this she felt uncomfortable and that she had to leave.[40]

While leaving much to the imagination, the personnel department's investigation into Kutějová's suicide showed the sharp upswing in nationalist fervour following Nazi occupation. A store that had served the community for fifteen years turned into a place of nationalist conflict. Kutějová's service was called into question by the townspeople solely for her place of origin. Through this incident we see the ways in which political change affected the everyday lives of people living in small-town Slovakia, as the Nazi occupation and the dissolution of Czechoslovakia significantly undermined the promise of a nationally indifferent workplace at Bat'a.

Blacklisted

Once the Second World War broke out at the beginning of September 1939, the Allies placed their own non-negotiable demands of loyalty on company executives. British authorities were unsure of what to do with the multinational behemoth that was Bat'a. Among government circles, there were conflicting accounts of Jan Bat'a's relationship to Nazi officials, and, given the national indifference of top management, the British had a hard time pinning down the company's allegiances. The British Ministry of Economic Warfare gave Jan five months to make a public statement in support for the Allies and deposit £100,000 in a British government account, which they told him was an expression of good faith. He did not do either of these things. Instead, he carried out negotiations with the British through an intermediary in Switzerland, the aforementioned George Wettstein, and dallied, claiming that he simply did not have that kind of cash.[41] As the company had $1,000,000 in reserve cash just to account for operating losses at the Belcamp plant for 1940, Jan was simply lying to British authorities.[42] Later he would write, "I felt humiliated, when in February of 1940, the Ministry of Economic Warfare came with questions and conditions which indicated their mistrust."[43] Perhaps because of this feeling of humiliation, from January to May 1940, Jan made the British wait.

While they were waiting for the statement of loyalty, Jan bought some 2,000 square miles of land in Brazil from German owners in the state of Matto Grosso. He used accounts from the mother company, Bata A.S. Zlín, to make the purchase. As the Allies were trying to freeze German bank accounts, allowing funds from Bat'a Zlín to go to German nationals infuriated the British Ministry of Economic Warfare (MEW). After discovering the transaction, they had had enough. Officials at MEW put Jan and the Bat'a Company on the "Statutory List," also known as the blacklist, in May 1940.[44] The British government then vested the majority of stock for the Bat'a satellite companies in the British Empire, and the Canadian government did the same for the Bata Shoe Company of Canada Ltd.[45] At that, Jan lost financial control over all of Bat'a's operations in the British Empire and Commonwealth.

The British decision to blacklist Bat'a emboldened enemies in the United States, such as rival shoe companies and labour unions, who moved the government to eliminate the company from American soil. Their campaign was assisted by a political mistake of some magnitude.

Senator Millard Tydings, while technically in Franklin D. Roosevelt's Democratic Party, was one of the president's least favourite people.[46] Tydings was a conservative Democrat, fiscally and socially, and had criticized the New Deal since its inception. Furthermore, he decided to try to upset Roosevelt's re-election in 1940. Especially problematic for Bat'a was that Tydings's campaign was at least partially financed by Jan, who had made statements in the company press about the dangers of "Red Roosevelt." Financing a challenger to FDR proved foolish. Tydings took a drubbing in the primaries, gaining only 9 of 1,093 total votes at the Democratic National Convention.[47]

There was considerable retaliation, and Jan's foray into American politics reversed hard-earned concessions from the United States. Just two years before, in the spring of 1938, the United States had reached a historic trade agreement with Czechoslovakia, an agreement which raised the quota of Czechoslovak shoes (almost entirely Bat'a-made) allowed into the United States from

650,000 to 4.8 million pairs per year.[48] Now, after a "policy shift" in Washington, which occurred a few months after Tydings's announcement that he would challenge FDR in the primaries, only 10 of the requested 100 work visas for Czech specialists to build Belcamp were permitted to Bat'a.[49]

Still, work continued at a furious pace. Bat'a telegrammed Zlín in September 1939 for more workers to "tour the world's fair," obviously a way to get workers into Belcamp and circumvent the new restrictions on work visas. This too would prove harmful for Jan's American plans. For in that same month, the FBI launched an investigation into Jan's supposed "Nazi drive in the Americas," eventually accusing him of bringing in illegal Czech "teachers," some 350 of them. Most of these workers got to Maryland through tourist visas to see the New York World's Fair.[50]

To make matters worse, building a new Zlín in Maryland was creating a culture clash as Belcamp's residents began to sour on Batism. One of the first major issues concerned the company's desire to create a Bat'a Industrial School for young women and men along the lines of the Bat'a School of Work in Zlín. Company employees fanned out in Belcamp neighbourhoods and went to the area's high schools to distribute recruiting pamphlets for the school. They promised recruits a week of forty hours of work at the factory, ten hours of instruction, room and board, and recreation. They would have to live in Bata dormitories, and would be paid $12.63 a week, out of which $7.00 would be taken for room and board, and $3.00 for entertainment and education. The other $2.63 would go into a Bat'a savings account for the adolescents. The area residents were alarmed by the idea and the recruiting tactics. "Violent" protest erupted at a school meeting and city officials fielded calls from outraged parents. Bat'a had to abandon the school entirely.[51]

Like the parents, local Maryland workers were suspicious of the company's business culture. Three independent American contractors, interviewed by an agent for the Immigration and Naturalization Service (INS), reported that

> the company is known of its "sharp-practice"; that it is slow in paying its bills; that it is generally believed the company intends to make Belcamp into a foreign town, exploit American labor, keep the workers under subjugation by paying them small wages and requiring them to purchase all the necessities of life from company stores and saving their money in a company-controlled bank.

They further stated the company hires persons only under twenty-five years of age and has a speed-up system that borders on slave-driving. They said the company charges workers $30 a month for a four-room apartment which could be rented for less in the neighbourhood.[52]

The report revealed just how quickly Bat'a's reputation in Maryland was sinking. Having arrived only in June 1939, Bat'a had worn out its welcome by September 1940. In turn, the US government was becoming increasingly suspicious of Jan's loyalty and the company's business practices. Something had to be done quickly to save Bat'a in the UnitedStates.

In order to try to persuade the government of his apolitical intentions, Jan decided to move to Washington, DC, in the autumn of 1940. While there, Jan did nothing but harm to the Bat'a cause. In what was perhaps his defining moment in the United States, Jan refused to publicly denounce the Protectorate government or publicly support the Czechoslovak resistance. Accounts of the incident suggest he both feared for the fate of his company back home and deeply mistrusted Edvard Beneš. Bat'a, a critic of the government in the late 1930s, thought Beneš too leftist, too weak, and too bureaucratic for the country.[53] When Vladimir Hurban, one of the chief organizers for the Czechoslovak government-in-exile, visited Bat'a in Washington to ask for financial support for the resistance movement, now under the leadership of Beneš, Bat'a is reported to have said, "If he will be president, then you can expect not even a cent from me."[54] What is worse, according to former foreign minister Jan Masaryk, while in Washington Jan might have become slightly unhinged. Masaryk reported to the interdepartmental Bat'a Committee, set up after the United States had joined the war solely to keep track of the Bat'a Company, about a meeting in the fall of 1940. According to Masaryk, Jan Bat'a arranged to meet on a Washington street corner "at a certain hour one evening" so that Jan could "take him to an obscure restaurant," and there told him that "he planned to move 10 million Czechs to Argentina."[55]

While Jan was saying strange things to the wrong people in Washington, federal judge Calvin W. Chesnut enjoined Bat'a because of a violation of the US child labour laws – and this shortly after the company pleaded guilty to a wage and hour violation charge. The wage charge forced the company to make restitution of $10,000 to its employees.[56] The violation of child labour laws would be accompanied by further inspections and a fine. Both findings were the result of House Resolution 432 of the 76th Congress, which passed on 19 March 1940: "Resolved that the Committee on Labor shall immediately make an inquiry as to the un-American conditions of employment imposed upon workers at the plant of the Bata Shoe Company, Belcamp, Maryland … [and that the company] openly and willfully violated the Fair Labor Standards Act."[57] All of this was terrible public relations for the embattled firm. The Czech model of the ideal city as seen through American eyes was becoming highly problematic. In the United States, Bat'a had become saddled with the rhetoric of "mass dictation."[58]

The attack on Bat'a cast together unlikely allies. Endicott-Johnson, an early source of inspiration for Bat'a but now a rival, used its political muscle to push for an investigation into the company's operations in Maryland.[59]

EJ's CEO, George F. Johnson, criticized Bat'a on patriotic grounds: "the Czechoslovak threat of invasion in our own market, with politicians negotiating what they call a reciprocity agreement ... they come in here now, with their shoes made with 50 to 60% cheaper labor than ours, and sell certain patriotic (?) merchants, who in turn can sell this foreign stuff to patriotic (?) citizens."[60] Powers Hapgood, president of the National Boot and Shoe Workers Union, a group long at odds with the anti-union policy of Endicott-Johnson, joined EJ in its fight against Bat'a. Hapgood offered all of his union's evidence of the un-American practices of the company – including links to the Nazi Party (these were spurious at best) – to the investigators and the press. The *Baltimore Sun* picked up the story and ran a series of articles that linked Bat'a to "the Nazi War Machine."[61] Kenneth Crawford, a journalist for the New York daily *PM*, wrote on 26 September 1941 that the Bata Company was "potentially, if not actually, the most dangerous unit of the Hitler fifth column on the march today."[62]

The State Department, the FBI, and the Department of Commerce seemed to agree. Unlike Jan, the FDR administration did not dally. In just a matter of months after the initial House Resolution, Immigration and Naturalization began an investigation into the Belcamp plant. This was the investigation that led to the fines and charges relating to wages and child labour. It was also the one that would quickly break up Jan's vision of reassembling the best and brightest *Batovci* on the shores of the Chesapeake.

The investigation found that 100 "instructors" from Czechoslovakia were not simply instructing. They were managing and participating in nearly every aspect of operations. As a result, most of their visas were voided. These instructors and Jan Bata were expelled from the United States. Immigration agents gave almost all of the highly talented Bat'a men and women in Maryland "a reasonable amount of time to prepare for departure."[63] In their eyes, this meant one month. After receiving the news, most of these young people went to South America to start subsidiaries there. They fanned out to create new factories in Chile, Bolivia, Argentina, Peru, Brazil, and Haiti, with very little start-up capital. Jan moved to Brazil.[64] A few decided to stay in the United States.

Interestingly, though sending a serious signal to Bat'a that their work practices and immigration tactics would not be tolerated, the United States did not want to close the plant down entirely. For it seems that Bat'a was far ahead of American shoe manufacturers in a crucial field. Part of the investigation turned up that Bat'a's vulcanization process and rubber shoe manufacturing process in general had no parallel among American manufacturers. As a result, the United States gave work visas to eight instructors in the rubber section, and the plant continued to operate.[65]

The Burden of Nazi Authority

Back at home, the city and company were losing the rationalized cosmopolitanism they had long crafted. At first, the loss seemed superficial rather than structural. After all, aside from a symbolic display on the town's square by the motorized German infantry company that first came into the city in March 1939, decision making for company, town, and its schools remained largely in *Batovci* hands. It would not be until the end of March 1941, in fact, that the city council would have to welcome Drs. Albrecht Miesbach and Maximilian Bittner as mandated council members for the German community. Even then, Miesbach had proven himself a reasonable and honourable person as director of the Bat'a factories, and he would go on to save managers from the horrors of concentration camps.[66]

Nevertheless, Nazi demands were far from light.[67] In May 1940, for example, the Gestapo turned the basement of the town hall into a jail for political prisoners. From then on, as the city council went about its day-to-day affairs, twenty-eight people languished below them for alleged political resistance.[68]

While the prison was a stark symbol of the occupation, things did not dramatically change until the beginning of 1941. For this was when Zlín and the surrounding areas were firmly put under the dictates of Nazi authority. It started with renaming the town square to "Main Square," from "Masaryk Square," and accelerated rapidly when the German authorities took over the schools.[69] A new German school, "for the purposes of school and the purposes of the NSDAP" opened that year. It was only for Germans. The Czech-speaking students' curriculum was significantly changed. German-language classes were no longer optional.[70] The city had to prepare and deliver a map of all of the Jewish-owned property in town to regional authorities by the end of February.[71] By November 1941, everyone working for the city had to be able to speak German.

Outside of Zlín, in 1941 Bat'a's customer first policies faced total collapse. One example of the dismantling of Bat'a's company culture is seen in the Aryanization of a run-of-the-mill retail store in Hodonín.

The pedicurists at the Bat'a "House of Service" in Hodonín, a small town on the border of Slovakia and Moravia, were having a typically busy Wednesday afternoon in 1941 when Mrs. Marie Tuplerová of Hodonín walked into the salon. Tuplerová walked past the small, crowded waiting room and directly to the pedicure "cabins," where she cut in front of a customer getting ready to sit in one of the recently vacated high-backed black leather chairs used for pedicures. Before Tuplerová could sit down however, Alice Králičková, a pedicurist at Bat'a for seven months, pointed to the woman behind Tuplerová and explained that customers were received in the order in which they appeared, to which Tuplerová replied, "that woman is a Jew!" Králičková paused before saying that, whether the customer was a Jew or not, the company's policy was first come, first served. Tuplerová shouted in response, "That woman is a Jew and you are protecting her!" and then stormed out of the store.

Tuplerová then walked directly to the police station, some one hundred metres away. There, she voiced a complaint against Králičková and the Bat'a store in general for being Jew-friendly. Her complaint received immediate attention, as Warrant Officer Ertlem quickly contacted the commissar of Hodonín, a Dr. Karl Boss. Boss immediately sent for Králičková upon hearing the story. The pedicurist arrived a few hours later. She explained. "The woman in the waiting room was Jewish. But then [Tuplerová] left immediately and I could not even get the opinion of my manager." [72] After Králičková gave her account, Dr. Boss arrived and demanded to see the manager of the store in Hodonín, Jan Trlida. Trlida would later describe the encounter in a report to corporate headquarters in Zlín:

> On the day of 31 July 1941, I was called on by Warrant Officer Ertlem to go with him to City Hall so that I could meet with the government commissar, Dr. Boss. I immediately complied with him and went to City Hall.
>
> Mr. Government Commissar Dr. Boss had maybe two pages of documents about the regulation of businesses on the table …
>
> The commissar said to me that I probably already knew why I was there and that the Gestapo was also aware of the circumstances. Then he said that they had discovered that the manager of our sales department makes Aryan staff wash the feet of Jews and he said loudly, "Jews can wash their filthy paws at home and not in cabins of the Bat'a pedicurist." He said it was misconduct, which required a radical remedy. Furthermore, he said we employ staff that gives preferential treatment to Jews. They apparently found a woman working for us who has had an affair with a Jew, and even lived with him. He then said that we knew about these Jew lovers and because of this we could suffer. Then he described in detail what mistakes we were making and what the new situation required.[73]

Over the next week, Trlida met twice more with Boss. At each meeting, the Nazi official became more congenial. At their last meeting, Boss informed Trlida that the whole affair was really Tuplerová's fault for not speaking German immediately upon entering the store. The store clerk, Králičková, simply did not have the chance to realize who she was dealing with, a member of the master race.

After learning "what the new situation required," Trlida implemented a policy that stipulated that Jews could only be served after hours, one day a week, and hung in the storefront a sign in German and Czech that read "Jews Are Forbidden to Enter." Trlida went on to say, "On my next visit I informed Mr.

General Commissar about my solution. [He] was satisfied with what I had done and promised that he would be visiting the store very soon as a customer."[74]

The incident in the pedicurist cabins in Hodonín provides striking evidence of the everyday erosion of civility brought about by Nazi racial policies. Essentially, a person could now use their "race," sanctioned by the use of the German language, to demand preferential service. As the scholars Frank Bajohr and Götz Aly have shown, average Germans directly benefited from the Holocaust through small, mundane interactions.[75] The state would now support Tuplerová's attitude of superiority. She should not have to wait for a pedicure now that she was considered an Aryan. Yet such privilege was far from immediate. The Nazi occupation had been on for two years before the local Nazi authorities mandated that Germans' feet must come first. The Bat'a customer first philosophy was tenacious, even in occupied Europe. Nevertheless, the incident in Hodonín happened just weeks after the German invasion of the Soviet Union. After June 1941, the cosmopolitan idea that all customers were to be treated as "lords" (a philosophy that would not return to the Eastern Bloc for fifty years), was systematically dismantled. No longer would first come, first served apply. From then on, Bat'a managers negotiated race policies with Nazi authorities. In this one case, it seems the Bat'a training of putting business over politics helped to allow Trlida to put his store above his morality. After all, he found a solution to keep the business moving, gaining a new customer in the process.

In the Nazi-occupied areas, including Zlín, the invasion of the Soviet Union turned the company's entire output toward the Third Reich. The company became the leading footwear producer for the German Army, and also contributed hundreds of thousands of tires for German army vehicles.[76] The factories in Chełmek and Ottmuth came to be used by the Nazi authorities as work camps, with nearby sites becoming extermination camps. Moreover, across Bat'a's vast retail empire in Central Europe, Nazi racial laws dramatically destroyed the culture of Bat'a. By so doing, one could argue that Czechs were then more likely to accept the national chauvinism of both the communists and Beneš' National Socialists. The outcome was that retail culture in Czechoslovakia would never really return to the Bat'a standards of the interwar era.

The United States versus Jan Bat'a

The *Batovci* who found themselves on the Allied side of the Second World War had to deal with new demands on their business operations, though none of these had to do with retail practices. Away from the dictates of Nazi authority, company personnel were nonetheless placed under considerable restrictions from Allied state actors. Once the United States entered the war in December 1941, American authorities carried Bat'a over from the British Statutory List and put it on the Proclaimed List, which was also commonly referred to as the "blacklist." Bat'a's operations in the Americas, Asia, and Africa were then put under strict surveillance and government oversight for the duration of the war.[77] The effects of the blacklist were immediate. All of Bat'a's liquid assets in North America were frozen. A regulatory body under the direction of the Treasury Department's Foreign Funds Control now had to approve the financial transactions of all of the subsidiary companies in the Allied sphere, and each manager of each subsidiary was now subject to a thorough investigation. Furthermore, the government intercepted and reported on the personal correspondence of employees routinely. One such instance of intercepted correspondence involved a B. Cekota, a Bat'a employee in Buenos Aires, and Vladimir Chlud, one of the major shareholders and investors in the Bata Company North America, who was living in New York. The exchange revealed the doubts that many of the rank-and-file managers of the company had come to have about their boss: "In 1941, Dr. Jab [short for Jan A. Bata] apparently counted on German victory and only from afar and indirectly did he flirt with the democratic powers, pretending to be a martyr, a victim of Nazism, which was only partly true. I think that he does deserve to be put on the blacklist because he did not permit the timely sale of the stock of shoes that Zlín had accumulated in Norway before the war, thus letting it fall into the hands of the Germans as war booty."[78] Cekota's suspicions would be later used by the leaders of postwar Czechoslovakia who tried Jan in absentia in 1947, before the communist coup. At the trial, the state prosecutors used the failure to sell off the large shoe supplies in Norway before the Nazis could seize them as evidence of Jan's collaboration.[79] He was found guilty.

As the war continued, Bat'a employees everywhere the company operated in Allied territory were put under new restrictions by the state. They struggled to maintain their stores and factories. Employees could no longer access savings accounts, and salaries almost altogether stopped for managers. The State Department's Division of World Trade Intelligence issued reports on Chile, Haiti, Peru, and Panama for the Interdepartmental Committee in 1942 and found in Panama two employees, John Albrecht and William Švab (the manager and assistant manager of two stores in the country) in desperate straits: "Meagre earnings from Bata ... Svab intends to close the [retail stores] in Panama City and Colon. He does not know what to do with the inventory, which he estimates is worth some $50,000 ... he claims that Bata owes him $5,000 and wonders if he could, since there are no funds on hand, take the equivalent of his claim in shoes for inventory ... he has urgently requested that he be relieved of his responsibility." Albrecht "is likewise anxious to free himself from Bata employment."[80] As employees pondered looting inventory to make up for back pay, the power of the United States was on full display vis-à-vis a transnational corporation.

Under such constraints, Bat'a tried desperately to be removed from the blacklist. On 15 September 1942, Jan Bata wrote to Jefferson Caffery, the US ambassador to Brazil, and offered to solve the Allies' rubber shortage: "Brazil can produce all the rubber that is needed, if the work is properly organized. I know how to organize it, and know how to achieve results, ones that will satisfy the need for crude rubber for the United States and the Allied Nations – in one to five years ... all that I would ask as compensation would be the delisting of my person and of the Bata Companies internationally before the end of 1942."[81]

The offer did little for the British or the Americans. In Washington, the State Department, the Treasury Department, and the Board of Economic Warfare assembled a Bat'a Committee in early 1942, because "an organization of world-wide ramifications and power cannot adequately be controlled by a system of Treasury operating licenses." The committee interviewed several key Bat'a personnel and Czechoslovak officials, including Jan Masaryk, the foreign minister of the Czechoslovak government-in-exile:

[Masaryk] stated that with his thousands of other interests Bata was only another problem with him, and that while he was interested in seeing everything possible to reach a satisfactory solution, he had no personal interest in the matter. He stated that his official interest is based on the fact that "Bata" is a great Czechoslovakian name, and that it is more or less a disgrace to his nation to have it on the Proclaimed List ... Masaryk stated that he knows Jan Bata intimately and that he is not the "great business man" he is reputed to be. In fact, Jan Bata has made rather a mess of the great enterprise and has alienated many of his leading men. He stated that Bata is "not a Nazi," but is more or less a "fool."[82]

Another key witness was Thomas Bat'a Jr., who had emigrated to Canada and set up another factory town there in 1939. There, Thomas carefully cultivated a positive relationship with Canadian authorities and allowed them full control over the factory's finances. He also turned over production entirely to produce military footwear to supply the Allies. Especially considering that his mother, Marie Bat'a, had returned to Zlín in 1940 to maintain control of Bata A.S. Zlín, Thomas's enthusiasm for the Allied cause threw into relief Jan's justifications for his noncommittal responses. Jan had repeatedly told officials that he dared not make a statement against the Axis powers for fear they would retaliate against loved ones in Zlín.[83] Soon after meeting with the committee members in 1942, Thomas was seen by American and Canadian officials as a reliable replacement to run Bat'a worldwide: "Thomas Bata Jr. impressed us with his straightforwardness and sincerity. He is about 27 years of age. He and his company are, we believe, well regarded by Canadian authorities. His company in Canada operates under the supervision of a committee of three government custodians and is manufacturing some 47 different articles for the Canadian war effort."[84]

The committee decided that the US response to the thorough investigation should be to place the company under the jurisdiction of the recently recreated Office of Alien Property, which had been reinstituted after Roosevelt signed Executive Order 9095 on 11 March 1942. The office, charged with managing and acquiring enemy assets, reported directly to the president and had considerable power. Any business or asset of a company deemed an enemy company could be seized. The United States placed all of Bat'a's holdings and businesses in the United States, the Caribbean, and Central America under the control of the Office of Alien Property.

Almost immediately after taking legal control of the Bat'a Company in the United States, Homer Jones, an agent in the Division of Investigation and Research, sent a confidential memorandum to the Executive Committee of the Office of Alien Property. In it, Jones claimed that all of the Bat'a executives operating in the United States were "acting for and on behalf of Jan Bata and are 'nationals' of a designated country [Germany]."[85] The report was followed by a vesting of all stock from the shareholders of not only Bata Shoe Company Inc. (the subsidiary organized in the United States) but all of the US-based subsidiaries. These were as follows: Westhold Corporation (shareholders Hoza and Vladimir Chlud); Anchor Mercantile Co. Inc.; New World Investment, Ltd. (Dr. George Wettstein, Zurich; Charles Jucker, Zurich, Wilhelmine Meier, Zurich; Leader A.G., Transoceanic); North River Securities Corporation (Donald Hill); Muscamo Corporation (Frank Muska).[86]

These companies would stay under the control of the Office of Alien Property for over three years, regaining their freedom only in March 1946. In the interim, the company split into three distinctly controlled enterprises: Bat'a Brazil, controlled by Jan; Bat'a Company N.S., controlled by the government of Czechoslovakia; and Bata Canada, controlled by Thomas Bata Jr., which gained control of nearly every subsidiary company outside of the Soviet sphere of influence and outside of Brazil in the coming years. How Jan was reduced to having control only over the emerging factory towns of Batatuba, Bataipora, and Bataguassu had much to do with the way in which US government officials handled the company between 1943 and 1946, and the way in which Edvard Beneš envisioned the socialist future of Czechoslovakia. These three years determined the next seventy-six.

By the fall of 1943, the Bat'a Committee decided to allow Bat'a companies to be removed from the Proclaimed List if they signed an agreement to legally disassociate with Jan Bat'a. The following example from Haiti is representative of dozens of contracts Bat'a managers had to sign to free themselves from the blacklists. In signed documents between the manager of the Bat'a enterprise in Haiti, Chaussures Bata Haiti S.A., Frank Votava, and the United States, signed 15 November 1943, Votava agreed "not to recognize any control by or on the part of or to have any relations of any kind with Jan Bata."[87] By signing the agreement, Bat'a Haiti could now control its own finances, and was free to enter into contracts without government approval. Severing all connections with Jan was the condition of continued operation. Across the Allied world, company managers signed similar agreements. And yet while the agreement to disassociate with Jan Bat'a floated around the Americas, Jan remained hopeful his name would be cleared and he could return to run the company.

As the war drew to a close, Jan wrote a letter to the British ambassador to Brazil, Donald St. Clair Gainor, on 15 March 1945, asking to have his name and his Brazilian companies taken off the blacklist. It was a passionate letter, full of feelings of betrayal and despair.

> For all years before the war, I have carried an economic policy based upon confidence to the British Empire. Our policy [after the Munich Agreement] was to tear the most of means from reach of Germans and turn them to friendly, British and American countries ... It was a dangerous game, which only centuries of tradition in this sort of fight and wisdom and confidence of British and American authorities made possible.
>
> Therefore, I felt humiliated, when in February of 1940, Ministry of Economic Warfare, came with questions and conditions, which indicated their mistrust ...
>
> My legal representative, whom I sent to MEW after publication [of the blacklist], wrote that he was surprised by the amount of enmity he found against us in London, for which he was unable to find an explanation. I am sure that industrial work in the British Empire, and whatever MEW mentioned to him against us as reason for distrust, would have brought me – after careful and impartial consideration – a British Knighthood – rather than blacklisting.[88]

A knighthood would not be in Jan's future. Instead, socialist imperatives in Central and Eastern Europe, and a resolute nephew in Canada, denied Jan a return to his kingdom.

The Czechoslovak, Yugoslav, and Polish states went on to nationalize all of the Bat'a factories in the immediate postwar period. Edvard Beneš, restored to the presidency of Czechoslovakia, enacted his plan of national socialism, which forcibly removed millions of German and Hungarian civilians and nationalized all large industries in the country. Bat'a, being the largest, was one of the first to be nationalized. On 14 May 1945, only four days after the end of the fighting in Prague, the National Council of Greater Zlín announced to thousands of workers gathered in the Bat'a courtyard that they, the workers, were going to be in control.[89] In the eyes of many nationalists, Bat'a's national indifference had been a problem for some time. Given the opportunity, prewar nationalists aligned with communists to seize all of Bat'a's assets in the country, including the massive industrial-social complex of Zlín – valued in 1945 at US$300 million. All of the executives who had remained throughout the war, such as Dominik Čipera and Hugo Vavrečka, were removed from their positions within the company. Two years later, in 1947, Czechoslovakia brought a charge of "crimes against the state" against Jan and found him guilty. He was sentenced in absentia to twenty years of hard labour and his personal holdings were confiscated by the state. The charges, levelled by the communist-controlled Ministry of the Interior, guaranteed that Jan could not press for compensation for losses due to the nationalization of his company.

Meanwhile, control over global operations passed to Thomas Bat'a Jr. By 1945 the Interdepartmental Committee, which had taken over control from Jan in all of Bat'a's operations in the Western hemisphere except Brazil, handed control over to Thomas. The British authorities in the Ministry of Economic Warfare, which had done the same to all of Bat'a's operations in Africa, the Middle East, and India, saw no reason to continue any sanctions. By November 1945, the MEW was arguing that the Bat'a enterprises should be removed from the blacklist, especially since "control of these firms lies in Switzerland and with Tom Bata and not in Jan Bata's hands nor in Czechoslovakia."[90] A new era in the company's history, one centred in Canada and Switzerland and in the hands of Thomas Bat'a Jr., had begun.

Conclusion

If Bat'a's rapid expansion across the globe from 1929 to 1937 provides powerful evidence of the futility of tariffs on a globalized manufacturing company, the freezing of company assets, the nationalization of company headquarters, and the fracturing of company leadership illustrate the power of the state and its primary motivation in relations to the transnational company. As seen through the saga of Jan Bata, the limit of globalization is loyalty.

By turning over the Canadian branch of the company to Canadian bureaucrats, dedicating production entirely toward military equipment, and openly professing his loyalty to the Allies, Thomas Bata Jr., unlike Jan, was able to convince British, American, and Canadian officials of his trustworthiness in a way that Jan never could. Jan's personal failings of Jan stood in the way. First there were his fascist predilections. If company founder Tomáš had looked to Henry Ford for inspiration, Jan had looked to Mussolini in the mid-1930s. Even his choice of Brazil as his refuge, where his close friend President Getulio Vargas had instituted the "Estado Novo," an authoritarian corporatist model based on that of fascist Italy, speaks of Jan's continued leaning to the far right.[91] Furthermore, he refused to spend money to mollify the British because of personal pride. He clung to his Patagonia Plan when there was no longer any tolerance for such silliness. He was unable to see that the Zlín model would not work in Belcamp. Chiefly, he failed to appreciate that a transnational company must choose a side in a world war. As Jan Masaryk said, he was no Nazi, but more or less a fool.

During the Second World War, loyalty to the state became the ultimate criterion for success in business. Jan and many *Batovci*, steeped in the national indifference of a transnational corporation, struggled to realize this. Others, though, used their indifference, and their ability to blend in, to free the company from government control and maintain global operations. When it was all over, the *Batovci* preserved control over global operations everywhere except in the emerging Soviet Bloc. Even after the collapse of imperialism in South Asia, Africa, and the Middle East, *Batovci* remained in control of the factories and retail outlets in the newly forming states.

Jan lived out the rest of his days in Brazil, the one country that allowed him to keep control over the Bat'a subsidiaries. He never stopped fighting in the courts to regain control of the company he lost in wartime. Branded a traitor at home, he died in 1965 a figure of some significance in Brazil, a country that had heartily embraced Jan even during his darkest days.[92] Eventually, Jan would be remade in Czech popular memory as an anti-communist hero after the fall of communism in the 1990s and 2000s. His conviction would be rescinded in 2007 when a Czech court officially cleared his name.[93]

Thomas Jr. carried on the rest of the operations around the world until he handed over power to his son in 1984. As he looked back at his life, Thomas would write that he felt Canadian, and that receiving the Order of Canada was "the only decoration that really matters to me."[94] Thomas's fierce loyalty to his adopted nation, and undoubtedly his unequivocal support for the Allied cause, allowed him and his company to emerge from the Cold War as untainted patriots of liberal democracy.

Bat'a remains a major brand in the global shoe industry. Perhaps owing to the blacklisting of the company, however, the Bat'a brand was never to become a household name in the United States. Instead, the company disguised Bat'a shoes under a plethora of different labels, such as Onguard, Power, and Bullets. Even under those names, Bat'a never made much of an inroad in the American market. Belcamp continued its operations all the way into the 1990s, under Canadian-based Bat'a management, but Bat'a never dominated the American market.

Overall, Bat'a's saga in the Second World War suggests that perhaps the world is flat only when there is a hegemony of military power. In times of global conflict nation-states will demand loyalty of the multinational, and, ultimately, the multinational corporation will have to pick a side. Perhaps walking the tightrope of national indifference is more dangerous for multinational companies than we currently realize.[95]

Conclusion

On 2 April 2007 the city of Zlín opened a conference to "morally cleanse the name of J.A. Bat'a." With a series of lectures, Czech academics made the case for Jan's "genius," innocence, and forthrightness. Milan Zelený, a professor of management systems at Fordham University, visiting professor at Tomas Bat'a University in Zlín, and long-time Bat'a acolyte, gave two talks that praised Jan's "thoughts, systems, and entrepreneurship." [1] While a relatively modest affair, the conference signalled that Jan's rehabilitation was under way. One month later, on the eightieth anniversary of Bat'a's 1937 May Day spectacle, a more public celebration of Jan took place. City officials, Jan's Brazilian-born family, a group of notable Zlínians, and a few dozen citizens unveiled a life-sized statue of Jan in University Park, just across from the old Bat'a administrative headquarters, the "21." At the ceremony, a spokesperson for the mayor announced, "the unveiling of this statue is the first step in cleansing the name of Jan Bat'a." A relative from Brazil added, "Jan Bat'a was a patriot who loved his country, he was a hero … I thank all the citizens of Zlín who helped the government clear his name." [2] In June, the court that had sentenced Jan in absentia in 1947 agreed to reopen his trial. In mid-November, the court ruled that the new prosecutor could find no evidence of a crime. [3] Jan's legal rehabilitation took less than a year. Condemned by the postwar Beneš regime as a collaborator, and then excoriated by the Communist Party as an oppressive industrialist, Jan is viewed by twenty-first-century Czechs with adoration for the most part. He is again a hero in Zlín.

Undeniably, official histories and commemorative events since the fall of communism have become crucial in shaping a positive public memory of the Bat'a legacy. Critics of Bat'a have fallen in the shadows of free market capitalism; far wealthier interests cast considerable shade and institutes financed by company executives and political parties are eager to make use of the "golden years" of the interwar era. In place of the lengthy diatribes against the company sponsored by the regime of the Czechoslovak Socialist Republic, there are now brief articles that infrequently appear on the website of the KSČM in Zlín (Komunistá strana Čech a Moravy).[4] Meanwhile, pro-Bat'a literature, once produced by only a handful of people who had emigrated to the West, has reclaimed Czech-language audiences over the last thirty years with a flood of popular and academic publications. A veritable army of institutions, Tomas Bat'a University (Univerzita Tomáše Bati), the Thomas Bat'a Foundation (Nadace Tomáše Bati), the J.A. Bat'a Foundation, and the Tomas Bat'a Archive, which all have strong links to the company, have moved into Zlín with clear mandates to promote the perception of Bat'a as a virtuoso enterprise. Add to this the drying up of state and university money for independent historical research in the 1990s and early 2000s, and the post-communist era has been one of a profound revisionism: so as to make Bat'a usable in the contemporary Czech Republic, this revisionism has smoothed out many rough edges – especially the mottled record of Jan Bat'a.

As with the earlier work of communist critics, the new interpretation of the Bat'a Company flattens history. Only now, the darker sides of the Bat'a project are removed instead of highlighted, and now, instead of questions about worker loyalty and managerial ingenuity, questions about how Bat'a manufactured consent and marginalized dissent go unasked. While vital scholarship continues to be produced by a handful of professional Czech historians, now public and amateur historians, politicians, filmmakers, city and regional governments, and business elites have by and large succeeded in grinding the positivist lens with which the public now sees the company. Consider the recently opened Bat'a Institute and Museum, whose permanent exhibit is entitled "The Bat'a Principle: Today's Fantasy, Tomorrow's Reality"; it provides an excellent example of just how the makers of history in Zlín create myth.

Housed in a former factory building, the Bat'a Institute's Museum offers today's visitors fun interactive experiences through games such as, "Can You Build a Shoe?" and "Can You Build Zlín?" It is clearly meant to squeeze entertainment out of industrial shoemaking. One board game on offer has players go through the everyday life of a fourteen-year-old enrolled in the Bat'a School of Work. Moving pieces across a large wooden gameboard, the players vie to be the first to race through an exhausting day that starts at 6:00 a.m. in the dormitory and ends only at 9:15 p.m. The game matches up well with the actual schedules of the Young Men.[5] Behind the games, visitors are given a narrative of Bat'a's history that would make any true *Batovci* from the 1930s stand and applaud. Indeed, much of the story, told in Czech and in English, reads as if lifted right out of company publications from the mid-1930s. This is because that is exactly what the curators have done. One wall of the exhibit is covered with maps and statistics taken directly from Jan Bat'a's book, *We Will Build a State of 40,000,000.*[6]

In addition, in 2017, only a few years after the opening of the Bat'a Insti-tute, the city of Zlín reconverted Tomáš Bat'a's memorial building, which had been the House of the Arts since 1948, back to a monument to Tomáš Bat'a.[7] As the shoe factories have fallen silent, the core of the former Bat'a world has become a massive memorial complex for the two managers who oversaw its construction.

This trend fits well with the ways in which Bat'a has become a political tool. Unlike when he wrote it in 1937, Jan's book caught the attention of the most powerful political figure in the country, the prime minister of the Czech Republic, Andřej Babiš. Babiš, like Tomáš Bat'a, grew a company into a large multinational enterprise (AGROFERT) before going into politics.[8] During his political career, Babiš has frequently referenced the company as a positive example for Czech business, and Tomáš as an influential example of the busi-nessman/politician.[9] In the summer of 2017, Babiš announced his grand vision for the country into the year 2035; as he laid his plan out to a live-streamed audience, he revealed his inspiration: Jan A. Bat'a's *We Will Build a State*. Just like Jan, Babiš called for massive infrastructure projects, and for reforming the political system. He added, with language that would have brought smiles to Jan and Tomáš's faces, "we have to depoliticize the legislative process."[10]

The memorialization project reached new heights in 2018 with an event enti-tled "11 Days of Jan Bat'a" ("11 dnů s J.A. Bat'ou"). Organized and funded by city and regional governments, private companies (the real estate company Cream being the primary sponsor), and the J.A. Bat'a Foundation, the event offered a series of talks (largely by the Brazilian-born descendants of Jan), documentary film premiers, and tours of various important locations in Jan's relatively brief tenure as chief executive.[11] Its aim was to celebrate the "120th birthday of Jan Bat'a – executive, entrepreneur, visionary, patriot, and carrier of the work of Tomáš Bat'a."[12] While a few respected historians did participate, their voices were overwhelmed by a tone of unabashed hero worship. Provid-ing historical nuance was not the point. Making money was the point. To put together such a celebration, a wide range of sponsors worked with a realty company deeply invested in the makeover of one Bat'a's old factory buildings – more evidence that being associated with Bat'a is good for business in the Czech Republic.

A growing number of cultural productions are raising the profile of the com-pany as well. While not all of these take a clear pro-Bat'a stance,[13] the vast majority of them do.[14] Among the handful of works aimed at a popular audi-ence in the English language, one will have a hard time finding a critique, though the use of the company for political ends is largely absent.[15] Czech-lan-guage cultural productions, however, deal with the company, and especially the two chief executives, as national icons. The theatrical production *Tomas Bat'a Lives!* (*Bat'a Tomáš, živý!*) ran in the theatrical season of 2015, and was popular enough to be filmed for Czech television. The play, the first in a planned trilogy, aims for high art with its surreal scenes of a resurrected Tomáš interacting with symbolic half men/half white horses, but nevertheless its message is clear – here was a titan of Czech entrepreneurship.[16] Soon, audiences will be able to watch a feature-length film about the experiences of Tomáš from 1904 to 1924. While it is impossible to gauge the way in which the film will portray the company, it looks nonetheless to be a major undertaking. The film, still unnamed at the time of the writing of this book, will be a big budget production, with one of the Czech Republic's rising actors, Martin Hofmann, in the starring role.[17]

At this point, one wonders if a Bat'a theme park is next. And, so what if it is? After all, the positive public memory that a host of Bat'a aficionados carefully crafted has a had a definitively positive economic effect on the city of Zlín. Without the myth of the genius Czech enterprise, when the shoe factories closed in the mid-1990s Zlín would more than likely have shared the fate of most post-industrial cities: high unemployment, real estate collapse, and vanishing city services. Drawing on the Bat'a legacy, especially the company's architectural legacy, the city has been able to successfully win a range of EU funds, most notably a European Investment Bank loan of 50 million euros on very favourable terms for general "rehabilitation."[18] Local commitment to preserving Bat'a's Zlín has been equally impressive. The Region of Zlín invested over 650 million Czech crowns to renovate the famous "21," Jan's "skyscraper," complete with an office in an elevator car, and turn it into the financial and administrative building for the Zlín Region in 2004.[19] Perhaps the biggest moment in the project to restore the equation that Bat'a equals Zlín, came when Václav Havel, the grandson of Bat'a executive Hugo Vavrečka, signed into law an act creating Tomas Bata University in Zlín. Originally comprising technical faculty that served the needs of shoe production for *Svit*, the university quickly pivoted to management training and is thriving. Creating a public university saved a significant portion of the city from urban blight; it saved most of the old dormitories while creating a powerful link between Bat'a and the town.

Yet, sitting in the film room of the Bat'a Institute and playing various Bat'a videos from its "golden era," one begins to see the positive projection as a mask that hides a much more unsettled past. For watching the gymnastics routines of the Young Women, the mass organized May Day parades, and the speeches of Jan Bat'a makes clear that the Bat'a principle, whatever that is taken to mean, belongs firmly in the context of its creation and makes little sense as a phenomenon to try to resurrect. Batism arose in era of mass politics and efficiency, an era in which trading privacy and independence for work and comfort had a much stronger appeal. Perhaps most of all, Bat'a's "golden age" existed in a world of utopian dreams. Humans were perfectible. They just needed rational organization.

And herein lie the two major problems of the current resurrection of the Bat'a Company as genius: in it we encounter both a country intent on rescuing the myth of a democratic First Republic of Czechoslovakia and the historical reality of a globalized company's national indifference, entrenched gender roles, and undemocratic spirit. At some point, more public intellectuals and politicians of the Czech Republic are going to have to come to terms with the tension between the company town and the First Republic's democracy and nationalism – something that more than a few writers have pointed out.[20] At no point between 1905 and 1945 can one assert that Batism embraced multiparty democracy or gender equality. In addition, affixing the label of Czechoslovak patriot, or national hero, to company executives of the 1930s is ahistorical. The executives were more often at odds with democracy and nationalism than they were championing them. Indeed, the present work points to a simple truth – the history of the Bat'a Company is a history of conflict between a rationalizing system of industrial production and a colourful cast of opponents – democrats, nationalists, communists, libertines, aristocrats, and small business owners.

At the heart of the tension was the fact that Bat'a's Zlín did not exist in an authoritarian state, but it became an authoritarian company town nonetheless. Because of its small size, poverty, and post–First World War turmoil, the Dřevnice Valley could do little to resist the revolutionary impulses of rationalization. Everyday life became enmeshed in a project designed to sweep away the past's daily rhythms as the Bat'a project turned a sleepy town into the nexus of a massive industrial enterprise. The dominant spaces became large, shared, and company-owned. Populating them were factory workers with personnel cards whose lives dropped into and out of a sophisticated system of surveillance and discipline that sought out the most intimate details of their lives. By some basic measures, their lives improved. Reports of declining infant mortality rates, low unemployment, and higher wages show this improvement. Against these, we have reports of the personnel inspectors detailing workers' private affairs. For women, careers were cut short, heads were patted, and value determined by motherhood. The system, to borrow from Noam Chomsky, was able to manufacture consent in a particularly modern way, as it offered a trade that few people at the time could refuse: personal privacy, lifestyle choices, and political participation in exchange for a relatively well-paid, secure, and comfortable life. Bat'a, then, provides ample evidence of both the light and dark sides of modernity.[21]

Another major source of tension in the history of the company concerns globalization. The Bat'a legend makers in today's Czech Republic have embraced Bat'a as a hero of the Czech nation, but they tend to ignore one of most important aspects of the company: Bat'a as a pioneer of post-colonial globalization. The company was and is much larger than Zlín and the Czech Republic. Its gaze knew no spatial limit.[22] It was the first to globalize the shoe industry and provide a democratic shopping experience to people across the world. The way in which it did so offers profound lessons for the role of national indifference in the process of globalization. After all, Bat'a's act of surviving the Second World War proved how the globalized corporation could be free from the nation-state. As it globalized from 1928 to 1945, it became transnational, making it impossible to be tethered to one state. The nationalization of Bata A.S. Zlín did not sink the company by any stretch of the imagination. Neither did the far-reaching blacklists of the Allied powers. The complexity and vastness of its organizational structures, as well as its advanced technology, allowed it to operate during and around those state restrictions.

At the same time, its globalization certainly did not provide evidence of the emasculation of state power. State actors around the world bent Bat'a to their will. The most dramatic illustration of this was the forced removal of Jan Bat'a from all operations save Brazil in 1944. If Bat'a's rapid expansion across the globe from 1929 to 1935 provides powerful evidence of the futility of tariffs on a globalized company, then the freezing of company assets, the nationalization of company headquarters, and the fracturing of company leadership illustrate the power of the state and its primary motivation in relation to the transnational company.

The company managed to navigate through precarious situations because of its globalism. Shoemakers committed to a national market and a set location, like Bat'a's former idol-turned-rival Endicott-Johnson, did not survive the deindustrialization of manufacturing in the Global North. To this day, Bat'a is one of the biggest shoe companies in the world; it sells on average one million pairs of shoes a day.[23] It remains the largest seller of shoes in India, and, while not nearly as large as Yue Yuen, the Taiwanese company whose 335,000-strong labour force makes huge numbers of shoes for Nike, Adidas, Puma, New Balance, Timberland, and ASICS, among others, for the world market, Bata remains active in manufacturing, currently running twenty-three factories in eighteen countries.[24]

As C.A. Bayly postulated, the fundamental feature of modernity was a growing global uniformity.[25] Food, political ideas, dress, sport, leisure, and commodities were becoming more homogeneous as people around the world engaged in this most complicated of project of modernity. If one only looks at the shoes themselves, the history of Bat'a supports Bayly's thesis of growing global uniformity. After all, Bat'a made shoes that were recognized across the globe for their modern style. And it made them in factory towns, built around the world, according to the principles of rationalization – that buzzword of the interwar era the globe over.

Yet in their remarkable similarity, these mini-Zlíns stood out in their local contexts. And so too did the people that came to manage them, Czech speakers who were educated as *Batovci* and were prized for their commitment to national indifference. Indeed, the Bat'a uniformity seemed quite unusual to the peoples of Belcamp, East Tilbury, and Calcutta when it arrived. Furthermore, the company quickly realized it needed to become recognized as a local company, and not part of a global, uniform business to succeed. Just as the standardized flat-roofed red-bricked buildings were going up, the *Batovci* began the task of blending in. All of this is to say that Bat'a, while being an agent of global uniformity through the mass distribution and production of shoes, was also forced to become highly sensitive to the local. Thus, while the oxford shoe and ladies' pump proliferated, so too did the winter boots made specifically for Canada, the basketball shoes for the United States, and the sandals for the Middle East. Additionally, by adjusting their branding to reflect local sensibilities wherever they operated, Bata executives guaranteed the company life in the post-colonial world: "In every country Bata operates, we are thought to be a local business."[26]

Such sensitivity is one of the major reasons one can buy the shoes today. It is why Bat'a was *sui generis* among the leaders of industrial shoemaking. It is also why the company culture, Batism, with its synchronized gymnastics routines, invasive disciplinary systems, and mass festivals did not survive into the second half of the twentieth century, when the company adapted to the much less collectivistic standards of industrial production in Canada and Western Europe.

While the company jettisoned its ideology as it reorganized after the war, remnants of Batism remained noticeable in its place of origin for quite some time. The large apartment blocks of the socialist era were largely the work of Bat'a-employed architects and designers.[27] Furthermore, once the socialist regime collapsed, a striking number of former *Batovci* in the area jumped at the opportunity to restore the integrity of Batism. The question of how Batism survived through the socialist era of Zlín, though, still waits for its historian.

In the end, we are left with a pastiche of reminiscence and misplaced optimism. The future will not return to the Bat'a world of the interwar era, largely owing to the globalization that Bat'a helped to accelerate. However, that does not mean there is nothing to gain from studying its history. The Bat'a story helps us understand the complexity of modernity and modernization by revealing the limits of a transnational corporation's ideology in the particularly volatile political landscape of the early twentieth century. Bat'a offered a striking example of a particular solution to the nefarious effects of industrialization. To create such an example, it borrowed widely and invented quickly. Its particular environments, first the Dřevnice Valley, then the Cisleithanian market, followed by global markets and the Second World War, all left their imprint. The overall impression, though, is not something from which we should make a mould.

Notes

Introduction

1 *Batovci* is used throughout the text to refer to the thousands of employees that outwardly demonstrated loyalty. It is an imperfect but helpful term, as it allows us to differentiate between workers and the true believers of Batism, the company ideology.

2 This description of May Day in 1937 is taken from photographs, newspaper accounts, and company records of the event found in the Bat'a Archive in the Moravský zemský archiv Brno – Státní okresní archiv Zlín (hereafter SOkA Zlín): Bat'a Fond, II, k. 50 č. 280.

3 This work uses Thomas for Thomas Bata Jr. and Tomáš for his father; Thomas spent most of his adult life in the English-speaking world, and, upon immigrating to Canada in 1939, spelled his name as such for the rest of his life. Tomáš, who died in Zlín in 1932, used the Czech spelling in most of his correspondence.

4 Built in 1933 in a functionalist style, the cinema held 2,200 seats. Eduard Staša, *Z historie zlínských kin. Zlínské noviny*, 1991. http://www.zlin.estranky.cz/clanky/novy-zlin/z-historie-zlinskych-kin.html (last accessed December 2019).

5 1 May 1937, Photo Archiv, SOkA Zlín, Bat'a Fond, k. 50 č. 280.

6 There was something unmistakably traditional in Bat'a's structure. Here was a company with a monarchical mentality folded into its organization. After all, loyalty to the chief executive mattered more than national identity, access to the executive level was largely restricted to family, and power was concentrated in the executives and directors. That the heir to the chief executive position would be a close family member was taken for granted. Such a structure was and is far from unique in the business world. The title is, therefore, not a rhetorical flourish, but part of an argument – the industrialization of shoe production was not without its continuities.

7 The historical eras referenced in this work are inspired by A.G. Hopkins and C.A. Bayly, whose writings on globalization organized the concept into archaic, proto,

modern, and post-colonial. Post-colonial refers to the late 1950s to the present. A.G. Hopkins, ed., *Globalization in World History* (New York: Norton, 2002) and C.A. Bayly, *The Birth of the Modern World, 1780–1914* (Cornwall: Blackwell, 2004).

8 James Hoopes has precisely shown how corporations operate from a totalitarian ethos. James Hoopes, *False Prophets: The Gurus Who Created Modern Management and Why Their Ideas are Bad for Business Today* (Cambridge, MA: Perseus, 2003).

9 Thornton Sinclair, "The Nazi Party Rally at Nuremberg," *Public Opinion Quarterly* 2, no. 2 (October 1938): 576.

10 Simonetta Falasca-Zamponi, *Fascist Spectacle: The Aesthetics of Power in Mussolini's Italy* (Berkeley: University of California Press, 1997), 93.

11 Malte Rolf, *Soviet Mass Festivals, 1917–1991* (Pittsburgh: University of Pittsburgh Press, 2013), 81.

12 Petr Dvořáček, *X Všesokolský slet roku 1938 a jeho ohlas ve společnosti* (dissertation, Charles University Prague, 2008), 29.

13 For mass spectacles see Falasca-Zamponi, *Fascist Spectacle*; Rolf, *Soviet Mass Festivals*; Andrew Rawson, *Showcasing the Third Reich: The Nuremberg Rallies* (Cheltenham: Spellmount, 2012).

14 See Stephen Meyer, *The Five Dollar Day: Labor Management and Social Control in the Ford Motor Company, 1908–1921* (Albany: State University of New York Press, 1981).

15 Greg Grandin, *Fordlandia: The Rise and Fall of Henry Ford's Forgotten Jungle City* (New York: Henry Holt, 2009), 319.

16 Photograph of parade, 1929, "Photographs of EJ Workers," in *EJ Ephemera*, Local History, Bartle Library Special Collections, Binghamton University, New York.

17 Kristina Knight, *Patriotism, Parades and Paternalism: How the Endicott-Johnson Corporation Controlled the Lives of Women in Johnson City and Endicott, New York, 1945–1965* (thesis, University of Binghamton, 2006).

18 Wolfgang Ribbe and Wolfgang Schäche, *Die Siemensstadt: Geschichte und Architektur eines Industriestandortes* (Berlin: Ernst & Sohn, 1985).

19 Ondřej Ševeček, *Zrození Baťovy průmyslové metropole: Továrna, městský prostor a společnost ve Zlíně v letech 1900–1938* (České Budějovice: Veduta, 2009), 45–6.

20 Eric Hoffer, *The True Believer: Thoughts on the Nature of Mass Movements* (New York: HarperCollins, 1951), 9.

21 Tomáš Baťa, "Nebojme se budoucnosti," *Zlín*, no. 14 (1931): 2.

22 Bohumil Lehár, *Dějiny baťova koncernu, 1894–1945* (Prague: Státní nakladatelství politické literatury, 1960), 209.

23 "Czechoslovakia: Bat'a," *Time Magazine*, 8 October 1928.

24 Lehár, *Dějiny baťova koncernu*, 227.

25 Endicott Johnson *could produce* 45.5 million pairs a year by 1934.. Bat'a *sold* 58 million pairs at home and abroad in 1936. See Inglis, *George F. Johnson*, 161, and Lehár, *Dějiny baťova koncernu*, 225.

26 Zahraniční obchod republiky Československé v roce 1937 (Prague: Státní úřad statistický, 1948).
27 Rationalization here is used in a Weberian sense. Max Weber used the word as a key to understanding modern society, which he saw as essentially a progression from emotions, values, and magical thinking to a society of specialization, order, and calculation. An excellent account of his work on this concept and some of his most important essays can be found in English in Tony and Dagmar Waters's translated and edited *Weber's Rationalism and Modern Society: New Translations on Politics* (New York: Palgrave, 2015).
28 SOkA Zlín. Bat'a, II, k. 1029 č.14. The number of paid informants from 1936 to 1940 is listed at 231. Yet, it is highly likely that this is only a fraction of the total number of informants used throughout the interwar period.
29 James C. Scott, *Seeing Like a State: How Certain Schemes to Improve the Human Condition Have Failed* (New Haven: Yale University Press, 1999), 5.
30 Scott, *Seeing Like a State*, 91.
31 Greg Grandin, *Fordlandia* (New York: Picador, 2010); Gerald Zahavi, *Workers, Managers, and Welfare Capitalism: The Shoeworkers and Tanners of Endicott Johnson, 1890–1950* (Urbana-Champagne: University of Illinois Press), 198; Patrizia Bonifazio and Paolo Scrivano, *Olivetti Builds: Modern Architecture in Ivrea: Guide to the Open Air Museum* (Milan: Skira, 2001).
32 Stephen Kotkin, *Magnetic Mountain: Stalinism as a Civilization* (Berkeley: University of California Press, 1995).
33 Kiran Klaus Patel and Sven Reichardt, "The Dark Side of Transnationalism: Social Engineering and Nazism, 1930s–40s," *Journal of Contemporary History* 51, no. 1 (2016): 11.
34 Jay Winter, *Dreams of Peace and Freedom: Utopian Moments in the Twentieth Century* (New Haven: Yale University Press, 2006), 1–2.
35 Take, for example, the scathing critique found in the book *Botostroj* (The Shoe Machine). Written by a former employee, Svatopluk Turek, the book is a fictionalized account of working in Zlín. In Turek's vision of Batism, company management has absolute control over every aspect of the workers' lives and the boss "thinks about everything." In *Botostroj*, Turek tried to convince the world of the evils of the Bat'a system through its omnipotent status in its employee's lives. The book was turned into a play for the National Theatre in 1947 (its reception was intensely political). Then in 1954, after having taking over the state in 1948, Communist Party officials made the book into a film, which did much to cement the idea that Batism meant the relentless oppression of workers in the minds of a generation of Czechoslovaks.
36 Because of his historical acumen, the fact that Lehár was beholden to the dictates of the Communist Party is obvious when reading the work. The state publishing house demanded that his book focus on the activities of members of the party who worked clandestinely in the company. This demand made for an awkward study – because the company became so good at marginalizing dissent, communist

activity within Zlín amounted to little more than crudely printed flyers by the mid-1930s. Bohumil Lehár, *Dějiny Baťova koncernu, 1894–1945* (Prague: Státní nakladatelství politické literatury, 1960).

37 Stanislav Holubec, "Silní milují život: Utopie, ideologie a biopolitika baťovského Zlína," *Kuděj* 11, no. 2 (2009): 30–55.

38 Antonín Cekota, *Thomas Bata: Entrepreneur Extraordinary* (Don Mills, ON: T.H. Best, 1968), 185–6.

39 *The Bata Phenomenon: Zlín Architecture, 1910–1960* (Zlín: Zlín Regional Gallery of Fine Arts, 2009), 8.

40 Milan Zelený, *Cesty k úspěchu: Trvalé hodnoty soustavy řízení Baťa* (Kusak: Vyškov, 2005).

41 *Tomáš Baťa: Doba a Společnost*, Sborník příspěvků ze stejnojmenné zlínské konference, pořádané ve dnech 30.listopadu – 1.prosince 2006 (Brno: Nadace Tomáše Bati, 2007).

42 Unfortunately, little of their work is available in English. An abbreviated bibliography is Lucie Galčanová and Barbora Vacková, "The Project Zlín: Everyday Life in a Materialized Utopia" *Lidě Města/Urban People* 11 no. 2 (2009): 311–17; Martin Jemelka and Ondřej Ševeček, *Tovární města Baťova koncernu: Evropská kapitola globální expanze* (Prague: Academia, 2016); Martin Jemelka and Ondřej Ševeček, eds., *Company Towns of the Baťa Concern* (Stuttgart: Franz Steiner Verlag, 2013); Martin Marek, *Středoevropské aktivity Baťova koncernu za druhé světové války* (Brno: Matice moravská, 2017); Vít Strobach and Martin Marek, "Batismus, urychlená modernita a průkopníci práce: Personální politika Baťova koncernu a řízené přesuny zaměstnanců v letech 1938–1941," *Moderní dějiny* (Prague: Historický ústav AV ČR), v. v. i., 2010, roč. 18, č. 1, s. 103–53; M. Marek and Vít Strobach. "Batismus, urychlená modernita a průkopníci práce: Personální politika Baťova koncernu a řízené přesuny zaměstnanců v letech 1938–1941," *Moderni dějiny: Sborník k dejínam 19. a 20. stoleti* 18, no. 1 (2010): 103–53. Barbora Vacková, Klára Eliášová, Jitka Ressová, and Markéta Reuss-Březovská, *Baťovský domek: Mizející prvky zlínské architektury* (Brno: Masaryková Univerzita, 2017).

43 Kimberly Elman Zarecor, *Manufacturing a Socialist Modernity: Housing in Czechoslovakia, 1945–1960* (Pittsburgh: University of Pittsburgh Press, 2011).

44 Petr Szczepanik, "The Aesthetics of Rationalization: The Media Network in the Bata Company and the Town of Zlín," in Katrin Klingan, ed., *A Utopia of Modernity: Zlín Revisiting Bata's Functional City* (Berlin: Jovis, 2009), 23.

45 Susanne Hilger, "Family Capitalism and Internationalization: The Case of the Czech Family Firm Bat'a up to the Early 1940s," in Christina Lubinski, Jeffrey Fear, and Paloma Fernandez Perez, eds., *Family Multinationals: Entrepreneurship, Governance, and Pathways to Internationalization* (New York: Routledge, 2013).

46 Tara Zahra, "Imagined Noncommunities: National Indifference as a Category of Analysis," *Slavic Review* 69, no. 1 (Spring 2010): 93–119.

47 Dominik Čipera, "Budoucnost," *Zlín*, 1 May 1933, 3.
48 Milan Zelený, *Cesty k úspechu: Trvalé hodnoty soustavy Baťa* (Kusak: Vyškov, 2005), 130.
49 Zahra, "Imagined Noncommunities," 119.
50 Sven Beckert, *Empire of Cotton: A Global History* (New York: Knopf, 2015), 164.
51 Lars Magnusson, *Nation, State, and the Industrial Revolution: The Visible Hand* (London: Routledge, 2009).
52 Beckert, *Empire of Cotton*, 164.
53 "Bat'a dal opět zabavit knihu!" *Tvorba*, 16 July 1937.
54 Lehár, *Dějiny Baťova koncernu*, 2.
55 Antonio Gramsci, Leon Trotsky, and Vladimir Lenin were fascinated by the idea of applying Fordism in a socialist manner. See John Schwartzmantel, *The Routledge Guide to Gramsci's Prison Notebooks* (London: Routledge, 2014), 25, 86.
56 Jan Bat'a, "Průmyslová budoucnost Zlína" *Zlín*, 28 June 1937, 1.
57 As to the presence of these individuals it is an assumption on the part of the author that Tauber, Fornoušková, and Stujlater were actually in attendance. Based on police and city records found in the Archiv Města Zlína (hereafter AMZ), which is found in the SoKA-Zlín, they were living in the city in May 1937. The others were most certainly in attendance, as the company required it and they were all under the company/city employ.
58 Alf Lüdtke, "Organizational Order or Eigensinn? Workers' Privacy and Workers' Politics in Imperial Germany," in *Rites of Power: Symbolism, Ritual, and Politics since the Middle Ages*, ed. Sean Wilentz (Philadelphia: University of Pennsylvania Press, 1985), 303–5.
59 John Eidson, "Compulsion, Compliance, or Eigensinn? Examining Theories of Power in an East German Field Site," Max Planck Institute for Social Anthropology Working Papers no. 61 (Halle, 2003), 1.
60 Giving attention to individuals' agency and the messiness of scientifically managed company towns resists the urge to classify company towns as having shared histories of totalitarian company control. This is the major conclusion of Neil White's *Company Towns: Corporate Order and Community* (Toronto: University of Toronto Press, 2012).
61 "Global South" is used here, as it is by Sven Beckert in his work *Empire of Cotton*, to refer to a large collection of areas that had little to no industrial manufacturing and were in a subjugated under imperial powers of the nineteenth century, but then rapidly industrialized during the post-colonial era. See Beckert, *Empire*, 379–90.
62 As it turns out, Hopkins was quite right when he speculated, "this picture (of globalization) might look rather different if other developments, such as the growth of import-substituting industries and joint ventures in a range of countries in the non-Western world, were taken into account. The period might then appear to be less like an interlude and more like the progenitor of changes that were to

become more visible after 1950." A.G. Hopkins, "The History of Globalization – and the Globalization of History?" in Hopkins, *Globalization in World History*, 36.

63 Bayly, *The Birth of the Modern World*, 1.
64 Timothy Brennan, "From Development to Globalization: Postcolonial Studies and Globalization Theory," in Neil Lazarus, ed., *The Cambridge Companion to Postcolonial Literary Studies* (Cambridge: Cambridge University Press, 2004), 137–8.
65 Robert Gilpin, *Global Political Economy: Understanding the International Order* (Princeton: Princeton University Press, 2011), 4.
66 The clearest political manifestation of the Bat'a agenda for Czechoslovakia can be found in Jan Antonín Baťa, *Budujme stát (pro 40,000.000 lidí)* (Zlín: Tisk, 1937).
67 Jan Janko and Emilie Těšínská, eds., *Technokracie v českých zemích, 1900–1950* (Prague: Archiv AV ČR, 1999).
68 Rudolf Kučera, *Rationed Life: Science, Everyday Life, and Working-Class Politics in the Bohemian Lands, 1914–1918* (New York: Berghahn, 2016).
69 Michel Christian, Sandrine Kott, and Ondřej Matějka, eds., *Planning in Cold War Europe: Competition, Cooperation, Circulations (1950s–1970s)* (Berlin: Walter de Gruyter, 2018).
70 Welfare capitalism generally refers to two types of structures, the one prevalent in the United States and the other in Europe. The American variety refers to the company town system of management, where companies provided a near total social service for their workers. Yet the term is best understood not through a bifocal lens but through historical context. In the interwar period in Europe several companies approximated the American definition, with company-controlled communities that tried to harmonize industry with a comprehensive social program for employees. One of the most curious aspects of welfare capitalism is its insistence on rationalizing *all* aspects of life, and yet maintaining a paternal system whose leadership is almost invariably familial and whose succession is almost always based on heredity. Thus, the title of this work, *In the Kingdom of Shoes*, makes a specific claim that the Bat'a system had significant parallels with absolutist monarchy, and indeed was subconsciously informed by the imperial structure of the Habsburgs. Thus while trying to eliminate the old, the Bat'a Company perpetuated a patriarchal hereditary organization. From the beginning of the system there was an inherent tension between the traditional and the modern, their synthesis was a radical departure in everyday patterns but provided a strong continuity in structures of power and matters of deference.
71 Melissa Feinburg, *Elusive Equality*, 1–10.
72 The multidirectional path of modernity seems best illustrated by Detlev Peukert's and David F. Crew's discussion of the "pathologies of modernity" and the rise of the Nazi Party. David F. Crew, "The Pathologies of Modernity: Detlev Peukert on Germany's Twentieth Century," *Social History* 17, no. 2 (1992): 319–28.

1 "A New Fixed Existence"

1 Sven Beckert, *Empire of Cotton: A Global History* (New York: Knopf, 2014), 144–5.

2 Josef Jančař, *Lidová kultura na Moravě* (V Brně Muzejní a vlastivědná společnost v Brně, 2000): 2–10.

3 Josef V Polišenský, *The Thirty Years War* (Berkeley: University of California Press, 1971), 61.

4 Ladislava Horňáková, P. Novák, and Zdeněk Pokluda, *Zlín – město v zahradách* (Zlín: Statutární město Zlín, 2002), 12.

5 Polišenský, *The Thirty Years War*, 253.

6 Ibid., 248.

7 Jindřich Bobák, *Procházky starým Zlínem* (Vizovice: Lípa, 1999).

8 Zdeněk Pokluda, *Zámek Zlín* (Zlín: Státní okresní archiv, 1998).

9 *Jurende's Mährischer Wanderer,* no. 43 (Vienna, 1854), 186.

10 Note by Claudius Bretton above the entrance of the Zlín chateau. In Josef V. Polišenský, *Aristocrats and the Crowd in the Revolutionary Year 1848: A Contribution to the History of Revolution and Counter-Revolution* (Albany: SUNY Press, 1980): 169.

11 Zdeněk Pokluda, *Sedm století zlínských dějin* (Zlín: Klub novinářů, 1991).

12 Stefan Haupt-Buchenrode, *My Memories* (Beau-Bassin: Doyen Verlag, 2012), 5.

13 This was a considerable sum – equivalent to about US$291,259 dollars in 1863. $291,259 would be about $6,000,000 today using a simple purchasing power calculation. Rodney Evisson, Historical Currency Converter, https://www.historicalstatistics.org/Currencyconverter.html (last accessed 21 August 2019). Purchasing power calculation done through Measuring Worth.com, https://www.measuringworth.com/calculators/uscompare/relativevalue.php, (last accessed 21 August 2019).

14 Haupt-Buchenrode, *My Memories*, 6, 32.

15 Photo by author taken of painted map on the walls of the Státní Okrésni Archiv Zlín, Klečůvka, 20 June 2014, illustrator F. Zedník.

16 Petr Škrabala, "Zlín ve víru politických změn let 1899–1914" (PhD diss., Univerzita Karlova, 2006), 9–11.

17 Katastrální mapy Zlína 1910–1915, SOkA Zlín, AMZ, č.1695.

18 Ibid.

19 The health version comes from Vincenc Hřbařík, a local investigator writing in 1933; the other account comes from a report created by police investigators (why the police were involved in investigating Florimont fifty years after his death is a mystery) in 1935. Both accounts are found in Různé policejní záležitosti 1911–1948, SOkA Zlín, AMZ, k. 581 č.1118.

20 "Šetření ohledně obuvnické továrny z roku 1873 ve Zlíně," 1935, SOkA Zlín, AMZ, k. 581 č.1118.

21 For an account of the demise of the cottage industry in the weaving profession see E.P. Thompson, *The Making of the English Working Class* (New York: Pantheon Books, 1964).

22 William H. Dooley, *A Manual of Shoemaking and Leather and Rubber Products* (Boston: Little, Brown, 1912), 253–4.

23 Alfred Chandler, *The Visible Hand: The Managerial Revolution in American Business* (Cambridge: Harvard University Press, 1993), 54.

24 As will be seen, "traditional" shoemakers throughout Europe fought Bat'a's expansion all the way into the Second World War.

25 Haupt-Buchenrode, *My Memories*, 13.

26 Ibid., 13.

27 "Šetření ohledně."

28 Carl Schorske locates the emergence of "modern movements" in Austria in the 1890s. Carl Schorske, *Fin-de-Siècle Vienna: Politics and Culture* (New York: Knopf, 1980), xxvii. Among the many excellent monographs on the subject of the middle-class revolution, see Colin Mooers, *The Making of Bourgeois Europe: Absolutism, Revolution, and the Rise of Capitalism in England, France, and Germany* (London: Verso, 1991); and Jerrold Seigel, *Modernity and Bourgeois Life: Society, Politics, and Culture in England, France and Germany since 1750* (Cambridge: Cambridge University Press, 2012).

29 Geoff Eley, *Society, Culture, and the State in Germany, 1870–1930* (Ann Arbor: University of Michigan Press, 1996), 31.

30 George Mosse, *The Image of Man: The Creation of Modern Masculinity* (Oxford: Oxford University Press, 2010).

31 Gary Cohen, "Nationalist Politics and the Dynamics of State and Civil Society in the Habsburg Monarchy, 1867–1914," *Central European History* 40, no. 2 (June 2007): 241–78.

32 Čtenářský spolek zlín, SOkA Zlín, AMZ, č. 13 K 2.

33 "Protokol," Čtenářský spolek zlín, SOkA Zlín, AMZ, č. 3 k. 1.

34 "Historie zlínské sokolovny," TJ *Sokol Zlín*, http://www.tjsokol-zlin.cz/?page _id=10 (last accessed 7 November 2019).

35 Yvona Činčová, *Sláva zlínského sportu* (Zlín: Muzeum jihovýchodní moravy ze Zlíně, 2011), 14.

36 Miroslav Tyrš, *Základové tělocviku* (Prague: Národní knihtiskárna, 1873), předmluva.

37 Činčová, *Sláva zlínského sportu*, 14.

38 "Protokol," 1900–3, Čtenářský spolek Zlín.

39 "Oldřich Říha interview of Josef Macka," November 1940, Hodáč Collection, SOkA Zlín, Bat'a fond I/3, č. 32 k. 20.

40 Rudolf Vachyněk to F. Hodáč, April 1940, SOkA Zlín, Hodáč Collection, Bat'a fond I/3, č. 32 k. 20.

41 Ibid.

42 Aloisie Mlýnková, "Vzpomínka z dob mého mládí," *Sdělení zaměstnání fy T. A. Baťa*, 15 December 1923, 5.

43 Ibid.

44 A fascinating account of the connection between the Oxford shoe and modernity can be found in Lou Ratté's *The Uncolonised Heart*, where he analyses Indian writers' responses to the "modern Bengali Babu" in 1895. Lou Ratte, *The Uncolonised Heart* (Calcutta: Orient Blackswan, 1995), 173–4.

45 Cekota, *Tomas Bata*, 37–8.

46 Ibid.

47 Bohumil Lehár, *Dějiny baťova koncernu, 1894–1945* (Prague: Státní nakladatelství politické literatury, 1960), 18.

48 Such a statement does not apply to other industries in Cisleithania, which steadily industrialized throughout the nineteenth century. See John Komlos, *The Habsburg Monarchy as a Customs Union: Economic Development in Austria-Hungary in the 19th Century* (Princeton: Princeton University Press, 2014).

49 Tomáš Baťa, *Úvahy a projevy* (Prague: Institut řezení, 1990), 24–5.

50 Richard Roe, "The United Shoe Machinery Company" *Journal of Political Economy* 22, no. 1 (January 1914): 43–63, http://www.jstor.org/stable/1821091 (last accessed 4 August 2020).

51 Tomáš Baťa, *Úvahy a projevy,* 25.

52 Eduard März, *Österreichische Industrie – und Bankpolitik in der Zeit Franz Josephs I* (Vienna: Europa Verlag, 1968), introduction.

53 Lehár, *Dějiny baťova koncernu,* 18.

54 Haupt-Buchenrode, *My Memories,* 32–3.

55 "Centralisace kapitalu," SoKA Zlín, Hodáč Collection, Baťa Fond I-3 č. 20 k. 19

56 Tomáš Baťa, *Úvahy a projevy,* 12.

57 Stanley Pech, "Political Parties among Austrian Slavs: A Comparative Analysis of the 1911 Reichsrat Election Results," *Canadian Slavonic Papers/Revue Canadienne des Slavistes* 31, no. 2 (June 1989): 170–93.

58 Jeremy King, *Budweisers into Czechs and Germans: A Local History of Bohemian Politics, 1848–1948* (Princeton: Princeton University Press, 2002), 134–9.

59 It was in 1905 that Austrian authorities instituted the Moravian Compromise, which offered a solution to the growing debate in the Moravian Diet over Czech- versus German-speaking representation by fixing seats around national identification.

60 Jakub Beneš, "Socialist Popular Literature and the Czech-German Split in Austrian Social Democracy, 1890–1914," *Slavic Review* 72, no. 2 (Summer 2013): 327–51.

61 William Mulligan, "Mechanization and Work in the American Shoe Industry: Lynn, Massachusetts, 1852–1883," *Journal of Economic History* 41, no. 1 (March 1981): 59–63.

62 Betsy Beattie, "Going up to Lynn: Single, Maritime-born Women in Lynn, Massachusetts, 1879–1930," *Journal of the History of the Atlantic Region* 22, no. 1 (Autumn 1992): 65–86.

63 Marie van Vorst, *The Woman Who Toils: Being the Experiences of Two Gentlewomen as Factory Girls* (New York: Doubleday, 1903), 171.

64 Thomas Dublin, "Rural-Urban Migrants in Industrial New England: The Case of Lynn, Massachusetts, in the Mid-Nineteenth Century," *Journal of American History* 73, no. 3 (December 1986), 629.

65 Paul Faler, *Mechanics and Manufacturers in the Early Industrial Revolution* (Albany: SUNY Press, 1981), 206–7.

66 "Women in Industry" *Monthly Labor Review* 13, no. 5 (November 1921): 149–51.

67 Mulligan, "Mechanization and Work," 62.

68 Cekota, *Tomas Bata*, 53.

69 *Machinists Monthly Journal* 1 (International Association of Machinists, 1906): 553. "Summary of Strikes Supported by Molder's Union, Showing Their Cause and Result," *The Review* (Detroit), March 1909, 28.

70 Stuart Brandes, *American Welfare Capitalism, 1880–1940* (Chicago: University of Chicago Press, 1976), 1–2.

71 Cekota, *Tomas Bata*, 55.

72 Bat'a estimated a Lynn shoe factory as being able to produce 1,200 pairs of shoes per nine-hour shift after the introduction of Matzeliger's lasting machine in 1895. Bat'a' estimated his workers produced a maximum of 800 pairs a day in 1905. Lehár, *Dějiny baťova koncernu*, 23.

73 Zdeněk Pokluda, "An Outline of the History of Bat'a and Zlín," in Katrin Klengan and K. Durst, *Utopia of Modernity: Zlín* (Berlin: JOVIS Verlag, 2009), 37.

74 B. Fimbingr, Letter from 1923, Hodáč kolekce, SOkA Zlín, Bata I-3 č. 32 k. 20.

75 "Interview with A. Ochsner," Hodáč kolekce, SOkA Zlín, Bata I-3 č. 32 k. 20.

76 Ibid.

77 "Protokol," January 1907, Spolek obuvníků Zlín, SOkA Zlín, č. 1 karton 1.

78 Ibid.

79 Eduard Malota, "Vzpomínky na Tomáše Baťu" (Zlín, 1939, unpublished, Bat'a fond SOkA Zlín), 89.

80 "Různé policejní záležitosti, 1911–1948," SOkA Zlín, AMZ, K 380 č. 954.

81 Malota, "Vzpomínky na Tomáše Baťu," 88.

82 Eduard Staša, *Kapitolky ze starého Zlína* (Zlín: Muzeum jihovýchodní Moravy ve Zlíně, 1991).

83 Staša, *Kapitolky ze starého Zlína*.

84 Some 4,000 people left from the Vizovice region to Texas alone in this period. Karel Kysilka, "Emigration from Vizovice and Zlín Counties to Texas before WWI." Paper presented at the Czechoslovak Geneological Society's 9th Annual Conference, Houston, Texas, 2003.

85 Between 1870 and 1910, 3,550,000 people emigrated from the empire. Heinz
    Faßmann and Rainer Münz, *Einwanderungsland Österreich?: Historische
    Migrationsmuster, aktuelle Trends und politische Maßnahmen* (Vienna: Jugend
    & Volk, 1995), 20.
86 Malota, "Vzpomínky na Tomáše Baťu," 127.
87 Ibid., 128.
88 Lehár, *Dějiny baťova koncernu*, 27.
89 The company reached 400 employees by 1914 and went from a net of 499,000
    crowns in 1907 to 2,121,736 in 1912. Cekota, *Tomas Bata*, 89.
90 Ibid., 90.
91 Lehár, *Dějiny baťova koncernu*, 31.
92 Nancy Reynolds, *A City Consumed: Urban Commerce, the Cairo Fire, and the
    Politics of Decolonization in Egypt* (Stanford: Stanford University Press, 2012),
    136.
93 Hodáč, *Osudy člověka a podniku*, unpublished, SOkA Zlín, Bata Fond I/3 č. 20
    k. 15.
94 Lehár, *Dějiny baťova koncernu*, 29.
95 For a thorough description of Austrian capitalism in this period see David Good,
    The Economic Rise of the Habsburg Empire, 1750–1914 (Berkeley: University
    of California Press, 1984), 186–236.
96 Hodáč Collection, Baťa fond I/3. č.29 k.19 SOkA Zlín.
97 Malota, "Vzpomínky na Tomáše Baťu," 126.
98 Lehár, *Dějiny baťova koncernu*, 30.
99 ANNO Österreichische Nationalbibliothek, Volltextsuche in Zeitungen und
    Zeitschriften (searched "Bata," and from 1905 to 1913, out of 630 hits, only two
    matched the Baťa Company). http://anno.onb.ac.at/anno-suche/#searchMode
    =simple&query=%22Bata%22&resultMode=list&from=51&selectedFilters
    =date%3A[1905+TO+1914] (last accessed 10 August 2020).
100 Two works which offer stunning scope and clarity into this process are Mosse,
    The Image of Man, and Bayly, *The Birth of the Modern World*. Both authors
    identify a specific, modern perspective emerging and moving around the world at
    roughly the same time.
101 Bayly, *The Birth of the Modern World*, 10–11.
102 Beckert, *Empire of Cotton*, 155.
103 Joseph A. Schumpeter and Redvers Opie, *The Theory of Economic
    Development; An Inquiry into Profits, Capital, Credit, Interest, and the
    Business Cycle* (Cambridge: Harvard University Press, 1934). Eduard März,
    Österreichische Industrie – und Bankpolitik in der Zeit Franz Josephs I (Vienna:
    Europa Verlag, 1968), 90–1.
104 David Good, *The Economic Rise of the Habsburg Empire, 1750–1914* (Berkeley:
    University of California Press, 1984), 248–9.
105 März, "The Austrian Economy," 90–1. See Good, *Economic Rise*, 249.

2 "Time Es Money"

1 From 1914 to 1922, German language newspapers (*Neues Wiener Tagblatt, Neue Freie Presse, Fremden-Blatt, Prager Tagblatt, Arbeiter Zeitung, Neues Wiener Journal, Pester Lloyd, Grazer Tagblatt, Verlustliste*) in six cities in the empire (Vienna, Salzburg, Prague, Olomouc, Budapest, Graz, and Linz) ran a total of seventy-five articles on Baťa. "Bata and Zlín search" on the Österreichische Nationalbibliothek's online database ANNO. http://anno.onb.ac.at/anno-suche #searchMode=simple&query=Bata+and+Zlin&resultMode=list&from =1&selectedFilters=date%3A[1904+TO+1922].

See, for example, "Mahre und faliche Demokratie" *Die Rohte Fahne*, Vienna, 16 September 1922, 4.

2 The best single collection on Americanization by its advocates can be found in Winthrop Talbot's edited volume *Americanization: Principles of Americanism, Essentials of Americanization, Technic of Race Assimilation* (New York: H.W. Wilson Company, 1920).

3 Korman, Gerd, "Americanization at the Factory Gate," *ILR Review* 18, no. 3 (April 1965): 396. *Business Source Complete*, EBSCO host (accessed 30 March 2017).

4 Robert Dunn was one of the first to systematically study the ways in which large industrial firms connected the open shop to Americanization. Robert Dunn, *The Americanization of Labor: The Employers' Offensive against the Trade Unions* (New York: International Publishers, 1927).

5 De Grazia's framework of Americanization holds that while the democratization of material wealth proved irresistible to a majority of Europeans, Americans in American organizations were what allowed it to spread dramatically over the continent. One of the primary actors is the Rotary Club, which, interestingly enough, was founded in Zlín in 1935 by Tomáš Baťa Jr. Victoria De Grazia, *Irresistible Empire: America's Advance through 20th Century Europe* (Cambridge, MA: Bellknap Press, 2005).

6 Tomáš Baťa, *Úvahy a projevy*, 32.

7 This would steadily increase to 4,000 pairs a day by 1915. Bohumil Lehár, *Dějiny baťova koncernu, 1894–1945* (Prague: Státní nakladatelství politické literatury, 1960), 31.

8 Lehár, *Dějiny baťova koncernu*, 33.

9 Regional newspaper clippings, 1910–45. SOkA-Zlín, Baťa Fond.

10 Anna Rektaríková, Kartotéky, SOkA-Zlin, Baťa Fond. k. 1014 č. 14.

11 Matthias Strohn, ed., *World War I Companion* (Oxford: Osprey, 2013), 136.

12 Josef Blažek, "Vzpomínky na Tomaše Baťu." Quoted in Lehár, *Dějiny baťova koncernu*, 36–7.

13 Lehár, *Dějiny baťova koncernu*, 35.

14 Antonín Cekota, *Tomas Bata: Entrepreneur Extraordinary* (Don Mills, ON: T.H. Best, 1968), 122.

15 Letter to the district office in Uherské Hradiště from F. Štěpanek, 13 October 1917, Různé policejní záležitosti 1911–18, SOkA AMZ č. 954.
16 *Sdělení zřízenectvu firmy T&A. Bat'a* (SOkA Zlín, Bat'a Fond, Noviny, 1917–18).
17 Lehár, *Dějiny bat'ova koncernu*, 40.
18 Okresní hejtmanství v Uherském Hradišti (Státní Okresní Archiv Uherském Hradišti, 1916/18 č. 422 and 615).
19 Lehár, *Dějiny bat'ova koncernu*, 42–4.
20 "Undernourishment and Working Overtime," 10 August 1918, *Sdělení zřízenectvu firmy T&A* (Bat'a, SOkA Zlín, Bat'a Fond – Noviny, 1917–18).
21 Rudolf Kučera, *Rationed Life: Science, Everyday Life, and Working-Class Politics in the Bohemian Lands, 1914–1918* (New York: Berghahn, 2016), 6–7.
22 Jan Kotěra, Vladimír Šlapeta, and Daniela Karasová, *Jan Kotěra, 1871–1923: The Founder of Modern Czech Architecture* (Prague: Municipal House, 2001), 66–8.
23 Marynel Ryan Van Zee, "Form and Reform: The Garden City of Hellarau-bei-Dresden, Germany, between Company Town and Model Town," in Marcelo Borges and Susana Torres, eds., *Company Towns: Labor, Space, and Power Relations across Time and Continents* (Palgrave Macmillan: New York, 2012), 42.
24 Ibid., 46.
25 Gerald Zahavi, *Workers, Managers, and Welfare Capitalism: The Shoeworkers and Tanners of Endicott Johnson, 1890–1950* (Chicago: University of Illinois Press, 1988), 23.
26 "Duševní spolupráce dělníka," 3 August 1918. *Sdělení zřízenectvu firmy T&A. Bat'a*, SOkA Zlín, Bat'a Fond, Noviny, 1917–18.
27 "Práci čest," 17 August 1918, *Sdělení zřízenectvu firmy T&A. Bat'a*, SOkA Zlín, Bat'a Fond, Noviny, 1917–18.
28 Mark Cornwall, *The Undermining of Austria-Hungary: The Battle for Hearts and Minds* (New York: Springer, 2000), 256–60.
29 For more about the Nazi use of terror on civilians to create defeatism and the like, see Ian Kershaw's *The End: The Defiance and Destruction of Hitler's Germany, 1944–45* (New York: Penguin, 2011).
30 František Obrtel, *Pojďte s námi* (Prague: Zemědělské knihkupectví A. Neubert, 1918), 208.
31 Ibid., 194.
32 T.G. Masaryk, statement in Pittsburgh, reported by the *Pittsburgh Daily Dispatch* on 31 May 1918, found in George Kovtun, *Masaryk and America: Testimony of a Relationship* (Washington: Library of Congress, 1988), 48.
33 The need to de-Austrianize is one of the central tenets of Thomas Masaryk's speeches from 1919 to 1920. T.G. Masaryk, *Projevy presidenta Ceskoslovenské republiky Prof. Dr. T.G. Masaryka od doby jeho zvoleni do dnu jubilejnich*, ed. Thomas Kratochvil (Prague: Nákladem Ceskoslovenskeho Kompasu, 1920). http://books.google.com/books?id=rvhBAQAAMAAJ.

34 "Der Amerikanismus in Wien," *Neues Wiener Tagblatt*, 18 December 1913, 12.
35 Viktor Grschen, "Amerikanismus," *Freie Stimmen*, 29 September 1918, 2.
36 F. Hodáč, *Osudy Clověka a podniku* (unpublished) Bata Fond I/3 č. 20 k.15 SOKA Zlín.
37 Léhar, *Dějiny baťova koncernu*, 49.
38 F. Hodáč, *Osudy Clověka a podniku* (unpublished) SOkA Zlín, Bata Fond, I/3, č. 20 k. 15.
39 Lehár, *Dějiny baťova koncernu*, 51.
40 *Boj o zlínskou radnici: Komunistická radnice*, kapitola II: 1919–23. http://www
   .zlin.estranky.cz/clanky/pele-mele--odkazy/-37-nazvoslovnik-ulic-a-namesti
   ---cast-6_7.html (last accessed 17 April 2017).
41 Author unknown, *Boj o zlínskou radnici, kapitola II 1919–1923.* http://www.zlin
   .estranky.cz/clanky/pele-mele--odkazy/-37-nazvoslovnik-ulic-a-namesti
   ---cast-6_7.html (last accessed 28 February 2017).
42 The change to the Communist Party was in line with what was going on nationally. In 1920, the governing Social Democratic Party lost its clear majority in parliament because of internal conflicts between those advocating a Bolshevik line and those advocating a more liberal position. By May 1921, the Czechoslovak Communist Party had been officially organized and applied for membership in the Third International. The best treatment of this remains Bernard Wheaton's *Radical Socialism in Czechoslovakia: Bohumír Šmeral, the Czech Road to Socialism and the Origins of the Czechoslovak Communist Party, 1917–1921* (Boulder: East European Monographs, 1986).
43 O. Ševeček, *Zrození Baťovy průmyslové metropole* (Němec: České Budejovice, 2009), 103.
44 Letter to T&A Baťa Company from Fr. Novák, 14 May 1921, SOkA Zlín, AMZ, č. 1093.
45 Yvona Činčová, *Sláva Zlínského sportu* (Zlín: Muzeum jihovýchodní Moravy ve Zlíně), 28–9.
46 Jana Šetřilová, *Alois Rašín: Dramatický život českého politika* (Prague: Argo, 1997), 67.
47 "Bata Shoe and Leather Company Lynn U.S.A," 17 January 1920 (Zlín: Sdělení zaměstancům firmy T.A. Baťa), 1.
48 Classified and Opportunities Department, Chilton Co. *Boot and Shoe Recorder* 77 (17 April 1920): 166.
49 Stephen Mostov, *Immigrant Entrepreneurs: Jews in the Shoe Trades in Lynn, 1885–1945* (Marblehead, MA: North Shore Jewish Historical Society, 1982), 86.
50 Jaroslav Pospíšil, *Rub a líc baťovských sporů* (Zlín: Kniha Zlín, 2012), 11.
51 Cekota, *Tomas Bata*, 146.
52 Ibid., 148.
53 Letter from T. Baťa to Henry Ford, February 1920, SOkA Zlín, Bata Fond, I/3 č. 29 k. 19.

54 Stuart Brandes, *American Welfare Capitalism, 1880–1940* (Chicago: University of Chicago Press, 1976), 89.

55 Zahavi, *Workers, Managers, and Welfare Capitalism*, 53.

56 Ibid., 41.

57 Cekota, *Tomas Bata*, 149.

58 "Czecho-Slovakia Representatives Praise Endicott," *News Dispatch* (Endicott, NY), 21 April 1921, 1.

59 Ed Aswad and Susan Meredith, *Endicott-Johnson* (Mount Pleasant, SC: Arcadia Publishing, 2003), 48–56.

60 Johnson's attitude was very much for public consumption. In private correspondence, Johnson frequently referred to workers as "the help." George F. Johnson, letter to E.H. Ellison, 11 September 1937, George F. Johnson Papers, Box 15, Syracuse University Library Manuscript Collections.

61 "The Worker at the Machine," *Sdělení*, 8 October 1921.

62 J. Soušek, "Experiences from America (Zkušenosti z Ameriky)," lecture for the Society of Architects and Engineers, 12 March 1920, Prague, reprinted in *Sdělení*, April 1920.

63 Nový Lid, "Amerikanismus," *Sdělení*, 20 March 1920.

64 One very interesting article on the souring of Czech opinion on "amerikanismus" is A. Pimper, "Reformátoři," 21 July 1921 (Prague: Národní Listy), 1.

65 *Boj o zlínskou radnici.*

66 J.V. Neumann, "Zločin, spáchany státu," *Reforma*, 1 October 1921.

67 Haupt-Buchenrode, *My Memories*, 98.

68 Jan Bat'a, *Sdělení*, 13 August 1921, 3.

69 "Prázdniny u nás," *Sdělení*, 1 October 1921, 8.

70 "Tovární hlídka," *Sdělení*, 17 December 1921, 2.

71 W.A. Sunday, "Staň se abstinentem," *Sdělení*, 7 January 1922, 5.

72 R.A. Bruns, *Preacher: Billy Sunday and Big-Time American Evangelism* (Urbana-Champaign: University of Illinois Press, 2002).

73 "Šarlatanský kazatel," *Štít, Věstník organizačního komitétu Strany katolického lidu pro diecézi královéhradeckou* 32 (22 December 1938): 4.

74 T. Bat'a to H. Ford, 9 January 1931, SOkA Zlín, Hodáč Collection, Bat'a Fond I/3 č. 29 k.19.

75 "Naše dítě," *Sdělení*, 3 March 1923.

76 "Co s volným časem?" *Sdělení*, 4 August 1923; "Dítě a povinnost," *Sdělení*, 3 February 1923; "Jak žíti," *Sdělení*, 1 December 1923*).*

77 Léhar, *Dějiny baťova koncernu*, 82.

78 Cekota, *Tomas Bata*, 179–81.

79 Léhar, *Dějiny baťova koncernu*, 83.

3 "An End to Politics"

1 Tomáš Bat'a, "Náš závod a město Zlín," in *Naše volby* (Zlín: 1925), 5, SOkA Zlín, Bat'a Fond, I.

2 Pavel Hajný, "Boj o zlínskou radnice: komunální politika ve Zlíně, 1908–1946," http://www.zlin.estranky.cz/clanky/pele-mele--odkazy/nazvoslovnik-ulic-a -namesti-ve-zline_gottwaldove.html (last accessed 8 November 2019).

3 Ondřej Ševeček, *Zrození Baťovy průmyslové metropole Továrna, městký prostor a společnost ve Zlíně 1900–1938* (Ostrava: Veduta, 2009), 165–70.

4 Hajný, "Boj o zlínskou radnice."

5 Tomáš Baťa, "Náš závod a město Zlín," in *Naše volby* (Zlín: 1925), 6, SOkA Zlín, Baťa Fond, I.

6 Karel Meisel, "Letter to T & A Baťa," 10 September 1923, in *Naše volby* (Zlín: 1925), 40, SOkA Zlín, Baťa Fond, I.

7 Alois Outéřický, "Letter to T & A Baťa," 30 September 1923, in *Naše volby* (Zlín: 1925), 36, SOkA Zlín, Baťa Fond I.

8 F.L. Gahura, "Letter to T & A Baťa," 6September 1923, in *Naše volby* (Zlín: 1925), 37, SOkA Zlín, Baťa Fond I.

9 Jon Hoza, "Duch Ameriky," in *Naše volby* (Zlín: 1925), 28, SOkA Zlín, Baťa Fond I.

10 Ibid., "Volby ve Zlíně a jejich výsledek."

11 "Občané a dělníci města Zlína!,",collected in *Naše volby*,(Zlín: 1925), SOkA-Zlín, Bata Fond, I.

12 Protokol, městké úřady, 1923–8. SOkA-Zlín, AMZ, k. 65 č. 1. The city budget continued to climb; in 1931 the city had a weekly budget of slightly over a million crowns.

13 Protokol, Městké úřady, 1923–8. SOkA-Zlín, AMZ, k. 65 č. 1.

14 Bohumil Lehár, *Dějiny baťova koncernu, 1894–1945* (Prague: Státní nakladatelství politické literatury, 1960), 99.

15 Peter Scott, "The Wolf at the Door: The Trade Union Movement and Overseas Multinationals in Britain during the 1930s," *Social History* 23, no. 2 (May 1998): 208.

16 Léhar, *Dějiny baťova koncernu*, 95.

17 Pavel Machonin and Jaroslav Krejci, *Czechoslovakia, 1918–92: A Laboratory for Social Change* (Basingstoke: Macmillan, 1998), 61–2.

18 "Lež – Hanba," in *Naše volby* (Zlín: 1925), n.p., SOkA Zlín, Baťa Fond, I.

19 Milan Zelený, *Cesty k úspěchu: trvalé hodnoty soustavy řízení Baťa* (Zlín: Univerzita Tomáše Bati, 2001), 20–58.

20 By 1928, the company had six organized sports teams competing on the international level and could boast of having trained Olympic champion Ladislav Vácha, gold medallist on the uneven bars. *Sdělení*, August 1928, no. 33, p. 1.

21 Vilém Vesely, *600 Hesel Baťa* (Zlín: Tisk, 1938), 4.

22 Though a complete picture of middle management is not possible, a careful study of managers' biographies published in the company newspaper from the years 1936 to 1938 as well as thirty-four middle managers' personnel cards reveals that nearly two-thirds of them began as factory labourers. SOkA Zlín, Baťa, II/6, Osobní kartotéky.

23 Osobní kartotéky, SOkA Zlín, Baťa, II/6 k.1021, 1023, 1024, č. 13, 14.

24 While the city council did have the authority to restrict both business and liquor licences, they did so sparingly in the lean years between 1919 and 1923. Rather, most of the city council's energy was spent on levying taxes on the major enterprises of the town, specifically Baťa, and building a relatively expensive town hall. *Městká rada protokol*, 1924, SOkA-Zlín, AMZ, k. 65 č .1.

25 Yvona Činčová, *Sláva zlínského sportu* (Zlín: Muzeum jihovýchodní Moravy ve Zlíně, 2011), 28.

26 *Lidové listy*, 8 May 1931.

27 T. Baťa Jr., *Tomas Bata: Shoemaker to the World* (Toronto: Stoddart, 1990), 23.

28 May Day 1924, SOkA-Zlín, Fotoarchiv, Baťa Fond, k. 10.

29 May Day 1925, SOkA-Zlín, Fotoarchiv, Baťa Fond, k. 10 č. 443.

30 Ševeček, *Zrození Baťovy průmyslové*, 60.

31 J. Novosad, "Boj o hospodu na Sokolovně," *Sdělení*, 20 June 1925, 2.

32 "Kdo chce s námí," *Sdělení*, 3 October 1925, 1.

33 Jan Laichter, "VIII mezinárodní sjezd proti alkoholismu ve Vídni," *Naše doba: Revue pro vědu, umění a život sociálni, Volume 9* (Chicago: University of Chicago, 1902), 666.

34 "T. Baťa at Autoclub," 1931. SOkA-Zlín, Fotoarchiv, k. 1. č. 4.

35 Tomas Baťa, convinced of the evils of alcohol around the time of his first trip to the Ford Motor Company, started his own temperance movement and began to use his significant power as both mayor and chief executive to rid Zlín of alcoholism. Within five years of its founding, the Abstinence Club stopped holding weekly meetings, and eventually disbanded altogether in 1936. It seems, that for new chief Jan Baťa, who took over after his half-brother's death in 1932, abstinence was to be a personal commitment, and much like political criminals, alcoholics were to be dealt with away from the public eye, that is, watched, studied, and expelled with little if any publicity.

36 *Sdělení*, 1 March 1924, 9.

37 "Hospodu nebo čítárnu?" *Sdělení*, 22 November 1924.

38 A. Cekota, "Školy a hospoda," *Zlín*, 6 September 1930, 1.

39 "Máca v. Baťa," SOkA-Zlin, AMZ, č. 860.

40 16 November 1928, City Council resolution, SOkA-Zlín, AMZ, č. 860.

41 SOkA-Zlín, Bata Fond, k. 124 č. 802.

42 T. Baťa, "O Hospodu.," *Zlín*, 12 February 1930, 1.

43 "Proti zalkoholisování obcí," *Zlín*, 5 December 1930, 1.

44 *Sdělení*, 1924; one such example is an advertisement on 27 September.

45 Articles regarding the back and forth between the teachers and the company appear numerous times in the company newspaper, *Zlín*, 1924–6.

46 "Boj o novou školu," Příloha, *Sdělení*, 24 June 1925, 2.

47 Charter Statement for the Baťova Škola Práce, SOkA-ZLÍN, Baťa Fond, k. 1187 č. 3.

48 Henry Ford's ideas about where to look for a modern factory's workforce can be found in his autobiography, *My Life and Work*. The book was reprinted in the company newspaper in Zlín over the course of four years between 1924 and 1927.

49 Capitalization of Young Men and Women denotes the position of student in the Bat'a School of Work; it was used by the company as a proper noun.

50 This parochialism would not last long. By 1937, the BSP received approximately 10,000 applications from all over Europe for 1,500 openings. The Great Depression, which left approximately one million people unemployed in Czechoslovakia, greatly increased interest in the BSP. Školy," studíjní Ustav výchova prumyslového člověka, SOkA Zlín, Bat'a Fond, k. 1192 č. 39.

51 Information List about the Dormitory for Young Men (1929–30), SOkA Zlín, Bat'a Fond, k.1187 č. 2.

52 Information List about the Internat for Young Men (1929–30), SOkA Zlín, Bat'a Fond, k. 1187 č. 2.

53 "Dlouhé vlasy," Sdělení, 12 July 1924, 3.

54 The clearest evidence of the city government's lack of interest in moral policing can be found in the minutes o the City Council, 1922–3, SOkA Zlín, k. 65 č. 1.

55 Thomas J. Bata with Sonja Sinclar, Bata – Shoemaker to the World (Toronto: Stoddart, 1990), 25.

56 L.F., Trestní spisy, SOkA-Zlín, AMZ, K581 č. 1118.

57 Ibid.

58 Why she stayed in the hospital so long is unknown, since she did not have an STD.

59 L. F., Trestní spisy, SOkA-Zlin, AMZ, K581 č. 1118.

60 "Jak se oblékáme do práce?" Sdělení, 18 September 1926, 4. "Vážná debata," Sdělení, 21 January 1928, 1. "Babičky jsou špatnými vychovatelkami," Zlín, 20 April 1936, 4.

61 Berta Ženaty, "Dívky nově doby," Zlín, 15 September 1928, 1.

62 A concise account of the Bat'a feminine ideal can be found in "Naše Žena," Zlín, 19 February 1928, 7.

63 "Osobní referent," Osobní oddělení, SOkA-Zlín, Bat'a Fond. k. 1506 č. 2.

4 "Speak Briefly"

1 "The Ten Commandments of Saving Time," Sdělení, 2 January 1926, 3.

2 "1924–25 Baťa," Národní archiv, Ministerstvo průmyslu, obchodu a živností, (hereafter NA-MPOŽ) k. 1878 č. 498211.

3 A recent article by Tomáš Kasper and Dana Kasperová asserts that Czechs first took the term "scientific management" from the French "l'organisation scientifique" before moving to the "Rationalisierung" of German. Kasper and Kasperová, "The Bat'a Company in Zlín: A Shoe Company or a School Company?" History of Education 47, no. 3 (2018): 323.

4 Čas, 18 November 1922, 7. For 1930, Kramerius shows seventy occurrences of the word in newspapers.

5 Jan Stocký, Hospdářská racionalisace (Prague: Karel Nepodal, 1930), 7.

6 Weber first developed the term in The Protestant Ethic and the Spirit of Capitalism (1905).

7 Frederick W. Taylor, Scientific Management (London: Routledge, 2004), 46.

8 Judith Merkle, *Management and Ideology: The Legacy of the International Scientific Management Movement* (Berkeley: University of California Press, 1980), 1.

9 Mary Nolan, *Visions of Modernity: American Business and the Modernization of Germany* (Oxford: Oxford University Press, 1994), 7–9.

10 Elisabeth van Meer, "The Transatlantic Pursuit of a World Engineering Federation for the Profession, the Nation, and International Peace, 1918–48," *Technology and Culture* 53, no. 1 (2012): 121.

11 Václav Verunáč, *Racionalizace, vědecká organizace, a otázka sociální* (Prague: Sociálni ústav republiky Československé, 1930), 11.

12 Otto Smrček, "Expanze technického myšlení," in Jan Janko and Emilie Těšínská, eds., *Technokracie v českých zemích (1900–1950)* (Prague, Archiv AV, 1999), 37–56.

13 Verunáč, *Racionalizace*, 14.

14 Ibid., 91.

15 Ladislav Dvořák, *O účelnosti ideí a metod Spojených států amerických pro národní hospodářství československé* (Prague: Česká národohospodářská společnost, 1928), 11.

16 V. Verunač, *Zásady laboretismu* (Prague: Nákladem Parlementu, 1928). See Kasper and Kasperová, 324.

17 Antonie Doležalová has done excellent work connecting Bat'a to laboretism. See Doležalová, "Bat'a's Search for Social Reconciliation in the Changing World of Social Justice," in *Company Towns of the Bat'a Concern*, ed. O. Ševeček and M. Jemelka (Stuttgart: Franz Steiner Verlag, 2013), and Doležalová, 'Nebylo úniku? Kontinuita a diskontinuita v ekonomickém vývoji ve 30 a 40. letech XX století," in *1938: Československo a krize demokracie ve střední Evropě ve 30. a 40. letech XX. století*, ed. Ivan Šedivý, Jan Němeček, Jiří Kocian and Oldřich Tůma (Prague: AV ČR, 2010), 461–77.

18 Rudolph Philipp, *Der unbekannte Diktator Thomas Bat'a* (Vienna and Berlin: Agis-Verlag, 1928), 185.

19 Ibid., 38.

20 Ibid., 26.

21 Ibid., 28.

22 Ibid., 190.

23 "Poznámky k berlínskému rozsudku," *Sdělení*, 17 August 1929, 1.

24 "Racionalisace podle Pana Srby," *Sdělení*, 19 January 1929, 3.

25 Ibid.

26 *Sdělení*; this number is taken from a random sample of one hundred advertisements August–September 1923 and August–September 1927. There are twice as many advertisements for wristwatches in 1927 (13) in 1927 compared with 1923 (6).

27 "Jak řešit snídani," *Zlín*, 5 February 1930, 3. "Strach z telefonu," *Zlín*, 9 January 1931, 2. "Jak si stráviti dovolenou", *Sdělení*, 2 July 1927, 8.

28 "Jak se oblekáme do práce?" *Sdělení*, 18 September 1926.
29 Nicholas Antongiavanni, *The Suit* (New York: HarperCollins, 2006). Geraldine Biddle-Perry and Sarah Cheang, *Hair: Styling, Culture and Fashion* (Oxford: Berg, 2008).
30 "Buď rychlý," *Sdělení*, 5 February 1928.
31 Vilém Veselý, *600 Hesel Baťa* (Zlín: Tisk, 1938), 7.
32 James C. Scott's premise that high modernism promoted an aesthetic of efficiency rather than actual efficiency best explains this paradox. James C. Scott, *Seeing Like a State: How Certain Schemes to Improve the Human Condition Have Failed* (New Haven: Yale University Press, 1998).
33 "Dopis z ciziny" *Sdělení*, 24 July 1926.
34 Bohumil Lehár, *Dějiny baťova koncernu, 1894–1945* (Prague: Státní nakladatelství politické literatury, 1960), 110–16.
35 "Naše Desatero," *Sdělení*, 27 February 1926, 5.
36 "Ladislav Vácha," *Sdělení* (Zlín), August 1928, 1.
37 Lewis H Siegelbaum, *Stakhanovism and the Politics of Productivity in the USSR, 1935–1941* (Cambridge: Cambridge University Press, 1988), 1–15.
38 George Mosse, *The Image of Man: The Creation of Modern Masculinity* (Oxford: Oxford University Press, 2010), 53.
39 Katrin Klingan and Kerstin Gust, eds., *A Utopia of Modernity – Zlín: Revisiting Bat'a's Functional City* (Berlin, Jovis, 2009), 12.
40 Eduard Staša, "Vznik a vývoj továrny na obuv z pohledu architekta," http://www.zlin.estranky.cz/clanky/batovy-zavody/vznik-a-vyvoj-tovarny-na-obuv-z-pohledu-architekta-1-2.html (last accessed 20 November 2019).
41 Ondřej Ševeček, *Zrození Baťovy průmyslové metropole Továrna, městký prostor a společnost ve Zlíně 1900–1938* (Ostrava: Veduta, 2009), 21.
42 "Sociální ochrana ženy v naší práce," Osobní odděleni, SOkA-Zlín, Baťa fond, k. 1020 č. 49.
43 "Rekapitulace propuštěných pro pololetí 1938," SOkA-Zlín, Bata Fond, k. 0 č. 11.
44 Employment statistics, Personnel Department, 1930–40. SOkA-Zlín, Bata Fond, k. 121 č. 121.
45 "Výssí škol mladých žen fy Baťa a.s. ve Zlíně: zásady výchovné," SOkA-Zlín, Bata Fond k. 1192 č. 39.
46 Ibid.
47 "Učební hodiny ženských škol Baťových," SOkA-Zlín, Bata Fond, k. 1192 č. 39.
48 Školy – studíjní Ustav výchova prumyslového člověka, SOkA-Zlín, Bata Fond, k. 1192 č. 39.
49 "Daňové přiznání Spolek rodičů ve Zlíně," SOkA-Zlín: AMZ, k. 1189 č. 23.
50 Ibid.
51 Vladmír Jůva, *Stručné dějiny pedagogiky* (Brno: Paido, 1994), 69.
52 Stanislav Vrána and Josef Cisař, *Deset let pokusné práce na měšťanských školách ve Zlíně 1929–39* (Zlín: Tisk, 1939), 13.

53 "Zpráva o činnosti pedagogického oddělení, 1935–38," SOkA-Zlín, AMZ, k. 1190 č. 28.

54 Vilém Veselý, *600 hesel* (Ve Zlíně: Univerzita Tomáše Bati, Fakulta managementu a ekonomiky, 2007), 4.

55 Anna T., Trestní spisy, SOkA-Zlín, AMZ, č. 1118.

56 Michel Foucault, *The History of Sexuality* (New York: Pantheon Books, 1978).

57 Zdravotní policie, SOkA-Zlín, AMZ, č. 1123.

58 Ibid., 1931–4

59 Jaroslav Kříž, "Zapomenutá historie zdravotní policie," *Hygiena* 54 (2009): 136–7.

60 Pavel Macek and Lubomír Uhlíř, *Dějiny policie a četnictva protektorát Čechy a Morava a Slovenský stát, 1939–1945* (Prague: Police History, 2001), 65–8.

61 See Joy Parr's *The Gender of Breadwinners: Women, Men and Change in Two Industrial Towns, 1880–1950* (Toronto: University of Toronto Press, 1990); Thomas Klubock's *Contested Communities: Class, Gender, and Politics in Chile's El Teniente Copper Mine, 1904–1951* (Durham: Duke University Press, 1998); and Laura Putnam's *The Company They Kept: Migrants and the Politics of Gender in Caribbean Costa Rica, 1870–1960* (Chapel Hill: University of North Carolina Press, 2003).

62 Alois Samohýl, "Production of Tires and Automobiles at the Bata Company," in *The Bata Phenomenon: Zlin Architecture 1910–1960* (Zlín: Regional Gallery of Fine Arts, 2009).

63 Susan Porter Benson, *Counter Cultures: Saleswomen, Managers, and Customers in American Department Stores, 1890–1940* (Urbana-Champagne: University of Illinois Press, 1987); Donica Belisle, "Negotiating Paternalism: Women and Canada's Largest Department Stores, 1880–1960," *Journal of Women's History* 19, no. 1 (Spring 2007): 58–81.

64 While complete statistics for all managers in the Bat'a era have yet to be compiled, several snapshots of management in the period reveal a profoundly male-dominated organization. All of the general directors, as well as the vast majority of department managers, were men throughout the period: there were 3 female directors out of 120 in 1937. Osobní oddělení, SOkA-Zlín, Bata Fond, K 0. In 1938, out of 198 city government positions 13 of them went to women. Protokol městká řada 1938, SOkA-Zlín, AMZ, k. 71, č. 153.

65 In 1938, for their world collection, the company had 350 types of shoes for women, 96 for men, and 128 for children. "Světová kolekce 1938," Prodejní odděleni, SOkA-Zlín, k. 1573, č. 289.

66 Lehár, *Dějiny baťova koncernu*, 122.

67 Ibid., 129.

68 K. Růžička, "Racionalizace českého prumyslů," *Národní listy*, 19 February 1930, 1.

69 "Anketa o Baťovy," *Přítomnost*, 11 February 1931.

70 Martin Jemelka, "Ottmuth: A German Enclave of Batism?," in *Company Towns of the Bat'a Concern*, 24–5

71 "Our Shoes in America," *Sdělení*, 25 June 1927.
72 "Made in Czechoslovakia," *Sdělení*, 9 February 1929, 5.
73 Belavsky quoted in Antonín Cekota, *Tomas Bata: Entrepreneur Extraordinary:* (Don Mills, ON: T.H. Best, 1968), 311.
74 A. Cekota, "10 let práce," in *Hospodářská politika čs. průmyslu v letech 1918–1928* (Prague: Ústřední svaz průmyslníků, 1928), 257.
75 Ústředna čs. obchodních a živostenských komor, 24 June 1936, "Vliv racionalisace na zdraví dělnictva." NA, MPOŽ, k. 1013 č. 68810–36.
76 Ibid.
77 Nolan, *Visions of Modernity*, 11.

5 "Half the World Is Barefoot"

1 See Jeffry Freiden, *Global Capitalism: Its Rise and Fall in the Twentieth Century* (New York: W.W. Norton, 2006); and Robert Boyce, *The Great Interwar Crisis and the Collapse of Globalization* (New York: Palgrave Macmillan, 2009).
2 John Maynard Keynes, *The Economic Consequences of the Peace* (New York: Harcourt Brace, 1920).
3 For a thorough account of the international trade of consumer items in the Austro-Hungarian Empire see David Good, *Economic Rise of the Hapsburg Empire, 1750–1914* (Berkeley: University of California Press, 1984).
4 Of the multitude of definitions of globalization, this work uses the following, set forth in Jagdish Bhagwati, *In Defence of Globalization* (Oxford: Oxford University Press, 2006), 3: "Globalization constitutes integration of national economies into the international economy through trade, direct foreign investment (by corporations and multinationals), short-term capital flows, international flows of workers and humanity generally, and flows of technology."
5 A.G. Hopkins, ed., *Globalization in World History* (New York: Norton, 2002), 9.
6 Douglas A. Irwin, *Peddling Protectionism: Smoot-Hawley and the Great Depression* (Princeton: Princeton University Press, 2017), vii–xviii.
7 G.F. Johnson letter to John Clarke, 17 January 1929, George F. Johnson Papers, Box 10, Syracuse University Library Manuscript Collections.
8 "Ocheana výroby obuvi v Juhoslávii," *Slovák* (Bratislava), 25 April 1928)
9 "Německo chce zvýšením cel na obuv znemožniti čsl. Konkurenci," *A.Z České Slovo* (Prague), 10 December 1929, 1.
10 James Harold, *The End of Globalization: Lessons from the Great Depression* (Cambridge: Harvard University Press, 2001), 126.
11 The list is compiled from Ondřej Ševeček, "The Case of Company Towns of the Bat'a Concern" in Ševeček and Jemelka *Company Towns of the Bat'a Concern* (Stuttgart: Franz Steiner, 2013), 35, and the website "Bat'a's World," which is managed by Tomas Bata University, http://world.tomasbata.org/. During

the 1940s, Jan Bat'a also built three company towns in Brazil, and other Bat'a employees built small factories in Chile and Bolivia.

12 These were Otrokovice/Bat'ov, Třebíč-Borovina, Ratíškovice, Svit/Batizovice, Zruč nad Sázavou/Baťov, Šimonovany/Baťovany, and Sezimovo Ústí/Baťov. Excellent short histories of each of these can be found in Martin Jemelka and Ondřej Ševeček, *Tovární města Baťova koncernu* (Prague: Academia, 2016).

13 "Bata's World," http://world.tomasbata.org/ (last accessed 22 February 2018). Bat'a would construct modern factories in Batapur, Baghdad, and Alexandria after the Second World War.

14 Hopkins best understood this transition as integration through imperialism (1850–1950) to integration through international organizations (1950–present). Hopkins, *Globalization in World History*, 34–5.

15 "Bata's World," http://world.tomasbata.org/ (last accessed 22 February 2018).

16 Mark Ovenden and Maxwell Roberts, *Airline Maps: A Century of Art and Design* (New York: Penguin, 2019), 14.

17 Lucy Budd, "Global Networks before Globalisation: Imperial Airways and the Development of Long-haul Air Routes," *GaWC Research Bulletin* (Loughborough: Loughborough University, 2007), 2.

18 "Bata's World: Egypt," http://world.tomasbata.org/africa/egypt/.

19 Max Rodenbeck, *Cairo: The City Victorious* (New York: Knopf Doubleday, 2017), 217.

20 Nancy Reynolds, *A City Consumed: Urban Commerce, the Cairo Fire, and the Politics of Decolonization in Egypt* (Stanford: Stanford University Press, 2012), 140–2.

21 Salim Tamari, *The Great War and the Remaking of Palestine* (Berkeley: University of California Press, 2017), 123.

22 "Bat'a's World: Israel," http://world.tomasbata.org/asia/israel/.

23 "Bat'a's World: Iraq," http://svet.tomasbata.org/asie/irak/.

24 Other compelling evidence for the local elite's interest in Bata can be found in Nehru's close relationship with Thomas J. Bata, son of Tomáš, as well as in Subhas Chandra Bose's links with Bat'a. See Thomas Bata and Sonja Sinclair, *Bata: Shoemaker to the World* (Toronto, Stoddart, 1990), 186–7.

25 Satadru Sen, *Benoy Kumar Sarkar: Restoring the Nation to the World* (London: Routledge, 2015), 6.

26 Tomáš Bat'a, "Dvě rasy," *Sdělení* (Zlín), 30 May 1925, 1.

27 Julie Marie Robinson, *Race, Religion, and the Pulpit: Robert L. Bradley and the Making of Urban Detroit* (Detroit: Wayne State University Press, 2015), 89.

28 Maria Noguez, *Ford and the Global Strategies of Multinationals: The North American Auto Industry* (London: Routledge, 2003), 46.

29 Cekota, quoting T. Bat'a, in *Tomas Bata*, 357.

30 Zuzana Hrnčířová, *Baťovy závody a život Čechoslováků v Indii v letech 1934–1950* (dissertation, Univerzita Karlova, 2017), 17–20.

31 Ibid., 25–6.

32 Tomáš Smetánka, "From Central Europe to Singapore: Bata and Baťa," in Yeo Lay Hwee and Turner Barnard, eds., *50 Years of Singapore-Europe Relations: Celebrating Singapore's Connections with Europe* (Singapore: World Scientific, 2015), 89–91.

33 Frank Zephyr and Also Musacchio, "The International Natural Rubber Market, 1870–1930," *EH.Net Encyclopedia*, ed. Robert Whaples, http://eh.net /encyclopedia/the-international-natural-rubber-market-1870-1930/.

34 Adrian Vickers, *A History of Modern Indonesia* (Cambridge: Cambridge Press, 2013), 67.

35 Clifford Geertz, *Peddlers and Princes: Social Development and Economic Change in Two Indonesian Towns* (Chicago: University of Chicago Press, 1963), 57.

36 His speech can be found on youtube: https://www.youtube.com/watch?v=jvUegwf Gs5o&feature=related (last accessed 21 February 2018).

37 "Top Shoe Manufacturing Countries by Country," worldatlas.com, https://www .worldatlas.com/articles/top-shoe-manufacturing-countries.html (last accessed 22 February 2018).

38 Cizinci v firmě, Baťa A.S., Zlín, Baťa Fond, SOkA-Zlín, k. 1192 č. 39.

39 "Indičtí mladí muži ve Zlíně" *Zlín*, 15 May 1933.

40 Reg Field, Bata Reminiscence and Resource Center, http://www.batamemories .org.uk/MAIN/ENG/00-EN-Pages/Memories/Field.html (last accessed 11 May 2018).

41 Cizinci v firmě, Bat'a Fond, SOkA-Zlín, K. 1350 č. 4.

42 Stephen Meyer, "Adapting the Immigrant to the Line: Americanization in the Ford Factory, 1914–1921," *Journal of Social History* 14, no. 1 (Autumn 1980): 77.

43 Tara Zahra, "Imagined Noncommunities: National Indifference as a Category of Analysis," *Slavic Review* 69, no. 1 (Spring 2010): 93–119.

44 Paul Lerner, *The Consuming Temple: Jews, Department Stores, and the Consumer Revolution in Germany, 1880–1940* (Ithaca: Cornell Press, 2015).

45 There are many such examples of Bat'a personnel and the city of Zlín participating in patriotic days – Masaryk's visit in 1928 to Zlín, the procession for his funeral, an official visit to Zlín by Beneš in 1937, etc.

46 Chad Byrant's work on the Nazi occupation of Prague argues that we should look at the ways in which people acted nationally and how they gave meaning to such actions in their day-to-day lives. Chad Bryant, *Prague in Black* (Cambridge: Harvard University Press, 2007).

47 "Batastory," http://batastory.net/cs/hlavni/ (last accessed 9 December 2019).

48 Austin Doležal, "Augustin Doležal, jeden z prvních a nejvěrnějších," Batastory. net, http://batastory.net/cs/stopa/augustin-dolezal-jeden-z-prvnich-a-nejvernejsich (last accessed 15 May 2018).

49 A. Cekota quoted in Milan Zelený, *Cesty k úspechu: Trvalé hodnoty soustavy Baťa* (Kusak: Vyškov, 2005), 130.

50 Dominik Čipera, *Ve službách práce a lidu: soubor úvah, projevu a vzpomínkových poznámek 1919–1944* (Zlín: Tisk, 1944), 92.

51 *Výběr a výchova průmyslového člověka* (Zlín: Tisk, 1937), SOkA-Zlín k. 1012 č. 17. Also Kalergi is found in *Vedení osobního oddělení* (Zlín: Tisk, 1938), SOkA-Zlín k. 1010 č. 12. Both books were required reading for managers.

52 Dominik Čipera, as quoted in Jaroslav Pospíšil, *Rub a líc baťovských sporů* (Zlín: Kniha Zlín, 2012), 23.

53 Bohumil Lehár, *Dějiny baťova koncernu, 1894–1945* (Prague: Státní nakladatelství politické literatury, 1960), 202.

54 Martin Jemelka and Ondřej Ševeček, *Tovární města Baťova koncernu* (Prague: Academia, 2016), 57–8.

55 In fact, one of the Bat'a Company's role models, Endicott-Johnson, would not globalize in the same period. EJ was essentially content with the large internal market of the United States and lobbied politicians to raise shoe tariffs, specifically on shoes coming from Czechoslovakia throughout the 1930s.

56 "Character Traits of the New Industrial Man," Conference of the Personnel Department, 29 November 1937, Bat'a Fond, SOkA-Zlín. k. 1010 č. 10.

57 Maksimovic quoted in Jemelka and Ševeček, *Tovární města Baťova koncernu*, 419.

58 The quotes and information about the contents of this article are from a series of memoranda between Czechoslovakia's Ministry of Industry, Ministry of Social Affairs, and Ministry of Foreign Affairs found in the National Archive of the Czech Republic (NA), Ministerstvo průmyslu, obchodu a živností (MPOŽ), 1918–42. k. 967 č. 86576.

59 Ondřej Ševeček, "The Case of Company Towns of the Bat'a Concern," in Ševeček and Jemelka, 35.

60 Anne Sudrow's as yet unpublished paper illustrates the European-wide anti-Bat'a movement: "Fighting Slavic Expansionism in Western Europe: A Transnational European Movement against the Bat'a Company during the Interwar Years." Presented at the Company Towns of the Bat'a Concern Conference in Prague, 24–25 March 2011.

61 Maixner to Girsa, 5 April 1935. NA, MPOŽ, 1918–42, k. 967 č. 86576.

62 Janusz Gruchała, *Czeskie środowiska polityczne wobec spraw polskich 1920–1938* (Katowice: Wydawnictwo Uniwersytetu Śląskiego, 2002).

63 Letter from Václav Girsa to the Ministry of Foreign Affairs, 28 June 1935. MPOŽ, k. 967 č. 86576, NA.

64 Ibid.

65 By 1935 the Bat'a School of Work was giving a unique educational experience to over 5,000 adolescents. Školy, studijní Ustav výchova prumyslového člověka, 1936. SOkA-Zlín, Baťa Fond, k. 1192 č. 39.

66 Letter to the Ministry of Social Affairs from the Ministry of Industry, 14 September 1935. MPOŽ, k. 967 č. 80445, NA.

67 Ibid.
68 Letter from Hugo Vavrečka to the Minister of Social Affairs, 27 July 1935. MPOŽ, k. 967 č. 80445, NA.
69 Letter from Maixner to Ministry of Foreign Affairs, 12 October 1935. Forwarded to other ministries in May 1936. MPOŽ k. 958, NA.
70 Much excellent work has been done tracing nationalists' fears of the "amphibians." See Pieter Judson, *Guardians of the Nation: Activists on the Language Frontiers of Imperial Austria* (Cambridge: Harvard University Press, 2006); Jeremy King, *Budweisers into Czechs and Germans: A Local History of Bohemian Politics, 1848–1948* (Princeton: Princeton University Press, 2002); Tara Zahra, *Kidnapped Souls: National Indifference and the Battle for Children in the Bohemian Lands, 1900–1948* (Ithaca: Cornell University Press, 2011).
71 "Živnostenský," November 1935. Baťa Fond, SOkA-Zlín, k. 376. The party's slogan was "poctivého nacionalismu, důsledné demokracie a zachování soukromého podnikání" (honest nationalism, vigorous democracy, and the protection of private business).
72 "Věstník živnostenský, úřednický, zřízenecký a dělnický," *Národní politika*, 14 September 1934, 9.
73 Kramerius search of "zrušení správkáren" revealed advertisements placed in 16 different Czech language dailies in 1934. http://kramerius.nkp.cz/kramerius /Search.do?text=zru%C5%A1en%C3%AD+spr%C3%A1vk%C3%A1ren+ &resultPage=6&documentType=periodical (accessed 6 June 2017).
74 Tobias Ehrenbold, "Putting Möhlin on the Map," in Jemelka and Ševeček, 129–45.
75 Ibid., 131.
76 Martin Jemelka and Ondřej Ševeček, *Tovární města Baťova koncernu* (Prague: Academia, 2016), 550.
77 Ibid., 551.
78 Ibid., 552.
79 Ehrenbold, "Putting Möhlin on the Map," 132–3.
80 Ibid., 134.
81 Jemelka and Ševeček, *Tovární města Baťova koncernu*, 552.
82 Ehrenbold, "Putting Möhlin on the Map," 137.
83 Ibid., 135.
84 Ibid., 145.
85 Jan Baťa, "Poznámky z Indie," *Zlín*, 1 March 1937.
86 Návštěvy v podniku, Baťa Fond, SOkA-Zlín. k. 12 č. 505.
87 For more on Baťa and India see Sreeparna Bagchi, "The Zlin Enterprise: A Profile of the Role of the First Multinational Organization in the Leather Industry in Bengal (1931–1945)," *Calcutta Historical Journal* 25 (2005), 47–63.
88 Robert Holton, *Globalization and the Nation State* (New York: Palgrave, 2011), 182–9.
89 Dominik Čipera, "Nejlepší z nejlepších," *Zlín*, 1 May 1933, 2.

90 The same is true, as has been discussed, of Ford.

91 Sven Beckert, *Empire of Cotton: A Global History* (New York, 2015), 426.

92 Ibid., 426.

6 "The Path of Perfection"

1 Bohumil Lehár, *Dějiny baťova koncernu, 1894–1945* (Prague: Státní nakladatelství politické literatury, 1960), 176.

2 From the variety of police records in the Archiv Města Zlín, the only records on police brutality before the Nazi occupation can be found in Bezpečností stráž města Zlína-personální záležitosti, č. 635.

3 Jane Jacobs, *The Death and Life of Great American Cities* (New York: Random House, 1961), 21.

4 Alf Lüdtke, *Eigen-Sinn: Fabrikalltag, Arbeitererfahrungen un Politik vom Kaiserreich bis in den Faschismus* (Hamburg: Ergebnisse Verlag, 1993), 14–15.

5 Manager's Guidebook, Bat'a Fond, SOkA-Zlín, p. 6.

6 J.A. Bat'a, "Jakých lidí si máme nejvíce všímat?" Bat'a Fond, SOkA-Zlín k. 1015. č 30, 1937 (exact date unknown).

7 "Svět Žen," *Zlín*, 10 August 1938, p. 8.

8 Lehár, *Dějiny baťova koncernu,* 231.

9 "Vedoucím oddělení," 28 September 1933. Bat'a Fond, SOkA-Zlín k. 1009 č. 7.

10 "Vedení osobního odděl. v průmyslových podnicích," Bat'a Fond, SOkA-Zlín k. 1009 č. 8.

11 "Katechismus pro vedoucí odd," Bat'a Fond, SOkA-Zlín k. 1010 č. 9.

12 Photographs of Jaroněk can be found in Jaroněk's personnel card, Bat'a Fond, SOkA-Zlín k. 1023 č. 14.

13 Jaroněk to personnel inspectors, 11 February 1935, Osobní odděleni, Bat'a Fond, SOkA-Zlín k. 1009 č. 7.

14 V. Jaroněk, personnel card, Bat'a Fond, SOkA-Zlín k. 1023 č. 14.

15 Ibid.

16 Ibid.

17 Konference osobních referentů, 29 November 1937, Osobní odděleni, Bat'a Fond, SOkA-Zlín k. 1010 č. 10.

18 Socialní služba prodejní oddělení, Bat'a Fond, SOkA-Zlín k. 0 č. 37.

19 Osobní inspektoři to S. Štetkař, Osobní odděleni, Bat'a Fond, SOkA-Zlín k. 1017 č. 10.

20 Osobní odděleni, Bat'a Fond, SOkA-Zlín.

21 "Ve Zlíně u Baťů: Ze vzpomínek baťovce Aloise Šafaříka," http://batastory.net/cs /abs/ (last accessed 5 June 2018).

22 Ibid.

23 Form for Store Managers, Prodejní Oddělení, 1938. Bat'a Fond, SOkA-Zlín k. 1506 č. 6.

24 Roy Jacques, *Manufacturing the Employee: Management Knowledge from the 19th to 21st Centuries* (London: Sage Publications, 1996), 1–15.
25 "Růžena Urbancová," Trestní spisy 1924–48, Archiv města Zlína (AMZ), SOkA-Zlín č. 1118.
26 Ibid.
27 The Minister of the Interior declared the *Bat'ovak* illegal in September 1931 under the new Defence of the Republic Law. Národní Archiv (NA), TS-IČ Baťovák k. 4 č. 32.
28 Among the many examples of guilt through familial connection, see the personnel cards of Anna Čevelová, Bohumíla Polašková, and Jan Kotas. Kartotéky KSČ, Bat'a Fond, SOkA-Zlín k. 1032 č. 17.
29 "Josef Vancura," personnel card, Bat'a Fond, SOkA-Zlín k. 1095 č. 17.
30 "Václav Berka," Kartotéky KSČ, Bat'a Fond, SOkA-Zlín k. 1032. in the police archives in the AMZ I found eighty-seven other cases of anonymous informants turning in suspected communists.
31 Tábory Lidu, AMZ, SOkA-Zlín k. 433 č. 962.
32 Ibid.
33 Police Report, 20 September 1936, AMZ, SOkA-Zlín. k. 579 č. 1118.
34 "Ilegální komunistický leták," 1936, AMZ, SOkA-Zlín k. 579 č. 1118.
35 Police letter from Jaroněk, AMZ, SOkA-Zlin k. 579 č. 1118.
36 "Ilegální komunistický leták" 1936, AMZ, SOkA-Zlín k. 579 č. 1118.
37 "Pan Josef Simajchl," 29 November 1935. AMZ, SOkA-Zlín č. 263.
38 "Trestní spisy," AMZ, SOkA-Zlín k. 579–84.
39 See Stephen Kotkin, *Magnetic Mountain: Stalinism as a Civilization* (Berkeley: University of California Press, 1995).
40 For the clearest work to date on the Soviet civil police see David Shearer, *Policing Stalin's Socialism: Repression and Social Order in the Soviet Union, 1924–1953* (New Haven: Yale University Press, 2009).
41 J. Bat'a, "Nevěrní lidé," *Zlín*, 16 August 1937.
42 While prostitution was never outlawed before the creation of Czechoslovakia, it was up to the municipal and regional authorities to determine its legality. Not surprisingly, prostitution was against the law in Zlín, and no sanctioned brothels existed. For a history of prostitution in Czechoslovakia, see Petr Hulinský, *Z dejin pražské prostituce* (Prague: Police History, 2009).
43 Marie. U., Trestní spisy, AMZ SOkA-Zlín k. 518 č. 1118.
44 Ibid.
45 Ibid.
46 Another woman, Anna T., became the focus of a two-month police investigation for having sex in a parking lot at a dance. A.T., Trestní spisy, AMZ SOkA-Zlín k. 581 č. 1118.
47 "Sociální ochrana ženy v naší práce," Osobní odděleni, Bat'a Fond, SOkA-Zlín k. 1020 č. 49.

48 These records can be found in individual employee personnel cards, which are not categorized, as well as in the minutes of meetings of the social and personnel inspectors. Each department had its own personnel inspection reports, though these too are not categorized in the company archive at Bat'a Fond, SOkA-Zlín.

49 Osobní odděleni, 1939, Bat'a Fond, SOkA-Zlín k. 0 č. 31–8.

50 Osobní odděleni, Bat'a Fond, SOkA-Zlín k. 0 č. 37.

51 "Sociální ochrana ženy v naší práce," Osobní odděleni, Bat'a Fond, SOkA-Zlín k. 1020 č. 49.

52 "Statisticky úřad, propuštení zaměstnanci, " Bat'a Fond, SOkA-Zlín k. 0 č. 11.

53 For more on abortion in Czechoslovakia see M. Feinberg, *Elusive Equality: Gender, Citizenship, and the Limits of Democracy in Czechoslovakia, 1918–1950* (Pittsburgh: University of Pittsburgh Press, 2006). It would be interesting to try to find cases of illegal abortion in Zlín through an examination of health records. Unfortunately, these documents were not found in the company, city, or national archives. No mention of abortion was made in company or city records.

54 One of the first examples was Tomáš's sister Marie, who was a manager in the stitching department until she got married to Josef Hlavnička in 1923 and left the firm to become a housewife. Osobní kartotéky Bat'a Fond, SOkA-Zlín k. 1021 č. 13.

55 Statisticky úřad, "propuštění zaměstnanci", Bat'a Fond, SOkA-Zlín K 0 č. 11.

56 For a good description of the typical female dormitory, see Ondřej Ševeček, "Socio-spatial Aspects of Zlín's Urbanization," in *The Bata Phenomenon: Zlin Architecture, 1910–1960* (Zlín: Regional Gallery of Fine Arts, 2009).

57 Domink Čipera, "Jak bude vypadat Zlín za 40 let?" insert, 40 let baťových závodů, *Zlín*, 25 January 1934, 9.

58 V. Karfík, "Domy služeb v roce 1974," in *The Bata Phenomenon: Zlin Architecture 1910–1960* (Zlín: Regional Gallery of Fine Arts, 2009).

59 "Moderní mladá žena a sport," *Zlín*, 19 February 1934. "Proč žena miluje Ameriku," *Zlín*, 9 March 1936. "Žena a letadlo," *Zlín*, 5 October 1936.

60 Endicott-Johnson did not routinely use air travel until after the Second World War, nor did the Ford Company.

61 "Příklad pro naše žen," *Zlín*, 21 March 1938, 4.

62 By 1932 Zlín had one car for every forty-four citizens as compared with Prague which had one car for every sixty-two citizens. By 1936 the ratio was 1:29. Doprava Silniční, AMZ, SOkA-Zlín k. 144 č. 144.

63 For a good discussion of women and the automobile in American society see Virginia Scharff, *Taking the Wheel: Women and the Coming of the Motor Age* (Albuquerque: University of New Mexico Press, 1992).

64 The *celibát* laws dated to the 1867 Austrian Constitution, and required that females in the civil service be abstinent and single. See Feinberg, *Elusive Equality*.

65 Several excellent works that trace the rise of the idea of woman as consumer-citizen elsewhere are Victoria De Grazia and Ellen Furlough, *The Sex of Things:*

Gender and Consumption in Historical Perspective (Berkeley: University of California Press, 1996); Lisa Tiersten, *Marianne in the Market: Envisioning Consumer Society in Fin-de-Siècle France* (Berkeley: University of California Press, 2001); Erica Carter, *How German Is She?: Postwar West German Reconstruction and the Consuming Woman* (Ann Arbor: University of Michigan Press, 1997).

66 The numbers fluctuated over time; these numbers are taken from 1937.

67 Letter to Jaroněk from J. Bat'a, 20 February 1934. Bat'a Fond, SOkA-Zlín k. 1020 č. 49.

68 Denní rozkazy, 12.1.1937–12.31.1937, Policejní úřady městká Zlína, AMZ SOkA-Zlín k. 217 č. 299.

69 One such story is found in the police record of Josefa Danielová, trestní spisy, AMZ SOkA-Zlín k. 580 č.1118.

70 Of the hundreds of personnel cards examined, not one of them was for someone of Roma descent, and the company's nationality breakdown of 1938 makes no mention of Roma either. Osobní oddělení, statistiky, Bat'a Fond, SOkA-Zlín.

71 Geza Štujlater, Trestní spisy, AMZ, SOkA-Zlín k. 581 č. 1118.

72 Mention of the Roma labourers can be found in various police records as well as in company documents. Bat'a Fond, SOkA-Zlín k. 121 č. 121.

73 Anna Šubertová, Trestní spisy, AMZ SOkA Zlín č. 1118 k. 582.

74 Ludvík Daniel, Trestní spisy, AMZ SOkA-Zlín č. 1118 k. 580.

75 Gabriel Daniel, Trestní spisy, AMZ SOkA Zlín č. 1118 k. 580.

76 Vladislav Daniel, Trestní spisy, AMZ SOkA Zlín č. 1118 k. 580.

77 A few notable histories of Zlín that have no mention of Romani communities are Zdeněk Pokluda, *Zlín* (Paseka: Praha-Litomyšl, 2008), and Karel Stloukal, *550 let města Zlína* (Zlín, 1948).

78 Of 2,748 arrests from 1923 to 1937 by city police, some 1,640 were cases of vagrancy. Public health statistics, 1937, AMZ SOkA-Zlín č.1123.

79 J. Bubík, Trestní spisy, AMZ SOkA-Zlín, k. 579 č. 1118.

80 Petr Šula a spol., Trestní spisy, AMZ, SOkA-Zlín. k. 579 č. 1118.

81 Public health statistics, 1937, AMZ, SOkA-Zlín č. 1123.

82 For an excellent account of the statistics on interwar Czechoslovakia's school system in the English language, see US Department of the Interior, Office of Education, Bulletin. No. 11, 1935.

83 Spolek rodičů, school budget, 1939–40, AMZ, SOkA-Zlín k. 1217 č. 161.

84 The steady stream of increased expectations can be found in Ředitelství BŠP různé osobní záležitosti internátů, 1936–9. Bat'a Fond, SOkA-Zlín k. 1223 č. 192.

85 "Zařidte kalendař," Bat'a Fond, SOkA-Zlín k. 1027 č. 14.

86 Ibid.

87 "Mladí muže," Schedule for 1936, Bat'a Fond, SOkA-Zlín k. 1508 č. 6.

88 James C. Scott, *Seeing Like a State: How Certain Schemes to Improve the Human Condition Have Failed* (New Haven: Yale University Press, 1999), 195.

89   Application letter, Baťa School of Work, Baťa Fond, SOkA-Zlín k. 1192 č. 39.

90   "Mladí muže" Schedule for 1936, Bat'a Fond, SOkA-Zlín.k. 1508 č. 6.

91   Ibid.

92   Eduard Staša, "Zlínský prospekt internátů," *Naše pravda*, 1990, http://www.zlin
     .estranky.cz/clanky/novy-zlin/nam_-t_g_-masaryka---zlinsky-prospekt-internatu
     .html (last accessed December 2019).

93   Jan Bat'a to engineers Drkoš and Kovárník and directors Hradil and Jaroněk, 15
     June 1937, Baťa Fond, SOkA-Zlín, k. 1223 č. 192.

94   Školy – studíjní Ustav výchova prumyslového člověka, Baťa Fond, SOkA-Zlín
     k. 1192 č. 39.

95   Svatopluk Jaburek, "Vznik, smysl a úspěchy Baťovy školy práce," http://
     batastory.net/cs/abs/vznik-smysl-a-uspechy-batovy-skoly-prace (last accessed
     December 2019).

96   Stanislav Štětkář, *Internát – Baťová škola práce* (Unpublished), SOkA-Zlín AK
     0/563/2: 9.

97   "Zemřel František Šumpela," Klub ABŠ, absolventů Baťovy školy práce. http://
     batastory.net/cs/abs/ (last accessed 18 October 2019).

98   Ibid.

99   Personnel card, Antonín Vavra. Bat'a Fond, SOkA-Zlín k. 1095 č. 57.

100 Denní rozkazy – Policejní úřady městská Zlína, AMZ, SOkA-Zlín k. 217 č. 299

101 Ibid., 8 December 1937.

102 Madla Vaculíková, "Ja jsem oves: rozhovor s Pavlem Kosatíkem," *Máj* (2002):
     20.

103 J.A. Bat'a, "Podnikatelská univerzita," *Zlín*, 22 November, 1937, 1.

104 Internáty – Minutes from the boys' dormitory Tomášov, 8 March 1940, Bat'a
     Fond, SOkA-Zlín k. 1027 č. 101.

105 Ibid.

106 A. Grác, *První tři léta Pedagogického oddělení 1935–38*, SOkA-Zlín k. 1190 č.
     28.

107 Newspaper clippings about the Adult Education program. SOkA-Zlín k. 1190 č.
     29.

108 Ibid.

109 Interestingly, the charter for the school was carefully worded so that the regional
     schoolboard's nationalism would be appeased. The charter assured that the
     school would be run by a Czechoslovak and that all classes taught in Czech
     would be by a Czechoslovak. In addition, it promised that the teacher of German
     would be a Czechoslovak national. Soukromná měštánská škola, AMZ, SOkA-
     Zlín č. 735.

110 Due to the state of the Bat'a archives, there is no way to know how many
     of these students actually became Young Men and Women. After the Nazi
     occupation, Jan Bat'a, who at that point had become the chairman of the regional
     schoolboard in Brno, revised the language program to focus on German. The

chief teacher of English, John Crubb from England, was fired and soon arrested by the Gestapo.

111 Odborná škola pro ženské povolání (1935–48) AMZ SOkA-Zlín, č. 734.

112 Letter from Vlček to the city council, 18 August 1938. Odborná škola pro ženské povolání (1935–48) AMZ SOkA-Zlín č. 734.

113 For the battle for children's national allegiance, see Tara Zahra, *Kidnapped Souls: National Indifference and the Battle for Children in the Bohemian Lands, 1900–1948* (Ithaca: Cornell University Press, 2008).

114 J. Durdik, 25 November 1937, AMZ SOkA-Zlín k. 217 č. 299.

115 Ibid.

116 Osobní Oddělení, 25 November 1937, Bat'a Fond, SOkA-Zlín k. 0 č. 37.

117 In 1937, for example, 68 per cent of their cases concerned financial support, wage issues, and requests from workers. Osobní Oddělení, 25 November 1937, Bat'a Fond, SOkA-Zlín k. 0 č. 37.

118 For an account of the lives of the workers in the dormitories see Ondřej Ševeček, *Zrození Baťovy průmyslové metropole: Továrna, městký prostor a společnost ve Zlíně v letech 1900–1938* (České Budějovice: Veduta, 2009).

119 From the variety of police records in the AMZ, the only records on police brutality before the Nazi occupation can be found in Bezpečností stráž města Zlína – personální záležitosti, č. 635.

120 That all of these activities were going on that day is an assumption of the authors based on evidence from 1937. For Bat'a reports on tardy workers see SOkA-Zlín 1937 For a report on Roma and the shell game in 1937, see AMZ Trestní Spisy k. 579 č. 1118. For *Máca v. Bat'a*, see AMZ SOkA-Zlín č. 860.

121 Jan Martinec, Trestní spisy, AMZ SOkA-Zlín k. 580 č. 1118.

7 "Everyone Gives Their Soul to Their Country"

1 "O schůzi národní obce fašistické ve Zlíně," 11 February 1937, Policejní záležitosti, AMZ SOkA-Zlín č. 1125: 1–6.

2 Ibid., 1.

3 Ibid.

4 "O schůzi národní obce fašistické ve Zlíně," 11 February 1937, Policejní záležitosti, AMZ SOkA-Zlín č. 1125: 1–6.

5 "Záznam – O schůzi národní obce fašistické ve Zlíně," 11 February 1937, Policejní záležitosti, AMZ SOkA-Zlín č. 1125: 4.

6 "O schůzi národní obce fašistické ve Zlíně," 11 February 1937, Policejní záležitosti, AMZ SOkA-Zlín č. 1125: 1.

7 Ibid., 6.

8 Ibid., 5.

9 J. Bat'a, "V Turíně," *Zlín*, 18 January 1937, 1.

10 J. Bat'a, "Na autostradě Turín – Milan," reprinted in J. Bat'a, *Za obchodem kolem světa* (Zlín, 1937), 12.
11 J. Bat'a, untitled, *Zlín*, 25 January 1937, 1.
12 Ibid.
13 J. Baťa to Vrána, Hradil, Kohn, and Čekota, 18 January 1937, Osobní Oddĕleni, Baťa Fond, SOkA-Zlín k. 1223 č. 192.
14 Ibid.
15 Chad Byrant, *Prague in Black* (Cambridge: Harvard University Press, 2007), 22.
16 Jan. A. Baťa, *Budujme stát pro 40,000,000* (Zlín: Tisk, 1937).
17 "Pět vedoucích knih politických a sociologických," *Lidové Noviny*, 5 December 1937, 1.
18 "Jak budujme stát," *Všehrd* 2 (1937–8): 172; "Literární souběh na téma budujme stát," *Přítomnost* (1938): 123; *Moravská orlice*, 21 January 1938, 1; *Český deník*, 6 March 1938, 5; "vzrůstajícímu rozvoji motorismu," *Národní listy*, 9 December 1938, 1.
19 *Budujme stát* has become required reading for a new brand of politicians in today's Czech Republic. Andřej Babiš, for example, cited the book as one of his most important sources of inspiration. Jan Pavec, "Budujme stát pro 40 milonů lidí: Přečtěte si, u koho se inspiruje Babiš," e15.cz. https://www.e15.cz/nazory /budujme-stat-pro-40-milionu-lidi-prectete-si-u-koho-se-inspiruje-babis-1328951 (last accessed 26 June 2018).
20 Jan. A. Baťa, *Budujme stát pro 40,000,000*, 16.
21 Jan. A. Baťa, *Budujme stát pro 40,000,000*.
22 Tomáš Fránek, "Jan Antonín Baťa prezidentem? Jednalo se o tom ale dostala firma," *Český rozhlas*, 21 February 2018. https://zlin.rozhlas.cz/jan-antonin-bata -prezidentem-jednalo-se-o-tom-prednost-ale-dostala-firma-6857351.
23 "Nová tvář zlínského pracovního máje," *Zlín*, 2 May 1938,18.
24 "Ideální průmyslové město budoucnosti – kniha zkušeností a rad z podnikání fy Bat'a," MZA-Zlin, Osobní oddĕlení, II/6.
25 Petr Szczepanik, *Konzervy se slovy: Počátky zvukového film a česká mediální kultura 30.let* (Brno: Host, 2009), 421–2.
26 The nine major exhibits were as follows: Baťa Exhibit at Prague's Spring/Fall Trade Fair, 1934–9; World Fair of Posters in Zlín, 1935; Brno Provincial Fair, 1935; The National Airplane Fair in Prague, 1937; World's Fair, Paris, 1937; Trade Fair, Cairo, 1938; Slavic Exhibition in Uherské Hradiště, 1937; NYWF 1939–40; May Semi-Permanent Exhibition in Zlín, 1938–9. Records of the Baťa company's foray into all of these exhibitions can be found in the collection "Výstavy," Bat'a Fond, MZA, SOkA-Zlín k. 319.
27 There are several excellent resources for the student of Batism, and undoubtedly the best way to access its philosophy is a thorough reading of the company and town's main newspaper, *Sdělení* (later to become *Zlín*), where company elites

routinely publicized their visions for the future. See, for example, "Baťovi mladí muži roku 1974," *Zlín,* 21 May 1934, 1.

28 Stanislav Holubec, "Silní milují život. Utopie, ideologie, a biopolitika batovského Zlína," *Kuděj* 11, no. 2 (2009): 30–55.

29 Antonín Cekota, "Zlínská práce a sport," *Zlín,* 20 August 1934, 1.

30 T. Baťa, "Co budeme dělat," *Zlín,* 29 April 1932, 1.

31 "Výsledky voleb v Československu," Český statistický úřad, https://www.czso.cz /documents/10180/20536128/422008k03.pdf/ (last accessed December 2019).

32 "Zaměstnanci dle národnosti a dle příslušnosti," department 20305, Osobní odděleni, Baťa Fond, SOkA-Zlín H 1134 k. 1011 č. 15.

33 "Zaměstnanci dle národnosti a dle příslušnosti," for vedoucí, Osobní odděleni, Baťa Fond, SOkA-Zlín H 1134 k. 1011 č. 15.

34 Ibid.

35 Thomas J. Bata and Sonja Sinclair, *Shoemaker to the World* (Toronto, Stoddart: 1990), 100.

36 A. Cekota, "Instrukce osob. Oddělení," Osobní odděleni. Baťa Fond, SOkA-Zlín, H 1134, k. 1506 č. 2.

37 "Výpadky," *Zlín,* 18 January 1938, 1.

38 "Vlajka a občan," *Zlín,* 17 January 1938, 3.

39 Zdeněk Pokluda, *Baťa v kostce* (Zlín: 2013), 83.

40 J. Baťa, "Úkol čsl. podnikatele," Honorary Doctorate Speech, 26 March 1938, Beneš Technical College in Brno. Found in "Promoce Jana Antonína Bati" http://www.zlin.estranky.cz/clanky/tomas-bata--jan-antonin-bata/promoce-jana -antonina-bati.html (last accessed 5 July 2018).

41 M. Wein, *The History of the Jews in the Bohemian Lands* (Leiden: Brill, 2015), 117.

42 Ibid., 118.

43 H, Vavrečka, quoted in Bohumil Lehár, *Dějiny baťova koncernu, 1894–1945* (Prague: Státní nakladatelství politické literatury, 1960), 237.

44 Lehár, *Dějiny baťova koncernu,* 235.

45 "Budoucnost průmyslového člověka," *Zlín,* 2 May 1938, 2.

46 J. Baťa, May Day Speech recorded in *Zlín,* 2 May 1938, 1.

47 "Velký Zlín," *Zlín,* 30 May 1938, 1.

48 Igor Lukes, "The Czechoslovak Partial Mobilization in May 1938: A Mystery (Almost) Solved," *Journal of Contemporary History* 31, no. 4 (1996): 72.

49 Pokluda, *Baťa v kostce,* 82–3.

50 "Mobilizace" *Zlín,* 26 August 1938, 1.

51 "Propuštených němců," SOkA-Zlín, Baťa Fond, k. 1350 č. 4.

52 30 September 1938 issue of *Zlín.*

53 V. Krejčí, *Poznamenaný: Deset měsíců s Janem Baťou a jak to bylo dál* (Zlín: Kniha Zlín, 2019), 66–7.

54 Ibid., 68.

55 Ibid., 69.

56 For an account of the Munich crises from Beneš perspective, see Milan Hauner, "Edvard Beneš's Undoing of Munich: A Message to a Czechoslovak Politician in Prague," *Journal of Contemporary History* 38, no. 4 (October 2003): 563–77.

57 Interview with J. Syrový, *Reportér* 30 (October 1968), found in Vojtěch Šír, "Armádní general Jan Syrový o situaci v září 1938," 9 October 2003. https://www.fronta.cz /armadni-general-jan-syrovy-o-situaci-v-zari-1938 (last accessed 1 July 2018).

58 Jan Kuklík, *Sociální Demokraté ve druhé republice* (Prague: Univerzita Karlova, 1992), 42.

59 Beran quoted in Kuklík, *Sociální Demokraté*, 42.

60 Kuklík, *Sociální Demokraté*, 9–10.

61 J. Baťa, "Rozhlasový projev po kapitulaci v září 1938," as quoted in Stanislav Vrbík, http://www.pozitivnisvet.cz/jan-antonin-bata-rozhlasovy-projev-po -kapitulaci-v-zari-1938/ (last accessed 28 June 2018).

62 Jindřich Dejmek, "Československá diplomacie v době druhé republiky," in *Pocta profesoru Janu Kuklíkovi* (Prague: Karolinum, 2000), 9–26.

63 Peter Demetz, *Prague in Danger: The Years of German Occupation, 1939–1945* (New York: Macmillan, 2009), 13.

64 Pokluda, *Baťa v kostce*, 82–3.

65 Ibid., 83.

66 "Prácovní tábory pro budování státu," *Zlín*, 14 October 1938, 1.

67 J. Baťa, "Soucit a pomoc," *Zlín*, 23 January 1939, 1, 3.

68 "Instrukce k protokolům pro kontrolu prodejen v území obsazaném Německem," Prodejní oddělení, Baťa Fond. SOkA-Zlín k. 1607 č. 385.

69 J. Baťa, "Kam s uprchlíky?" *Zlín*, 31 October 1938, 1.

70 J. Baťa, *Budujme stát pro 40,000.000 lidí.*

71 J. Baťa, "Kam s uprchlíky?," 1.

72 City Council Minutes, November 1938. AMZ, SOkA-Zlín k. 72.

73 Personnel card for Alexander Reinhartz, Osobní kartotéky, Baťa Fond, SOkA-Zlín k. 1036 č.18.

74 The first Baťa department store to open in the region was in Užhorod in 1929. When the company began operations, they reported that "Rusyn footwear is the most primitive imaginable." *Zlín*, 15 May 1931, 2. The clearest picture of economic differences between the different regions in Czechoslovakia can be found in the 1930 National Census for the country.

75 Letter from Miksha Reinhartz to the Baťa Company, 4 December 1939. Reinhartz, Osobní kartotéky, Baťa Fond, SOkA-Zlín k. 1036 č. 18.

76 Personnel card for Alexander Reinhartz.

77 Letter from Rosalia Reinhartzová to Baťa Company. Alexander Reinhartz, Osobní kartotéky, Baťa Fond, SOkA-Zlín k. 1036 č. 18.

78 "Report on a Young Man/Young Woman Facing Termination," 18 December 1938. A. Reinhartz, Osobní kartotéky, Baťa Fond. SOkA-Zlín k. 1036 č. 18.

79 There is no company record of Alexander during the war, but he resurfaces in Zlín in the fall of 1945 in the form of two "witness" reports about his time in the company before the war. These testimonials were for the "Factory Council," the group that assumed leadership of the factory complex after the government nationalized the company. Most likely, Alexander was looking for work. Unfortunately, such remarks would fall in the realm of speculation. It remains to be known where Alexander went during the war. Assuming that he went home, his survival is remarkable. The Jewish population of the former Czechoslovak territory of Subcarpathian Ruthenia fell from 122,000 in 1939 to 15,000 by the end of the war.

80 The report from 18 December 1938 evaluates his entire time thus far in the factory and school. It finds his "work good," his behaviour "good," and his "overall quality good." "Report on a Young Man/Young Woman Facing Termination," 18 December 1938.

81 "Cestovní zpráva Horák z Chelmeku," 13 October 1938. SOkA-Zlín, B.F., Prodejní oddělení, k. 1601 č. 385.

82 Report on Emil Seidel, 25 November 1938, SOkA-Zlín, B.F. Prodejní oddělení, k. 1011 č.15.

83 Krejčí, *Poznamenaný*, 79.

84 Ibid., 81.

85 Ibid., 82.

86 Larry Carmichael, *Bata Belcamp: The Story of the Bata Shoe Company in Harford County, Maryland, 1932–2000* (Waters Edge, MD: Carmichael Enterprises, 2014), 1–5.

87 Eric J. Jenkins, "'A Bit of Europe in Maryland': The Bat'a Colony in Belcamp," in Martin Jemelka and Ondřej Ševeček, eds., *Company Towns of the Bat'a Concern* (Stuttgart: Franz Steiner, 2013), 179–80.

88 Jenkins, "A Bit of Europe in Maryland," 182.

89 *Ideální průmyslové město budoucnosti*, SOkA-Zlín, Baťa Fond k. 8 č. 1669.

90 Undated, unnamed letter, Ředitelství BŠP různé osobní záležitosti internátů, 1936–9, SOkA-Zlín, B.F., k. 1223 č. 192.

91 "Národní jednota na Zlínska," *Zlín*, 30 January 1938, 1.

92 Ibid.

93 J. Bat'a, "Hledejte spolupráci, nenávist je neplodná," *Zlín*, 3 March 1939, 1.

94 D. Čipera, "Osud naší vlasti leží v rukou každého z nás," *Zlín*, 4 January 1939, 1.

8 "Not a Nazi but More or Less a Fool"

1 "Protiněmecké různé akce 1939–1944," AMZ, SOkA-Zlin č. 1152. Oberlandrat was a title for Nazi-appointed local head administrators – the "governors" of the seventy counties of the Protectorate of Bohemia and Moravia.

2 "Protokol městská rada 1941," AMZ SOkA-Zlín k. 73.

3 These claims are taken from the extensive previously classified records of the Department of Justice records at the National Archives of the United States (NA-USA), Department of Justice Foreign Funds Control Docket Files, Records of the Office of Alien Property, Docket Files of Business Enterprises, Record Number 131, Container Number 902.

4 Jan Langmeier, "Proces s J.A. Baťou před národním soudem v roce 1947," *Právnehistorické studie* 43 (Karolinum 2013): 327–46.

5 19 February 1942 Master Memorandum. NA-USA, Department of Justice Foreign Funds Control Docket Files, Records of the Office of Alien Property, Docket Files of Business Enterprises, Docket # 371-B.

6 Jan Baťa, "Osídlování," *Zlín*, 4 April 1938, 1.

7 Thomas Bata Jr., *Bata: Shoemaker to the World* (Toronto: Stoddart, 1990), 151.

8 *Shoemaker to the World*, 151.

9 "Pan šef k Mladým Ženám v aule Masarýkových škol dne 13. dubna 1939." Ředitelství BŠP – různé osobní záležitosti internátů 1936–1939, Baťa Fond, SOkA-Zlin k. 1223 č. 192.

10 Ibid.

11 Ibid.

12 "Schůze v aule Masarýkových škol dne 15. května 1939," Ředitelství BŠP – různé osobní záležitosti internátů 1936–1939, Baťa Fond, SOkA-Zlín k. 1223 č. 192.

13 Ibid.

14 Ibid.

15 Ibid.

16 Letter, unknown author, Ředitelství BŠP různé osobní záležitosti internátů 1936–1939, Baťa Fond, SOkA- Zlín k. 1223 č. 192.

17 Jan Baťa, 10 September 1939. Ředitelství BŠP různé osobní záležitosti internátů 1936–1939, Baťa Fond, SOkA- Zlín k. 1223 č. 192.

18 Karel Aster, Osobní kartotéky, Baťa Fond, SOkA-Zlín k. 1123 č. 89.

19 "Slovácké děvče instruktoru na Haiti," *Telegraf*, Morávské Ostrava, 1 April 1941. The story also ran in the *Večerník Národní Práce*, Prague, and the *Severočeské vydaní*.

20 M. Kouřilová. Osobní kartotéky, k. 1123 č. 89, MZA-Zlín.

21 John Nash, "Jan Bata's Underground Railroad Rescues Czechoslovak Jews," 2008 (unpublished) found through https://issuu.com/martfumedia/docs/bata_assists _jewish_exodus (last accessed 31 July 2018).

22 Přísežné prohlášení, Marie Mogernstern, 21 July 1969, to Willard C. Holt. On the website of Marek Belza Publishers, "Jan Antonín Baťa," http://mbelza.sweb.cz /jan%20bata.htm (last accessed 31 July 2018).

23 Martin Marek, "Z baťovského Zlína do světa: Směry transferu a kvalifikační kritéria přesouvaných baťovských zaměstnanců v letech 1938–1941," *Moderní dějiny: Časopis pro dějiny 19. a 20. století* 19, no. 1 (2011): 157–97.

24 Martin Marek, *Středoevropské aktivity Baťova koncernu za druhé světové války* (Brno, Matice moravská, 2017), 1–10.

25 Marek and Strobach, "Nový český svatý?" Nový prostor, č. 367. http:
    //novyprostor.cz/clanky/367/novy-cesky-svaty (last accessed 31 July 2018).

26 Otto Heilig, in his affadavit now at the US Holocaust Museum, even states that "it
    was a known fact [at Bata] that religion was about as important in a candidate's
    qualifications as was the colour of his eyes." Heilig in Nash, "Underground
    Railroad," 2.

27 Zachary Doleshal, "Imagining Bat'a in the World of Tomorrow," in Martin
    Jemelka and Ondřej Ševeček, eds., Company Towns of the Bat'a Concern
    (Stuttgart: Franz Steiner, 2013), 61.

28 "Bata Held by Mistake," New York Times, 21 November 1938.

29 Ivan Brož, Chlapi od Baťů: Osudy baťovců v době, kdy šefoval Jan Baťa (Prague:
    Epocha, 2002), 72.

30 Letter from Frank Muska to Mr. J.S. Brock, Chairman of the Interdepartmental
    Committee, 26 June 1942. Department of Justice Foreign Funds Control Docket
    Files, Records of the Office of Alien Property, Docket Files of Business Enterprises,
    Record Number 131, Container Number 902: Docket # 371-B (NA-USA).

31 "New Bata Factory in USA, 1939," British Pathé, 1 March 2021. https://www
    .britishpathe.com/video/new-bata-factory-in-usa (last accessed 1 August 2018).

32 Ibid.

33 "Seznam osob odjíždějících dne 14. dubna 1939 na práci do Německa," Protokol,
    1939, AMZ SOkA-Zlín č. 802.

34 Jaroslav Pospíšil, Hubert Valášek, and Hana Pospíšilová, Herr Direktor a ti druzí
    Albrecht Miesbach, protektorátní ředitel Baťových závodů (Zlín: Kniha Zlín,
    2015).

35 Letter to the "Oberlandratovi ve Zlíně," 16 June 1939, Bezpečnosti stráž města
    Zlína – personální záležitosti, AMZ SOkA-Zlín č. 635.

36 "Rušení při promitání filmu Olympia, 6 March 1940," Protiněmecké – různé akce,
    AMZ SOkA-Zlín č. 1118 k. 1152.

37 Protiněmecké – různé akce, AMZ SOkA-Zlín k. 1152.

38 "Helena Kutějová," Socialní Služba prodejního oddělení, 1936–1939. Bat'a Fond,
    SOkA-Zlín k. 0 Č. 37

39 Ibid.

40 Ibid.

41 Memorandum, Interdepartmental Committee on the Proclaimed List on 21 May
    211946, Department of Justice Foreign Funds Control Docket Files, Records of
    the Office of Alien Property, Docket Files of Business Enterprises (NA-USA)
    #371-D, Record Number 131, Container Number 902.

42 Letter from Frank Muska to Mr. J.S. Brock, Chairman of the Interdepartmental
    Committee, 26 June 1942. This letter makes clear the financial status of the
    company in regard to its "Swiss Trust." There were undoubtedly significant cash
    reserves elsewhere.

43 Jan A. Baťa, Letter to the British Ambassador to Brazil, Donald St. Clair Gainor, 15 March 1945. NA-USA, Department of Justice Foreign Funds Control Docket Files, Records of the Office of Alien Property, Docket Files of Business Enterprises #371-D, Record Number 131, Container Number 902.

44 Memorandum, Interdepartmental Committee on the Proclaimed List on 21 May 1946. NA-USA, Department of Justice Foreign Funds Control Docket Files, Records of the Office of Alien Property, Docket Files of Business Enterprises #371-D, Record Number 131, Container Number 902.

45 Confidential memo sent out from the Chief of the Division of Investigation and Research for the Department of Justice, Homer Jones, date unknown. NA-USA, Department of Justice Foreign Funds Control Docket Files, Records of the Office of Alien Property, Docket Files of Business Enterprises, Record Number 131, Container Number 902.

46 Marian C. McKenna and Joseph McKenna, *Franklin Roosevelt and the Great Constitutional War* (New York: Fordham University Press, 2002), 551–2.

47 David Leip, "1940 Presidential Election Results," *Dave Leip's Atlas of US Presidential Elections* (31 July 2005).

48 "Czechoslovak Shoes," *New York Times*, 13 March 1938.

49 "Policy Shift Puts Immigration Ban on Baťa Shoe Men," *New York Times*, 29 December 1939.

50 Edvard Valenta, *Žil jsem s miliardářem* (Brno: Blok, 1990), 145.

51 "Digest of a Confidential Report of an Investigation by Agents of the Immigration and Naturalization Service into the History, Activities and Financial Transactions of the Bata Shoe Company," 21 August 1940, NA-USA, Department of Justice Foreign Funds Control Docket Files, Records of the Office of Alien Property, Docket Files of Business Enterprises, Record Number 131, Container Number 902.

52 Ibid.

53 Valenta, *Žil jsem s miliardářem* (Brno: Blok, 1990). During Jan's exile in New York, the men met in a hotel to discuss the fate of their country. Brož, *Chlapi od Baťů*, 72.

54 Brož, *Chlapi od Baťů*.

55 "March 17, 1942 Meeting of the Bata Sub-Committee," National Archives, Department of Justice Foreign Funds Control Docket Files, Records of the Office of Alien Property, Docket Files of Business Enterprises, Record Number 131, Container Number 902, Docket # 371-B.

56 "Bata Concern Enjoined", *New York Times (1923–Current File)*, 4 June 1940, 36, https://ezproxy.shsu.edu/login?url=http://search.proquest.com/docview/105292960?accountid=7065.

57 House Resolution 432 of the 76th Congress March 19, 1940, NA-USA, Department of Justice Foreign Funds Control Docket Files, Records of the Office

of Alien Property, Docket Files of Business Enterprises #371-C, Record Number 131, Container Number 902.

58　George F. Johnson as reprinted in "'Geo. F.' Renews Pledge to High Ideals of E.J.," *Endicott Bulletin*, 9 June 1931, 1–2.

59　"Under Fire from Congressman Hall," *Endicott Daily Bulletin*, 28 March 1940, 1.

60　George F. Johnson to E.H. Ellison, 11 September 1937, George F. Johnson Papers, Box 15, Syracuse University Library Manuscript Collections. Johnson's parenthetical remarks.

61　"Bata Maryland Plant Linked in US Files to Nazi War Machine," *Baltimore Sun*, 20 July 1941, 1.

62　Kenneth Crawford, found in Robert Chodos, *Let Us Prey* (Toronto: James Lorimer, 1974), 62.

63　"For Immediate Release," Department of Justice, 26 September 1940, NA-USA, Department of Justice Foreign Funds Control Docket Files, Records of the Office of Alien Property, Docket Files of Business Enterprises #371-C, Record Number 131, Container Number 902.

64　Having travelled to Brazil in 1940 at the request of President Vargas, Baťa had the necessary political connections to start again there.

65　21 August 1940 – "Digest of a Confidential Report," NA-USA, Department of Justice Foreign Funds Control Docket Files, Records of the Office of Alien Property, Docket Files of Business Enterprises #371-C, Record Number 131, Container Number 902.

66　Jaroslav Pospíšil, Hubert Valášek, and Hana Pospíšilová, *Herr Direktor a ti druzí Albrecht Miesbach, protektorátní ředitel Baťových závodů* (Zlín: Kniha Zlín, 2015).

67　"Protokol městská rada 1939–1941." AMZ SOkA-Zlín k. 73 č. 15.

68　"Žádost o příděl mýdla pro měst. Vězníci," 20 December 1940. *Věznice policejního úřadu města Zlína*, AMZ SOkA Zlín č. 1115.

69　17 January 1941, "Protokol městská rada - 1939–1941." AMZ SOkA-Zlín K. 73 č. 15.

70　"Německé školy ve Zlíně v období okupace, 1939–1943," AMZ SOkA-Zlín č. 741.

71　"Židovský majetek 1940–1948." AMZ SOkA-Zlín č. 782.

72　Alice Králičková, Deposition taken in Hodonín, 30 July 1941. Prodejní Oddělení, Bat'a Fond, SOkA-Zlin k. 1530 č. 72.

73　"Letter from Jan Trlida zast: Obchovedoucího," 14 August 1941, Prodejní Oddělení, Bat'a Fond, SOkA-Zlin k. 1530 č. 72.

74　"Letter from Jan Trlida," 14 August 1941.

75　Götz Aly, *Hitler's Beneficiaries: Plunder, Racial War, and the Nazi Welfare State* (New York: Picador, 2005); Frank Bajohr, *"Aryanisation" in Hamburg: The Economic Exclusion of Jews and the Confiscation of their Property in Nazi Germany* (New York: Berghahn, 2002).

76 *Plan práce, 1941*, Bat'a Fond, SOkA-Zlin k. 11 č. 13.

77 "Digest of a Confidential Report," NA-USA, Department of Justice Foreign Funds Control Docket Files, Records of the Office of Alien Property, Docket Files of Business Enterprises #371-C, Record Number 131, Container Number 902.

78 "Government Intercept of B. Cekota of Buenos Aires to Vladimir Chlud in NY, NY from December 13, 1944," NA-USA, Department of Justice Foreign Funds Control Docket Files, Records of the Office of Alien Property, Docket Files of Business Enterprises, Docket #371-D.

79 Hana Kuslová, *Národní Soud versus Jan Antonín Bať a* (Zlín: Muzeum jihovýchodní Moravy, 2015), 62.

80 Report by the World Trade Intelligence for the Interdepartmental Committee, 1942. NA-USA, Department of Justice Foreign Funds Control Docket Files, Records of the Office of Alien Property, Docket Files of Business Enterprises, Docket #371-B.

81 Jan Bat'a, Letter to Jefferson Caffery, 15 September 1942, NA-USA, Department of Justice Foreign Funds Control Docket Files, Records of the Office of Alien Property, Docket Files of Business Enterprises, Record Number 131, Container Number 902, Docket #371-B.

82 Bata Committee Memorandum, 17 March 1942, NA-USA, Department of Justice Foreign Funds Control Docket Files, Records of the Office of Alien Property, Docket Files of Business Enterprises, Docket #371-B.

83 Jan Bat'a as quoted by GT Coleman, United States Consular Officer, in a letter to the Secretary of State, 17 May 1946. NA-USA.

84 Memorandum for Mr. Pehle from Walter M. Day, Division of Foreign Funds Control, Treasury Department, 5 February 1942. NA-USA, Department of Justice Foreign Funds Control Docket Files, Records of the Office of Alien Property, Docket Files of Business Enterprises, Docket #371-B.

85 Homer Jones, "Confidential Memorandum to the Executive Committee of the Office of Alien Property Custodian from the Division of Investigation and Research," exact date unknown, winter 1943. NA-USA, Department of Justice Foreign Funds Control Docket Files, Records of the Office of Alien Property, Docket Files of Business Enterprises, Record Number 131, Container Number 902.

86 Ibid.

87 Undertaking between Chaussures Bata Haiti S.A and USA, 15 November 11943, NA-USA, Department of Justice Foreign Funds Control Docket Files, Records of the Office of Alien Property, Docket Files of Business Enterprises, Record Number 131, Container Number 902.

88 Jan Bat'a, letter to Donald St. Clair Gainor, 15 March 1945. NA-USA. Department of Justice Foreign Funds Control Docket Files, Records of the Office of Alien Property, Docket Files of Business Enterprises, Record Number 131, Container Number 902.

89 Bohumil Lehár, *Dějiny baťova koncernu, 1894–1945* (Prague: Státní nakladatelství politické literatury, 1960), 258.

90 Ministry of Economic Warfare Foreign office letter to US Secretary of State, 17 November 1945, NA-USA, Department of Justice Foreign Funds Control Docket Files, Records of the Office of Alien Property, Docket Files of Business Enterprises, Record Number 131, Container Number 902.

91 Daryle Williams, *Culture Wars: The First Vargas Regime, 1930–1945* (Durham: Duke University Press, 2001), 66–86.

92 Davi Costa da Silva, "The Brazilian Agrarian-Industrial Towns of Jan Antonin Bat'a (1940–1965): Bata Shoe Company's Ideal Industrial Town as Transnational Crossings of Urban Planning Ideas," master's thesis, Charles University, Prague, 2018.

93 Daniela Lazarová, "Jan Bat'a's Name Cleared After Sixty Years," Radio Prague, http://www.radio.cz/en/section/curraffrs/jan-antonin-batas-name -cleared-after-sixty-years.

94 Thomas Bat'a Jr., *Bata: Shoemaker to the World*, 326.

95 For a defence of the need for the "cosmopolitan corporation" see Thomas Maak, "The Cosmopolitan Corporation," *Journal of Business Ethics* 84 (2009): 361–72.

Conclusion

1 "Socha Jana A. Bati a conference o něm." http://batastory.net/cs/milniky/jan -antonin-bata-zivot-a-dilo-pokracovatel-prace-tomase-bati (last accessed 12 May 2019).

2 Adam Bartoš, "Zlín napravuje šedesátiletou křivdu, odhalil sochu Bati," 2 May 2007, idnes.cz. https://www.idnes.cz/zpravy/domaci/zlin-napravuje-sedesatiletou -krivdu-odhalil-sochu-bati.A070502_114541_domaci_adb (last accessed 23 May 2019).

3 "Justice po 60 letech očistila Jana Antonína Baťu," 15 November 2007. https:// www.idnes.cz/zpravy/cerna-kronika/justice-po-60-letech-ocistila-jana-antonina -batu.A071115_135917_krimi_cen (last accessed 23 May 2019).

4 One telling example of the way in which criticism has become more and more watered down is Vítězslav Vystavěl's article "Marný boj s baťovskou legendou" (The Vain Battle with Bat'a's Legend), 3 May 2008, KSČM ve Zlíně, http:// www.kscm.zlin.cz/old/precetli_jsme_1.php (last accessed 6 May 2019). In it, Communist Party member Vystavěl concludes that there is no point anymore in trying to downplay Bat'a's achievements.

5 "Jeden den mladého muže Baťovy školy práce," in "The Bat'a Principle: Today's Fantasy, Tomorrow's Reality," permanent exhibit, Bat'a Institute Museum, Zlín.

6 "The Bat'a Principle: Today's Fantasy, Tomorrow's Reality," permanent exhibit, Bat'a Institute Museum, Zlín.

7 "Zlínský Dům umění se mění zpět na památník Tomáše Bati," ČT24, 13 January 2017. https://ct24.ceskatelevize.cz/regiony/2010605-zlinsky-dum-umeni-se-meni -zpet-na-pamatnik-tomase-bati?_ga=2.132564878.1604207853.1558363725 -1875442663.1551730014 (last accessed 20 May 2019).

8 The similarities and differences between the two men are many and interesting. See Veronika Pehe, "Babiš jako novodobý Baťa?" A2LARM 22 November 2017, https://a2larm.cz/2017/11/babis-jako-novodoby-bata/.

9 Babiš is quoted in one article as saying, "Actually, Tomáš Baťa was also a politician. He became a politician just like me, with my own vision." Jan Tvrdoň and Hana Manzacová, "Co dělají velcí státníci a není Baťa jako Baťa: Ověřili jsme Babišový výroky z rozhovoru pro Deník N," Deník N, 10 January 2019. https://denikn.cz/50439/co-delaji-velci-statnici-a-neni-.bata -jako-bata-overili-jsme-babisovy-vyroky-z-rozhovoru-pro-denik-n/.

10 "Babiš představil vizi do roku 2035: Prý se inspiroval Baťou," Lidovky.cz, 22 June 2017. https://www.lidovky.cz/domov/babis-predstavil-vizi-do-roku-2035-pry-se -inspiroval-batou.A170622_151049_ln_domov_ELE.

11 "11 dnů s J.A. Baťou," Konference a doprovodný program. http://jabata120.cz/ (last accessed 12 June 2019).

12 Ibid.

13 For an example, the 2018 documentary Baťa, První Globalista, by Peter Kerekes, offers a nuanced portrait.

14 A few examples of the way in which recent filmmakers have mythologized interwar Baťa are Karolina Zalabáková, Batalives (Cinebonbon, 2017); Jakub Motejzík, Zlínský klenot (Česká televize, 2018).

15 Karen Guthrie and Nina Pope's movie Bata-ville, We Are Not Afraid of the Future (Commissions East, 2005) and Mariusz Szczygiel's wonderfully entertaining essays about Baťa in Gottland: Mostly True Stories from Half of Czechoslovakia (New York: Melville House, 2014) are among the best examples of how interwar Baťa is being constructed as a trendy, quirky company that should be approached with the curiosity of a nineteenth-century ethnographer.

16 Dodo Gombar, Baťa Tomáš, živý, 24 May 2016, Česká televize.

17 "Po seriálu Most! má Martin Hofmann hlavní roli ve filmu Baťa." Zdroj: https:// www.idnes.cz/kultura/film-televize/bata-martin-hofmann-most-jan-pachl .A190331_144216_filmvideo_spm (last accessed 20 May 2019).

18 Dušan Ondrejička, "Czech Republic: EUR 50 Million for the Development of the Zlín Region," 8 December 2005, The European Investment Bank. https://www.eib .org/en/press/all/2005-130-czech-republic-eur-50-million-for-development-of-the -zlin-region (last accessed 24 May 2019).

19 "Obnova Správní budovy č. 21 – Baťova mrakodrapu ve Zlíně pro sídlo Zlínského kraje a Finančního úřadu," http://www.transat.cz/obnova_spravni_budovy_21 -batova_mrakodrapu_ve_zline.php (last accessed 9 September 2019).

20 The works about Baťa by Martin Marek, Martin Jemelka, Barbora Vacková, Lucie
    Galčanová, Ondřej Ševeček, Vít Strobach, Edvard Valenta, and Petr Sczepanik
    provide excellent theoretical and analytical examples of the tension between the
    myth of Baťa and the myth of the First Republic. Barbora Vacková and Lucie
    Galčanová, "Project Zlín. Everyday Life in a Materialized Utopia," *Lidé města/
    Urban People* 11, no. 2 (2009): 311–37.
21 Detlev Peukert's work on modernity informed this work throughout. Peukert's
    work offers an outstanding insight into the contradictions of modernity. For him,
    modernity, with its emphasis on the power of science to solve all social problems,
    created new social and cultural forms that were politically malleable. See Peukert,
    The Weimar Republic: The Crisis of Classical Modernity (London: Allen Lane,
    1991).
22 Such a construction is inspired by Saladdin Ahmed's introduction in his
    Totalitarian Space and the Destruction of Aura (Albany: SUNY Press, 2019),
    xiii–xv.
23 Average global footwear statistics for Bata are a combined number based on
    the individual companies' sales that the Bata Company compiled. Amazon, the
    world's largest online retailer of shoes, sells approximately twice that of Bata.
24 "Bat'a Company Info," https://thebatacompany.com/assets/Uploads/Bata
    -company-info.pdf (last accessed 14 October 2019).
25 C.A. Bayly, *The Birth of the Modern World, 1780–1914* (Blackwell, 2004), 1.
26 "Bata Life," http://batalife.com/ (last accessed 27 August 2018).
27 Kimberly Zarecor, *Manufacturing a Socialist Modernity: Housing in
    Czechoslovakia, 1945–1960* (Pittsburgh: University of Pittsburgh Press, 2011).

Bibliography

Primary Sources

Archival and Manuscript Collections

"1924–25 Baťa." Ministerstvo průmyslu, obchodu a živností, Národní archiv, Prague, CZ.

Archiv města Zlína, Moravský zemský archiv Brno – Státní okresní archiv Zlín.

Baťa Fond, Moravský zemský archiv Brno – Státní okresní archiv Zlín.

Baťovák, Národní Archiv, Prague, CZ.

EJ Ephemera, Local History, Bartle Library Special Collections, Binghamton University, New York.

Fotoarchiv, Baťa fond, Státní okresní archiv Zlín.

George F. Johnson Papers, Syracuse University Library Manuscript Collections.

Hodáč Collection, Baťa Fond, Moravský zemský archiv Brno – Státní okresní archiv Zlín.

Malota, Eduard. *Vzpomínky na Tomáše Baťu.* Zlín: 1939, unpublished, Baťa fond, Státní okresní archiv Zlín.

Naše volby, Zlín: 1925, Baťa fond, Státní okresní archiv Zlín.

National Archive of the Czech Republic, Ministerstvo průmyslu, obchodu a živností, 1918–42, Prague, CZ.

National Archives of the United States, Department of Justice Foreign Funds Control Docket Files, Records of the Office of Alien Property, Docket Files of Business Enterprises, College Park, MD.

Okresní hejtmanství v Uherském Hradišti, Státní Okresní Archiv Uherském Hradišti, 1916/18.

Štětkář Stanislav. "Internát – Baťová škola práce", Moravský zemský archiv Brno – Státní okresní archiv Zlín.

Trestní spisy, Archiv města Zlína, Moravský zemský archiv Brno – Státní okresní archiv Zlín.

Government Documents, Articles, and Other

ANNO: Österreichische Nationalbibliothek's online database.

Bat'a, Jan Antonín. *Budujme stát (pro 40,000.000 lidí)*. Zlín: Tisk, 1937.

Baťa, Tomáš. *Úvahy a projevy*. Prague: Institut řezení, 1990.

Cekota, Antonín. "10 let práce." In *Hospodářská politika čs. průmyslu v letech 1918–1928*. Prague: Ústřední svaz průmyslníků, 1928.

Čipera, Dominik. *Ve službách práce a lidu: Soubor úvah, projevu a vzpomínkových poznámek 1919–1944*. Zlín: 1944.

Dvořák, Ladislav. *O účelnosti ideí a metod Spojených států amerických pro národní hospodářství československé*. Prague: Česká národohospodářská společnost, 1928.

Haupt-Buchenrode, Stefan. *My Memories*. Beau-Bassin: Doyen Verlag, 2012.

Ideální průmyslové město budoucnosti, SOkA-Zlín, Baťa Fond.

Krejčí, V. Edited by Martin Jemelka. *Poznamenaný: Deset měsíců s Janem Baťou a jak to bylo dál*. Zlín: Kniha Zlín, 2019.

Masaryk, T.G. *Projevy presidenta Československé republiky Prof. Dr. T.G. Masaryka od doby jeho zvoleni do dnu jubilejnich*. Prague: Nákladem Československého kompasu, 1920.

Obrtel, František. *Pojďte s námi*. Prague: Zemědělské knihkupectví A. Neubert, 1918.

Philipp, Rudolph. *Der unbekannte Diktator Thomas Bat'a*. Vienna and Berlin: Agis-Verlag, 1928.

Talbot, Winthrop, ed. *Americanization: Principles of Americanism, Essentials of Americanization, Technic of Race Assimilation*. New York: H.W. Wilson Company, 1920.

Tyrš, Miroslav. *Základové tělocviku*. Prague: Národní knihtiskárna, 1873.

US Department of the Interior, Office of Education. Bulletin No. 11, 1935.

van Vorst, Marie. *The Woman Who Toils: Being the Experiences of Two Gentlewomen as Factory Girls*. New York: Doubleday, 1903.

Verunáč, Václav. *Racionalizace, vědecká organizace, a otázka sociální*. Prague: Sociálni ústav republiky Československé, 1930.

Veselý, Vilém. *600 Hesel Baťa*. Zlín: Tisk, 1938.

Výběr a výchova průmyslového člověka, Zlín: Tisk, 1937.

Zahraniční obchod republiky Československé v roce 1937. Prague: Státní úřad statistický, 1948.

Newspapers and Journals

Baltimore Sun
Boot and Shoe Recorder
Die Rohte Fahne

Endicott Daily Bulletin
Freie Stimmen
Jurende's Mährischer Wanderer (Vienna, 1854)
Lidové Noviny
Machinists Monthly Journal (International Association of Machinists).
Monthly Labor Review
Národní Listy
Naše doba: Revue pro vědu, umění a život sociální
Neues Wiener Tagblatt
The New York Times
News Dispatch (Endicott, NY)
Přítomnost
Sdělení zaměstnání fy T. A. Baťa
Sdělení zřízenectvu firmy T&A. Baťa
Time Magazine
Tvorba
Zlín

Secondary Sources

Ahmed, Saladdin. *Totalitarian Space and the Destruction of Aura*. Albany: SUNY Press, 2019.

Aly, Götz. *Hitler's Beneficiaries: Plunder, Racial War, and the Nazi Welfare State*. New York: Picador, 2005.

Bagchi, Sreeparna. "The Zlin Enterprise: A Profile of the Role of the First Multinational Organization in the Leather Industry in Bengal (1931–1945)." *Calcutta Historical Journal* 25 (2005).

Bajohr, Frank. *"Aryanisation" in Hamburg: The Economic Exclusion of Jews and the Confiscation of Their Property in Nazi Germany*. New York: Berghahn, 2002.

Baťa, Thomas, Jr. with Sonja Sinclair. *Bata: Shoemaker to the World*. Toronto: Stoddart, 1990.

The Bata Phenomenon: Zlín Architecture, 1910–1960. Zlín: Zlín Regional Gallery of Fine Arts, 2009.

Bayly, C.A. *The Birth of the Modern World, 1780–1914*. Cornwall: Blackwell, 2004.

Beattie, Betsy. "Going Up to Lynn: Single, Maritime-Born Women in Lynn, Massachusetts, 1879–1930." *Journal of the History of the Atlantic Region* 22, no. 1 (Autumn 1992).

Beckert, Sven. *Empire of Cotton: A Global History*. New York: Knopf, 2015.

Beneš, Jakub. "Socialist Popular Literature and the Czech-German Split in Austrian Social Democracy, 1890–1914." *Slavic Review* 72, no. 2 (Summer 2013).

Benson, Susan Porter. *Counter Cultures: Saleswomen, Managers, and Customers in American Department Stores 1890–1940.* Urbana-Champagne: University of Illinois Press, 1987.

Bhagwati, Jagdish. *In Defence of Globalization.* Oxford: Oxford University Press, 2006.

Bobák, Jindřich. *Procházky starým Zlínem.* Vizovice: Lípa, 1999.

Bonifazio, Patrizia, and Paolo Scrivano. *Olivetti Builds: Modern Architecture in Ivrea: Guide to the Open Air Museum.* Milan: Skira, 2001.

Borges, Marcelo, and Susana Torres, eds. *Company Towns: Labor, Space, and Power Relations across Time and Continents.* New York: Palgrave Macmillan, 2012.

Boyce, Robert. *The Great Interwar Crisis and the Collapse of Globalization.* New York: Palgrave Macmillan, 2009.

Brandes, Stuart. *American Welfare Capitalism, 1880–1940.* Chicago: University of Chicago Press, 1976.

Brennan, Timothy. "From Development to Globalization: Postcolonial Studies and Globalization Theory." In *The Cambridge Companion to Postcolonial Literary Studies,* edited by Neil Lazarus. Cambridge: Cambridge University Press, 2004.

Brož, Ivan. *Chlapi od Baťů: Osudy baťovců v době, kdy šefoval Jan Baťa.* Prague: Epocha, 2002.

Bryant, Chad. *Prague in Black.* Cambridge: Harvard University Press, 2007.

Budd, Lucy. "Global Networks before Globalisation: Imperial Airways and the Development of Long-Haul Air Routes." *GaWC Research Bulletin* (Loughborough University, 2007).

Carmichael, Larry. *Bata Belcamp: The Story of the Bata Shoe Company in Harford County, Maryland, 1932–2000.* Waters Edge, MD: Carmichael Enterprises, 2014.

Cekota, Antonín. *Tomas Bata: Entrepreneur Extraordinary.* Don Mills, ON: T.H. Best, 1968.

Chandler, Alfred. *The Visible Hand: The Managerial Revolution in American Business.* Cambridge: Harvard Press, 1993.

Chodos, Robert. *Let Us Prey.* Toronto: James Lorimer & Company, 1974.

Christian, Michel, Sandrine Kott, and Ondřej Matějka, eds., *Planning in Cold War Europe: Competition, Cooperation, Circulations (1950s–1970s).* Berlin: Walter de Gruyter, 2018.

Činčová, Yvona. *Sláva zlínského sportu.* Zlín: Muzeum jihovýchodní moravy ze Zlíně, 2011.

Cohen, Gary. "Nationalist Politics and the Dynamics of State and Civil Society in the Habsburg Monarchy, 1867–1914." *Central European History* 40, no. 2 (June 2007).

Cornwall, Mark. *The Undermining of Austria-Hungary: The Battle for Hearts and Minds.* New York: Springer, 2000.

Costa da Silva, Davi. "The Brazilian Agrarian-Industrial Towns of Jan Antonin Bat'a (1940–1965): Bata Shoe Company's Ideal Industrial Town as Transnational

Crossings of Urban Planning Ideas." Master's thesis, Charles University, Prague, 2018.

Crew, David. "The Pathologies of Modernity: Detlev Peukert on Germany's Twentieth Century." *Social History* 17, no. 2 (1992): 319–28.

De Grazia, Victoria. *Irresistible Empire: America's Advance through 20th Century Europe.* Cambridge, MA: Bellknap Press, 2005.

Dejmek, Jindřich. "Československá diplomacie v době druhé republiky." In *Pocta profesoru Janu Kuklíkovi,* 9–26. Prague: Karolinum, 2000.

Demetz, Peter. *Prague in Danger: The Years of German Occupation, 1939–1945.* New York: Macmillan, 2009.

Dooley, William H. *A Manual of Shoemaking and Leather and Rubber Products.* Boston: Little, Brown, 1912.

Dublin, Thomas. "Rural-Urban Migrants in Industrial New England: The Case of Lynn, Massachusetts, in the Mid-Nineteenth Century." *Journal of American History* 73, no. 3 (December 1986).

Dunn, Robert. *The Americanization of Labor: The Employers' Offensive against the Trade Unions.* New York: International Publishers, 1927.

Dvořáček, Petr. "*X Všesokolský slet roku 1938 a jeho ohlas ve společnosti.*" Dissertation, Charles University Prague, 2008.

Ehrenbold, Tobias. "Putting Möhlin on the Map." In *Company Towns of the Baťa Concern: History, Cases, Architecture,* edited by Martin Jemelka and Ondřej Ševeček. Stuttgart: Franz Steiner, 2013.

Eidson, John. "Compulsion, Compliance, or Eigensinn? Examining Theories of Power in an East German Field Site." *Max Planck Institute for Social Anthropology Working Papers* no. 61 (Halle, 2003).

Eley, Geoff. *Society, Culture, and the State in Germany, 1870–1930.* Ann Arbor: University of Michigan Press, 1996.

Faßmann, Heinz, and Rainer Münz. *Einwanderungsland Österreich?: Historische Migrationsmuster, aktuelle Trends und politische Maßnahmen.* Vienna: Jugend & Volk, 1995.

Falasca-Zamponi, Simonetta. *Fascist Spectacle: The Aesthetics of Power in Mussolini's Italy.* Berkeley: University of California Press, 1997.

Feinberg, Melissa. *Elusive Equality: Gender, Citizenship, and the Limits of Democracy in Czechoslovakia, 1918–1950.* Pittsburgh: University of Pittsburgh Press, 2006.

Foucault, Michel. *The History of Sexuality.* New York: Pantheon Books, 1978.

Freiden, Jeffry. *Global Capitalism: Its Rise and Fall in the Twentieth Century.* New York: W.W. Norton, 2006.

Geertz, Clifford. *Peddlers and Princes: Social Development and Economic Change in Two Indonesian Towns.* Chicago: University of Chicago Press, 1963.

Gilpin, Robert. *Global Political Economy: Understanding the International Order.* Princeton, 2011.

Good, David. *The Economic Rise of the Habsburg Empire, 1750–1914.* Berkeley: University of California Press, 1984.

Grandin, Greg. *Fordlandia: The Rise and Fall of Henry Ford's Forgotten Jungle City.* New York: Henry Holt, 2009.

Gruchała, Janusz. *Czeskie środowiska polityczne wobec spraw polskich 1920–1938.* Katowice: Wydawnictwo Uniwersytetu Śląskiego, 2002.

Harold, James. *The End of Globalization: Lessons from the Great Depression.* Cambridge: Harvard University Press, 2001.

Hoffer, Eric. *The True Believer: Thoughts on the Nature of Mass Movements.* New York: HarperCollins 1951.

Holton, Robert. *Globalization and the Nation State.* New York: Palgrave, 2011.

Holubec, Stanislav. "Silní milují život: Utopie, ideologie, a biopolitika batovského Zlína." *Kuděj* 11, no. 2 (2009).

Hoopes, James. *False Prophets: The Gurus Who Created Modern Management and Why Their Ideas Are Bad for Business Today.* Cambridge, MA: Perseus, 2003.

Hopkins, A.G., ed. *Globalization in World History.* New York: Norton, 2002.

Horňáková, Ladislava, P. Novák, and Zdeněk Pokluda. *Zlín – město v zahradách.* Zlín: Statutární město Zlín, 2002.

Hrnčířová, Zuzana. "*Baťovy závody a život Čechoslováků v Indii v letech 1934–1950.*" Dissertation. Univerzita Karlova, Prague, 2017.

Inglis, William. *George F. Johnson and His Industrial Democracy.* New York: Huntington Press, 1935.

Irwin, Douglas A. *Peddling Protectionism: Smoot-Hawley and the Great Depression.* Princeton: Princeton University Press, 2017.

Jacobs, Jane. *The Death and Life of Great American Cities.* New York: Random House, 1961.

Jacques, Roy. *Manufacturing the Employee: Management Knowledge from the 19th to 21st Centuries.* London: Sage Publications, 1996.

Jančař, Josef. *Lidová kultura na Moravě.* Brno: Muzejní a vlastivědná společnost v Brně, 2000.

Janko, Jan, and Emilie Těšínská, eds. *Technokracie v českých zemích, 1900-1950.* Prague: Archiv AV, 1999.

Jemelka, Martin, and O. Ševeček, eds. *Company Towns of the Bat'a Concern.* Stuttgart: Franz Steiner, 2013.

– *Tovární města Baťova koncernu.* Prague: Academia, 2016.

Judson, Pieter. *Guardians of the Nation: Activists on the Language Frontiers of Imperial Austria.* Cambridge: Harvard University Press, 2006.

Jůva, Vladimír. *Stručné dějiny pedagogiky.* Brno: Paido, 1994.

Keynes, John Maynard. *The Economic Consequences of the Peace.* New York: Harcourt Brace, 1920.

King, Jeremy. *Budweisers into Czechs and Germans: A Local History of Bohemian Politics, 1848–1948.* Princeton: Princeton University Press, 2002.

Klengan, Katrin, and K. Durst, eds. *Utopia of Modernity: Zlín.* Berlin: JOVIS Verlag, 2009.

Knight, Kristina. "Patriotism, Parades and Paternalism: How the Endicott-Johnson Corporation Controlled the Lives of Women in Johnson City and Endicott, New York, 1945–1965." Master's thesis, Binghamton University, 2006.

Komlos, John. *The Habsburg Monarchy as a Customs Union: Economic Development in Austria-Hungary in the 19th Century.* Princeton: Princeton University Press, 2014.

Kotěra, Jan, Vladimír Šlapeta, and Daniela Karasová. *Jan Kotěra, 1871–1923: The Founder of Modern Czech Architecture.* Prague: Municipal House, 2001.

Kotkin, Stephen *Magnetic Mountain: Stalinism as a Civilization.* Berkeley: University of California Press, 1995.

Kučera, Rudolf. *Rationed Life: Science, Everyday Life, and Working-Class Politics in the Bohemian Lands, 1914–1918.* New York: Berghahn, 2016.

Kuklík, Jan. *Sociální Demokraté ve druhé republice.* Prague: Univerzita Karlova, 1992.

Kuslová, Hana. *Národní Soud versus Jan Antonín Baťa.* Zlín: Muzeum jihovýchodní Moravy, 2015.

Langmeier, Jan. "Proces s J.A. Baťou před národním soudem v roce 1947." *Právnehistorické studie* 43 (2013): 327–46.

Lehár, Bohumil. *Dějiny baťova koncernu, 1894–1945.* Prague: Státní nakladatelství politické literatury, 1960.

Lerner, Paul. *The Consuming Temple: Jews, Department Stores, and the Consumer Revolution in Germany, 1880–1940.* Ithaca: Cornell University Press, 2015.

Lüdtke, Alf. "Organizational Order or Eigensinn? Workers' Privacy and Workers' Politics in Imperial Germany. In *Rites of Power: Symbolism, Ritual, and Politics since the Middle Ages,* edited by Sean Wilentz. Philadelphia: University of Pennsylvania Press, 1985.

– *Eigen-Sinn: Fabrikalltag, Arbeitererfahrungen un Politik vom Kaiserreich bis in den Faschismus.* Hamburg: Ergebnisse Verlag, 1993.

Lukes, Igor. "The Czechoslovak Partial Mobilization in May 1938: A Mystery (Almost) Solved." *Journal of Contemporary History* 31, no. 4 (1996).

Macek, Pavel, and Lubomír Uhlíř. *Dějiny policie a četnictva protektorát Čechy a Morava a Slovenský stát, 1939–1945.* Prague: Police History, 2001.

Machonin, Pavel, and Jaroslav Krejci. *Czechoslovakia, 1918–92: A Laboratory for Social Change.* Basingstoke: Macmillan, 1998.

Magnusson, Lars. *Nation, State, and the Industrial Revolution: The Visible Hand.* London: Routledge, 2009.

Marek, Martin. "Z baťovského Zlína do světa: Směry transferu a kvalifikační kritéria přesouvaných baťovských zaměstnanců v letech 1938–1941." *Moderní dějiny. Časopis pro dějiny 19. a 20. století* 19, no. 1 (2011): 157–97.

– *Středoevropské aktivity Baťova koncernu za druhé světové války.* Brno: Matice moravská, 2017.

Marek, Martin, and Vít Strobach, "Nový český svatý?" *Nový prostor,* č. 367 http:// novyprostor.cz/clanky/367/novy-cesky-svaty (last accessed 31 July 2018).

März, Eduard. *Österreichische Industrie – und Bankpolitik in der Zeit Franz Josephs I.* Vienna: Europa Verlag, 1968.

Meyer, Stephen. "Adapting the Immigrant to the Line: Americanization in the Ford Factory, 1914–1921." *Journal of Social History* 14, no. 1 (Autumn 1980).

– *The Five Dollar Day: Labor Management and Social Control in the Ford Motor Company, 1908–1921.* Albany: State University of New York Press, 1981.

Mooers, Colin. *The Making of Bourgeois Europe: Absolutism, Revolution, and the Rise of Capitalism in England, France, and Germany.* London: Verso, 1991.

Mosse, George. *The Image of Man: The Creation of Modern Masculinity.* Oxford: Oxford University Press, 2010.

Mostov, Stephen. *Immigrant Entrepreneurs: Jews in the Shoe Trades in Lynn, 1885– 1945.* Marblehead, MA: North Shore Jewish Historical Society, 1982.

Mulligan, William. "Mechanization and Work in the American Shoe Industry: Lynn, Massachusetts, 1852–1883." *Journal of Economic History* 41, no. 1 (March 1981).

Nash Bata, John. "Jan Bata's Underground Railroad Rescues Czechoslovak Jews," 2008 (unpublished). https://issuu.com/martfumedia/docs/bata_assists_jewish _exodus (last accessed 6 March 2021).

Noguez, Maria. *Ford and the Global Strategies of Multinationals: The North American Auto Industry.* London: Routledge, 2003.

Nolan, Mary. *Visions of Modernity: American Business and the Modernization of Germany.* Oxford: Oxford University Press, 1994.

Parr, Joy. *The Gender of Breadwinners: Women, Men, and Change in Two Industrial Towns, 1880–1950.* Toronto: University of Toronto Press, 1990.

Patel, Kiran Klaus, and Sven Reichardt. "The Dark Side of Transnationalism: Social Engineering and Nazism, 1930s–40s. *Journal of Contemporary History* 51, no. 1 (2016): 3–21.

Pech, Stanley. "Political Parties among Austrian Slavs: A Comparative Analysis of the 1911 Reichsrat Election Results." *Canadian Slavonic Papers/Revue Canadienne des Slavistes* 31, no. 2 (June 1989).

Peukert, Detlev, J.K. *The Weimar Republic: The Crisis of Classical Modernity.* London: Allen Lane, 1991.

Pochylý, J. *Baťova průmyslová demokracie.* Prague: UTRIN, 1990.

Pokluda, Zdeněk. *Sedm století zlínských dějin.* Zlín: Klub novinářů, 1991.

– *Zámek Zlín.* Zlín: Státní okresní archiv, 1998.

– *Baťa v kostce.* Zlín: Kniha Zlín, 2013.

Polišenský, Josef V. *The Thirty Years War.* Berkeley: University of California Press, 1971.

– *Aristocrats and the Crowd in the Revolutionary Year 1848: A Contribution to the History of Revolution and Counter-Revolution*. Albany: SUNY Press, 1980.

Pospíšil, Jaroslav. *Rub a líc baťovských sporů*. Zlín: Kniha Zlín, 2012.

Pospíšil, Jaroslav, Hubert Valášek, and Hana Pospíšilová. *Herr Direktor a ti druzí Albrecht Miesbach, protektorátní ředitel Baťových závodů*. Zlín: Kniha Zlín, 2015.

Rawson, Andrew. *Showcasing the Third Reich: The Nuremberg Rallies*. Cheltenham: Spellmount, 2012.

Reynolds, Nancy. *A City Consumed: Urban Commerce, the Cairo Fire, and the Politics of Decolonization in Egypt*. Stanford: Stanford University Press, 2012.

Ribbe, Wolfgang, and Wolfgang Schäche. *Die Siemensstadt: Geschichte und Architektur eines Industriestandortes*. Berlin: Ernst & Sohn, 1985.

Rodenbeck, Max. *Cairo: The City Victorious*. New York: Knopf Doubleday, 2017.

Rolf, Malte. *Soviet Mass Festivals, 1917–1991*. Translated by Cynthia Klohr. Pittsburgh: University of Pittsburgh Press, 2013.

Scott, James C. *Seeing Like a State: How Certain Schemes to Improve the Human Condition Have Failed*. New Haven: Yale Press, 1999.

Scott, Peter. "The Wolf at the Door: The Trade Union Movement and Overseas Multinationals in Britain during the 1930s." *Social History* 23, no. 2 (May 1998).

Schumpeter, Joseph A., and Redvers Opie. *The Theory of Economic Development; An Inquiry into Profits, Capital, Credit, Interest, and the Business Cycle*. Cambridge: Harvard University Press, 1934.

Sen, Satadru. *Benoy Kumar Sarkar: Restoring the Nation to the World*. London: Routledge, 2015.

Šetřilová, Jana. *Alois Rašín: Dramatický život českého politika*. Prague: Argo, 1997.

Ševeček, Ondřej. *Zrození Baťovy průmyslové metropole: Továrna, městský prostor a společnost ve Zlíně v letech 1900–1938*. České Budějovice: Veduta, 2009.

Shearer, David. *Policing Stalin's Socialism: Repression and Social Order in the Soviet Union, 1924–1953*. New Haven: Yale University Press, 2009.

Siegelbaum, Lewis H. *Stakhanovism and the Politics of Productivity in the USSR, 1935–1941*. Cambridge: Harvard University Press, 1988.

Sinclair, Thornton. "The Nazi Party Rally at Nuremberg." *Public Opinion Quarterly* 2, no. 2 (October 1938).

Škrabala, Petr. "Zlín ve víru politických změn let 1899–1914." PhD dissertation, Univerzita Karlova, 2006.

Smetánka, Tomáš. "From Central Europe to Singapore: Bata and Baťa." In *50 Years of Singapore-Europe Relations: Celebrating Singapore's Connections with Europe*, edited by Yeo Lay Hwee and Turner Barnard. Singapore: World Scientific, 2015.

Staša, Eduard. *Kapitolky ze starého Zlína*. Zlín: Muzeum jihovýchodní Moravy ve Zlíně, 1991.

Szczepanik Petr. *Konzervy se slovy: Počátky zvukového film a česká mediální kultura 30.let.* Brno: Host, 2009.

Tamari, Salim. *The Great War and the Remaking of Palestine.* Berkeley: University of California Press, 2017.

Taylor, Frederick W. *Scientific Management.* London: Routledge, 2004.

Thompson, E.P. *The Making of the English Working Class.* New York: Pantheon Books, 1964.

Vacková, Barbora Lucie Galčanová. "Project Zlín: Everyday Life in a Materialized Utopia." *Lidé města/Urban People* 11, no. 2 (2009): 311–37.

Valenta, Edvard. *Žil jsem s miliardářem.* Brno: Blok, 1990.

Van Zee, Marynel Ryan. "Form and Reform: The Garden City of Hellarau-bei-Dresden, Germany, between Company Town and Model Town." In Marcelo Borges and Susana Torres, eds., *Company Towns: Labor, Space, and Power Relations across Time and Continents.* Palgrave Macmillan: New York, 2012.

Vickers, Adrian. *A History of Modern Indonesia.* Cambridge: Cambridge University Press, 2013.

Vrána, Stanislav, and Josef Cisař. *Deset let pokusné práce na měšťanských školách ve Zlíně 1929–39.* Zlín: Pokusné školy, 1939.

Waters, Tony, and Dagmar Waters, eds. and trans. *Weber's Rationalism and Modern Society: New Translations on Politics.* New York: Palgrave, 2015.

Wein, Martin. *The History of the Jews in the Bohemian Lands.* Leiden: Brill, 2015.

Wheaton, Bernard. *Radical Socialism in Czechoslovakia: Bohumír Šmeral, the Czech Road to Socialism and the Origins of the Czechoslovak Communist Party, 1917–1921.* Boulder: East European Monographs, 1986.

Williams, Daryle. *Culture Wars: The First Vargas Regime, 1930–1945.* Durham: Duke University Press, 2001.

Zahavi, Gerald. *Workers, Managers, and Welfare Capitalism: The Shoeworkers and Tanners of Endicott Johnson, 1890–1950.* Chicago: University of Illinois Press, 1988.

Zahra, Tara. "Imagined Noncommunities: National Indifference as a Category of Analysis." *Slavic Review* 69, no. 1 (Spring 2010): 93–119.

– *Kidnapped Souls: National Indifference and the Battle for Children in the Bohemian Lands, 1900–1948.* Ithaca: Cornell University Press, 2011.

Zarecor, Kimberly. *Manufacturing a Socialist Modernity: Housing in Czechoslovakia, 1945–1960.* Pittsburgh: University of Pittsburgh Press, 2011.

Zelený, Milan, *Cesty k úspechu: Trvalé hodnoty soustavy Baťa.* Kusak: Vyškov, 2005.

Index

Printed and bound by CPI Group (UK) Ltd, Croydon, CR0 4YY

16/04/2025

14658336-0001